AF411945

One Man's Life

One Man's Life

*From Wagon Wheels to the
Space Age*

Don and Eugenia Hummel

A FREE ENTERPRISE AMERICANA BOOK

The Free Enterprise Press

BELLEVUE

Distributed by  *MERRIL PRESS*

FIRST EDITION
Published by the Free Enterprise Press

Typeset in Palatino typeface on Iconix computers by the
Free Enterprise Press, Bellevue, Washington

The Free Enterprise Press is a division of the Center for the Defense of
Free Enterprise, 12500 N.E. Tenth Place, Bellevue, Washington 98005.

This book is distributed commercially by Merril Press, P.O. Box 1682,
Bellevue, Washington 98009. Additional copies of this book may be
ordered from Merril Press at $14.95 each.

LIBRARY OF CONGRESS CATALOGING-IN-PUBLICATION DATA

Hummel, Don, 1907—
        One man's life : from wagon wheels to the space age / by Don
and Eugenia Hummel. — 1st ed.
                p.   cm.
        "A Free Enterprise Americana book."
        Includes index.
        ISBN 0-939571-03-X : $14.95
        1. Hummel, Don, 1907 —   . 2. Businessmen—United States—
Biography. 3. Politicians—United States—Biography. 4. United States
—Officials and employees—Biography. 5. National parks and reserves
—United States—History—20th century. 6. Concessions (Amusements,
etc.)—United States—History—20th century.
I. Hummel, Eugenia. II. Title.
CT275.H697A3 1988
973.9′O92′4—dc 19
[B]   88-6093
                                                                    CIP

PRINTED IN THE UNITED STATES OF AMERICA

To our three daughters
Donna, Diane and Charlene
and the memory of our son Cliff

Books by Don Hummel
Stealing the National Parks

with Eugenia Hummel
One Man's Life

Contents

Foreword   ix
Preface   xi

Beginnings

1. Ancestors   1
2. Childhood   7
3. High School   25
4. University of Arizona   31
5. Law School and Lassen   43

Into the World

6. Work Projects Administration   59
7. World War II Service   77
8. War and the Impact on the National Parks   113
9. Return to Lassen   127
10. Conference of National Park Concessioners   145

Politics

11. My First Experience in Politics   153
12. Democratic Politics in Arizona   187
13. American Municipal League   189
14. Mount McKinley National Park Company   195
15. My Experience in City Government   209

Concessions

16. Glacier National Park   229
17. Challenges to Concessions Policy   259
18. Growing Restrictions   269

Contents

Concessions (continued)

19. Controversy Over Souvenirs   273
20. Public Law 89-249 - Concessions Policy   291
21. Study of Concessions on Federal Lands   307
22. Department of Housing and Urban Development   313
23. U.S. Natural Resources - Yosemite Park
       and Curry Company   355
24. A Christian Ministry in the National Parks   363

Losing Our National Parks

25. Centennial Commission for the National Parks   365
26. Attempted Closure of Zion, Bryce Canyon
       and the North Rim of the Grand Canyon   383
27. Lassen Closure   399
28. Return to Glacier Park   415
29. Incorporation of the Conference of
       National Park Concessioners   437
30. Committee on Government Operations and
       Committee on Small Business   445
31. Reducing Concessioner Ability to Perform by
       National Park Contract Provisions   461
32. Master Plans: Instruments to Reduce
       Visitor Facilities   475
33. Glacier Personnel   489

Legacy

34. National Parks for a New Generation   499

Index   503

Foreword

Don Hummel is as close as you can get to being a living monument to the public's right of access to our national parks. From his early days building Lassen Volcanic National Park's first visitor concession in 1933 to his retirement in 1980 from two decades as Glacier National Park's concessioner, he has fought for the visitor's right to visit America's national parks. Where ever exclusionary forces have tried to shut down visitor facilities or keep people out of the parks for some trumped-up reason, Don Hummel has been there to challenge their legitimacy.

This book is the story of his whole life, and a fascinating life it is. With his wife Genee, Don Hummel tells us here how an Arizona ranch kid who didn't start at the valley's one-room schoolhouse until he was nine years old could find himself one day serving as a federal subcabinet officer under President Lyndon B. Johnson and becoming the bane of Park Service bureaucrats as a savvy and successful concessions businessman.

I've read many biographies of noteworthy Americans, but none with the homespun flavor and authentic American accent of *One Man's Life*. The early chapters are full of the grit and gristle you'd expect of a good pioneer story, while the final ones reflect a sophisticated assessment of how the contemporary environmental movement uses its political clout to keep people out of our national parks. What comes between is the personal pilgrimage of triumph and tragedy that is the life of Don and Genee Hummel, exemplifying the human condition and all its hopes and pangs.

This book is not the tightly constructed work that Don's *Stealing the National Parks* was — it is a delightfully more leisurely ramble down many roads taken, full of chugholes

Foreword

and breathtaking vistas both. There was no need here to give source notes for every little fact, and so the yarn can spin itself out freely with a directness that reads like good conversation around the campfire — the campfire of a long memory. And it was Utah Phillips who said that the most revolutionary thing on earth is a long memory.

I have known Don Hummel for many, many years. There are few people in America that I respect more. He's a fighter who can get bullheaded at times, but never for mere personal pique, always for the benefit of those to whom he is responsible. His toughness is that of a man who takes his responsibilities seriously.

America has in *One Man's Life* a portrait of itself, a motion picture of its own growth from the closing of the Western Frontier to the opening of the final frontier, the space age. Follow Don and Genee Hummel across the pages of that American landscape as I have. You'll be all the richer for it.

Garner Hanson
National Park Concessions, Inc.

Preface

We have long hoped to pass on the story of "One Man's Life" to our children, to our many relatives and to our friends. When the writing was all done, though, this book turned out to be more than just a private memoir for a close circle of intimates: Upon re-reading its many pages we found it to be a biography of America as much as of a man.

Our joint opinion rests upon more than simple pride of authorship. After conferring with Free Enterprise Press editor-in-chief Ron Arnold, who published Don's *Stealing the National Parks*, we received his enthusiastic support to turn *One Man's Life* into a major work. "You've mined an untapped vein of classic American experience here," he told us. "And its no-nonsense story-telling approach is refreshing after reading the overdecorated literary efforts that frequently cross my desk. It will be a welcome addition to our Free Enterprise Americana series."

The reader will find here not only the fascinating biography of a widely experienced and respected Southwesterner, but also the original draft manuscript "national park chapters" that Don later rewrote to meet the publisher's demanding standards of verification in *Stealing the National Parks*. Since the autobiographer has a freer hand than the advocate and no need of footnotes or bibliographies, we decided to include Don's "thinking out loud" initial draft chapters for two special reasons: First, the national parks specialist as well as the interested layman will find in them much more detail than could be included in *Stealing the National Parks*, especially on the business end of the concession business; and second, the historian will discover here the original version of much that later became *Stealing the National Parks*, which will reveal the evolution of

Don's ideas and also provide a basis for comparison that should be illuminating.

But to overemphasize the national parks aspect of *One Man's Life* would be to miss its whole point. This is the story of the full life of a family man, a successful businessman, a politician and public servant, an organizational leader, a fighter for the cause of the national parks — and as such it touches the heart as well as the mind. It is a personal testament that speaks to the personal in all of us. In a way, you could say of it what Walt Whitman said of his *Leaves of Grass*:

> Camerado! This is no book!
> Who touches this, touches a man.

And while we're invoking Walt Whitman, let's devote a sentence or two to the writing style of *One Man's Life*. As Walt Whitman was a journalist turned poet, wordsmith and image-maker, Don Hummel is a lawyer turned businessman turned public advocate, and he uses the language in an all-business, no-frills manner. If it sounds in places like a lawyer's memo, take it at face value: Don Hummel has a tough message about our laws and institutions. His writing is light on adjectives and heavy on nouns and verbs. It favors narrative and shuns description. It avoids figures of speech and relies upon blunt and plain expression, which we believe gives this book the great virtue of being understandable. When you read Eugenia Hummel's "Christmas Letters," see if you don't think that they reflect her Stanford education and her experience as a schoolteacher — and catch the flavor of the times. The total reading experience is one of absolute sincerity and unadorned straightforwardness — and, we think, rewarding human understanding.

This book would not have been possible without the help of many hands. We would like to thank Ron Arnold, editor-in-chief of the Free Enterprise Press, for his editorial assistance and his personal encouragement. Our thanks to Alan M. Gottlieb, president of the Center for the Defense of Free Enterprise for accepting this project for publication in the Free Enterprise Americana series. Special thanks to Garner Hanson for making the special effort to provide this book's Foreword — Garner has been a long-time friend and fellow national park concessioner.

Our thanks to Emily Moke and Lynda Karjola for their expertise in typing and computer services — and more, for their very real help and advice along the way.

We hope this book informs and entertains, that it calls forth a smile and a tear from page to page, that it brings both uplift and deep concern. It is our humbly offered testament and our legacy to America.

Don and Eugenia Hummel
Tucson
January, 1988

1
Ancestors

My father, Louis G. Hummel, was born December 1, 1864, the son of German immigrants Christian Hummel and Louise Goetz Hummel. He was the only son among four children, all born in Cincinnati, Ohio.

My mother, Emma Yockey Hummel, was born in Ripley, Ohio, July 16, 1867. Mother's parents also came from Germany. Her mother's maiden name was Elizabeth Reichman, from Baria Ungstein. Her father was Jacob Yockey, from Westphalia Hevschthol.

Grandfather Christian Hummel was a distilling engineer — he worked in the manufacture of alcoholic beverages. He was, as he called himself, a "testallar" who tested the product by taking a mouthful and then spitting it out. In the well-known practice of the trade, he never swallowed it.

Grandmother Hummel came to the United States at the age of sixteen. She was the daughter of the caretaker for the livestock of the royal family of Bavaria. In her youth she knew Maria Feodorovna, the girl who later married Alexander III and became the Czarina of Russia. Grandmother Hummel was an intellectual and was often sought out by German immigrants who wanted word on the gossip of the royal families in Germany. She was a poor housekeeper.

Great Grandfather John Hummel was conscripted by Napoleon as he moved through Germany to attack the Russians. As is well known, Napoleon fought through to Moscow, but the Russians refused to surrender and set the city afire as they vacated. Napoleon's army found itself without food resources. With winter approaching, many soldiers died on the retreat to Europe. Great Grandfather was one of the fortunate twenty-three per cent to survive.

I had a two-ounce whiskey ration bottle which he carried in the War of 1812. My brother Louis carried it in World War I in France, and I carried it in China in World

War II. I had it mounted but it was stolen when my office in Tucson was robbed. A sentimental loss.

My father dropped out of school in his sophomore year of high school and went to work as an entry clerk at Ames and Doeptke Department Store in Cincinnati. While he worked twelve hours a day and made only $2.00 per week, he spent most of his money on law books, which he read at night by candlelight. He had decided he wanted to be a lawyer, but was told by the Dean of Cincinnati Law School that he would have to take an examination to enter as he did not have a high school diploma.

Dad asked if he could see the type of questions asked. The Dean showed sample questions to him and asked if he could answer them. Dad replied, "No, but I'll be back next year." When he returned the following year the Dean exclaimed, "Well, the kid's back. I never expected to see you again." Dad passed the entrance exam and entered law school.

Three years later Dad graduated as the youngest man in his class. It turned out to be a prestigious class, including Charles G. Dawes, later Vice President of the United States; Atlee Pomerene, later U.S. Senator from Ohio and one of the prosecutors of the Tea Pot Dome oil scandal; and Horace Taft, brother of William Howard Taft, Cincinnati alumnus and President of the United States.

As soon as he graduated, Dad decided he wanted to go West. He procured a ticket to Seattle, Washington. En route, he joined four other young men, one of whom was a resident of Seattle attending West Point Military Academy. His name was Peterson, and as he had made the train trip several times, he was familiar with the procedures and customs, including some less than honest conduct by the train's crews.

There was no such thing as dining car service, so the train stopped at specified locations for food service. Each person paid the station concessioner for his meal and was served family style, but the food was delayed and served just when the train attendant would call "all aboard." You had a choice: miss either the meal or your train.

Young Peterson alerted this group and when the train

crew called "all aboard," one passenger grabbed the platter of meat, another the potatoes, the bread, etc. Dad said he thought this was the first "dining car service" on the railroads.

As they were going through the valley just north of Yellowstone National Park, the government put on a carload of soldiers to protect the train, as the Indians were on the warpath. This was in 1886 and one of the last Indian uprisings. Dad said that, looking back, he thought they were in more danger from the drunken soldiers than from the Indians. He said the soldiers shot out all the train windows, perforated the car roof, and blazed away at anything that moved within sight. Dad said he saw some tepees, but no Indians.

On arrival in Seattle, Dad was appointed Assistant City Attorney, handling all police court cases. Many of the cases involved Indians out of the Yukon and Canada, and the cases had to be tried in the Chinook jargon, a trade language including words from English, French, Chinook, Nootka and various other borrowings, which prevailed as a means of communication.

Dad used to tell me that the local Indians, mostly of the Duwamish and Suquamish tribes, would sit in a circle around a small campfire at night. He said they never seemed to talk to each other but just sat together. In an attempt to start a conversation with the Chief of the group, Dad asked, "Don't those boys get cold?", referring to numerous Indian youngsters running around stark naked. The old Chief looked at Dad and said, "Your face get cold?" Dad said, "No." The Chief replied, "Them all face." (This apocryphal old chestnut has been attributed to Indian Chiefs all over America.)

One evening Dad sat in his Seattle law office reading a legal text when he heard his door being slowly opened. He pulled out his desk drawer and reached for his revolver. As the door swung wider, a wizened face appeared and said, "Are you a lawyer?" Dad said, "Yes," and told his uninvited guest to come in. The man did. He was naked as a jaybird. He had been shanghaied aboard a lumber vessel anchored at the wharf down by Henry Yesler's sawmill and the press gang had taken his clothes to prevent him from "jumping ship."

Dad got a writ of habeas corpus to secure the abducted man's release and took it on board the offending ship. As he stood on the deck trying to serve his papers on the ship's captain, two crewmen pulled up the boarding plank. Dad said he thought his legal career was coming to an end — perhaps to begin a seagoing vocation — but the Captain accepted the papers, released the victim's clothing, and extended the plank once more to allow Dad back into the sawdust and mud streets of Seattle.

Dad returned to Cincinnati in 1887 to marry his boyhood sweetheart, Emma Yockey. They were married on June 12, 1888, in Hamilton County, Ohio, my mother's birthplace. They were destined to have nine children, two of whom died in infancy. Surviving children were Villette, Louis, Floss, Gene, Della, me and Gail. But that's getting ahead of ourselves.

Dad immediately opened his private law firm in Cincinnati, Ohio, having been admitted to practice before the Supreme Court of Ohio back in March of 1886, before he left for Seattle. He tells of one early case in which he was hired to represent a party in the hill country of Kentucky. The families in litigation were both prominent and great interest had been generated. So many people came to see the trial that the judge moved the case to an old vacant warehouse — the courtroom was too small to accommodate the observers.

Dad and the opposing counsel agreed on a six-man jury which was placed behind the table used by the attorneys and their clients. Dad said his opposing counsel didn't know much law, but he was a good haranguer who stomped around and often banged the table with his fist to make a point.

Dad decided that he would have to follow suit if he was to convince this backwoods jury. When it came his time to argue, he also banged the table and the whole jury dropped from sight. They had been seated over the doors to the basement and with all this commotion the door hinges gave way dropping the jury onto the stairs to the basement.

Dad said his first thought was "There goes my case." He was both surprised and delighted when the jury nevertheless gave him the verdict.

Dad was fascinated by mining which was opening up in the West. At one time he controlled several zinc mines in Joplin, Missouri. He made trips to Colorado on behalf of financial backers interested in the mines in Cripple Creek, Fairplay and Leadville. He also represented backers who built a railway into Pittsburgh, Pennsylvania, and who financed the construction of a narrow gauge railroad into Georgia.

He lost his fortune in 1907 during the so-called financial crisis. He had backed a formula which was to be a substitute for gas street lights. During the crash, he was unable to provide the product and was closed out. As he had mining interests in Greaterville, Arizona, he moved his family to Tucson in 1907, where he continued his law practice as best he could.

As a lawyer, Dad was very sympathetic to minorities and often represented them in court. This did not set well with the "establishment" and as a result, they tried to intimidate him by shooting through our house at night. These were unruly days and intimidation prevailed as a means of persuasion.

One minority that received little or no protection from the law consisted of Chinese merchants, who had stores located mostly in the Mexican-occupied and poorer sections of town. These minority store owners were periodically robbed and sometimes the proprietor was injured with no recourse to the law.

One evening while we were attending our Saturday night movie, a group of Chinese came and got Dad from the theater. A Chinese merchant had been robbed and murdered. The Chinese community wanted to put up a $5,000 reward for the perpetrator. Dad had a hard time talking them down to $1,500. He told them with so much money at stake, the local law enforcers would convict someone, whether innocent or guilty. Five thousand dollars in those would be equal to at least $50,000 today.

The reward of $1,500 was offered and the man apprehended within a week. A Tucson detective paid a Mexican official $100 to push the man across the border at Nogales, Sonora, where he had fled. Dad participated in the prosecution. The man was convicted and hanged at the state prison in Florence, Arizona.

Dad suggested and organized the Chinese Chamber of Commerce to protect the Chinese from all kinds of depredations. If they were solicited for a contribution, it was submitted to the Chamber and Dad would check out whether or not it was legitimate. If it was, the contribution would be made through the Chamber of Commerce. This prevented the "shakedowns" that the Chinese had often suffered.

If any Chinese merchant was robbed, the Chinese Chamber of Commerce offered a reward. This soon stopped most offenses against the Chinese, as the culprits were usually caught and convicted.

As a result, Dad represented practically all of the Chinese people in Southern Arizona. They tried to get Dad to move to San Francisco to be the legal representative of commercial transactions between Chinese in the United States and China. Dad declined to move from Tucson. He practiced law for over sixty years.

Dad died on December 7, 1955, at the age of 91. Mother predeceased him October 5, 1937, at the age of 70.

2
Childhood

I ARRIVED in Arizona on December 24, 1907. I was an infant of three months, born September 9, 1907 in Cincinnati, and came to Tucson with my mother, my brother Gene and sister Della. As the family had just suffered great financial reverses in Ohio, we had only one berth for the family of four. Needless to say, there was very little sleeping on that trip, except for me!

My father had preceded us to Tucson and rented a house for the family on Franklin Street, where we lived for a short time. I do not know just how long. At that time Tucson was a dusty little unpaved town with hitching posts on Congress Street, many bars, and numerous saddle shops, blacksmith shops and stables. During my early years in the area I never saw a motor vehicle. Two railroads came through Tucson, the Southern Pacific line and the El Paso Southwestern.

My mother liked to tell about an event from our first days in Arizona: there were few fair-skinned children in Tucson as most of the population was of Mexican descent. As a baby, I was extremely blond and fair-skinned and when my mother would hold me on the porch, a number of Mexican mothers stopped and crossed themselves. I am not asserting claim to any special significance in this, but simply to relate an incident told to me by my mother. It impressed her!

Some time thereafter, my father took up a homestead out near Cortaro, west of Tucson. The homestead laws required that certain improvements be made including the building of a house. My father had no money, so he accumulated a number of old abandoned railroad boxcar doors and built our first home with them. Of course there was only dirt for a floor. It was a tremendous change for my mother who was used to rather luxurious quarters in our country home in Cincinnati, Ohio, a fine residence called "Sweetwine." It was there that I had been born in a room with hand-decorated walls and hand-carved furniture.

From Cortaro, we moved to the Santa Rita Placers, named for its location in the Santa Rita Mountains. It was not really a community in the proper sense, but rather a collection of placer mining claims, the site of my father's mining interests. In the midst of the mining operations stood a tiny post office bearing the name "Greaterville." The post office was about all there was to Greaterville. I do not know the exact arrangement that my father had, but we lived in an old frame house on these premises. I know that my father did not practice law there.

Santa Rita Placers was the center of some sporadic mining and a great deal of smuggling out of Mexico. Santa Rita had been established as a placer mining property by George MacInney, one of the five very successful mine operators in the early days, along with William Randolph Hearst and Leland Stanford, who established Stanford University in 1885. They were known as part of the "big five" successful miners.

We were one of the few Anglo families in the Greaterville area. Practically all the rest were of Mexican descent. We had one of the few houses in that area with a wooden floor. On occasion a group of Mexican-Americans would call on Dad and ask if they could give a dance in our home. Dad would say "yes," and wanted to know when and they would say, "tonight." Dad would ask, "How in the world can you get people here tonight?" "Oh," they would say, "we can do that." Then they would send five or six men on horseback, spread out in every direction, and at about dusk families in wagons and individuals on horseback started arriving.

Music for these impromptu shindigs was provided by a man who had a concertina and a peculiar ritual. He would take an old wooden box and set it up in front of him. On the box he laid a large gold plated watch and a six shooter. Then he began to play. After he played for an hour, he stopped, the crowd passed the hat and paid their musician. If the concertina artist didn't think he got enough money, that was the end of the music. The dancers had to pass the hat again for additional funds. He trusted them — but only for an hour at a time!

I remember being fascinated by the practice that prevailed in those days of showing interest in a girl by breaking an egg filled with confetti over her head. They called it a *cascarone*.

Our family's next move was to a homestead which mother and my maternal Grandmother Yockey (who had come to live with us after we moved to Arizona) filed on about eight miles north of Sonoita upslope in the Cienega Creek valley between the Santa Rita Mountains and Apache Peak. The land came with an old frame house which had been moved from another location. You might visualize this region as the scrub desert it is today, but you'd be wrong. In the early 1900s this whole area was a sea of grass as high as a horse's belly. Sacaton bunchgrass six feet tall can still be found in places along Cienega Creek, but it was so abundant during my childhood that everyone called the local valleys "Sacaton bottoms."

This ranch facing the rugged Santa Catalina Mountains to the north, the Santa Ritas to the west and Apache Peak to the east became our home for several years. For reasons that were never explained to me, my father gave up his law practice entirely during this time to live the spartan life of a rancher. On the ranch lived my father, mother, Grandmother Yockey, my sisters Floss and Della, my brother Gene and myself — along with my niece, Aline Seibold. My older sister Villette (Aline's mother) lived in Tucson and my brother Louis, age sixteen, worked as a delivery boy for a produce firm in Tucson. Louis was the sole source of cash for the entire family.

It was on the ranch that my brother Gail was born on January 11, 1911. I will never forget the day, because Aline and I were told to go up into the pasture. It was raining and we didn't want to go, but the family insisted upon it. In our absence, my father delivered Gail. Grandmother Yockey was bathing him on the oven door when we returned. This was often the place where children were bathed because it was the warmest place in the house.

Life on a ranch during these pioneer days was not easy, particularly for the adults. There was little food except that which was homegrown, and then only in season. Refrigeration was unknown. Preservation of food was primitive, and included such processes as curing in brine or smoking or salting down. The few vegetables and fruits not consumed during the season were canned or preserved.

The women cooked in iron pots or skillets over wood-burning stoves. No fancy Teflon-coated utensils existed. Iron skillets and pots were difficult to clean. We washed them in a dishpan with water heated on top of the stove. We had no running water. All our water was pulled from a well by the bucket with a windlass or scooped up from a tank attached to the windmill.

Life for my mother was particularly burdensome, having to prepare three meals each day for an extended family. The drudgery began in the early morning after Dad built a fire. Mother baked biscuits; there was mush to fry, eggs to prepare and butter to churn, then the perennial dishes to wash and wipe after dressing the children, getting them ready for school and preparing lunch pails.

Once each week, mother would prepare the dough for twelve to fourteen loaves of bread which she left overnight to be raised in the heating oven above the stove and baked the following day.

Then, too, there was the weekly wash, which was done in a washtub with a corrugated washboard with water heated on top of the stove. This same washtub served for our Saturday night baths. We dreaded this event as mother wanted us *clean* and she was far from gentle as she scrubbed us from head to foot.

Nighttime, after we children had been put to bed, Mother did the sewing and darning. She had no forty-hour week and no days off. I still marvel at the work she did and marvel more that she sang as she worked! The older children helped, but essentially the household work of cooking, baking, cleaning, sewing and responding to the needs of the children were hers.

Dad's and my older brothers' work started early, too. The cows had to be rounded up and brought in from pasture — often a distance of two to three miles — then milked and watered. There were chickens and pigs and dogs to feed, wood to be chopped and water to be pulled from the well. Rounding up the horses for the work teams, harnessing them and going to the fields to plow, or to cultivate or to disc or to harvest was a daily chore depending on the season. It was all the more difficult as my dad was educated as a lawyer, not a farmer. Life on the ranch was particularly distasteful for my brother Gene, who lacked an education and detested farming, particularly since any emoluments from the work went to support the family and were never distributed to individual members. Cash was almost nonexistent and individual recognition just as scarce.

Repairs on a ranch are endless — fences to build and mend, equipment to repair, windmills to be put in order — be it the blades on the tower or the valve in the water at the bottom of the well. Work was more difficult as we had to make do with what we had. There was no such thing as running to a hardware store to purchase a needed valve or a length of pipe.

On February 14, 1912, the Act of Congress making Arizona a state was signed by President Taft. At that time Tucson was about four square miles, population approximately 14,000. There were a police chief, two sergeants, and six patrolmen. There were five firemen and 30 volunteer firemen; four hospitals; six newspapers, 23 real estate firms, 12 blacksmith & horseshoe businesses; four hay & grain stores.

Also in 1912, author Harold Bell Wright arrived in Tucson and bought 160 acres at the SW corner of Broadway and Speedway (then four miles outside the city) to build a home, which he did in 1922. It is now the Harold Bell Wright Estates.

On very rare occasions we would take a trip to Tucson to get supplies. This would be by horse and wagon. The distance was fifty miles and took almost two days each way. Most of the trip was made in dry washes as there were a minimum of established roads. We followed the route that the army used going from Tucson to Fort Huachuca, established to protect settlers from the Apache Indians. Fort Huachuca is still there, now serving as an intelligence communications center for the armed forces.

On these occasions Dad would try to buy a box of fruit or a string of bananas to take to the ranch. On one trip we ran into a snowstorm and dad asked if I'd like an ice cream cone. Of course, I said "Yes," so he cut an orange in half, piled some snow on it and that was my ice cream cone! I didn't know any better so it was a treat.

Another treat I'll never forget came at Christmastime. Dad bought a gramophone. It was a tubular type and the music came out of a big horn that had a picture of a dog listening to his master's voice. This was our first real encounter with music in the home.

On one of our trips to town Dad was alone returning to the ranch. A mountain lion scared off his horse and treed him. He spent the night in a tree with a rifle across his knees. He had to walk home, leaving the wagon. The horse turned up at the ranch about six months later.

In 1916 my life changed. Neighbors built a one-room schoolhouse about a mile and a half from our house. It was the only school for many miles around. Students came primarily from the local Mormon community: the Johnsons, Binghams and the Williamses. Kenneth Putnam was our next door neighbor. He and I were the only non-Mormons attending the school.

You might say that my education began late. I was nine years old when this little school in Cienega Creek Valley opened, and it was my first formal instruction. I recall that a woman named Burdette Rhork was our schoolteacher. Because I was older than some of the others, she gave me special help, teaching me some second grade lessons along with first grade material.

After my first year in school we moved to a new location farther down Cienega Creek Valley about two miles north of the old site where Gail had been born. We called it "Cottonwoods" because of its huge cottonwood trees reaching 110 feet in height, one in particular measuring 36 feet in circumference.

Cottonwoods was about three or three and a half miles from the schoolhouse. During my second year, my brother Gail and I rode horseback to school. Gail was not yet of school age but insisted on going, so he rode behind me on Old Sam, the horse that belonged to Della. On one occasion

I remember going under a branch of a palo verde tree and not warning Gail. The branch swept him off the back of the horse, so he went home crying and I continued on to school by myself.

One weekend Gail and I went up in the pasture to get our horse to ride to school the following day. There had been a protracted drought and cattle were dying all around us. When we finally found our horse, we started toward him, but a cow charged us. It was obviously half-starved and had a wild look in its eyes. We were always told that if we could not get to a fence, we should lie down on the ground so the cow could not gore us. Gail did not take any chances. He threw a rock (which he had lots of experience doing, as his main defense against me whenever he was mad was throwing a rock at me). He hit the cow in the head and we dropped to the ground. The cow stumbled and fell on top of us. One horn went through my pocket. Fortunately, the cow was not too heavy and did not land its full weight directly on us. I will never forget seeing those wild eyes as I laid under the cow's shoulders with her trying to hook me. I was told that an animal would not hurt you if you played dead. I alternated between closing my eyes as if I were dead and trying to get away. I got out from under the cow and looked for Gail, but he had headed for the fence and was long gone. The cow never did recover or regain its feet. It died at that very spot.

Another thing I recall while I was going to the one-room schoolhouse was a remark made by Joe Kennedy, the son of a local cowboy. He asked me why I kept that old rag in my lunch basket. The "old rag" he was referring to was the napkin my mother always put in my lunch pail. Without wishing to acknowledge that I carried a napkin, I said I didn't know. When I got home I told my mother. She was furious with me for having said that I didn't know what a napkin was for!

Tucson's Southern Pacific Roundhouse was expanded in 1916 — it had been built in 1904. Once it was the biggest engine repair facility between El Paso and Los Angeles.

The freedom of time spent on the ranch is one of the highlights of my life. We played, roped calves, milked cows and rode horseback. We hunted rabbits every morning before leaving for school. I had a single shot .22 caliber rifle. My hunting was the source of most of the meat for our family. The family seldom butchered an animal for home use. Stock was the source of our scarce cash revenues. Gail often went with me as I hunted. Someone asked him if he ever shot any rabbits. He said, "No, all I do is carry the `wrabbits'."

While I never became a good bronc rider, I broke my share of horses. The wild horses that roamed the country were the source of all of our steeds except dray horses, which we had to buy. Rounding up these wild horses and driving them into a corral was an exciting activity. Usually, when a band of wild horses was spotted, we would get two or three riders and circle the animals and try to drive them into a corral. It would be a wild chase with the horses trying to break away and avoid capture.

I remember how mad my brother Gene would get if I failed to turn the running herd in the right direction. He was also fearful that my horse would fall with me, as there were arroyos and ditches to traverse as we rode at a gallop. I was only ten years old at the time. As a youth I was fearless and oftimes stupid in not recognizing the danger I was in. This not only made Gene apprehensive, but also exasperated with me.

Back to school. In the second year my teacher gave me some additional work and told me that if I would spend six weeks in summer school, I could advance to the fourth grade. I wasn't enthralled by the prospect of spending a summer in school, but I recognized the value of an education and I made up my mind to do it.

That, coincidentally, was the summer Dad gave up on ranching and decided to re-establish his law practice. So we moved from the ranch and my little one-room schoolhouse to Tucson, where I enrolled in summer school. I will never forget the difficulty in adjusting to the city school right after skipping parts of two grades. The stuccoed brick building of Safford Elementary School was pleasant enough, but everything about my new situation seemed strange. The sheer number of fellow students — about thirty even in summer school — felt like a crowd compared to the dozen or so back in my rural school. And probably seventy percent were Hispanic; we seldom encountered Mexican-Americans on the ranch and that was something else to get used to.

I quickly learned to get along with the other students, but the schoolwork gave me real problems. I had entered a fourth grade preparatory class without mastering the first three years of material. The first day the teacher put an assignment on the board and told the class to copy it, which I dutifully did, but didn't know what the word "assignment" meant. I had difficulty the following day, as I had merely copied the words from the chalkboard but had done no homework. No one told me to do otherwise, so I continued in this fruitless copy-board routine for nearly half the summer school session. It was a trying time for me, but somehow I managed to do the work and was promoted to the fourth grade. That fall I proudly enrolled as a regular fourth-grader in Safford Elementary School.

As most of the students were of Hispanic origin, Spanish was commonly spoken in the school yard. In order to get children to speak English, our teachers and school administrators chastised us if we attempted to speak Spanish. After being sent to the principal's office on several occasions for speaking Spanish, I stopped trying. This was unfortunate, as I never did learn the Spanish language, much to my regret in later years.

The following year when I started the fifth grade, my teachers felt that I could take sixth grade work, so they skipped me to the sixth grade. I found this disconcerting, as they made no effort to fill the gaps when I jumped from one grade to another, especially when something came up that I had never heard of. Phonics was one of these subjects. I also remember that I had never been given instruction in punctuation. The Arizona education department that year mandated a statewide test to determine how effective their schools were at teaching English. Our class was high on the list until they graded my paper. It was obvious that I knew nothing about punctuation. Fortunately my teacher saw to it that I was drilled in punctuation. In fact, I was at the blackboard almost daily getting instruction. I received considerable praise when the follow-up six-week test was given and I made only one mistake. I put the apostrophe after the "t" instead of before on the word "won't." So, I have had the experience of being held up as the dumbest kid in the class and the brightest!

During this time about 1917 America's first municipal airport was developed in Tucson, named after its builders Dwight Davis and Guy Monthan, two aviation enthusiasts. Called Davis-Monthan, it was the first in the United States. It's now a strategic Air Force Base.

I completed my grammar school education in five years and caught up with my age group. When it came to graduation from grade school, a group of boys contacted me and asked if they could put me up for president of our graduating class. I had always been told to "be modest" so I demurred and they elected someone else. This gave me a good lesson and I never made that mistake again.

My first summer job came right after I graduated from Safford School. My manual training teacher, Mr. Byron Morton, had gone into the construction business and since I received the highest grade in manual training, he offered me a job as a carpenter's helper. Carpenter's helper is a high sounding name for general flunky. I mixed cement and held up the end of a wheelbarrow, carried lumber — and toward summer's end actually got to put shingles on house roofs. This was a difficult job in the middle of the summer particularly since the asphalt shingles tended to melt and stick to your hands. The hot tar could really burn. Then, too, we had to bend over to nail the shingles on the slope of the roof below our feet. We could not stand on the already-laid shingles while nailing them onto the next row. It was backbreaking work, for which I received $15.00 per week. Thus began my work career.

Summers were not only welcome because we were out of school, but because we usually went to the ranch to spend the summer. We could not wait to leave Tucson and go back to the ranch. The ranch was now run by my sister Floss, who was homesteading it. Gene and Della lived there also. As time went on, Della and Floss married and moved to their own homes. Gene then continued to live at the ranch alone.

It was our practice to invite friends to stay with us at the ranch during the summer. I remember particularly Ade

Abbott, who had just moved from Ohio, and his brother, Leonard. Ade and I were about twelve years old and Leonard and Gail were nine or ten. On one occasion I remember, we were left alone: my older brother Gene was gone for some reason. We had to do our own cooking and dishwashing, feed the chickens and pigs and do the evening chores. As you might expect, there was a minimum of work performed, particularly along the lines of washing dishes. We often went until we had used practically every dish and pot and pan in the house, and then would of necessity have a dishwashing splurge. When some of the family came to pick up Ade and Leonard two weeks later, they found that we had just about run out of food; in fact, the last meal we had was one small can of sardines and some biscuits we had baked. Gail had been asleep on the couch while I was baking biscuits; when we finally sat down to eat, Gail took all the sardines on his own plate. It was with some difficulty that we got him to divide them. Needless to say one small two-ounce can of sardines did not go very far!

When we still lived on the ranch the old transcontinental road came within a half mile of our house. It was just a couple of tracks across the land. No grading at all. Automobiles often broke down nearby and many times drivers sought help from us. One man decided to leave his car and catch a ride to Tucson. He left his car almost two and a half miles from our house. He agreed to pay me twenty-five cents per day to go over and check on it. Gail and I dutifully trudged the five mile round trip each day and ran up a bill of $11.75. I was really put out when Dad settled with the car owner for $3.00 because of some hard luck story. We had made 47 five-mile walking trips for $3.00 and Dad kept the money for the family. I never forgot this injustice!

Despite the hardships we had our diversions. One was to explore the limestone caves in the Santa Rita Mountains. One cave had a big hole that we called the bottomless pit. You could drop a rock and hear it hit the sides and then nothing. Whether it stopped or continued to fall we did not know. On one occasion my older brother Gene and I decided to see if we could explore this pit. I went down a three-eighths inch rope about thirty-five feet. I had great difficulty getting back as the rope got wet and slippery. I should have known better and my older brother Gene certainly should have assessed the danger to me. I do not know what we expected to find at the end of a thirty-five-foot rope.

Another time we attempted to find buried treasure. We had found a map and document written in Spanish called the "Mine With The Iron Door." We translated it and learned of a number of mines purportedly worked by the Spanish Padres. The story went that the King of Spain thought the padres were not sending back all the gold so he sent out instructions for the padres to return. The King's instruction packet was not to be opened until a given date but the padres of the Tumacacori Mission opened it upon receipt. Being thus forewarned of their imminent recall to Spain and thinking of their possible return to Arizona years hence, the padres hastily secreted forty burro loads of gold and silver into a mine shaft known but to them, and blasted the tunnel shut with such thoroughness that all evidence of the mine entrance was obliterated forever. So went the story.

We found out about the map and document through a Mexican prospector who hired Dad to protect him because he thought he had found the legendary lost mine of Tumacacori Mission. The prospector showed Dad the evidence, which is how we gained access to it.

My brother Gene, a friend named Frank Beetson and I went there. The document's description fit the site we saw, but we could make out no mine entrance and ended up merely taking an interesting walk. On our way back we saw a snake going through a pool. It must have been a boa as it was over twenty feet long. I wanted to kill it but my brother, who was opposed to killing anything, forbade it. Seeing the snake was the most remarkable thing about our adventure looking for the lost mine of Tumacacori Mission. Some legal battles followed the discovery of this alleged mine. The lawyers made some money but no treasure was ever found.

On another trip to look for the mine, Gene and I discovered a bottomless pit. We threw stones into and they bounced until no sound came. Gene had a lariat and I shinnied down. The rope got wet and slimy and I could hardly hold onto it wrapping my legs trying to get a grip and work myself up. I've often wondered how Gene and I could have been so stupid.

Our family celebrated the traditional holidays, such as Christmas, Thanksgiving, Easter, Fourth of July, etc. On these occasions most of the family would gather at home. Christmas, particularly, was a command function for all the children to come home.

At the ranch, while we were young, the myth of Santa Claus was maintained. Gene or Louis would drive up to the Santa Rita Mountains to cut a tree which was hidden from us until Christmas morning. The tree was decorated at night, after we children were sent to bed. Our first look at the tree was in the morning, when Dad would blow a horn for us all to march in single file with the youngest in front. The lights on the tree were small candles; a real fire danger, except that the trees were cut fresh, not months ahead, as they do now. There were presents for all. I remember getting a BB gun at the age of four and a single-shot .22 rifle at the age of six. We were taught that all guns were always loaded (and they were). Even pointing a stick as a make-believe gun in play was taboo. A gun was for a serious purpose and never to be used in play.

Mother, of course, had been busy for weeks making cookies and fruitcake. My sister Floss was a great candy maker and one year made a hundred-ten pounds of candy, including fudge, chocolates and fondants.

The first automobile I remember was a Cadillac, which my brother-in-law, Alfred S. Donau (Villette's husband), drove up to the ranch for Christmas. It was an open car. I do not believe there were any closed cars in those days. The lights were carbide lamps, the hand brake was on the outside on the running board and the horn was a large bulb that you squeezed. Al always had a chauffeur to drive him. I was very impressed!

Dances were held about once every three to four months. These were usually held at the schoolhouse in Sonoita, Elgin or Patagonia. On these occasions the older children would ride horseback and Dad and Mom and we younger ones would go by wagon. It was an eight- to eighteen-mile drive each way, depending on where the dance was held. The dance band usually had a makeshift assortment of musical instruments. Benches were lined up along the wall for the people to sit on and later for the young children to be bedded down to sleep. Occasionally, there would be trouble when some cowboy didn't want to take off his spurs while he danced. Some were real hazards as they danced the two-step, or what they interpreted as the two-step. At midnight the lunch pails were opened and everyone ate and at the first crack of dawn, the dancers mounted their horses and the families got into wagons for the long trip back to the ranches. Some cowboys would ride fifty miles to attend a dance, as this was the only entertainment available. Radios had not been invented and the only music in the home was a Gramophone with the big horn, and these were rare indeed. We were fortunate to be one of the first families to own an early gramophone.

About once every two years Dad would order two hundred-pound blocks of ice which were shipped by railroad from Tucson to Sonoita. Gene would pick them up in a wagon and bring them to the ranch. For several days before the ice was due, we'd save up all the cream we could keep sweet and make ice cream as long as the ice held out. We ate ice cream far beyond our capacities until it was gone. It was a case of eat it now or lose it!

On occasion dad would invite everyone for miles around to a "Settlers Picnic" at our ranch at the Cottonwoods. This was a gala affair and we often had up to a hundred people come from all over the valley. Some merchants from Tucson would attend. The merchant I remember best was the owner of Fishers' Music Store. At one of thse picnics he gave me a harmonica left over after some sale. There were fireworks and speeches — aspiring politicians attended. These were indeed gala events.

While attending Safford School, I joined the Boy Scouts of America. Byron Morton, my manual training teacher, was the scoutmaster of Troop Four. He was an excellent leader and inspired those who joined. I was a member of his troop. The scouts provided one of the few outlets for youngsters of that time.

Occasionally, we would go out to Sabino Canyon on an

overnight camping trip. It was fifteen miles with most of the road running along the sand washes in the dry stream bed. It was a very difficult fifteen miles on a bicycle. The scoutmaster would take our bedrolls and camping gear up with his truck. Then he would return and relay us up to the campsite at Sabino. These were memorable events. Capture the flag was one of the main games. We would divide up into two camps and each side would try to capture the other's flag. If you were touched in "enemy" territory you were out of the game. As it was played at night it required stealth to find the flag without being caught.

A man by the name of James Ogle became the Scout Executive for Tucson. He was an energetic sponsor of the scouting program and made special efforts to hold the older boys in the program. As a result, I stayed in during part of my high school days. There were five of us who stayed together while in Tucson High. They were John Windram, John Chamberlin, Frank Beetson, Cliff Wyatt and myself. We remained friends all through high school and in the case of Frank Beetson and Cliff Wyatt, through college.

John Windram went to the Naval Academy and was released after his second year for health reasons. He died some time thereafter of tuberculosis. Frank Beetson graduated and spent the rest of the life as a property man for Warner Brothers motion picture organization. Cliff Wyatt had to drop out of college because he too had contracted tuberculosis. He studied in bed and finally graduated from University of Arizona Law School. He finished first in his group that took the Arizona Bar examination. He joined Dad and me in our law firm under the name of Hummel, Hummel and Wyatt. His ill health finally put him to bed and he died at the age of 45 of tuberculosis. My son Cliff was named for him.

It was through the Boy Scout movement that Burton Hall, Frank Beetson and I were selected to pack all the bedrolls and supplies for the Boy Scout Summer Camp at Camp Lawton on Mount Lemmon. I could not afford the price of attending camp so this labor-in-lieu provided me an opportunity to attend.

We were given twelve burros and packs which unfortunately were for mules and much too large for burros. This made packing exceptionally difficult as the packs would not stay on the burros. We started out walking from Tucson, driving these burros, many of which had never been packed before. We were met in lower Sabino Canyon by a truck carrying the scouts' bedrolls and clothing which we packed on the burros and started up the trail to Mount Lemmon. The total pack trip was forty-five miles. It took us two days.

The only road to Mt. Lemmon in those days circled from Tucson around the Santa Catalina Mountains by way of the little mining town of Oracle, a 75-mile trip. The mountain portion was a one-way controlled road. At certain hours you could only go up. You had to come down at alternate times.

When our little pack train arrived at Camp Lawton, we unpacked and then traversed a three-mile trail to Soldiers Camp, where the tents, food supplies, etc., had been previously trucked up by local scout volunteers — the road did not extend all the way to Camp Lawton. We were to set up Camp Lawton for the first contingent of scouts.

As the packs didn't fit well and some of the burros bucked and ran into trees trying to dislodge their packs, we had supplies spilled all over the ground. One burro had knocked off a pack loaded with toilet paper which was strung on the trail. In fact, when families would drive up to Soldiers Camp and ask the rangers the way to Camp Lawton, they were told to just follow the toilet paper along the trail. This was somewhat of an exaggeration!

When the first contingent of Scouts was scheduled to come to the camp, we took our burros down the trail to lower Sabino Canyon to pick up their luggage and escort them to the camp, a hike of thirty miles each way.

They were supposed to stop at the Basin, a distance of fifteen miles where we were to camp. Many of these boys had just joined the scouts to go to camp, so we had an assortment of bedrolls, some properly bundled, some so loose and sloppy they hardly qualified as "bedrolls." As we moved up the trail, we were picking up bars of soap, toothbrushes and an assortment of articles falling out of the bad bedrolls.

The Scoutmaster escorting this contingent of thirty scouts went ahead with the boys. In their enthusiasm they reached the Basin in early afternoon and decided to go on. They did not consider the slower pace of the burros. We arrived at the Basin midafternoon, saw that they had thoughtlessly gone on ahead, and as we had all their blankets, we decided to push on after them.

About midway between the Basin and the Camp, the burros, which were carrying pretty heavy loads, began to lay down. They absolutely refused to get back up. We had no choice but to camp on the trail. We opened some bedrolls and went to sleep. About midnight we heard a periodic whistle on the trail. Then Sutton Menard appeared — a scout sent by the Scoutmaster to bring us to camp. I don't now how the Scoutmaster expected him to do this. We explained the situation to Sutton and suggested he take a bedroll and go to sleep. He did. We arrived the next morning about ten o'clock. The scouts had spent a cold night in front of a campfire.

Thereafter, they decided to truck the scouts up to Soldiers Camp. On this high note my scouting career ended and I went on to other things. However, the packing experience thus gained was to stand me in good stead when I became a park ranger in Grand Canyon National Park during my college days.

3

High School

AFTER MY graduation from Safford Elementary School, we moved to the northern part of the city, where my father rented a home at 1125 N. First Avenue. This made it easier for us to attend Roskruge School, which was being used as the High School while a new high school building was being erected. At that time there was only one high school in Tucson. Unfortunately, I found High School rather easy and therefore never really developed any good study habits and, as I was getting good grades, I had no pressure from home. In fact, some brothers and sisters said that I didn't have to worry about remembering things, because if I understood, I could figure out the answer. They said there was no reason to rely on memory. I found in later years that this was bad advice and that memory is as equally important as the ability to work out solutions to problems. The failure to improve my memory plagued me all of my life. I could have drastically improved my knowledge had I made a real effort to improve my memory.

Radio came into existence during my high school career. There was only one channel and it was full of static. Many students made crystal sets to listen in on radio broadcasts. And Arizona's first citrus industry was developed by Maurice Reed in 1923.

In my sophomore year, I was elected President of the Debate Club, but was not too interested and not too successful. I paid little attention to the responsibilities of debating and ended up by not making the Debate Team.

In my junior year, I went out for the football team. There were eighty-two out for the team, with eleven lettermen returning. It didn't look promising for me, as I was of a light build, weighing only 130 pounds, not particularly fast on my feet and not a good ball handler. As a result, I was put on the line as a guard. The 130 pounds was a distinct disadvantage. During one session, Coach Sylvester Paulus told Harold Patton (or "Porque" as we called him) and me that we should go in and take our suits off, as he did not have time to use us. I did not realize that this was a polite dismissal to leave the football squad. Porque Patton went in and did not return until the following year. The next night I dressed and went out for football and was on about the third team. One night during scrimmage, with a particularly poor player opposite me, I was making a lot of tackles and the coach noticed me for the first time. That evening, which was Friday, we were all at a local dance hall, and the coach came to check on how many football players were out that night. He said to me, "I may play you tomorrow, so go home early." This was the wrong thing to say to me, because I didn't sleep all night!

The next day we were playing Douglas, a team which we should have beaten by several touchdowns, and as we got near the end, it was a scoreless tie and the coach was walking up and down in front of the bench saying, "Who can I put in — who can I put in?" Finally, Jake Meyer, the line coach, said "Try Hummel." I was sent in when we had a little over three minutes left to play. Douglas had the ball and I got lined up and caught the eye of one of the backfield men. I knew he was going to get the ball by the look in his eyes. I dove over my man and caught the backfield man by one foot. He was so surprised that he fumbled and we recovered the fumble. When I went back in, the coach told me to tell the quarterback, Brigham Young (Brigham was his nickname), to pass, but he called for an end run. I immediately called the signals to be checked and told the quarterback, "The coach said to pass." He threw a pass. It was knocked into the hands of our end, who ran for a touchdown, making the score 7 to 0 in our favor. Coming off the field, the coach said, "Anybody who can tackle like that can play ball for me." Thereafter, I was a regular on the first team and made honorable mention for All-State.

Sylvester Paulus was an emotional but wonderful coach. The players worshiped him. He brought out the best in his players. He was demanding, but fair. He died at a very early age. I do not believe any other coach would have given me the opportunity he did. I'm pleased at how he summed up my sports career, as he wrote in my year book: "Your fight put you on the team. What you do in the future will always be of interest to Your Coach."

Several football games stand out vividly in my memory. One was when we played the first football team in Tombstone, Arizona. They had only 12 players try out for the team so everyone who had come out was on the team. When we played, the businesses in the community closed all their stores so the citizens could turn out to watch their boys play football. There were no bleachers and the citizens moved up and down along the sidelines. We played terrible ball, which was often interrupted as we waited for some Tombstone player to revive, because when more than one was knocked out, they had no substitutes. Our team was in top shape through our schedule of keen competition. Theirs was in very poor physical condition. During one play, when the Tombstone team had the ball and came through the center of the line, their player was tackled by Nelson Thompson, our fullback, and the Tombstone fellow really folded up. The mother of the knocked-out player came out on the field with a black umbrella (which women commonly carried in those days) and started beating our fullback over the head. The local citizens figured that we were a very dirty football team as their men were knocked out so often.

Another game I remember vividly was one we played in El Paso, Texas. Texas had no eligibility rules and anyone could play as many years as he was in school. It so happened that the fellow who lined up opposite me was the captain of the team and this was his fourth year of competition. What made matters worse was that he weighed 210 pounds and I was still only 135 pounds. He played poor football, but he certainly beat me over the head the entire game. The game was written up in *Spaulding Sports Magazine*. The timekeeper did not know the timekeeping rules. He would take time out everytime the ball was blown dead until it was snapped again. As a result, we played two full games; the first quarter was 60 minutes long. We won what should have been the end of the first game, but we lost in the final game. Our players were not only out-matched, but were up against what would have equaled four teams. They were on their own field, with their full squad, while we had only about a team and a half, who had traveled to El Paso.

Being active in school athletics had some extra attractions. It provided an opportunity to go to surrounding communities such as Phoenix, Douglas, Bisbee, Nogales, etc. We would be released from school on Friday afternoon to drive to the community, play ball on Saturday afternoon, and drive home on Sunday.

Most high schools would provide a school dance on Saturday night and a good time would be enjoyed by all. There were exceptions and these occurred in mining communities such as Bisbee or Douglas. The miners took their sports seriously and feelings would run high if we beat the local team, particularly if they thought the refereeing was not to their liking. On one occasion, after a basketball game, the school had to call the police and fire departments to let us out of the basketball court. We had to go to the next community to shower and dress. This happened in Douglas, Arizona.

As Tucson has grown and the population has moved to the outskirts, many schools have been left with a declining neighborhood population. Tucson High School is one of these. In order to utilize the facilities, there has been a movement to expand the curriculum which would appeal to a wide variety of educational needs. They call these schools "Magnet Schools". Tucson High is now a Magnet School and the Badger Foundation (after the school's athletic mascot), was formed to support this new designation. As part of the support mechanism, the school started a Hall of Fame. I was pleased to be selected as one of the first five. There were three teachers and two students selected. The other student was Frank Borman, the astronaut and recent past President of Eastern Airlines. Frank was the commander of the first crew to circle the moon on December 21-27, 1968 (10 times).

In addition to two letters in football, I made a letter in basketball and was elected Senior Class President. This was the class of 1925 and the first class to graduate from the new Tucson High School building. As president I was responsible for senior class affairs which included assembly announcements, collection of class dues, arrangements for the senior class dance, etc. Our principal, O. W. Patterson, was a Baptist and very strict in his views. He did not like dances. When I announced the senior class dance at our assembly, he called me into the office and asked what right I had to announce a dance. I told him as class president it had always been done that way and that I had approval of our class advisors, Helen Jones and Danny Romero. The principal said, in effect, that dancing was just an appeal to the sensual. Being rather brash, I said I thought it was just his evil mind. He almost threw me out of the office. He should have. However, the class advisors and the students' mothers insisted that a public school had a right to have a senior class dance. It was held. The principal made a rule that the dancers had to stay six inches apart. This made me the brunt of many jokes, as I was asked if I had my ruler to see that they all stayed six inches apart as they danced.

In 1975, the class had its 50th Reunion and enjoyed it so much that we have had a class reunion every year since. This year (1987) will be our 11th Reunion, representing 61 years since graduation day!

4

University of Arizona

IN SEPTEMBER, 1925, I enrolled as a freshman at the University of Arizona. With my inauspicious beginnings in the educational process back on the ranch and the difficulties I had struggled with while mastering high school materials, actually entering college seemed a pinnacle of achievement for me. However, I soon discovered that enrollment in college was just the beginning of a long path strewn with many obstacles.

At first my social life occupied my attention. I pledged Phi Delta Theta. I had graduated from Tucson High School and this fraternity emphasized selection of members from the Tucson community. Many fraternities had overlooked Tucson High School graduates, as they lived at home, and most frats were looking for pledges who would live in the house. As a result, Phi Delta Theta pretty much dominated and selected whom they wanted from Tucson High School. While I was "rushed" by a number of fraternities, I selected Phi Delta Theta.

In those days fraternities engaged in a great deal of hazing. Some hazing antics were dangerous to say the least. The most perilous situations arose during initiation. Among their favorite trials was an especially hazardous undertaking: They blindfolded us naked and told us to find five pennies in the bottom of a tub of water. Then they stuck electric wires directly out of a socket into the tub. It is a wonder no one was killed. It was a harrowing experience.

At the close of my freshman year at the University of Arizona I was invited by a fellow Phi Delt named Lawson Baxter and his sister Ethel to spend the summer at their parents' home in Wyandotte, Michigan. Their father, Howard Baxter, was chief chemist at the Michigan Alkali Plant in Wyandotte. He arranged a job for me at the plant and I took the opportunity, despite having to pay my own round trip transportation costs from Tucson to Wyandotte.

At Michigan Alkali my work involved taking samples from various locations in the plant every hour and making tests to determine whether the product was being properly processed. Shortly after I had settled into the new job a vacancy occurred which permitted me to work twelve-hour shifts — two weeks on days and two weeks on nights. I had some difficulty adjusting from day to night shifts each two weeks, but I welcomed the extra hours and the extra money as the round trip train fare from Tucson to Michigan was considerable.

Working away from home that summer exposed me to some new and fascinating experiences. For one thing, I worked with a deaf-mute who taught me sign language. We got along famously. For another, I traveled to the plant by street car but had to hang my head out the window because the workmen smelled so strongly of garlic that I could hardly breathe.

In my sophomore year, fellow Phi Delta Theta pledge Kenneth Bechtold and I got fed up with school. "Beck" and I were old friends: we had played football side by side in Tucson High. The two of us decided to take our bedrolls, cooking gear and rifles and go down into Mexico to live off the land by hunting! Mexican border officials nipped our bold plan in the bud when they would not allow us to take our guns into Mexico.

So! We were out of school, with no place to return to but home. Back in Tucson I got a job pumping gas at a filling station for Shell Oil Company, which was just starting to do business in Arizona. "Beck" got married and never returned to school.

But dropping out had taught me the value of education. I re-enrolled at the beginning of the next year. There I was, a semester behind. And once again I got by with a minimum of study and made average to better-than-average grades. It is unfortunate that someone did not get me started in the right direction and help me establish good study habits.

In my junior year, I went out for spring football. I now weighed 155 pounds, still playing as a guard. The University of Arizona's team was not good and the coach was short of material. I played in the spring game, but did not return to football the following fall. One autumn day the coach approached me and asked why I had not gone out for football during the regular season. I told him that I was tired of too much scrimmaging and too little chance to play. U of A's line coach felt that if you did not weigh 200 pounds, you couldn't play football. I never did get a letter in college sports.

During the remainder of my undergraduate studies I worked in gas stations after school in order to get enough money to stay in school. Of course, I lived at home and had my room and board furnished by my family.

During my college years I would still go out to the ranch on occasion. I recall that my sister Floss's husband Wert (Wick) Fenter had been raised on a cattle ranch and even after becoming a chiropractor loved to go to the ranch at roundup time and help brand the stock. One weekend during college Wick and I went to the ranch. The usual routine was to go to the corral and rope an unbroken horse for me to ride. We caught and saddled a bronc.

We never put a bit in a bronc's mouth but used only a hackamore (a rope around the nose) attached to the reins. On this occasion the horse bucked around the corral as usual, but then started to run. When the beast charged toward a barbed wire gate I pulled back to try to stop him, but the horse hit the gate and tore it down. The hackamore broke and I was without reins. The horse started running down alongside the corral fence and made for a narrow slot between the fence and a mesquite tree. I swayed to try to miss the tree, but the gap wasn't wide enough and I caught a mesquite trunk hard on my shoulder. The blow almost jerked me out of the saddle. Fortunately the tree was not one of those massive old deep-rooted mesquites: this one broke off at the bottom when I hit it. The horse then began bucking around one tree after another, with me trying to avoid the branches. Wick rode after me trying to rope the bronc with a small noose, hoping to avoid getting me entangled with the horse. He finally caught the ornery critter and I dismounted.

For weeks thereafter, as I walked on the University of Arizona campus, my legs would give out. Looking back, it was kind of foolish to get on a bronc when I was not riding regularly. I also was black and blue from my shoulder to my elbow and on my thighs as a result of having hit the mesquite tree and being pulled up over the bucking rolls on the saddle.

It was 1928. Tucson was growing. The Catalina Foothills development had just been started by John Murphy — ordinary things in my ordinary world. One night after school my sister Villette Donau invited me to her house, as she wanted me to meet some of her friends. The friends turned out to be Minor R. "Tillie" Tillotson and his wife, Winifred. Tillie was the Superintendent of Grand Canyon National Park. This was indeed a fateful introduction, because it set me on the path that was to shape my entire career in the national parks: During our conversation, Tillie offered me a job as a temporary ranger in Grand Canyon.

I was astonished at the invitation, but decided to apply. However, when I received the instructions and noted the price of the regulation park ranger's uniform, I felt this summer job would not leave me any money for school. The pay was $150 per month with fifty cents deducted for each meal. I told my dad I thought I would not accept the job. He told me to go ahead and take it and he would help me with my finances. He said, "The people you will meet at Grand Canyon may mean a lot more to you than the money you earn." This turned out to be more than true.

I reported to the Park Service in Grand Canyon in June 1928. When I was asked to fill out the application and looked at the "Year of Birth" question, I realized I was not of age. I was only 20 years old and the minimum was 21. I lied and showed my birthdate as 1906 instead of 1907. Evidently nobody checked up on me, because Assistant Superintendent Pat Patrow swore me in as a temporary ranger. Since the federal government at Grand Canyon had concurrent jurisdiction with the county and state, I was also sworn in as a deputy sheriff.

In those days we carried a gun in certain situations. In fact, the chief ranger often called me to go with him on raids in an attempt to stamp out bootlegging which was being carried on in the park. On these cases, we always carried a gun. It was a cat and mouse experience. We knew that a former Fred Harvey Company wrangler was selling bootleg, but since he knew the park as well as we did, we were never able to catch him. It was particularly amusing when we would meet him in the hotel lobby and exchange greetings, and then he would go out one door and we would dash out the other to try to catch him with liquor in his possession. We never did.

I was assigned to the Hopi fire tower on the ponderosa pine-covered Coconino Plateau south of the canyon to watch for forest fires. I was also placed on road patrol to and from the fire tower. Because there was only one tower — instead of several, from which triangulation could locate the fire precisely — I had to estimate the distance when a smoke was sighted. The smoke often lay beyond the horizon and correct estimation was difficult. I was congratulated for my accuracy. If you were too far off on your estimate, you could send the fire fighters on a wild-goose chase. This would not make you popular.

In the evenings I was on Rim patrol until 9:00 p.m., which meant that each evening I had to go up on the Rim of the canyon and walk back and forth on the walkways and trails to answer questions and to enforce the park's regulations. I was usually joined by other rangers and Park Service people. Sitting on the Rim watching the girls go by and watching the sunset over the canyon was a favorite pastime for everyone.

Having had stock and packing experience, I was assigned special trips across the Grand Canyon and odd jobs of packing supplies into the canyon. The Park Service was in the process of reconstructing the suspension bridge across the Colorado River in the lower gorge. The bridge was made of wooden planks suspended from cables across the canyon, some 420 feet in length. This bridge was obsolete and the Park Service was in the process of substituting a steel suspension bridge. The project took all the regular packers, so other packing jobs fell to my lot. This pleased me, as I loved to go off on my own with a saddle horse and a string of pack mules.

One day I was called by the superintendent and told that he and his wife and I were to go across Grand Canyon to pick up some important people. They were a nationally known naturalist, John C. Merriam; Wallace W. Atwood, President of Clark College in Worchester, Massachusetts;

and two employees from the National Park Service Branch of Operations in Washington, D.C.: senior auditor Charles L. Gable and his assistant Wilson A. Blossom.

The saddle horses and pack mules assigned to the job totaled 14 head of stock. I had never seen these particular mules before. Six of them had full packs and the balance had saddles. I knew at the end of the day I had to turn these mules into a corral with seventy-five other mules assigned to the regular packing contingent at the bottom of the canyon. The next morning I would be expected to identify my mules and re-pack them.

I spent the entire trip down the trail trying to memorize the identity of each mule and his pack so I could match them again the next morning and avoid a lot of adjusting of harnesses and packs.

That night when I went to bed I kept saying to myself, "I have to get up at four o'clock, I have to get up at four o'clock." It would be essential for me to have that time to pick out the mules, get them saddled and packed and be ready to start out at 7:00 a.m. with the superintendent and his wife.

I awoke with a start, lit a match to look at my dollar watch, and saw it was 11:30 p.m. I did this for the rest of the night about every 45 minutes to an hour, until I finally got up at 3:30 a.m. and set out to select my pack mules. The superintendent was there ahead of me. He was probably apprehensive about my ability to identify and pack our mules. Between the two of us we got the job done. The trouble was we finished so early the mules had to stand several hours with full packs and they were as tired as I was by the time we reached the top of the Canyon on the North Rim.

We returned the next day with our V.I.P. guests Merriam, Atwood, Gable and Blossom. The seven of us stopped in the bottom of the canyon at Phantom Ranch that night. This was an overnight guest accommodation operated by the Fred Harvey Company, the concessionaire for Grand Canyon National Park. Gable, who headed what was soon to become the concessions division of the National Park Service in Washington D.C., asked me if I would join him and two others in a bridge game. I said "yes." We had just sat down to play when someone turned the lights off.

Mr. Gable got up and turned them back on. A Fred Harvey Company employee, the manager-chef at that location, jumped up and turned them off again. Mr. Gable protested, stating that he wanted to play bridge. The manager berated Mr. Gable, not telling him that they were having generator problems. If that simple fact had been explained, there would have been no altercation, but words were exchanged and Mr. Gable, a very small statured person, offered to fight the manager, a 6' 2" tall man. The Fred Harvey people were notified about this offending manager and he was terminated for his lack of diplomatic behavior. I guess he had been isolated too long in the Canyon and was tired of dealing with visitors and erratic generators.

During my first year at Grand Canyon the rangers lived in tents. I shared a tent with Harvey Holtz, a medical student from Oklahoma. In order to save money we ate only two meals a day and substituted a quart of milk, crackers and cheese for lunch.

I'll never forget a conversation with Fred Johnson, the assistant superintendent in Grand Canyon National Park. Fred and I were sitting on the Rim waiting for Chief Ranger James P. Brooks to come out of the canyon. I was to leave for school the next day. Fred told me about his life. He was the thirteenth child of a Mormon family from Kanab, Utah. He said he had a third grade education. He said, "It probably doesn't seem like much to you, but to get to be assistant superintendent here is a great achievement for me, but one thing scares me. That's the Colorado River. I can't swim a lick, and if they told me to go on the river, I think I'd quit."

I didn't think too much about this until about two months later at college, when I read in the paper that Fred Johnson and Joe Sturdevant, the park naturalist, had been drowned in the Colorado River. Chief Ranger Brooks had arranged for Sturdevant and Johnson to run the rapids to get into a side canyon and plant some fingerling trout. Fred tried to get Brooks to let him climb down the walls and avoid the river. Brooks said, "Fred, this will take about five minutes and your way will take three days." Joe Sturdevant asked to go too. The boat turned over and only Brooks got out alive. Joe's body was recovered, but Fred's body was never found. The silt in the Colorado River pulls a body to the bottom, where it gets lodged among the rocks.

Feeling among the rangers ran high against Brooks, as we all knew of Fred's reluctance to go into the river and Fred was undoubtedly the most popular man in Grand Canyon National Park. Jim Brooks was a fearless man and couldn't understand why others expressed fear. Two instances will demonstrate his attitude:

One involved a couple of Kentuckians working in the park. One day they were drinking and one was waving a Colt automatic, daring Brooks to come and get him. The other Kentuckian said, "Brooks, let me talk to him — he'll shoot you." Brooks's response was, "This is my job." He walked up and took the gun out of the drunk's hand.

Another involved me. I was in the Hopi fire tower when Brooks called me and said to get my gun and motorcycle and meet him at headquarters. I did and was instructed as follows: "Three fellows have held up a service station in Williams and shot the attendant. They're headed this way and we believe they're in the park. They're travelling in an old rattletrap car. Two are about your size and one is a little guy. Get on your motorcycle and go out toward Desert View. If they get hard with you, beat the hell out of them." I went to Desert View but fortunately I never found them. I just brash and foolish enough to have tried.

Later I was invited to share quarters with Eddie McKee, the park naturalist who replaced Joe Sturdevant. Then I moved in with Carl and Gordon Cox, George Collins and Bob Williamson. Gordon and George were permanent employees and entitled to real housing rather than tents, housing which they shared with us.

While I was at Grand Canyon fellow ranger Carl Cox bought a new ranger's hat for $12.00 but lost it in a wind gust over the canyon. I offered to retrieve it. I tied a 250-foot rope to a tree and went over the ledge. When I cleared the last ledge I saw the rope dangling seventy-five feet short. I then started to climb out when my fingers cramped. I held on to the rope with my legs and talked out loud to myself not to panic. I finally inched my tortuous way to the top and out. A foolish thing to do for a $12.00 hat.

Carl and Bob, who slept downstairs in the group cabin, were great pranksters and, as I was always on rim duty, I could expect a pan of water over the door when I came home at night. I adapted by always pushing the door open with my foot to let the water spill out. They adapted by putting a five-gallon can of water under the porch roof with a rope to the door. As I stepped back and pushed the door open with my foot, I was drenched.

My tormentors had locked the upstairs door to the room where George, Gordon and I slept. Intent upon retribution, I went to the ranger supply storage and got a ladder and a back-pump used to fight forest fires. I pumped about ten gallons of water into Carl and Bob's beds. Though they were in bed at the time, they never gave me the satisfaction of uttering a word.

To get even, George bought a bottle of cheap perfume and saturated my pillow and bed with it. I had to sleep with my head hanging over the edge as the perfume gave me a terrific headache. It was a fun but hazardous place to live.

We have remained lifetime friends. George and Gordon still keep in touch. I handled the purchase of the V.T. Ranch (now the Kaibab Lodge) for Carl Cox when he left the Park Service. Carl died of cancer and Bob of a burst appendix.

As I said, my dad's statement that I would meet people who would mean more than just a job was certainly true. I established friendships that lasted the rest of my life. In fact it altered my legal career as I spent much of my life as a park concessionaire, where I gained more lifelong friends.

One day I was called to take a string of pack mules across to the North Rim of the Grand Canyon. I had my saddle horse and 12 mules. It is remarkable that park regulations would not permit the Fred Harvey Company regular packers to have more than six mules to a guide, but they sent me out with 12. That is the way the government operates. Regulations can be overlooked if it isn't convenient for the government. The Harvey guides were far more experienced and competent than I.

I got down to the suspension bridge which, as I said, was made of 2x12 planks hung from cables across the inner gorge about 75 feet above the water. This bridge was supposedly limited to one horse and rider at a time. I was tying up my horse when three of the mules broke loose and started back up the trail. I hastily tied up my horse by the bridge and ran after the mules.

I tried to pass them, but the faster I ran the faster they ran, until finally I got to a wide place in the trail where I could pass. The mules were packed with kayak boxes. These packs could easily knock a man off the trail to fall five or six hundred feet, so I was careful not to pass until the trail was wide enough. When I did, I made the mistake of shooing the mules down the trail. Unfortunately, they didn't stop when they got to the bottom, but pushed into the rest of the mules and broke the reins on my saddle horse. My horse and twelve fully-packed mules went out on this bridge officially limited to a single horse and rider. The bridge buckled and bounced up and down and swayed while the mules fought for a foothold .

My heart almost came out of my mouth, for all I could see was the bridge breaking and all of my mules and my horse seventy-five feet below in the Colorado River, and my job with them! Fortunately, one mule got a foothold and got out and that was enough to let the others scamper off the bridge. My job was saved! I did not tell anyone about this for a long time. I do not know whether this incident contributed to it, but in a heavy windstorm that next fall, the bridge went down. I am afraid I may have contributed to its destruction.

Packing and getting away from the hotels and people-concentrated places was the most enjoyable part of the job. Because I could pack, I got the prime assignments.

One assignment that stands out in my memory in-volved a trip to the basin area on the South Rim, about 30 miles west of the Bright Angel hotel. Chief Ranger Brooks furnished me a saddle horse and two pack mules and instructed me to go down into the canyon and locate seep-ing springs, dig them out and make cement catch basins. The purpose was to provide water holes for the wild game.

On this trip Chief Ranger Brooks gave me a rifle and told me to shoot any of the wild burros I encountered. This wasn't exactly a pleasant task and I was fortunate that I never did come across any wild burros. The shooting of burros many years later caused a considerable uproar, par-ticularly among the humane societies. The uproar led to the

"Adopt A Burro" program which asked people all over the country to adopt a burro so they could catch them and turn them over to adoptive homes rather than shoot them. The uproar also convinced Congress to pass the Wild Horse and Burros Protection Act of 1971.

The reason Park Service officials wanted the burros eliminated was that they are great foragers. They eat the grass and browse the vegetation so low that wildlife does not have much of a chance to survive. There are pictures showing a tremendous crisscross of trails and completely eroded hillsides devoid of all vegetation in the lower end of the Grand Canyon — a result of the excessive burro population.

At the close of the visitor season in 1930, as I was preparing to return to school, George Collins and I were waiting for Chief Ranger Brooks to arrive so I could take my leave. George said to me, "Don, I don't understand you. You're a damned good ranger and cow-punching material and can live in these great outdoors in the parks, but you're going to law school to be a lawyer and sit behind a desk in some stuffy office."

Well, I went on to become a lawyer. But I also went on to become a concessions operator and spent a good part of my life in the national parks. What happened to George Collins?

He was a very talented man with leadership ability, so he was promoted to Washington, D.C. and spent most of his time behind a desk! I never let George forget his remark to me. Every time I visited him I asked, "How does it feel, George, to be in the National Park Service and live in the great outdoors?"

5

Law School and Lassen

In 1930, after graduating from the University of Arizona with an AB degree in history and political science, I enrolled at the University of Michigan Law School in Ann Arbor.

My college friend Lawson Baxter enrolled with me. Bax's father — who remained chief chemist at Michigan Alkali — was anxious to have his son become a lawyer but Bax didn't like it and dropped out at Christmas time. Bax subsequently followed in his father's footsteps and became a chemist.

A number of University of Arizona friends lived near Ann Arbor, which made possible some very enjoyable weekend get-togethers at the Baxter home. Bax's sister Ethel had married a man named Thomas Bate who was attending medical school at Wayne University in Detroit. Our college friend Hudson Smart had a job flying Ford trimotor experimental aircraft out of Dearborn, Michigan.

Law school changed me. I learned to study properly and for the first time in my life actually learned my academic material thoroughly. I also got a harsh introduction to the realities of law school and the legal profession. The first-year class had three-hundred students. It was school policy to graduate only one hundred per year. We were informed of it at our first class. The room was large and formed a semicircle in tiers with the professor in the center. Professor Grover C. Grismore, who taught contracts, opened the class by saying, "Introduce yourself to the man on your right, now to the left. Only one of you will be here to graduate in three years."

While we got periodic quizzes, the only grade that counted was on our final examination. As a result, the pressure increased as the completion of the class approached. This was intended to prepare us for our state bar examination where only our examination determined whether we would be authorized to practice law.

One incident I remember distinctly occurred in Professor Waite's Crimes class (I can't recall his first name). The professor was explaining the legal concept that if you had no duty, you could not be held responsible. Charley Jones, a student from Kansas who spoke in very precise terms and smacked his lips between words, said, "You mean to tell me (smack) that if I go out of my house and a baby has been left on my doorstep (smack) and it is cold and stormy and I know that the baby will die if I do nothing to protect it (smack) and the baby dies (smack) that they can do nothing to me?" Professor Waite said, "That's right." Charley retorted, "By God, that ain't right."

In a contracts class, Professor Grismore presented a case in which a man had contracted to have a house built and midway through construction, the house burned down. Professor Grismore wanted to know what, if the owner of the house came to you to represent him, would you do? The professor went from one student to another without getting an answer.

Homer Kripke held up his hand. Homer was a brilliant student of Jewish ancestry. He said, "I'd have a fire sale." This really brought down the house — no pun intended. Homer Kripke was the only student in our class who graduated with a perfect grade record.

I was nominated for student member of the Board of Governors but was defeated after a tie vote. I had made quite a number of enemies as head waiter at the Lawyers Club where most of us lived. I refused to let students in for breakfast after the dining room doors had closed. I was often rebuked by the late arrivals. I was also nominated but defeated for senior class president.

I graduated with a Juris Doctor degree in June 1933 but did not wait to attend the graduation exercises as I had work to do in Lassen.

In 1930, on the recommendation of my friend, George Collins, whose brother, Walker Collins, was the Superintendent of Lassen Volcanic National Park, California, I applied for a job at Lassen as a temporary ranger. I knew nothing about Lassen except that George had told me there were no concession facilities within the park; that it was a small park, but a beautiful place to work; in fact, it was where he started and was one of his favorites. I sent an application and George followed with a letter of recommendation to his brother. I then returned to law school but heard nothing in response to my application. It was nearing time to return for summer employment when I received a telegram from Chief Ranger Brooks asking whether or not I was returning to Grand Canyon. As I had to have a job, I immediately sent a wire stating that, yes, I was returning for my fourth season.

About three days later, I received an offer of a temporary ranger's job at Lassen Volcanic National Park. Don Ford, who was in the class ahead of me at law school, was from Hollywood, California. As Westerners, we got acquainted and I told Don of this offer of a second job. This was unheard of during the depression. He asked me to recommend him to Mr. Collins for the job at Lassen. I agreed, but warned him that I knew neither Mr. Collins nor anyone else at Lassen and he knew nothing about me except what his brother had told him. I doubted whether my recommendation would carry much weight; however, I sent it off and much to both of our surprises, Don Ford got an offer to be a ranger at Lassen National Park.

Don Ford and his roommate, Lawrence Curfman, who lived in Pittsburg, Kansas, were returning home. Since Don and I both had jobs in the national parks, we bought a secondhand 1929 Ford Roadster and agreed to take Curfman home. We also agreed to take Kingsley Chadeyne, who had graduated and lived in Van Nuys, California, to Los Angeles for $30.00.

The four of us started out on our trek to the west. We stopped first at Grand Canyon to allow me to disembark and then they went on to Los Angeles. Curfman had no job so he was going to see if he could get the job that Don Ford had had delivering ice for ice boxes around the Hollywood area. He did, and lived with the Ford family. Don and Curfman drove up to Lassen Volcanic National Park for Don to report to his job and Curf returned to Los Angeles.

At the close of the season I went to Los Angeles and Curfman and I drove up to Lassen National Park to pick up Don. We returned by a circuitous route through Coos Bay, Oregon, so Don could see his girlfriend, Siri Ann Enegren.

The following season Don Ford and I applied for and received jobs as temporary rangers in Lassen Volcanic National Park. We were to be stationed at Summit Lake Ranger Station which is located roughly in the middle of the park. We were assigned a pick-up truck but no horses. If we had to go to the back country, we had to have some saddle horses. Time passed and still we received no horses.

Don decided the best way to avoid further delay was to give a dinner for Superintendent Collins and his wife, Clara. We put on a regular menu and Don invited the Superintendent and his wife. The invitations were named "the `horse bait' dinner." I did most of the cooking, but did not feel capable of baking a pie. Eddie, a cook for the construction camp, had a reputation of being an excellent pie baker, so we had him bake us a raisin pie, which we then heated in the oven and served at our dinner. We got our horses about three days later.

One of our ranger duties was to contact people in the campgrounds. We were to visit with them and find out if there were any problems. This gave us an opportunity to get acquainted with park visitors.

Often when campers departed for home, they dropped their leftover supplies off at the Ranger Station. This lightened our grocery bill; in fact, we lived on $7.00 a month for each of us. Both Don and I were rather frugal in our habits and I, as the cook, found that Spanish rice was easy, a good dish and very inexpensive. To this day, Don tells how he lived on Spanish rice all summer. This was not quite factual, but I admit that we did have our share. I did the cooking and Don washed the dishes.

Occasionally we went to a dance in Chester, California, which was nicknamed "Little Reno" because of its wide-open gambling. This was a typical small town dance which would last into the wee hours of the morning and was about our only diversion from the regular duties as rangers.

Toward the end of the season, Don Ford was called into headquarters to help on the preparation of the budget as he had worked on the budget the previous year, and they welcomed his assistance. After that he returned to Los Angeles.

This left me alone at Summit Lake. We were badly in need of a trail from Summit Lake to Echo Lake. I laid out a trail of about two miles, following pretty much the contours of the land so as not to require too much cutting and filling. I marked the trees with a big "T" by cutting the bark with an axe. This was a rather arduous job and difficult. I had no plan or way to lay out a route except as I advanced on the ground. I would have to go forward and put a temporary mark and go back and see if it was the proper way to arrive at Echo Lake and not bypass it. I finally completed the Echo Lake Trail and was pleased when the park adopted it as the regular trail. The following year the park assigned a trail crew to take out the rough spots and cut some of the banks to level out the trail, but they followed my route.

Toward the end of the season, I was doing road patrol over the Lassen Peak Road. I arranged my schedule so that I would end at Manzanita Lake, where Charles Keathley, the ranger-naturalist, was living. He and I prepared our evening dinner together instead of each of us cooking alone. It was at one of these dinners when I said to Keathley that someone was going to make money if they put in some concessions. I had given away quite a bit of gasoline to tourists who came into the park expecting services, only to discover that they did not have enough gasoline to get out of the park to a service station. I jokingly suggested that maybe we ought to put in for the concessions. Keathley thought this was an excellent idea. In our subsequent discussion we got rather enthused and I said that I would go in to see the superintendent the next day to find if there was a possibility of us applying for the concession.

The following morning I went to see Superintendent Collins, who advised me that the Park Service was looking for a concessioner; in fact, they had offered it to the Yosemite Park & Curry Company, but had been turned down, it being too small for their interest. I asked Mr. Collins if he would recommend Charles Keathley and me for the concession and he advised me he would. He said the people who ran the lodge at Childs Meadows were also interested in applying.

I gave this information to Keathley and together we prepared an application. When we came to the portion concerning financing the facilities, we were stumped. We finally ended up by saying that we had "sufficient financial backing to insure this venture." This was rather an overstatement, as I had signed notes for all my tuition at law school and was working as a waiter at the Michigan Law Quadrangle for my board and room. Keathley was in worse condition. He had to borrow money from his fiancée to buy his uniform to take this ranger-naturalist job!

As the season closed and I had been notified that I had been promoted from waiter to head waiter at the law school, I got a coach ticket on the Southern Pacific Railroad to return to Tucson to see my parents preparatory to going back to Ann Arbor. The train stopped in Sacramento and I got off to stretch my legs.

I was walking when two men came up beside me, one with a British accent and very well dressed. The other was a short, fat man in suspenders and shirt-sleeves. He asked where I was going and I said I was on the train headed for Tucson. He said, "Oh, you are on the train and just stretching your legs like we are." They walked along with me, just sort of talking between themselves. The so-called Englishman said he had just come over from England to settle his sister's estate and that he was glad he had come because he had already been offered more money than they had indicated they were willing to pay for the estate's assets by letter. I said I thought that would please the family and he said, "Oh, they won't know about this, because I am going to have a good time while I am in the West." The discussion ranged from, but always came back to, money when finally the so-called Englishman said, "Why don't we flop a coin for the drinks?" The other man winked at me and said, "We say in this country `flip a coin'". "Well," the Englishman said, "flip or flop — how about it?" About that time we were approaching a bar which was down in a cellar off the street.

I was becoming increasingly suspicious. The conversation was going too well and the emphasis was too much on money. When they proposed to go off the street, I told them they should go without me and that I would continue on as I didn't want to miss my train. Whereupon the Englishman said, "Come on in — you don't have to participate — you can be the judge." I said, "I think you people need a jury, not a judge."

The Englishman persisted and the little fat man grabbed him by the coat and said to him, "Come on, come on — he's wise." So they took off down the street and I returned and boarded the train.

About Easter time I was putting on my waiter's coat at Ann Arbor to go to work when a friend brought a telegram to me from Charles Gable of the National Park Service. The substance of the wire was that they would like a "more definite statement of our financial position." I made some hurried telephone calls to Keathley, who was at the University of Missouri. We both decided that we would see what financial support we could secure.

I had become acquainted and had been quite friendly with Dallas W. Dort, who was a graduate of Princeton University and who was reputed to have some money. Dort's father had been one of the organizers of General Motors. I approached Dal, who had heard of national parks but had never heard of Lassen Volcanic National Park. I produced the wire from the National Park Service, so Dal and I worked out an agreement and that afternoon we sent a wire giving Dal Dort's financial position.

We were notified that we could have a four-year permit. This was quite disturbing to me as I did not see how we could possibly invest the necessary funds with such a short-term contract. The Park Service assured us, however, that if we showed a satisfactory performance, the contract would be extended. We decided to proceed on their assurances.

I immediately called my dad and asked him to set up a California corporation which he did under the name Lassen National Park Camps, Ltd. This was rather a lengthy name for such a small beginning.

Keathley immediately quit school where he was working on his masters degree in paleontology. He married Mary Ann Hutchinson, the fiancée from whom he had borrowed money to buy his uniform. He then bought a second-hand Ford and he and his bride headed for Lassen.

As I was not yet out of school, I continued for two weeks. When Dal and I graduated, we went to Flint, Michigan, and bought a second-hand Ford van for two hundred dollars. We bargained quite successfully for the car, stating that we didn't have any more money. When Dal gave the car salesman his check showing the name "Dort," which was of course well-known in Flint he thought we had taken advantage of him in our bargaining.

Lawson Baxter, whom I had started law school with in Ann Arbor, and who had quit at Christmas time, decided he would like to go back to California and work for us in this new venture, so the two of us started west. We found that we had not made quite as good a deal as we thought on the automobile. The tires were so old and rotten we spent half our traveling time fixing flat tires as we drove to Lassen Volcanic National Park.

When Keathley arrived at the park, he had contacted Superintendent Collins, who had been advised that a concession contract had been granted to us for a lodge at Manzanita Lake, a scenic spot ideal for tourist accommodations. The superintendent immediately helped Keathley make contact with various suppliers in the area. The principal one was the Diamond Match Company, which had agreed to deliver lumber for the start of construction in the park. We received about $5,000 worth of lumber without even a credit rating. The fact that it was being spent for construction in the park led the company to think they were secure in furnishing us lumber. After all, it was the bottom of the depression and every business was willing to take a chance in order to sell its product.

Walker Collins again assisted us by putting Charlie Keathley in touch with employees who had previously worked in the park, either as laborers or carpenters. Appropriations from the federal government had all been held up pending approval of emergency funds. (The regular appropriation was to be replaced with emergency appropriations in support of the program to hire the unemployed.) The delay meant that many workers were eager to find a job. As a result, Keathley hired some carpenters and some laborers to help start our Manzanita Lake construction program. We were paying carpenters $5.00 per day, and laborers $1.00 per day.

When I arrived in the park two weeks later, I found our first payroll waiting for me. It amounted to $750 and it was due on Saturday — the day I arrived! Dal Dort had given me a checkbook on a Michigan bank, but I had no notice of the deposit having been made. This was Saturday afternoon and, of course, all the employees were anxious to get to town to cash their checks, as most of them had been out of work for some time. I telephoned every number I could think of, but was unable to contact Dort to determine whether or not a deposit had been made.

Keathley and I frantically discussed the matter. We felt it would be better to issue paychecks immediately and get in touch with Dal in time to clear them in Michigan, as it would take almost a week, rather than tell our new employees that they would have to wait for their money. They all knew us from our previous year's summer employment as ranger and ranger-naturalist, and knew that we personally had no money. A delay in payroll would have been disastrous. Fortunately, later that night, Dal Dort called and advised me he had deposited $2,000 in our bank in Flint, Michigan. It was a tremendous relief for us both. I do not know what would have happened if the checks had arrived before Dal made the deposit.

The architect for Yosemite Park & Curry Company, Eldridge (Ted) Spencer, had designed the lodge for Manzanita Lake, which was to be a rock building. The specifications called for rock no larger than one man could handle. The Park Service sent an architect to supervise the construction. Their architect wanted huge boulders, but we were not prepared to handle them. One day I stopped to watch the work on the walls. They were taking an hour or more to put one rock in the building. I realized we could not continue in this manner so I left for Redding, California, to see if I could get a truck with a boom to lift the rocks into place in the wall. Keathley had been offered a truck at $25 per day, and we were to furnish the driver, maintenance and fuel. This seemed to be a completely unreasonable price.

While in Redding I heard about a farmer who had just had his truck returned from another job, and that it would probably be available for hire. I went to the farmer's home and talked with him through a screened porch where he had gone to bed. To this day I have never seen the man's face. We made an agreement that he would rent us the truck for $15 per day and he would provide a driver, maintenance and fuel. The truck was brought up to our job the following day.

During this period of construction, Charles and Mary Ann Keathley were living in a tent that also served as a store. Their bed was separated by a counter at which we sold candy, beer and groceries, along with sandwiches that Mary Ann made. It was not a very modern operation but a practical one under the circumstances. Our most distinguished visitor was Herbert Hoover, the former President of the United States, who had just been defeated. He was quite a fisherman and often went to Lassen to fish. We thought we had struck a real bonanza as his party bought every thing we had for sale and then left half of it for our own use.

The lodge we were building was a small structure. I do not recall the exact size, but in the lodge was a lobby, a six-seat food counter, a few shelves for groceries, a kitchen and a counter for registration and another counter for the sale of gifts. We also had a slot for a Post Office and Mary Ann Keathley was appointed Postmistress. At the side of the building was a two-pump service station for the sale of gasoline. Gasoline was pumped by hand into the glass cylinders, the usual practice in those days. It was not exactly ideally located, as the cars blocked the side entry into the lodge.

Dal and Betty Dort had been touring the country, as Dal tried to land a job with some law firm. I know he had an appointment with Robert LaFollette, the Progressive Party candidate for President of the United States, but nothing came of it. Dal thought he should go to Lassen to see what progress was being made with the funds he had pledged and advanced.

It was a surprise to Keathley and me when Dal and Betty arrived. We soon found work for them. Dal took over painting the lobby ceiling. Most of it was gray overglaze accomplished by putting on brown stain and then painting over it with green paint, which had to be immediately wiped off, leaving a very pleasing but somewhat mottled texture. As a result Dal had paint on his clothes, his arms, head and hair. Betty became a maid and subsequently our first wait-ress. As I recall, Dal received no wages and Betty's were minimal at best.

We also had under construction ten duplex cottages, each one with two bedrooms and individual bathrooms with showers and a connecting kitchen. The kitchen was ar-ranged to be shared if there was a family party, or could be locked off with one being rented as a bedroom only and the other as a bedroom with kitchen. The space heaters were wooden stoves that had been poorly placed in an alcove in the cabins. We had to set the stoves out in the middle of the rooms, for if we had placed them in the alcoves as the architect designated, we would have burned the cabins down. The hot water was heated by propane gas, using a Swedish invention called a Watrola. The Watrola was a very efficient unit. You did not have to store water in a tank. The water was heated as it went through a series of copper coils. They were excellent units.

There were occasional problems. We encountered one early in our construction of cabins in 1934. A Watrola's safety cutoff was malfunctioning. It would suddenly cut off the flame even though the pilot light still functioned. It was a shock when taking a warm shower to suddenly be dashed with cold water that came out of a snow bank. I had gone over to the cabin several times trying to fix the troublesome unit and even violated safety regulations by attempting to tie back the shutoff valve.

I was behind the desk in the lobby when the door flew open and a man entered with a bathrobe thrown over his shoulders, in his bare feet and with water dripping from his hair. He shouted, "The G— D——— thing is off again!" People were startled but unfortunately I laughed. He immediately returned to his cabin and checked out. He had had enough of our service.

As we were unable to utilize either the lodge or the cottages, which were unfinished, our total receipts for the summer were only $15,000. This came entirely from sales made over the counter in the tent occupied by the Keathleys.

In 1934 I arranged for a $15,000 loan through Mr. Frisbie, a banker in Redding, California. These funds were to be utilized for completion of the lodge and cabins and for purchase of equipment. We also planned an expansion to the lodge building by constructing an addition to the back of the lodge to provide for a real dining room with space for a grocery store at the lower level. The ground dipped sharply from the rear of the lodge, which would enable us to cut into the bank so that the dining room attached to the lodge was at ground level, with the store below the ground except that the entrance at the lower end of the store was also at ground level.

Because we wanted a fireplace at the end of the dining room, we had to secure a lot of large rocks which would complement the rocks in the lodge. The terrain dictated that we build a very high chimney. In order to get the rocks in place, we borrowed a power winch from the National Park Service. We then dug a hole in the ground, cut a pine tree and put it in the hole with guy-wires running about 40 feet in the air attached to several trees. The cable on the power winch ran through a block and tackle on the top of the tree.

The rocks were dumped several yards away to be easily accessible, but as the rock mason would select a rock from someplace in the interior of the pile, it became necessary to pull these heavy rocks over the tops of the others. The power put on to raise a thousand-pound rock which was lodged behind other rocks would cause the tree to bend like a bow and when the rock finally cleared the other rocks, the tree would snap back. I operated the power winch, and in order to avoid it dropping behind other rocks, I would have to keep power on it and then cut the power as it sailed through the air to prevent it from crashing into the building.

Our insurance agent came up one day to watch the operation. When he saw these large rocks flying through the air and the danger that was attendant to them, he climbed into his car and left. He didn't want to know anything about this operation! We never saw him again, but business in the depression was prized. He never canceled our insurance policy!

Although we had perishables, we had no refrigeration to protect them from spoiling. As a result, we built a screened box which we placed next to the mountain steam under the bridge, with water going over a burlap cover. The coolness of the stream and the evaporation on the burlap kept the produce in reasonable condition. It was a matter of amusement as someone would order a bottle of milk in the lobby, only to have the clerk run out the door, go down under the bridge, get the bottle of milk, return to the lobby, then have to go back again when the individual decided he also wanted a pound of butter. This worked reasonably well until the Park Service brought in a Veterans' CCC Camp. They learned where we kept the beer in the stream under bridge and it was with great difficulty that we were able to protect these supplies.

Once a week we had to go to Red Bluff and Redding,

California, to get supplies. The trip took us over Lassen Peak road and down to Red Bluff where we picked up fruit, vegetables, melons and produce.

We obtained these from a Japanese farmer, who later turned out to be part of the Japanese intelligence when World War II started. We then continued on to Redding for the balance of our supplies and then on Highway 44 to Manzanita Lake. The trip was a total of 170 miles and took the entire day, often up to midnight. Our truck was a three-quarter ton panel and was always overloaded. It was a slow trip climbing from almost sea level to six thousand feet.

We built a new full-size service station about 100 yards from the lodge. This relieved one of the big obstacles as the service station blocked the lodge side door leading to the cottages.

The employees now consisted of Charles and Mary Ann Keathley, Harriet Hutchinson, sister to Mary Ann, and myself.

I was helping on the construction of the new dining room and grocery store which required cutting into the bank adjacent to the lodge building. To expedite this, I borrowed a Caterpillar tractor from the Park Service. They told me it had been left in the forest where it was last used and I would have to go and get it.

I found the Caterpillar and started over the manzanita brush, when I ran over a length of pine log and it lodged between the tracks of the Caterpillar. The Caterpillar was turned half on its side, but the thickness of the manzanita kept it from turning over completely. As a result I was able to climb under the Caterpillar. I took the logging chain which was attached and ran it up over the log between the two tracks and then hooked the chain into one of the tracks. I then got on the machine and gunned the motor. I held the one track and the one with the chain on it jerked the log and flipped it out behind me.

I often sweated later when I realized that the chain could have swung around and cut me in half. It worked, however, and the log was unstuck, the machine righted and I continued over the manzanita to the lodge.

While I was digging next to the lodge, I went into the

lodge building. I was, of course, covered with dirt and grease and was a pretty disreputable looking person. I stepped behind the desk and heard a woman say, "I want to see the manager." The clerk turned to me and said, "This is the manager." I still remember the look of disgust on her face when she looked at me, probably thinking, "This dirty looking creature is the manager of this operation!" I do not remember whether she just turned around and left or whether she made some complaint, but she obviously was appalled at my appearance.

At the close of the season I contacted the National Park Service and asked for an extended contract on the basis that we had demonstrated our capacity to finance and operate our facilities. We still had two years to go on our permit, but that was obviously inadequate, if we were to proceed. I was successful and received a new 10-year contract in 1935.

During this period of time differences of opinion arose concerning the way Keathley wanted to operate the facilities and the way I thought appropriate. Keathley was rather strong-willed and arbitrary, and didn't get along very well with our employees.

In addition to those mentioned above, my nephew, Al Donau, and Marshall Keathley, the youngest brother of Charlie Keathley, began working for us. The animosity developed to such a point that Dal and I thought it would be best if we bought Keathley's interest in the operation. We contacted Charlie and he agreed to sell his one-third interest in the company for $20,000. This was a pretty good return for an individual who had gone in with nothing just seven years before, in fact a very generous purchase price, but we felt that in the long-term interest of the company, it would be well to separate our interests. You must remember that $20,000 in those days was a lot of money, when a laborer got $1.00 a day and carpenters got $5.00 a day and lumber could be pur-chased for $20.00 a thousand.

Keathley and Mary Ann went to San Francisco where Keathley began working with Government Services, Inc. in the Regional Office. He continued there until his retirement many years later.

The Lassen Company started with a minimum investment and a few facilities, but grew rapidly. We attempted to keep up with the demands for facilities by getting loans from the bank and reinvesting our depreciation account and what little profits were made. From its inception until the merger in 1970 no dividend was ever paid. We had invested a total of $15,400 starting in 1933 in the main lodge and the few cabins that were constructed as the first complement. As the cabins and lodge were not completed at this time, it took the next several years to finish improving the facilities and to add equipment for the operation.

My salary during this period was $30.00 per month. With the intercession of World War II, we constructed no additional facilities; in fact, the regulations adopted by the government prevented the expansion of any so-called recreational facilities.

The Park Service was interested in keeping as many concession facilities open during the war as possible. Arthur Demaray, the Associate Director, said he would get National Parks Concessions, Inc. to operate the Lassen facilities if we would agree. We made a contract with them to the effect that we would split the profits. Claude Galloway was assigned by National Park Concessions, Inc. to manage the operation.

6
Works Project Administration

AFTER GRADUATING from law school, I studied for the California Bar. This consisted of reviewing Widforst's Law Review Books and getting acquainted with courses in sales, mining and water law, partnership and other courses which I had never had in law school. The California Bar examination had a reputation of being one of the most exacting in the United States. It was a three-day examination of eight hours each. I took the bar in San Francisco in August 1933.

I have forgotten how many took the bar, but they only passed twenty-three percent. I was fortunate to be among them. There was quite an uproar at flunking so many, which included all the Stanford graduates, the Yale graduates and fifty percent of the Michigan graduates. The son of the Chief Justice of the California Supreme Court flunked. When we were admitted to the California State Bar the Chief Justice said, "I guess the exam can be passed as I see a few of you have, but we are going to find out why so many failed." On the next exam, they passed sixty-four percent. It was comprehensive but, in my opinion, a fair examination.

In December 1934, I took the Arizona Bar and was fortunate to get the second highest grade on the examination. My dad was delighted. The Arizona Bar exam was harder for me as it was more technical and often turned on Arizona statutory law. I did not think it was as good a test as the California examination.

I was admitted to both bars and maintained membership in both until my retirement in 1982. Arizona awarded me my fifty-year Certificate of Merit.

I entered practice with my father in Tucson, Arizona. There was plenty of law business but as no one had any money we seldom collected any fees. I was working as an attorney, but received little or no compensation. All the clients, of course, were my dad's and the income went to him.

One day while driving home from the office with my dad, a police car pulled ahead of us and surrounded a house on

North Second Avenue with machine guns at the ready. I pulled up to see what was going on when my dad ordered me out of there. This was the house that the John Dillinger bank robbery gang had holed up in. The Tucson Police captured the gang and they were extradited to other states for bank robbery and murder charges. The FBI killed Dillinger on the streets of Chicago in 1934 after he escaped from a Lima, Ohio, jail. They had been tipped off by a woman accompanying Dillinger to a movie — they were alerted by the "Woman in Red."

In 1935 Dallas Dort took a job with the Works Project Administration (WPA) in Washington, D.C. Dal had dropped in for a visit with his friend, Corrington Gill, who was an Assistant Director of the WPA under Harry Hopkins, Administrator. Corrington told him he was too busy to talk with him. He said, "Take off your coat and go to work."

Senator William Edgar Borah, Republican from Idaho and a powerful man in the U.S. Senate, made charges of waste and graft in the WPA. Dal was sent to investigate the charges. That was the beginning of the Division of Investigation of the WPA. The division was charged with the responsibility of investigating any alleged violation of criminal laws arising out of the usage of emergency relief funds. These funds included not only WPA appropriations, but many of the other emergency agencies such as the National Youth Administration and the Emergency Relief Agency (ERA).

In February 1936 I applied through Dal for a job as an agent with WPA. Shortly thereafter I was interviewed by another agent, hired, and told to report to Dallas, Texas.

In the interim, Carl Cox, who was a temporary ranger at Grand Canyon, had agreed to purchase the old V-T Ranch, now called the Kaibab Lodge, about twenty miles north of the North Rim of the Grand Canyon. He asked me to handle the arrangements for the purchase of this resort. I went to Flagstaff to check the title and then to the Grand Canyon to consummate the deal. I spent only a couple of days there, as I was required to report immediately to Dallas for my new job.

On arrival in Dallas, a message was awaiting me from Washington, D.C., advising me to report to WPA headquarters in Washington for training and instruction. I flew to Washington, D.C., where I spent two weeks familiarizing myself with the operations and the investigative procedures for the WPA. I was then told that there was trouble in the State of Washington and ordered to return to Dallas, pick up my car, and report to Nathaniel Rogers, Field Agent in Charge in Portland, Oregon, for assignment to the State of Washington. The Portland office covered the four states of Washington, Oregon, Idaho and Montana.

In Dallas I took my car to the Buick garage to be serviced prior to my departure and then went back to the office to check out. A courtesy car was returning me to the Buick agency when I saw my car being driven down the street. I said to my driver, "There's my car," whistled at the man driving it and pointed to it. When I arrived at the garage, the man said, "Your car is ready for you." I said, "I just saw it going down the street." He said someone was probably giving it a final test drive. I waited around for a couple of hours before it was finally decided the car had been stolen and the theft reported to the police. By this time it was late in the afternoon and I was advised to get a room in the hotel and return in the morning.

The following morning the police said a car had been picked up, but they didn't know whose it was. It was my car. It had been abandoned on a side street. When I whistled and pointed to the thief the day before he was probably led to believe he had been discovered and got rid of the car as soon as possible. All my clothing and everything in the car had been taken. I made arrangements with the garage to give them a couple of weeks to retrieve my belongings, and then demanded that I be reimbursed for my losses. They denied any responsibility as they had a sign posted: "Not responsible for any articles left in your car." I finally compromised for fifty percent of what I thought the value of my clothes were. They had more value than I estimated as there were many things in the suitcases I did not recall until later and which had not been listed.

I reported to Field Agent Nathaniel Rogers in Portland and was told to ready myself to go to Seattle where I would be assigned as the state agent.

Nat Rogers was preparing to go to Washington, D.C., for a Field Agent in Charge meeting. He took me to Seattle, introduced me to some of the WPA personnel and advised me to get acquainted with the personnel, but to do nothing until he returned.

Nat was way over his head as far as ability to run an investigative unit. He was somewhat apprehensive about having me as an agent, as I was a lawyer and he was not. He was also aware of my friendship with Dallas Dort (Director of the Division).

In Nat's absence, and after conversations with the Personnel Director of the State WPA, I prepared a statement taken from him to the effect that the WPA workers were being required to kick back money from their checks into a fund which apparently was to be used to support a political campaign for George Gannon, the State WPA Administrator. It was a strong affidavit with considerable positive evidence to support it. I was told, though, not to proceed with the investigation because of its sensitive political overtones.

After sitting for several days, I decided that I would at least interview some of these people named in the affidavit and take statements. It was obvious that some laws were being violated. I continued to interview witnesses while Nat Rogers was in Washington.

I called Dal Dort to advise him of what I was doing. He said since this was my first case, to hold off and he would send an agent out from Kansas City who had considerable experience in investigations. The agent's name was Tommy Stakem, later to become the head of the U.S. Maritime Commission.

Shortly thereafter, Tommy Stakem arrived and I briefed him on what evidence I had. He told me later that he thought I must have been a poor investigator because with the evidence I had, I certainly should have gotten some confessions. The fact was that these people knew they would be fired if they confessed to illegally soliciting the funds.

During the investigation Rex Nicholson, who was in charge of a transient camp in the State of Washington, came to me and asked if I was a federal agent. I said "yes." and he asked if I could tell him what I was doing. I said, "No, I can't." He said, "Well, I have been certified for relief — I've got a wife and a baby girl — I must have this job. Would you recommend that I resign?" I said, "No, certainly not; do your job. Don't engage in any activities which are beyond the law, but stay on the job." Rex Nicholson's name will appear many times in this book: a lasting friendship was started at that time.

Much to my amazement, I got a call from Harry Hopkins, top man in the WPA and right-hand man to President Roosevelt. Harry Hopkins was rather profane in his language, and we had an interesting discussion interposed by Harry saying, "The hell you say — the hell you say — is that what those bastards are doing?" Shortly thereafter, Dal Dort called to say, "Don't do anything further — we think we can handle this here in Washington." I was instructed to go on to other cases and Tommy Stakem was sent back to Kansas without having participated in the investigation.

I was working on a case in Tacoma, Washington, when I saw the morning newspaper headline, "Gannon Fired for Illegal Solicitation." I thought, "Gee, this outfit really means business, they don't fool around." Little did I realize that it was brought about by Washington State Senators Bone and Shellenbacher who felt that Gannon posed a threat to their positions as senators and they wanted him disposed of immediately. That ended the first case I had to investigate in WPA.

After Mr. Gannon was fired, Major B. M. Harloe, the Regional Director in Salt Lake City, sent Joe Tracy, Chief Regional Engineer, and a group of about five top administrators to reorganize the WPA in the State of Washington. At the end of their investigation, Joe Tracy asked, "What do you know about this man Nicholson?" I said I didn't know much, but that he had come to me with some concern during the Gannon investigation — and I related our conversation. Joe Tracy said that Rex Nicholson was probably the most capable man in the state to administer the program, but he didn't have political support. They expected to make Don Abel the WPA Administrator, but he was just a political figurehead. Nicholson was to be made the Deputy Administrator in the State of Washington and would actually run the show. Since I had found no adverse information concerning Nicholson's activities during my investigation, he was appointed and started up the ladder. Rex was an excellent administrator. He was a former cowboy from the Texas

Panhandle and had very little education, but he married a schoolteacher who educated him. He was an intelligent man with drive and ambition. He made great strides.

During my assignment to the Portland office, I was confidentially informed by Paul Sceva, the concessioner in Mount Rainier National Park, that the WPA was building a lodge to be used for commercial purposes on Mt. Hood, some sixty miles east of Portland, Oregon. The man behind this was E. J. Griffith, the WPA Administrator. Paul Sceva said he didn't think it was proper for the government to be using relief funds to build a hotel to compete with private sector lodges. In those days we were authorized to send in a complaint stating only that it was from a confidential source. We never had to disclose who that confidential source was.

During my investigation I discovered that Griffith had authorized the diversion of most of the non-labor costs of practically every project in the State of Oregon, to build the Timberline Lodge on Mt. Hood. WPA limited non-labor costs to ten percent of the cost. The program was designed to employ people.

As part of the investigation I examined the lodge. They had spent almost a million dollars on a beautiful structure with sumptuous lobby and dining room, but had only constructed nineteen rooms for rental to guests. There were numerous other mistakes, such as the construction of three huge fireplaces, with no place for the storage of wood; the kitchen crew had to cross through the lobby to get from their quarters to work. The worst was the setting of the lodge so that the snow piled up at the front door and blocked the entrance. They later had to go in and construct a huge culvert-like structure so that people could get into the lodge during winter, as the front door was completely under snow.

In the middle of my investigation our Washington office called and instructed me to interview E. J. Griffith, personally. He had complained to his friend, Eleanor Roosevelt, about the conduct of an investigation of his administration without anyone having obtained clearance from him as the head of the agency.

In compliance with his request Nat Rogers and I went to see Griffith. He was irate and greeted us with a haughty demeanor, demanding to know who made the complaint.

He said he knew it was started by one of his political enemies. I felt safe, as only I knew who the complainant was, not having disclosed it even to Nat Rogers.

After his tirade he turned to me and said, "Well!," as though he was now giving permission to proceed. I decided he was not going to take control of the investigation, so I said as innocently as I could, "Mr. Griffith, you sent for us, what do you have in mind?" He blew up! I proceeded to question him about the diversion of non-labor funds and the agreement with the Forest Service Supervisor and Jack Meier, of Meier and Franks Department Store, to operate the Timberline Lodge after it was completed. This, of course, was a diversion of funds as a public facility had to remain under public control.

As soon as we left, he apparently telephoned Washington, and referred to me as an "Investigator of extreme youth and badgering tactics." Thereafter, the agents in the Portland office referred to me as The Badger.

When my investigation was near completion, the WPA forced a reorganization, threw out those who had an agreement to operate the lodge, and put the contract up for public bid. But this did not rectify some of the basic faults. They had to authorize close to a million dollars in additional funds to build dormitories for skiers and other lodging facilities to enable the lodge to operate at a profit.

After the Griffith investigation in the State of Oregon, I was assigned cases primarily in the states of Washington and Montana. This suited me just fine, as it meant I collected $5.00 per diem for every day I was away from Portland headquarters or my station in Seattle. We were also paid five cents per mile for the use of personal vehicles. Distances were great in these states and many times our expense accounts exceeded our payroll checks. My salary was $3,100 per year.

Costs were cheap. I stayed in hotels for $1.00 per night and kept my food bills down to $1.00 per day. This meant 25 cents for breakfast, 25 cents for lunch and 50 cents for dinner. This enabled me to save $3.00 per day out of my per diem and most of my salary. Gasoline averaged about 15 cents per gallon, which enabled me to save money on the 5 cents per mile they paid for the use of my car.

Some of the other agents were not quite as frugal and often had to borrow money from me before they received their next salary or expense checks. This was understandable with Donald Ainsworth, who was supporting a wife, son and twin girls; not so for my boss, Nat Rogers, who was separated and supporting only himself. Ainsworth dubbed my frugality as "Hummelizing."

I remember one case in Butte, Montana, that backfired. I had driven close to 11 hours on very icy roads to get to Butte to keep an appointment at 7:30 in the morning. I arrived at about 5:00 a.m. and decided not to put my car in a garage to save a dollar (the cost of a heated garage). It was forty-seven degrees below zero. It cost me $42.00 to get my car started. The battery was frozen and had to be replaced and the car had to be steamed as all the grease in the transmission and differential had to be replaced. It was an expensive lesson in how not to save money!

It was during investigations in Montana that I met Mike Blinn, the State WPA Finance Director. While Mike had been born and raised in Butte, he did not go along with some of the free wheeling ways that prevailed in the political atmosphere of Montana. He used to tip me off to any skulduggery in the WPA for my investigation. Mike was extremely capable in financial affairs. He was a C.P.A. practicing in Chicago, but chose to return to Butte when his youngest son drowned in Lake Michigan. Mike was to get me out of a hole later, but that is getting ahead of my story.

Our principal problem in WPA concerned financial irregularities. Supervisors would divert labor and material to improve some private property. This immediately produced falsification of payrolls and material accounts. Padding of payrolls was usually followed by forgery of government checks. There were some thefts of government property and occasional collusion to advance an alleged community improvement such as building veterans' club houses or additions to private hospitals. Political kickbacks were rampant in states when local politicians attempted to take over WPA organizations for their own power bases.

In most instances restitution was achieved by administrative changes and reimbursement of funds. Occasionally the violations were serious enough to bring criminal prosecution by the United States Attorney. When this occurred, I sometimes encountered difficulty. I was usually thought to be much younger than I was.

I remember one forgery case in Oregon for which I had the written confession of the defendant. When the defense attorney started cross-examination, he sought to discredit me. He asked, "What qualifies you to make a criminal investigation?" I said, "I am a lawyer." He asked, "Have you been admitted to practice law?" I said, "Yes." He said, "Where?" I said, "Arizona and California." He asked, "Have you ever practiced?" I said, "Yes, with my father in Arizona." He said, "Say, how old are you anyway?" I replied, "Twenty-seven years old," and he dropped the cross-examination. I learned later that he thought I was an eighteen-year-old political appointee!

This was a stimulating job as we covered a wide jurisdiction and were permitted to complete the investigation wherever it took us. This was different from the F.B.I., which had agents all over the United States and if a lead went to another city or state, the investigating agent would have to refer it to another F.B.I. agent. The ability to complete an investigation made for a much more interesting experience. In fact, I was offered a position with the F.B.I. and turned it down.

Our investigations took us into many homes. I was often impressed by the attitude of the people we interviewed. They were ordinary Americans, down on their luck, not out of personal failure, but reduced to poverty by the failure of the economy. I've heard more than one man say, "I've worked all my life and I want to work now, but if I can't get a job, I'll steal before I see my family go hungry."

The country was near revolution. I am amazed that there was not a serious uprising with bloodshed. We would not be able to avoid it today if these economic conditions were to be repeated. Roosevelt, through his flexibility and political acumen, avoided a revolution. It's too bad the policies that were fine for those times have been continued long after their usefulness. This is one of the weaknesses of a democratic society. Politicians do not want to antagonize any constituency by removing their largesse.

In 1937 I married the secretary in the WPA office. Her name was Marion Christison, a Scotch girl. When Marion was hired as the secretary she was the only one in her family able to get a job. Jobs, of course, during the depression, were almost nonexistent. She had two brothers: Thomas, the eldest, and James, just slightly older than Marion. The mother was a widow and Marion was the sole source of support for the family. She said she was often irritated in that everybody told her what she could do and where she could go, when she was the one supporting the entire family. Marion had health problems which later proved to be tuberculosis. When she became too ill to work regularly, she resigned and I arranged for her to spend some time at my parents' home in Tucson, Arizona. She was there for several months and then returned to Portland.

Upon receipt of news that my mother was dying of cancer of the pancreas and if I wanted to see her I would have to go home, I resigned my job, married Marion, and we both returned to my folks' home at 1845 E. Adams, Tucson (now part of the University of Arizona Hospital grounds). We were married September 27, 1937. My mother died October 6, that same year.

I again started law practice with my father in Tucson, but it was evident Marion had to have constant care. I arranged to have her entered in a rest home on east Speedway. The cost was $350 per month, more than I made in law practice, so I contacted Roger Bounds, Director of the Division of Investigation of the WPA, and returned to the WPA in San Francisco as agent assigned to the State of California.

I was investigating a case in San Luis Obispo when I received word from San Francisco that WPA Washington D.C. was attempting to contact me. Washington ordered me to get my things together and report to the U.S. Attorney in Albuquerque, New Mexico, to aid in an investigation. The U.S. Attorney had indicted some 37 people, including the entire family of Senator Dennis Chavez, the U.S. Senator from New Mexico. The principal defendant was Assistant U.S. Attorney, Stanley Miller, son-in-law of the senator.

I reported to Everett Grantham, U.S. Attorney for the State of New Mexico. He advised me that the charges were solicitation of funds for political purposes through payroll padding, falsification of payrolls and forgery of checks, in addition to many other irregularities in the use of WPA funds. Donald Ainsworth, who had been an agent with me in Portland, Oregon, was also told to report to New Mexico. Actually he arrived before I did. I was to be there only a short period of time. I was there for eleven months.

Since an indictment had already been made of some thirty-seven people, we were given the charges to investigate and substantiate guilt; or to provide information so charges could be dismissed. It was obvious that with the amount of work we had to do and the trial fast approaching, we needed more help.

John Peckham and McGrath (whose first name I cannot recall) were assigned. I was put in charge of the investigation. I learned shortly after reporting to New Mexico that Rex Nicholson had previously been sent to New Mexico to check on the WPA administration after Everett Grantham had indicted this group. All were top people in New Mexico's WPA. Nicholson had told Harry Hopkins he would take the job of cleaning up the WPA in New Mexico, provided I was put in charge of the investigations. When I met with Rex in New Mexico, he filled me in on how corrupt he had found the operations. He warned that he expected attempts to thwart the investigation, including the framing of agents, himself, etc. He said he expected me to protect his backside if he was going to clean up the mess.

On completion of our investigation a jury was impaneled and we went to trial. The trial lasted six weeks and ended in a hung jury. The F.B.I. followed immediately with a jury tampering investigation but no charges were filed.

We tried again on the principal case which had been drastically reduced in scope. This trial lasted two weeks and all the defendants were acquitted. After the trial was over the jury foreman told U.S. Attorney Grantham that it was obvious there were people in the jury who would never vote for conviction so they decided to acquit and relieve the government of further expense. Thus ended that case in New Mexico.

Another case in New Mexico will shed some light on conditions in that state. A man named Barney Cruz was acknowledged to be the political boss in Mora County in Northern New Mexico. There were charges of diversion of funds, padding of payrolls and forgery of checks on a sewing project in Mora County. The principal defendant was Barney Cruz. I was sent to investigate.

Toward the end of my investigation, I was on a country road trying to locate a witness that was out cutting vigas (poles to be used in the construction of houses) when I noticed a highway patrol car following me. When I turned around to go back, the patrol car pulled in behind me and continued to follow. I stopped and asked him if he wanted to see me. He asked, "Are you a Federal agent?" I said, "Yes." He said, "I don't want to know what you are doing, but I was told to come out and protect you. You know they have killed two Federal agents this year (it was then April), and the Chief said to come out and see that you are not ambushed."

I went about my business and then to lunch. The Chief of the New Mexico Highway Patrol joined us. They told me that Barney Cruz was a bad actor and had cut the Sheriff's face with a broken beer bottle when the Sheriff tried to arrest him. I later talked to the Sheriff. His face was a mass of scars.

I was scheduled to interrogate Barney that afternoon, which I did without incident. I didn't get a confession from him although I had plenty of evidence to convict him. He was subsequently convicted and sent to a prison camp for a year and a day. I was informed later that when he was released the folks in Mora County greeted him back with a band and a celebration. New Mexico was an interesting place to conduct investigations.

During this time Marion was in a rest home in Tucson and her health had seriously deteriorated. I was able to visit her about every two weeks by driving from Albuquerque to Tucson for the weekends. I visited Marion on our first wedding anniversary, September 27, 1938, and I was greeted with a poem by Marion entitled *Marion Christison to Don Hummel - A Year Ago Today*. The poem read:

> To have lived long years and never to have your lips
>   soft on mine;
> Never to have your arms with mine entwined;
> Never to know the thrill of sweet surrender;
> Heard your whisper - gentle, tender "mine all mine";
> Oh, better short sweet days of living, loving,
>   dreaming,
> If one brief year is all there is to be,
> My joyous thanks for moments shared, for our loves'
>   immortality

During the latter part of May 1939 I was notified that Marion would have to be hospitalized. We took her to St. Mary's Hospital in Tucson. About ten days later one lung collapsed through a tear in the pleura lining. Roy Hewitt was her doctor, and no better doctor ever practiced. Marion had utmost confidence in him. One day, Dr. Hewitt could not visit her, so a senior associate from the Tucson Clinic made the visit. He decided to apply a butterfly valve so that the air breathed in could escape. I knew from Dr. Hewitt's expression when he visited Marion the next day that this was a consignment to death.

On the 15th day in the hospital, Marion awoke and said to her mother and me, "Last night I crossed too many hills of understanding. I've gone too far and I can't turn back. I'm going on. It's going to be hard on you both, but I want you to be brave." Just then Dr. Hewitt came in and Marion said, "Doctor, I had confidence that if anyone could help me, you could, but we've lost the fight and you've lost a patient." She died on the second day, after 17 days in the hospital. I buried Marion next to my mother in Evergreen Cemetery in Tucson, Arizona, on June 6, 1939, just 20 months after our marriage. No braver girl ever lived.

After the cleanup in New Mexico the Works Projects Administration was changed to Works *Progress* Administration and a new Regional Office was set up in Denver, Colorado. Rex Nicholson was designated as the Regional Director and I was sent up as Field Agent in Charge of the Division of Investigation. The agents assigned me were Ralph Hauser, Solbert J. Barsy, Paul Zempel and William Reifschneider. Our jurisdiction covered six intermountain states.

I held the office of Field Agent in Charge until 1940 when I was sent to Atlanta, Georgia, to take over the position of field agent in charge for seven of the southeastern states. In making this assignment to me, Roger Bounds, the Director, said to me, "Now, Don, they don't work as fast in the South as you do, so take it easy. You have a reputation of pushing your men and, as you know, your office has led in the number of cases resolved, but the South is a little different and you are going to have to relax and take it easier with these Southern agents."

Shortly after reporting to Atlanta, a new agent, Anthony F. Greco, was assigned to my office. He was from Neskahoning, Pennsylvania, a mining community. He had graduated from Fordham Law School in New York and had applied for an agent's job. He was asked if he would be willing to work for "twenty-six," meaning $2,600 per year. Tony said, "Yes," thinking they were talking about $26 a week. When he received his first paycheck, he carried it around for several days and finally got up nerve to ask how much he was being paid and they told him $2,600 a year. This was far more than he had agreed to work for. The result was that he married his college sweetheart, Jeanne O'Reilly. Jeanne's father was Irish and her mother was Italian.

They reported to Atlanta, Georgia, and that was the beginning of a lifetime friendship with the Grecos. In fact, the Grecos and I were playing badminton on Peachtree Road in Atlanta when a chap ran up and said the Japs had bombed Pearl Harbor. This was December 7, 1941. Needless to say, the badminton game was discontinued.

The country was gearing up for war and the WPA was winding down. It appeared that a change should be made in my own position. I went to Washington to see about a new office that was being created — the Office of Price Administration. It was to have rationing and price control. The net result was that I was appointed to organize, prepare rules and regulations and to staff the Office of Inspection and Investigation for the Office of Price Administration (OPA), covering the seven southeastern states with headquarters in Atlanta, Georgia.

I was halfway through completion of this job when I was moved to Denver to set up the new Office of Inspection and Investigation of OPA for the six intermountain states with headquarters in Denver. This transfer took place in 1942. Shortly thereafter I got a call from Tony Greco saying he wanted to move to Denver and join me in setting up the staff. This occurred with some opposition from Jeanne, who had never been west of Albany, New York, until she moved to Atlanta after marrying Tony.

I contacted Sol Barsy and Paul Zempel and asked if they would move to Denver to help. They agreed and so the triumvirate of Zempel, Barsy and Greco joined me as my three assistants to aid in organizing the staff and preparing the procedures for the new Office of Price Administration for the intermountain states.

It was during this time that the Greco's son Don, my namesake, was born. When it came time for christening, Tony arranged for the ceremony to be held in New York in the Fordham Chapel, where he had attended law school. As Tony was Catholic, and I a Protestant, I was not truly eligible to be the godfather. But this didn't faze Tony. During the ceremony, while I was holding my namesake in one arm and a candle in the other hand, Tony ducked his head, obviously chuckling. At the end of the ceremony I asked him what was so funny about the service. He replied that as he looked at me in a Catholic chapel, holding his son and a candle, if the walls of the church didn't fall down with this black Protestant holding a Catholic baby, he thought the world was on equilibrium!

Most of the principals in the Investigative Division in the Office of Price Administration were of draft age. Because of this, Roger Bounds, Director of the Division of Investigation, had proposed to the military services that we be issued commissions in the various branches of the services in the intelligence divisions, as we were experienced investigators.

I was the first to be notified by a telegram on June 1, 1942, addressed to Captain Don Hummel, advising me to report to Boling Field, Washington, D.C., on June 8th. I puzzled over the wire as I had not been notified that I had been approved as a commissioned officer in the Air Force, but the wire was addressed to "Captain" Don Hummel, so I assumed that my commission had been approved. It turned out later that I received one of the last direct commissions as a captain.

My government service in helping to organize the Office of Price Administration came to a close when I received that wire. In the meantime Tony was trying to qualify for a commission in the Marines. He had poor eyesight and was not able to qualify, even though he drank a quart of carrot juice before the examination, as he had one very bad eye. In his usual humorous way, Tony said the person examining and giving the test to him said, "Cover your left eye now, walk forward, and stop when you can read the chart with your right eye." Tony said, "I walked until I bumped my nose on the wall, and I still couldn't read it."

Paul Zempel was shortly thereafter approved as a lieutenant junior grade in United States Navy Intelligence. Solbert Barsy was the only unfortunate. The draft caught up with him and he was mustered in as a draftee and private. He was told to report to a location in Denver, and thereafter the OPA office force went to visit him on his birthday, as he was not allowed to leave the compound. They visited him through a chain fence. He said it made him feel like he was a jailbird. They brought a cake and he celebrated his birthday by cutting the cake and passing it through the wire fence.

Of my three OPA assistants, Paul Zempel went into the Navy, Sol Barsy was inducted into the Army, and subsequently Tony Greco, who kept trying, went in as a second lieutenant in the Marine Corps. This came about shortly after I reported to Washington, D.C. I went to Marine Corps headquarters to find out what had happened to Tony's application for a commission. The general advised me that his application had been held up because, although he was well qualified, they hesitated to give Tony a commission in intelligence because his parents had been born in Italy, and Italy was an enemy country.

I reiterated a story about Tony when he was an investigator in Atlanta. He was investigating another Italian who was charged with diversion of WPA funds. After establishing a good case against him, he inter viewed the subject. The subject said to him, "Paisano, we are both Italians — can't you do something for me?" Tony replied, "I don't have anything to do except make the investigation. Somebody else makes the decision; but I'll tell you, if I did have something to do with it, I'd throw the book at you, because it's your kind of 'Wop' that makes us all unpopular in this country!"

They cleared Tony as a loyal American citizen. He received his commission as a second lieutenant and his notice to report to Washington, D.C., where he served throughout the war. He was released as a captain. Sol worked his way up the ranks and was also released as a captain. He served in the European theatre.

7

World War II Service

I REPORTED to Boling Field in Virginia on June 8, 1942, where I was sworn in as a captain in the U.S. Air Corps. Believe it or not, the first job given to me was a speech to be delivered by the top general of the Air Corps, Hap Arnold, to a group of incoming Air Corps officers. I was instructed to examine the speech and determine whether it contained any security violations. Here I was, an officer for only a few hours and I was checking on the head of the U.S. Air Corps to be sure he didn't violate security! That is the way the armed forces operated.

Our counterintelligence unit was transferred from Boling Field to the new headquarters at Graveley Field, Washington, D.C. Graveley Field is now the Washington National Airport. I was assigned to a security unit which consisted of having informers throughout the Air Force reporting to us any statement or other evidence of disloyalty to the country by any member of the armed services. This was not only tedious, but far from my liking. Shortly thereafter, I was named as the liaison officer between the Air Corps and the Command and General Staff of the Army. I was transferred to an office in the Pentagon building, where I spent the next 11 months.

It was my responsibility to convey messages and to implement solutions to problems that had security implications between the Air Corps and the Army General Staff. I had a desk in an office shared by several other Army and Air Corps officers. Among them was Stanley Miller, the son-in-law of Senator Chavez, and the principal defendant in the suit we had prosecuted in New Mexico for soliciting political funds in the WPA. Also, there was an officer who had been given a direct commission from New York. He was from a high society group in New York but, unfortunately, was also homosexual. I was told by the Army that they were going to put a tap on our telephone, as they were uncertain whether or not he could be blackmailed by an enemy agent because of his sexual preferences. It was an interesting experience for me at the close of each week to sit down with Army counterintelligence officers and hear all the conversations, including my own.

I had been in this assignment as liaison officer for about three months when my commanding officer, Colonel Boberg, came to me and said that there were some promotions in the works and I should be among them, but he had withdrawn my name because he did not want to antagonize officers in the Army counterintelligence unit with whom I worked. Promotions in the Air Corps were much more rapid than in the Army and caused considerable friction between Air Corps and Army personnel. As a result of this, he held up my promotion and shortly thereafter promotions were frozen, so I waited another six months before I was promoted to Major. I always resented this, as I was selected as having the best relationship with the Army, but that militated against my promotion as a matter of diplomacy. It had the long-term effect of preventing me from being promoted to a full colonel.

During the next few months, and just before the invasion of South Africa by American forces under General Eisenhower, I was asked to help the F.B.I. in the investigation of an officer in the oceanography section. There were questions of his loyalty. This officer had been a German national. His unit was preparing for the invasion of Africa where General Rommel of the Wehrmacht held sway. He was to assist General Eisenhower, who was to lead the invasion, with information on what kind of tides he might encounter when he landed in Africa. It was, of course, a top secret assignment as any leak of information would be a tip-off as to where the invasion would occur.

Arrangements were made to have this man undergo a physical examination and when the doctor had him undress, I grabbed his clothes and gave them to the F.B.I. They photographed everything he had in his pockets and then I put his clothes back in the dressing room. As far as I know, he never knew that they had been purloined during his physical examination. The doctors were quite elated with having played a role in this operation. I never heard whether the F.B.I. had found any incriminating information.

You will recall that General Eisenhower had considerable problems dislodging the Germans from North Africa, but as they broke through the Kasserine Pass, the Germans left saboteurs and espionage agents behind as they retreated, exposing the Eisenhower rear forces. He wired headquarters for two competent counterintelligence agents to be sent to him to help guard against saboteurs and espionage agents. The letter arrived with a red border. Instruction for handling red border letters was to respond with the action required within 24 hours. In this case, the two officers had to be reassigned, put on an airplane going to South America and from there, fly the Atlantic to South Africa; and they had to be on their way in 24 hours.

I took this communication to my superior officer, Colonel Boberg. He said he was going to assign Colonel Cutting and Major Qualters, the latter having been with the New England Highway Patrol. Qualters had been assigned to President Roosevelt when the President visited New England. He had a repertoire of jokes and a quick wit. The President took a liking to him and had him assigned to the Secret Service, where he became part of the Presidential Protection Staff. He held this job until he was commissioned in the Air Corps.

When I learned from Colonel Boberg who he had assigned, I said, "Colonel, that's sabotage. You know those are not the most competent men. You should send your most competent officers."

Colonel Boberg said, "I could have you court-martialed for that." I answered, "I know you can, but I don't think you will." As a result, the colonel withdrew Cutting's assignment and substituted a more competent man, but sent Major Qualters to South Africa.

Several weeks thereafter another liaison officer, a major, came to me with a red bordered letter and said, "Will you take this?" I looked at the date — it was already three days old. I asked the major what he had done with it in the intervening days and he said, "Nothing." I said I would take it on the condition that I endorse upon the letter that I received it as of that hour and that day, and I would not be responsible for the delay in delivery or try to explain it. He was so glad to get rid of it, he gave it to me and I proceeded to clear the communication.

Shortly thereafter a captain in Army Counterintelligence came to me and said, "We have a special project. I can't tell you what it is, and you may not know for a long time. I can only say that it is extremely important to the United States and security is going to be the best we can provide. I would like to recommend your name for it. There is one drawback — you would be constantly on this same project, in Washington, D.C., for the duration of the war." I said, "No thanks." I did not learn until long after that it was the Manhattan Project, which was developing the atom bomb.

Colonel Boberg had promised he would send me to Harrisburg, Pennsylvania, to Combat Intelligence School, as I wanted to get out of counterintelligence and into the combat zone. He kept procrastinating and procrastinating, and finally I wrote a communication to him quoting his agreement and asking to be assigned to the next class, which was the last class that a person with Major rank could be assigned to. He held onto it without communication, although the regulations required that he endorse the memorandum, either rejecting my request or approving it.

He waited until a Saturday morning and then called me, saying that he was going to approve it. He did this on the telephone, without answering the communication in writing. He thought I would not be able to get necessary clearance, as I would have to leave the following day to be in Harrisburg for the beginning of the class Monday morning. He did not realize that as Liaison Officer, I was very familiar with operations in the Pentagon building.

I hand-carried this request for transfer to Harrisburg from one office to another with all the urgency I could muster. When I got the final required signature, a colonel said to me, "This does not specify whether you are to be assigned or whether you are to be sent on temporary duty to this school." I said, "Colonel, I have been here 11 months and if Colonel Boberg didn't specify, I think I have served my time here in Washington. I would like to have you approve this on an assignment basis." He winked at me and signed. I returned the papers and the following day was on my way to Harrisburg, Pennsylvania.

In Combat Intelligence School there was one lieutenant colonel who had been in combat overseas and was returned to the school for further instruction, as he wanted to transfer to Intelligence. There were only three majors assigned to the school: Bobby Jones, the famous golfer, one other whose name I do not recall, and myself. It was a six-week course and as we came to the end of the course, we were called in and asked to express our preference as to where we were to be assigned.

I asked the colonel in charge, a very arrogant sort of guy, whether I could speak frankly and he said, "Certainly." I said that I wanted to be assigned to the Chinese Theater. He asked why and I told him I thought that was the place the final war would be fought and the final peace determined. He snapped back at me, "You'll go where we send you." I said, "I understand that, colonel, but I thought you gave me permission to express my preference and that is my preference." I was rather shaken but pleased later to find that I was assigned to a group which became the Chinese-American Composite Wing, mobilized in Norfolk, Virginia, to be shipped overseas by boat.

When I stopped by Colonel Boberg's office to say goodbye, he was irate. Apparently Colonel Crandall, who had been in our Counter intelligence Division, had advised him that he and I were to be shipped to China. That was the first realization Colonel Boberg had that I was not to return to his counterintelligence unit and this made him furious. He said to me, "I have told those men in the Pentagon never to let this happen to me again," that he was going to let this assignment go through, but "never to take a man from my command without my approval." I said, "Yes, sir," and got out of his office. I knew that he had lost control over me.

The nucleus for the Chinese American Wing was assembled in Virginia and we were put on two liberty ships to cross the Atlantic. Ours had 618 men aboard. As is usual in the military, we were lined up by rank and when they divided us into two ships, we had all the rank on one ship and most of the noncommissioned officers and soldiers on the other. After two days of sailing, assignments had still not been made to lifeboats, so three of us went to see the skipper of the ship. We asked why no drills had been conducted and no assignments to lifeboats made, as we knew we had to pass through combat waters. The skipper's response was that if anything hit the ship, we would need a parachute and not a boat. We said we didn't understand and he said, "There are 1800 tons of TNT under you, and if anything hits this ship, we will all be blown sky-high." This was contrary to regulations, which prohibited transport of troops and explosives on the same vessel.

We also found that no arrangements had been made to feed our personnel on the ship. We had no galley, as that was reserved for the ship's crew. All there were were two big kettles heated by steam off the engines. For three or four days, we had nothing but steamed dehydrated food: dehydrated rutabaga, dehydrated eggs, dried beans and some bread and hot tea.

It was not a satisfactory arrangement and our group of officers designated me and two others to see the skipper of the ship. It was obvious that something was amiss. The skipper referred us to the ship's steward, who told us that he had signed on at the last minute and didn't know what the ship stores were and that he was sorry, but the stores were in complete disarray, so he couldn't help us. We said, "Well, we will make an inventory of the ship's stores so that you will have a record and we also want to prepare our peoples' food in the ship's galley and not be limited to steamed food."

The ship's crew were eating like kings — three meals a day. For dinner they would have prime rib or roast turkey or similar entrees; almost a gourmet selection. It got so bad that we had to put armed guards on the gangway because the soldiers started talking about throwing the ship's crew overboard. The ship's crew were taunting the soldiers for being foolish to have joined the Army (most of them had not volunteered, but had been called up). The ship's crew said they were getting combat pay as the ship was in a combat zone and this further agitated the soldiers.

We selected a crew and inventoried the ship's stores. It was fantastic! There was enough in that storeroom to cross the Atlantic five or six times. We did not learn until later that this was part of a plan to hoard the ship's stores and then sell them on the black-market in North Africa. In fact, when we got to North Africa, we could buy any kind of meal we wanted for a price; most of it came from foodstuffs which were to have fed the soldiers, but were never served to them.

We had made arrangements with the steward to alternate the use of the ship's galley. As soon as the ship's cooks got out of the galley, we put ours in to prepare our food and then return the galley to the ship's crew for the next meal. Only two meals per day were served to the military personnel, while the ship's crew had three regular meals, as they were on duty.

One time the steward objected to me using so much food for the soldiers, saying that they were going to run out. Since I had retained a copy of the ship's stores, I told him that was crazy, that we knew exactly what they had and we expected to see that the soldiers were well-fed on the way over.

A delegation representing the ship's crew came to see me about our use of the ship's stores for our soldiers. When I refused to accede to their demands, they advised me that they intended to go on "whack." I said I didn't know what that meant so they gave me a manual designating sailor's rights.

Going on "whack" was a term that allowed each sailor to demand the ingredients of the mess so he could prepare his own meal. This was a carry-over from sailing days when ships' cooks spoiled their food in the cooking process. The trouble was that the manual had never been updated. It provided the sailor a right to demand a cup of flour, a half tablespoon of salt, some grease, etc. I showed this to the sailors' delegation and urged them to go on "whack." That ended that threat.

Our arrangement continued until we were about a day out of Oran, Algeria, when the lieutenant in charge of the cooks came to me and said, "We can't get in the galley." I said, "You're a little late telling me, aren't you?" He said, "Yes, but I've had an argument with them and they won't let me in the galley." So I went to the galley. The ship's cook told me they had decided to stop feeding us from the galley, as we were using too much food. We got an armed guard, threw their cooks out of the galley, put our own cooks in, and continued to feed the soldiers.

We learned later that our sister ship with the non-commissioned men aboard had a worse fate. They were locked in the hold and fed a meager diet for most of the 33 days at sea.

Upon arrival in Oran, Algeria, we put into port and were assigned to a camp which was in the process of being erected. Actually, the camp was in a shambles and we were required to put up our own tents where we would be bivouacked until we could get transportation through the Mediterranean and the Suez Canal to India.

We were destined to form our unit at Karachi, which is now the capital of Pakistan. At that time it was still part of India. We were in camp in Oran for approximately two and a half months, with little or nothing to do. Occasionally, we were able to borrow a jeep and go down to Sidi Bel Abess. This was the headquarters of the famous French Foreign Legion in North Africa.

We whiled away our time until we were given notice that we were to board two transport ships (they were British ships) — the *Banfora*, on which I was assigned, and the *Rhona*, a sister ship. Here, again, the highest ranked officers were on our ship, with the captains and lieutenants on the *Rhona*. Both ships had noncommissioned officers and soldiers who were bunked in the holds of the ships under miserable conditions.

On the third day out we were hit with radio-controlled glide bombs coming from aircraft off the southern coast of Italy. No one fully realized what was happening, in that we could only see one or two aircraft in the air at one time, and then at quite some distance away. Then we would see a smaller aircraft underneath and somebody would yell, "There's a fighter up there," or "the fighter has been hit!" What really was happening was that a bomb with wings was dropped from the mother ship. A rocket would give the bomb momentum and they would bring this rocket bomb down in a steep glide to attack the ships.

During one attack, the Rhona, our sister ship and the one just ahead of us in line, was hit amidships. As we pulled hard to port to go around so as not to ram her, we saw the Pandemonium that was taking place. Flames were shooting 100 feet into the air and soldiers were trying to launch their lifeboats. It turned out that the Indian crew had deserted and the soldiers had to launch their own lifeboats. As the ship listed, the lifeboats would hit the roll of the ship, and be knocked off their davits. The boat would tilt, throwing all of the occupants into the water, and then the lifeboat itself would finally fall, many times on top of groups of soldiers below. They threw landing nets over the sides to allow the men to climb down, but as the soldiers reached the bottom of the net, they were still a couple of hundred feet above the water and if they hesitated, were pushed off as other soldiers climbed down above them. It was a horrible sight, with flames and smoke belching out of the ship.

The sinking of the Rhona was considered to be the worst disaster of the war in the transportation of troops. We lost 2,000 men out of 2,200 on the Rhona; most of them were trapped below deck and went to the bottom with the ship. There were harrowing tales by those who were picked up afterward. One officer spent all night hanging between the rungs of a ladder with a dead man's head bobbing up and down in another rung of the ladder just in front of his face. The dead soldier had tied himself to the ladder and his body surged with the waves. It was a disastrous affair!

We had a council of war that night and decided that if we were attacked again, we would take a chance on being strafed and bring all the soldiers from below onto the decks, as most of the casualties came from getting trapped below deck. We wanted to avoid a repeat of the Rhona tragedy. This attack occurred on Thanksgiving Day, 1943.

Three days later we had a lifeboat drill. I did not hear the announcement that the next would not be a drill, but would be the real thing. Apparently they had received word that there was a flight of enemy aircraft on the way to attack our convoy, or what was left of it. I went below deck and was taking a bath when the klaxon went off signaling an air raid. As we had just finished a drill, I assumed that they wanted to see how we would react, without warning. I started to dry off and just as I did, some of the guns started firing. I knew then that it was the real thing and not just a drill. Nobody dressed faster than I did!

I was in charge of a lifeboat on the top deck, and headed that way. As I went up the gangway, at the top of it was Colonel Crandall, the fat guy who had told Boberg that we were going to China. I did not know until then what the term "scared green" meant. He said, "The s.o.b.s are back." He was as green as grass. His face was green; his neck was green; his arms were green.

As I hit the top deck to go to my lifeboat, I saw twelve bombers in perfect formation starting to make their bomb run over our convoy. I thought, "We are in trouble." We had lost 2,000 men and some ships three days before and never saw more than one or two aircraft in the air at one time. Here were twelve bombers at about 4,000 feet getting ready to make their bomb run over the convoy.

We all cheered when we saw our flak ship and two destroyers head in the opposite direction and out to intercept the bombers. They made a turn and made the bomb run with the bombers with all guns blazing. You have never seen a Fourth of July display until you have seen highly armed ships with their tracer bullets and their shells bursting in the air. The fire was so intense that it broke up the bombing formation. The Germans decided to get out of there. They just dropped their bombs without aim to get rid of them. There were bombs going off all over the Mediterranean. Only one bomb hit a ship. It turned out to be a dud. It went right down the stack into the ship's hold but never exploded. The ship put into Port Said where it was removed. The attack was a sight to see, but not one to be repeated.

All of our crew were Air Corps with not too much love for the Navy, but we took up a collection that night and sent it to the Navy in thanks for saving us. We also learned later that some English Spitfires hit the returning group of German bombers and reportedly shot down every one of them.

After going through the Suez Canal we crossed the Indian Ocean and arrived in Bombay, India. We were not allowed off the ship, but an exception was made for me to go ashore and reconnoiter to determine what was in store for us. We soon learned that we were to disembark, but would not be allowed to stay in Bombay, but would take a train up the central portion of India to New Delhi.

As we had been out of communication with home for over three months, General Winslow Morris, our commanding general of the Chinese American Composite Wing (CACW), flew an airplane from Karachi to Bombay with mail for us. The train trip was interesting in that there were no aisles and no connections from one car to the next. In usual Army fashion, four of us officers were assigned to one car, which included a shower, while the noncommissioned officers and soldiers were jammed into cars like cattle, sleeping on wooden slats along the sides of the cars.

I remember distinctly that I had accumulated 142 letters. I put them in sequence by post date so I could start catching up with what was happening in the United States. Occupying the car with me was Captain "Rocky" Henderson, a bomber pilot, Captain Barry Malone, a fighter pilot, and Major George Hightower, an administrative officer. As news from home came, we would share it with one another.

All of a sudden, Barry Malone said, "Dammit, I told her it was her responsibility. Why didn't she do it?" We asked what he was talking about and he told us that he had just been informed by his wife that she was pregnant. He was pretty upset. He was rather fatalistic, feeling that he would never return to the United States. Rocky Henderson was shot down on his first mission as a bomber pilot in the South China Sea. He was not the pilot, but served as a co-pilot at his request. They were skip-bombing ships in the China Sea off the southern coast of China. Skip-bombing consisted of dropping bombs and skipping them into the side of the ship. As they did this, they misjudged their distance and when the ship blew up — it was a fuel ship — the explosion caught the bomber, killing all.

If we wanted to visit anyone in another car, we had to climb out the window, hanging onto the sills, and swing from one window to another until we got to the car we wanted, watching all the time to make sure we weren't scraped off by a signal pole!

Christmas Day was spent at a siding somewhere in Central India. There was, of course, no food operation on the train so we used cold rations. One of the cars had cooking facilities. They prepared a meal for us, so when we pulled into the siding about noon, we were served corned beef hash, bread and hot tea for our Christmas dinner. We were no sooner served, when several men had the unfortunate experience of having their mess kits knocked out of their hands. Crows would swoop down and try to take the food right out of their kits, so we walked around with one arm over our mess kit to protect it while we ate.

It was not long before quite a number of Indians came around. They seemed to crop up from everyplace and, as usual, they were just skin and bones. When they sat down, they would sit on their haunches, with their knees up alongside their chins. (Try this. I'll bet you can't do it!) After getting pretty much what we wanted to eat, and feeling sorry for the Indians who appeared not to have had a solid meal for some time, we turned over some of the corned beef hash to them. We were amazed to see these Hindus pick out all the meat and threw it on the ground and eat just the potatoes. They are forbidden by their religion to eat meat.

When we arrived in Karachi, which would be our home for a short period of time while we were organizing the CACW, we were assigned to an old military base that had been used by the British many years before. It was fairly comfortable, but we were anxious to get into China where our unit was to be stationed.

To get in to China, we had to fly The Hump, which meant going over the Himalaya Mountains in unarmed transport aircraft. Unfortunately, the Japanese had taken Myitkyina in Burma and had stationed a fighter squadron there to intercept American aircraft flying into China. The only protection you would have, if you were sighted by a fighter aircraft, would be to find a cloud and hope that there was no mountain in it. Those who were stationed in India and not scheduled to fly The Hump, had a gruesome sense of humor. They would line up while we were boarding the ship to fly into China and say, "Goodbye — I hope you make it." This didn't exactly receive a favorable response.

When it came my turn to fly The Hump, a number of us were assigned to a C-46, which was known among the Air Force as "The Flying Prostitute" (as it had no visible means of support), because of its small wingspan. These aircraft carried a heavy load, but if you lost an engine on takeoff, it was almost certain to be fatal. We had been told that a new regulation had come out and that we could only carry 66 pounds per man. This, of course, was ridiculous and everybody in Karachi realized it, so the word was passed down, "Just underestimate your weight."

This was equally foolish, because as we got on the plane, it obviously was way overloaded. We sat in bucket seats on the side, with loose cargo all down the center of the aircraft. What disturbed us most was one of the tires on this C-46 was completely bald, squashed down, and looked as though it would blow out at any moment. But we took off and landed in Agra, where the Taj Mahal is located, and had some lunch. As we were taxiing out onto the runway for takeoff, one tire blew out and we heaved a sigh of relief because we could now get a new tire. When we got out of the plane we saw to our dismay that it was the new tire that had blown and the old bald one was still intact. We laid on the runway in Agra for about two and a half hours before we got a new tire and finally took off.

The pilot lost his way and it was beginning to get dark. Word came back that they were not sure where we were and they did not know a place to land, so to be prepared if we had to bail out. I never did figure out how to be prepared for that! We were flying too low to use our parachutes, but they might have attempted to climb, although they were running short of gas and if the gas ran out in the climb, we would really be in trouble.

Finally word came back that the pilot had sighted the lights of the Chabua, which was the takeoff point to fly The Hump. We were flying in a terrible rainstorm when we landed. We held our breath as the aircraft bounced down the runway. We were sure that the bald tire was going to blow out every time we hit. But we made it, only to step off the runway and go up to our knees in mud. They had had rain there day after day. We had no more than gotten out of the aircraft when the air raid alarm sounded and we spent the next hour down in the trenches standing in water and mud up to our thighs while the Japs bombed the airstrip. When this was finally over we got a place to sleep and await our turn to fly The Hump.

We arrived in Kunming, China, and reported to the

14th Air Force, which was under the command of General Clair Chennault. Our unit was being organized so as to use Chinese personnel and lend-lease aircraft. They had experienced difficulty in the matter of face. A Chinese officer would not fly on the wing of a man who had graduated from flying school later than he had. They felt that they lost face when the other pilot was leading the flight, as he was in a subservient position. This caused considerable problems, as we had trained a lot of young Chinese pilots in the United States to fly the P-40, the fighter craft that we had. The ranking Chinese officers had never flown our equipment, nor did they know anything about our tactics or the use of the aircraft. The United States was also under pressure from Generalissimo Chiang Kai-shek to provide the Chinese with their share of lend-lease equipment. The Generalissimo was constantly threatening that he would make a separate peace with Japan. President Roosevelt was trying to keep him happy, so equipment was being shipped to them on a lend-lease basis but they did not have the personnel to fly, nor did they have an organization or structure to form tactical units. It was then that the idea of this Chinese American composite was born.

The idea was that there would be an American cadre with a Chinese counterpart for every position. Most of the noncommand functions were supplied by the Chinese. In other words, our tactical unit was composed of a commanding officer, an operations officer, an intelligence officer, a supply officer, a weather officer and a personnel officer. Each of us had a Chinese counterpart from the Chinese Air Force. We were supposed to teach them the methods of the United States in handling our particular functions. We also had noncommissioned officers in positions to instruct the noncommissioned officers of the Chinese Air Force. The Americans led the bombers and fighter groups in combat, with 75 percent of the personnel being in the Chinese Air Force.

The Chinese had no compunction or feeling of lack or loss of face by flying under the command or on the wing of an American officer of lesser rank. Our unit was designated the Chinese-American Composite Wing; composite because it contained both fighter and bomber groups within the wing. Normally a wing would be either a fighter or a bomber wing. Because of our combat record, this was one of the favorites of Generalissimo Chiang Kai-shek.

After a short stay in Kunming, the headquarters of the 14th Air Force, we were moved to Kweilin, where we were to be stationed at least temporarily. Kweilin is considered one of the beauty spots of China, and beautiful it was on the Lee River.

Rock spires stick up all over the area like inverted cones. These were hazardous to flying and the weather normally was miserable. In fact, an officer was supposed to meet us at the airstrip, but the weather was so bad he decided nobody would be foolish enough to come in at that time. Our pilot disagreed and took us in. In fact, we came between two of these spires which we could not see because of the poor weather. It was our good luck that we were in the middle, instead on either side.

During our assignment, we attempted to perfect our organization and learn how to deal with our Chinese counterparts. Our permanent base was to be a base called Chengtu, which was near Canton in the south of China. The United States had spent millions on this base. It was being finished so our unit was being moved from the present base to Chengtu—the name of the base, not to be confused with the city, Chengtu, in Western China.

We no more than got there than we were told that the Japanese were building up supplies along the Yellow River with the idea of transportation of supplies down the Lung-hai Railroad for an attack on the southern part of China. At this time the Japanese controlled all the coastal areas and everything north of the Yellow River. This drive would split China in half. The Generalissimos headquarters were established in Chunking after he had been driven out of Shanghai, Nanking and Wuhan.

General Chennault decided that we should move up north to destroy the supplies that were being deposited along the Yellow River so as to stall this drive into the south. This project was called Mission A.

I was selected as the Chief Intelligence Officer to accompany a survey group to decide where we should establish our Air Force units to enable us to attack the Japanese supplies and forces along the Yellow River. There were 12 of us selected, each one representing a discipline: one was a fighter pilot, one was a bomber pilot, one was an operations officer, a supply officer, a weather officer, etc.

With us was John Birch, the son of Baptist missionaries in China whose parents had returned to the United States. John had remained to become a missionary himself. He had been given a direct commission as a first lieutenant in the Air Force by General Chennault. John spoke fluent Mandarin and could write the language. He accompanied us as the interpreter for our group when we flew north in a C-47, which is in civilian life designated as a DC-3. This plane was considered the workhorse of the Air Force, but could not carry a heavy load. We were to be met at various locations where airstrips were being constructed.

A most incongruous situation occurred when we flew into one airstrip. There was lunch, waiting for us, prepared by some missionaries from Norway. It was served to us, complete with sterling silverware and goblets, beautiful china and tablecloths, in the shade beside a ramada on the airstrip.

We flew to a number of locations, only to get lost. A storm came up and the pilot did not know where he was. John Birch told him to go down and circle a little village. The villagers had been instructed to put Chinese characters on the ground, giving the name of the village so lost pilots could identify their location. John immediately identified our location and told the pilot so he could set a course to return to our base. The weather was bad, with very little visibility as we started up a canyon. The only difficulty was that the canyon came to an end. I will never forget the looks on the pilots' faces when the pilot tipped the plane on wingtip and made a 180-degree turn. The tip of the wing did not miss the canyon wall by more than 20 feet. We spiraled up and got out and finally got home. If John Birch had not been with us to identify and read the Chinese signs, we probably never would have gotten back.

It was decided that we would establish our forward base at Liangshan, south of the Yellow River, with the most advanced base at Laohoko. Liangshan was to have the fighter and bomber aircraft based there so we could attempt to destroy the Japanese supplies. Laohoko was the advance communications base.

I was assigned to the Liangshan base to set up the intelligence program as we had no intelligence data. My job was to photograph the enemy installations, get the pictures developed and interpreted so as to advise the commanding officer where the targets were, what type of targets they were and to make recommendations as to the type of bombs to be used by the group. I was the senior ranking person and therefore in control.

We lived in what the Chinese called hostels, which were made of split bamboo woven into a pattern and then plastered over with mud. They had a complement of cooks and houseboys.

Air Force personnel were coming in and out but I was responsible for the preparation of occupancy of the base. There was nothing to work with. There were no chairs, no tables or desks and no place to house the combat fighter units scheduled to arrive. I didn't have a cabinet of any kind where I could file the pictures of the targets we had photographed. I had to have the furniture made. This was accomplished by the Chinese carrying logs on their dong poles, then sawing boards off by hand and fashioning a file cabinet. There was no such thing as nails. They had to be put together with glue made of wooden pegs and affixed with pig's blood.

I had control of a P-38 photographic ship to direct what pictures I wanted taken; then I had three photo interpreters on my staff to put the photographs together, interpret them and give me a report. This provided me the list and location of the best targets to attack.

There was no place to develop the film after the pilots photographed the targets, so we had to build a photo lab. A young Chinese engineer was assigned to this task.   In addition to the lab, we needed water to develop the film. There was a huge wooden tank that had been sitting for days or months and the boards had shrunk. It would no longer hold water. I worked with this young engineer. We got the Chinese coolies to make a mound of earth and to put the tank up high enough so it would flow by gravity into the photo lab. I really put pressure on the engineer to rush the completion. The young engineer said we couldn't do it but I insisted that we had to. He was extremely pleased to tell me when he had finished it.

After he finished the construction, he put up a plank runway so the Chinese coolies, each one carrying a couple of five-gallon cans suspended from dong poles, could fill the tank. The tank was leaking badly as it had not had time to swell up enough to hold water. That evening the mound of earth on which the tank was built collapsed. You never saw a more downhearted young Chinese engineer in your life, but we got it back up again and by that time the tank had swollen enough to hold some water. We got our photo lab ready and started developing film.

The problem in getting the furniture we needed for our file cabinets and a desk and bench to sit on was a challenge. The Chinese used old abandoned temples as workshops. All the work of course was very primitive, with crosscut saws, pegs and glue, but they did do a creditable job. The only difficulty was that they had been given too many assignments and ours was supposed to have priority. Whenever I contacted them they would insist that I had to sit down and drink a glass of tea before we discussed business, which was discussed in pidgin English. After several visits, this got to be burdensome. We were fighting time because we knew the Japanese were about to launch their attack, and we had to be ready for it. I would tell them what they had to do first. They were very rank conscious. They did not want me to lift anything in or out of the truck, and they did not want me to get out of the truck without putting a stool for me to step on. Well, I had no time for that kind of foolishness and that upset them. I finally got across in pidgin English that this work had to have priority to meet the expected Japanese assault.

I had a Chinese interpreter, but he knew about as much English as I knew Chinese. It was very difficult to explain what I wanted and since they would always say, "Yes," I couldn't really know if they understood. I would then tell them exactly the opposite of what I wanted and if they still said, "Yes," I knew that I had to start over again. If they looked puzzled, then I would say, "Now, this is what I want you to do." As soon as I left, even though they were working on what was supposed to be a priority project, they would go to some other job. As a result, I had to come back every hour or so to see that they were still working on my project. This slowed things up considerably, but we did get the job done.

There was an amusing incident during this time. We received practically no American-made goods because of the cost of getting them flown over The Hump. Every gallon of gasoline cost over $6.00 per gallon by the time it was delivered to us. Air shipment into China was the only access we had to supply our forces. As Mission A was a top priority assignment getting ready to meet a new assault, they gave us some special attention. They sent a number ten tin of blackberry jam. There is so little sugar in the Chinese diet that you really craved something sweet. I would have paid ten dollars for a candy bar any time. I doled out the jam very, very carefully.

I turned over what was left in the can to the head houseboy to be responsible for it. About three days later, the head houseboy came to me and said, "Houseboys taste a little." I said, "What do you mean?" He said, "They taste a little." I said, "Taste a little what?" He explained, "That black sugar," speaking of the blackberry jam. I said, "Okay, what's left?" He said, "None left." They had eaten that whole number ten tin of blackberry jam. I was ready to kill a bunch of Chinese!

The lack of an interpreter was particularly difficult. We had a fighter control officer to warn us when the Japanese were going to bomb. China had been marked off in a grid pattern. The only warning system we had were spotters who would telephone on radio when they sighted an aircraft. There was no such thing as radar in the Chinese theater. We relied on those reporting stations. The Japanese controlled the principal centers and the lines of communications along the rivers and the roads. There were lots of friendly Chinese to report in by telephone and in some instances, by radio, to enable us to track the Japanese aircraft as they entered the warning net. These reports were charted on the grid map so we would know whether we were threatened.

A warning would occur if an unidentified ship penetrated the net. The warning would be signaled to the community by running up one ball to the top of a pole and another warning would be given by hitting one bong on a huge temple cymbal. If the aircraft was identified as being enemy ships and their location was advancing toward your location, two balls went up; that meant the village should get ready for an air raid. When three balls went up, that meant "get out" as they were definitely going to attack your area.

The difficulty was that these instructions were coming in in Chinese, and our Chinese interpreter could not communicate with us. Sam Rosenberg was the fighter control officer. He and I had to work very closely together with the interpreter so as to protect our people from these Japanese attacks. The Japanese had discovered that we were setting up an aircraft operation in the Liangshan area.

Some time later, we advised our headquarters that we were ready for our combat units to come up. These were fighter aircraft, bomber aircraft and the personnel to service and man them. We met disaster the day they were scheduled to arrive. Our flight of fighters got lost and almost ran out of gas before they finally located themselves and landed at Liangshan. Shortly thereafter, we were hit by Japanese bombers. Several of our fighters went up to intercept, and one Chinese pilot was shot down. I helped pick him up out of the field and take him across the rice paddies on a stretcher, but he died before we got help for him.

As we got better established, we moved up a considerable number of our remaining units and started regular operations against the Japanese from Liangshan.

It was always interesting when General Morris, our commander, would bring General Chennault to be briefed on the enemy situation as depicted by our photographs and intelligence reports. The General (Chennault) was rather hard of hearing and General Morris would stand next to me at the situation map and as I tried to brief General Chennault, Morris would keep punching me in the side, saying, "Louder—louder, he's hard of hearing." I don't know whether General Chennault heard him or not, but it was certainly disconcerting for me.

It was at that period of time when General Chennault issued instructions for me to send out six intelligence teams into the back country; each team to consist of an intelligence officer and a cryptographer with a coding machine and an interpreter.

I established the six units behind Japanese lines and in the areas considered dominated by friendly Chinese. We accomplished this by flying over Japanese lines, landing in some field, dropping the personnel with their equipment, and getting back to base as quickly as possible.

One of these teams was headed by John Birch. His was a two-man team as John was the intelligence officer who needed no interpreter. He had a cryptographer. Later I sent John his captain's bars behind the Japanese lines when he was promoted from first lieutenant to captain.

As the Japanese were driving closer and closer to us, it was determined that these advance bases were too dangerous and our whole unit moved back to Peyshi, which is west and about eight miles out of Chunking. The rest of the Chinese and American Composite Wing joined us here. This was the new headquarters for CACW. We also had fighter units in Sian and Changsha.

It was my job as the Intelligence Officer to brief the staff and the fighter groups each morning as to the developments that had occurred the previous day; and to interpret the intelligence reports that had come in. I'll never forget when I was briefing the staff, General Morris said, "What about the ten thousand Japanese soldiers that have moved down into the Yellow River? Why didn't you mention that?" I said, "Because it came from the Third Chinese War Zone, and there are no Japanese there. This type of report was typical. When the Chinese wanted more support they would exaggerate the Japanese threats.

Though the Generalissimo had general authority, he did not have actual control of all of the generals in many of the war zones. They did pretty much as they pleased, and if they wanted to put pressure on Generalissimo, they would falsify reports as to the Japanese strength and demand the Generalissimo headquarters send more support.

It was one of these reports that came to me saying the Japanese had moved ten thousand troops into the area. I told General Morris they weren't there. He said, "How do you know—you haven't been there?" I said, "We have spotters along the rail road and we have spotters on the river and the Japanese do not have enough aircraft to move that many men without us getting a report. And as this came from the third war zone, they are just putting pressure on the Generalissimo to give them more support." I said it would be foolish for me to make a report which I know to be false. He turned to his operations officer and said, "Call the 312 Fighter Squadron and have them send out a reconnaissance to check this report." They did, and found that there were no Japanese in the area whatsoever. The General never acknowledged this to me.

These were the kinds of reports that we learned to deal with as we became acquainted with the various sources that provided intelligence reports. Common sense sometimes told you that the reports you received were fabricated for some other purpose; that they were questionable or completely false.

Mission A, which was designed to destroy supplies being stored at the Yellow River and was supposed to last from two to six weeks, ended up as the beginning of a major confrontation with the Japanese. Our unit was now fully involved with fighting the war against Japan. While I was still assigned with this mission, our unit was moved from Kweilin to Chengtu, the multi-million dollar base from which we were to operate in southern China.

Shortly after I moved up to Liangshan on Mission A the Japanese, who had been watching the development of the Chengtu base, moved in with substantial ground forces and took over the base. The result was that we blew up the base before evacuation so as to make it unusable. We never even ran a bomber or fighter mission out of the Chengtu base. Since I was with Mission A in Liangshan while my unit was in Chengtu, I was not present when the unit was evacuated and I lost a good part of my clothes. I never saw my clothes again except those I had taken with me to Liangshan.

While I had access to all the intelligence pictures, I wanted a firsthand look at the areas we were to bomb. I accompanied a raid on the supplies stacked along the Yellow River. I went along as an observer. We encountered considerable flak as we made the bomb run. The pilot got nervous and did not maintain his elevation and direction as the fire became intense with shells exploding all around us.

As a result our bombs scattered all over the landscape and no damage was done to the Japanese supplies. It was a wasted mission.

It was toward the end of our stay in Liangshan that I heard that Captain Barry Malone, whom I had traveled with from Norfolk, Virginia, was missing in action. He had been hit on a strafing mission. He reported over the air that he "had been hit bad." That was all I could learn about Barry, who always felt that he would never return to the United States. He never saw the baby he read about on the train ride to India. He was too young to die.

My next big personal loss came when Sam Rosenberg, our fighter control officer whom I worked with when establishing the base at Liangshan, and Steve Evans, the officer in charge of the photo laboratory, and five others were lost in a storm flying from Liangshan to Kunming. They had been waiting for days for the weather to lift so they could go to Kunming for R&R. We were all playing poker when the word came that the ship to Kunming could take off. They dropped their cards and rushed to the airstrip. That was the start of the fatal flight. This brought to four the number of men that I had bunked and worked closely with that would never go home. It hurt, but you could not allow yourself to dwell on it. You put it out of your mind and went on with your duties. The ship was found after the war where it had gone into a mountain. The letters that had been written and recovered from the wreckage were sent on with an explanation so that relatives did not take hope that the writers were still alive.

The Chinese American Composite Wing was moved from Chengtu to Peyshi which was just west of Chunking. This was to be our base until we moved to Changsha later in the war. A few experiences come to mind. In setting up the intelligence program for our unit before they moved up, we had accumulated enough intelligence information and pictures of Japanese targets to start bombing and strafing raids. This was the most interesting aspect of my job. As the intelligence officer, I had access to all information we had on the Japanese. The intelligence officer is supposed to be the source of all information concerning the enemy. This gave me the opportunity to select the targets and make recommendations as to the bombs to be used. It was an exciting period of time.

Army and Air Corps regulations prohibited intelligence officers from going on combat missions for the reason that if they fell into enemy hands, we might disclose how much information we had acquired about their activities. Despite this, I was authorized on a number of occasions to accompany our missions. I felt that I could not adequately perform my functions unless I really understood the conditions that the pilots and crew members experienced.

I will never forget the first strafing mission I accompanied. The pilot was our operations officer, Dave Munson. I was a waist gunner and as we came to the enemy target, I wondered what all those flashing lights were. They looked like fireflies which lighted up the whole hillside. Then I realized that each of these lights was the flash of a bullet intended for us. It was a shocking revelation! We made several strafing runs, really more than we should have, and then returned to our base. The disturbing part of the raid was that the Chinese ground forces never followed up with an attack. This was not unusual for our Chinese allies to request a raid, but not get involved. It was typical of Chiang Kai-shek's policy of having others fight while he conserved his own forces.

One of our bomber pilots, who had a tremendous reputation for bravery as a skip bomber in the South China seas, often led the bombing missions. I accompanied one of these and to my dismay, the mission turned back before reaching the target. The pilot had reached that psychological stage where he felt his luck had run out. General Morris called me and asked me to express my opinion as to whether or not the mission should have been canceled because of bad weather, as the leader had reported. I told him I saw no reason to cancel the mission and was astounded when it was. This led to recognition that this bomber pilot had reached the end of his usefulness. He needed to return to the United States for R&R. Once a man had convinced himself that his luck had expired, he was useless in battle thereafter.

All our supplies were flown over The Hump, the Himalaya Mountains, into Kunming and transported to the outer bases. Occasionally, we had to go into headquarters to transact some business in person. When we did, we returned on some transport ship which in most instances was piloted by a new pilot who had just been assigned to the China Theater and knew little of the terrain or the weather conditions that existed.

One time I recall especially was when I boarded a transport at Kunming to return to our base at Peyshi. The pilot said, "Fasten your seat belts." Every man who had been flying in China for some time looked at one another, knowing that this was a brand new pilot. No one ever fastened seat belts in the China area. As I relaxed, trying to read a book, I heard the pilot say, "We are going down to Chialumpo." The weather was miserable. You could hardly see the wing tips of the plane. I looked at my watch and thought, "We are in trouble if we are going into Chialumpo." This airfield was below the level of the Chialing River banks on a sand bar next to the river. To make an approach, you had to come in high and drop down very rapidly and hit exactly at the end of the runway. It was too short for most aircraft and if you didn't get the aircraft stopped, you went off the end of the runway into the Chialing River.

Just then, we zoomed to clear a house and I knew immediately we were not at Chialumpo, but at Peyshi, as I saw some of our aircraft in their revetments. We made a 180 degree turn and headed back to make an appropriate landing. Flying conditions were absolutely minimal. I will never forget the pilot as he stepped off the plane perspiring and opening the collar on his shirt and making the gesture, "Boy, that was close!" And it was. In fact, we lost more people in transport in China than we did in combat. A transport that went into a mountain usually took a plane load, while in combat it was usually just a pilot, or in the case of a bomber, a crew of three to five men.

Of the six men that I roomed with going overseas, only two of us returned. The rest lost their lives in aircraft disasters.

As the intelligence officer, I was also the person responsible for censorship of all public relations dispatches and all letters had to be reviewed by the Intelligence Division. We had a reporter assigned to us who was a good reporter, but an alcoholic. I recall one day when he had gone into Chunking, he did not return for three days. When he returned he said, "There is something wrong with this liquor — it poisoned me — I can't remember a single thing." I thought this was impossible. The reporter was soon ushered out and returned to the States.

I mention this because of an experience a short time later. It was during Christmas holiday season that the Generalissimo gave a party for the American Chinese Composite Wing and some of his officers in Chunking. We had a weather officer who never drank at all and in fact he was the one who always set up the chairs for the religious services. He was a rather modest, retiring man. I have forgotten his name. When we were invited to go to this Christmas party, his Chinese alternate gave him a bottle of Chinese wine. Although he was not used to it, the Chinese officer insisted that the weather officer drink with him in the truck transport. Refusing to drink when toasted was considered insulting.

When he reached Chunking he was completely inebriated. He knocked out a number of windows in the hotel where the party was to be held and pushed some of the food off the stove in the kitchen. He was subdued when he started chasing a houseboy in the hotel with a pair of scissors. General Wedemeyer, who had been assigned as the new theater commander, sent word that this event was to be investigated and if the man was guilty, he was to be dishonorably discharged.

I was assigned to make the summary investigation. In interviewing the weather officer, he advised me that he did not remember a thing except people holding him down and not permitting him to do what he wanted to do. He stated that he had no recollection of the events and I believed him, as by then I had had a similar experience in loss of memory.

It was during this same Christmas period that the Generalissimo had invited us to a banquet. Each table was to set up to serve eight officers. There were about 50 Chinese Air Force officers at the banquet. One of the men sitting at the same table as I was, a major, said, "You know, I was educated in the United States. I went to the University of Michigan." I said, "I graduated from the University of Michigan Law School," whereupon he jumped up and said, "Let's drink to Michigan."

That was the signal and about 30 to 40 Chinese officers lined up behind him to drink to Michigan. I was supposed to drink with each one. It was considered very bad taste to refuse to drink and the normal procedure was to "gambay." This means "dry the cup," or in our words, "bottoms up." I was faced with the prospect of gambaying with about 40 Chinese officers. Much of the rest of the story they told me. Chinese wine, which is served hot, apparently goes directly into the bloodstream, and its effect is almost immediate.

After the banquet, our host was performing his ceremony preparatory to awarding a number of gifts (Chinese are great for ceremony). During his presentation, he described each of the gifts that was to be given away. When he picked up a little chop, which is a Chinese instrument they use to sign their name (they do not write their names as we do), he said, "This is the most valuable of all—it's over 300 years old." My roommate, Colonel McGhee, who had not taken any drinks because he was on sulfa (sulfa forms crystals in the kidneys if you drink any alcohol), was there. McGhee told me what happened: I said, "Fine," reached out, picked up the chop, and put it in my pocket, much to the consternation of my host. McGhee said, "Put it back," and I put it back. Our host continued with the ceremony and then he turned around and noticed the chop was missing. Colonel McGhee came to me and said, "If you have it, put it back," whereupon I took it from my pocket and reached around behind my back and handed it to him and he had to put it back.

The next thing Colonel McGhee knew, I was missing, so he started looking for me. He went outside the building and found me in the back seat of a station wagon with two Chinese drivers. He said I told him I had had enough, that I was going back to the barracks. I remember none of this.

During my investigation of the weather office, I recounted this experience in drinking hot Chinese wine. I spent more time on that as a justification of the man's actions than in investigating his actual activities. As a result, I saved his commission. General Wedemeyer accepted the explanation.

I will never forget the day I met General Stillwell, who was a former theater commander. Word came in that the General was on a plane and would land at our base. I was designated to meet his plane. A four-star general stepped out and said, "My name is Stillwell." As if everyone in the theater did not know who the four-star general was!

Stillwell was a very modest man. It is unfortunate that the records do not fully disclose what a wonderful individual he was. He probably was not the best theater commander, but perhaps knew more about China and Chinese than any other living American. He also saw through Chiang Kai-shek. He referred to him as Peanut.

There were many dreary days in China, as the weather was abominable. Day after day no aircraft could take off. It was on one of these days that we were routed out with the call that the Japanese were going to bomb our base. With the three-ball alert, and the three bongs on the cymbal, we left the hostel to man our guns.

We had no real ground defense. There never were any American ground units to defend us. We relied entirely on Chinese ground forces, which were not very satisfactory, to say the least. As a result, Major Ashmead, our supply officer, had resurrected a number of 50 caliber guns from crashed P-40 aircraft. He had fashioned mounts so that we could use these guns for the defense of our base against bombers. As these were makeshift mounts, the cartridges had to be fed in from one side by a soldier while an officer operated the machine gun. They had no blast tubes, so as you fired, the flash of the gun would blind you and you would have to wait until you could see again; not exactly an effective operation! To make matters worse, Major Ashmead had installed the guns in pits in direct line with what served as a control tower.

I manned one gun, which was about 30 or 40 yards from one side of the control tower. Ashmead manned one about 30 or 40 yards the other side. The idea was that the bombers would come close enough that we might be able to shoot them down. Sgt. Eller was my top sergeant in intelligence. He fed the ammunition for me as I manned the machine gun.

I can still hear the Japanese aircraft as they dived. They toggled their bombs to make the bomb run. Toggling is to drop one bomb at a time in a stepped-up procedure, rather than drop ping all the bombs at once. We could hear the bombs hitting closer and closer to our gun pit. When one hit within about fifteen yards of the pit, Sgt. Eller dropped the ammunition belt and ducked. Our heads were below the ground, but as we were standing in water up to our thighs, we could not get down too low. That ended my shooting on that raid, as the gun was jammed.

When we got into the weapon carriers to return to our hostel, Colonel Ashmead was covered with mud and straw and I said, "What happened?" He answered, "I didn't know how I would react under fire." The next bomb, after the one that hit near our gun pit, went over the building and landed to within a few yards of his gun pit where it exploded. He jumped out of the gun pit and dove into a rice paddy, with all the muck that you get in a rice field.

It didn't take him long to move the gun pits from the direct line of attack up to the side of the hill. My new gun position was interesting in that it was located in an old cemetery. We had three wooden caskets sticking out of the side of our gun pit. As Chinese use an extra heavy wooden casket hollowed out of coffin trees, the coffins made an excellent place to hang up our helmets and guns when we were not under attack. It was not exactly consoling to be in a cemetery when we are there trying to protect our air base. It could have become permanent!

As the Japanese intensified their attacks on ground forces from the south, our unit was transferred to Changsha to meet this new threat. It was here that we finished out the war.

Sometime before our transfer, the new B-29s were moved into Chengtu in western China. This was done with utmost secrecy. They never even advised our own unit that they were in Chengtu. They were stationed to attack the Japanese on the east coast of China. The result was Pandemonium, as we had all kinds of alerts of strange aircraft in the reporting net. We used valuable and scarce gasoline to send our fighters up, only to learn that it was our own aircraft out of Chengtu. The B-29s were the biggest bombers in the war. The mission result was also disastrous, in that the B-29 bombers ran out of gasoline. If they had been briefed, they could have landed on friendly fields which we occupied. Some had to parachute out and abandon the aircraft. One landed at Chialumpo. How the pilot ever got that B-29 down on that little sand bar I'll never know, but he did! He later stripped the aircraft to lighten it and flew it out!

We of the Chinese American Wing in the intelligence section spent the next three to four months trying to extricate our B-29 pilots who were downed behind the Japanese lines, but in friendly Chinese territory. This was quite an operation. Chinese (civilian) forces would take in our pilots, dress them in Chinese clothes, hide them and attempt to return them to our units.

In order to avoid the confusion that existed with that first raid by the B-29s, one of our men, either Colonel MacAlenan or I, would go to Chengtu, the headquarters of the B-29s. We would then keep our U.S. units advised of the mission and what route they would be flying, so as to avoid falsely alerting the air raid net. This avoided the need for our fighters to go up to intercept them.

This is where I met General Curtis LeMay, who was in command of the first B-29s. He had previously flown with the 8th Air Force out of Great Britain and was known as "Old Ironpants," as he flew through the flak barrage put up by the Germans. He subsequently became the Chief of Staff of the United States Armed Forces after the close of the war.

I do not know the circumstances but General Morris was released from command and transferred and Colonel Earl Bennet was placed in command of CACW. Lyle Shepard was the executive officer throughout the formation and operation of CACW. Lyle provided the real stability of the unit. He was a civilian involved in the investment business in New York. He had volunteered out of patriotism. He was the stabilizing influence and a complement for some of General Morris's shortcomings.

Some time later, I was advised that the manager who was taking care of the Lassen operation had been recalled by National Park Concessions, Inc., and that we would be without a manager. Dal was in the State Department and unable to leave, so I asked for 30 days R&R to return and take care of securing a manager for Lassen. It is rather ironic that I was permitted to fly from China to the United States to take care of my own personal business, but I had spent some two and a half years in China, and was entitled to 30 days R&R.

I flew into the United States and went to Oakland, California, to interview Fred L. Taber, a principal of a school who had worked a season or two at Lassen during the summer. We spent about an hour making arrangements. I gave him the keys to the Lassen facilities, authorized him to sign on our bank account, and prepared to return to China. I decided to visit Dal Dort in Washington, D.C. before I left the country.

Upon arrival in Washington, D.C., Dal advised me that he had an option to buy the Yosemite Park & Curry Company for $1,750,000, but Government Services, Inc., headed by Park Service Associate Director Arthur E. Demaray, had the first right to buy. Dal asked if I would go to Yosemite and look over the operation and advise him what I thought of the purchase of the company. I agreed to do so.

Hilmer Oehlmann, president of Yosemite Park & Curry Company, met me in San Francisco and we drove to Yosemite. We spent about a day going over the facilities owned by the company. I recommended to Dal that he do everything possible to acquire Yosemite Park & Curry Company. He would have, except that Arthur Demaray, being an Associate Director of the National Park Service, and holding first option, kept requesting extensions from Don Tresidder. Demaray was in a conflicting position acting as both purchaser and for the government as a contractor.

Don Tresidder had been the president of Yosemite Park & Curry Company, but had taken the position of President of Stanford University. This left them without a general manager, except for Hilmer Oehlmann, who was not a major stockholder. They were not too certain how long the war was going to last, so decided they would sell the operation.

Arthur Demaray did not play a very fair game. He kept putting pressure on Tresidder to extend his option, even though he could not comply with the terms. Finally, Government Services, Inc. employees struck their company, as they wanted more money. Arthur Demaray raised their wages. This resulted in Government Services losing about $20,000 per month on the operation of the cafeterias in the government buildings in Washington, D.C. Under the pressure of the strike, Arthur Demaray raised the meal prices. O.P.A. stepped in and said, "You can't do that." Mr. Demaray said, "Well, I'm losing money," to which they replied, "That's what everybody tells us." They forced him to cancel his increases.

This was the final act for Demaray. He had to give up his right to buy. The difficulty was that the war with Japan was coming to an end, and not long afterward rationing and price controls were removed. The pent-up demand for recreation as a result of restrictions of the war were lifted and the parks filled up overnight. Yosemite Park & Curry Company then decided they did not want to sell the facilities after all and Dal Dort lost his option to purchase.

Upon completion of my trip to Yosemite, I got passage to Manila in the Philippines, where I was scheduled to go on temporary duty for 30 days. The purpose of sending me to the Philippines was to be sure we coordinated the intelligence activities of the 14th Air Force in China and the 5th Air Force, which was stationed in the Philippines. I was to get acquainted with the intelligence organization in the Philippines to ensure closer liaison.

The B-29s had since been moved from Chengtu, China to Saipan. Our forces were attacking the Japanese out of Saipan and Guam. It was obvious that we were converging on the Japanese mainland and that the final assault was soon to become effective. They expected a major drive would come out of the Philippines area, Saipan, Guam and mainland China.

I was in Manila, but no one seemed to be particularly interested in getting down to real work. I spent the 30 days, but don't believe that I accomplished anything.

I then received word that I was to return to my unit which was now located in Changsha. Instead of going over

The Hump, we had things sufficiently under control that we were able to overfly the Japanese in Kowloon, and the southern part of China. This, of course, shortened my trip considerably and I returned to my unit in Changsha.

It was just after this that we dropped the atom bomb on Hiroshima and shortly thereafter on Nagasaki. It was after this occurred that the Japanese sued for peace. The first step of the surrender was for the Chinese Army, headed by Generalissimo Chiang Kai-shek, to take the surrender of the Japanese forces that were on the China continent. We were amazed to find out that the Japanese had over a million soldiers on the mainland of China. The surrender of these forces was made at our base in Changsha.

I had a special written invitation to the surrender cere-monies, but unfortunately I don't know what happened to it. On my way home, we flew over Hiroshima and Nagasaki. It's hard to describe the desolation. Only a few walls and chimneys were left standing in Hiroshima. All else was obliterated.

Don Ford, who was teaching at the Command and Staff School, had been ordered to India and then transferred as one of the principal intelligence officers in the theater head-quarters on the Chinese mainland. He asked if I would like to transfer to the main headquarters from the CACW unit. I said I would and was transferred thereafter to the theater headquarters for China.

I was fortunate thereafter to be named and awarded the Legion of Merit for my services in China. I had previously received the Bronze Star for my services in setting up the intelligence organization in Liangshan. I also received two awards from the Chinese government.

Shortly after General MacArthur took the surrender of the Japanese forces on an aircraft carrier in Japan, I was sent to Shanghai. Three of us were sent and as the airport was out a number of miles from Shanghai, we had to move into the city by Jeep. I will never forget going through about seven miles of Japanese forces marching along each side of the road we were traveling. They were good soldiers and tough ones. Although they were completely armed, the Japanese soldiers had been told that the war was over. The Emperor had ordered hostilities to cease. I imagined what might have happened if American G.I.s had been there and somebody told them not to shoot these enemy officers traveling in an unarmed jeep...what some of them might have done!

We encountered no difficulties and got into Shanghai without incident. Shortly thereafter I was told to go out and demand that the Japanese headquarters in Shanghai be vacated as we wanted to utilize those buildings. It was an eerie feeling walking past Japanese soldiers and into their headquarters alone, with no support. I then asked that the general release the quarters to the Americans. True to Japanese tradition, the Emperor had told them that the war was over and no attempt was made to harm me.

Don Ford and the office staff were later moved to Shanghai. He and I occupied a room together in a hotel taken over for American quarters. We were there several months when I was ordered home, as I had more than enough points for discharge.

I flew back to the United States and was released at the Marysville center in California. This ended my military career, except that I stayed in the Air Force Ready Reserves until I was discharged, having reached retirement age.

8
War and the Impact on the National Parks

THE WAR YEARS were difficult ones for the national parks, as appropriations were reduced from 21 million to five million, a diminishing point, with the result that government facilities were allowed to fall into disrepair from lack of maintenance; concession facilities had also deteriorated through failure of maintenance and use. Many areas were closed and unoccupied.

Following the end of the war and the lifting of price and rationing controls, the parks felt the full impact of a recreation-starved population. They overflowed the parks. This only aggravated the use of deteriorated facilities, both government and concessioner. The concessioners, who had to rely on private financing to restore their buildings and to replace obsolete furniture and fixtures, were experiencing difficulty in securing financing on terms they could live with. Various proposals suggesting government acquisition of concession facilities resulted in the formation of a Citizens' Advisory Group in 1946, to propose solutions. Clem Collins, an accountant from Denver, was named chairman. Committee members were AAA Travel Director Elmer Jenkins, George D. Smith from the hotel industry, Charles P. Taft, representing the general public, and Charles G. Woodbury, conservationist.

After two years of inquiry and studies, the group recommended government ownership but not operation of visitor facilities in the national parks. At the same time they acknowledged that congressional appropriation of acquisition funds appeared highly unlikely. In view of the lack of acquisition funds, they recommended that operations by concessioners be continued under policies which would protect the government's interest and give the concessioners the security to which they were entitled and sufficient incentive to provide a high standard of service to the public.

This citizens' group also recommended that concessioners of known reliability who had provided satisfactory service should have their contracts renewed. They stated that public interest would best be served by the existing policy of granting preferential contracts to concessioners who had performed to the satisfaction of the National Park Service.

Horace M. Albright, former Director, also questioned whether Congress would provide funds for acquisition of concessioners' facilities and doubted the desirability of government ownership.

He questioned whether the Park Service could run the parks and at the same time operate tourist facilities. He questioned whether the Park Service might erect visitor facilities too far removed from areas attractive to visitors to make them profitable, stating that the policy of protecting scenic features would probably predominate.

The recommendations of the Citizens' Advisory Group, while recognizing the problems, did little to provide a solution, but opened the door for the Department of the Interior to seek to acquire concession facilities.

A Department of Interior's solicitor would propose the means to acquire the concession facilities without obtaining congressional appropriations by declaring the forfeiture of the concessioners property interests. It would also make it impossible for concessioners to acquire the financing necessary to upgrade and expand facilities needed to meet park visitors' demands. All these proposals would add another five-year delay in upgrading visitor facilities while building costs escalated.

It was at this stage that the Western Conference of National Park Concessioners became actively involved. It would also be the first time that the concessioners resorted to congressional assistance in dealing with the Department of the Interior and the National Park Service. The Park Service and the concessioners had "grown up together." Problems had often been solved jointly with few or no precedents to guide them, but with a shared responsibility to provide service to the park visitor. This spirit of cooperation overcame many obstacles until shattered by the Department of the Interior's proposal for government acquisition of concession facilities.

When World War II started, rationing was instituted and prices were controlled on a national basis. No provision had been made for recreational activities and most of the park concession operations ceased for the duration of the war. Yosemite Park & Curry Company had leased the Ahwanee Hotel to the Navy for a rest and recreation center for returning submarine crews. The Park Service had moved its headquarters from Washington, D.C., to Chicago, Illinois, with a reduced staff to make way for defense-oriented services in Washington, D.C.

At the end of the war, and as concessioners started to reestablish their operations, most of their contracts had expired. Concessioners met with the Park Service and the Assistant Secretary for Parks to discuss the renewal of our contracts in 1946.

The Assistant Secretary for Parks was C. Gerard Davidson, whose nickname was "Jebby." At this meeting Jebby Davidson said he had a Solicitor's opinion which he wanted to read to the Conference members to get their reaction. Harry Edelstein was Assistant Solicitor for Parks. Mastin G. White was the author of the opinion, but Edelstein was the one who made the presentation.

The substance of the opinion was that our contracts did not protect our property interests. Structures that we had built on park land and paid for in accordance with the concession contracts, belonged to the government! Harry Edelstein stated that we still had a right to sell to a successor concessioner — as if anyone would buy under those conditions. But, if we signed a new contract, all our property rights would be forfeited. This was based on the position that the Secretary had no right to recognize our property ownership; that buildings built on government-owned land belonged to the government, as the title to the buildings followed the title to the land. In other words, the government owned all our facilities and our only rights were to sell to successor concessioners, as our rights arose out of and expired with our contracts. As this announcement was being presented, I was sitting next to Don Tresidder, President of Yosemite Park & Curry Company, who was usually a reserved man in control of his emotions. He was urbane in his demeanor. In fact he had the ability to state in straightforward language, his position in a most gentlemanly and unantagonistic manner.

I could see Tresidder getting worked up as the Assistant Solicitor read the opinion. He had hold of the chair in front of him, squeezing it until the white showed on his knuckles. He was on his feet immediately, protesting in the strongest manner that this was repudiation of the understanding that they had with the National Park Service when the contracts were negotiated. This was the beginning of a five-year-long fight between the Conference and the Secretary of the Interior.

In this connection the Park Service was definitely on the side of the concessioners, but as a bureau under the Department of the Interior, they were restricted in how much they could express their opinion. They were appalled, as we were, at the attitude of the Secretary's office; in fact, the former Secretary of the Interior, Harold L. Ickes, met with Tresidder one day and commented on the Department of the Interior's approach. His statement to Tresidder was, "You know I wanted to take you over, but I didn't intend to steal the facilities."

There then ensued a series of negotiations and maneuvers by the Department of the Interior and by the Conference of National Park Concessioners. A congressman from Iowa by the name of Ben Jensen, of the Appropriations Committee, was reported to have heard about these maneuvers. He was upset by them. At our Conference in 1946 members discussed these problems and debated what steps should be taken, they always ended up saying, "It's going to have to be settled in Congress." During a recess of the Conference, I went to see Congressman Jensen and discussed the Solicitor's opinion. He, too, was appalled, and indicated that he wanted to intercede on behalf of the concessioners. On the reconvening of the Conference session, I reported the results of my visit with the congressman. We were nearing the end of our Conference and without any comment on what I had said, Bryon Harvey, who was the Conference Chairman at that time, announced that he would entertain a motion for adjournment.

I strongly protested, saying that I had listened for several days to their discussions and the general consensus was that we would have to go to Congress for relief, and now that a congressman had expressed interest in pursuing this problem on our behalf, we were going home without consulting him. I advised the Conference that if I were in the congressman's shoes and they did not follow through with his offer, and later asked for assistance, I would tell them all to go to hell!

As a result of this, a discussion took place and the Chairman appointed Herman Hoss, the Conference attorney, and me to go see Congressman Jensen. This we did, and after some discussion the congressman suggested that we take the matter up with the Public Lands Committee. This committee was the predecessor to the Interior and Insular Affairs Committee, and had legislative jurisdiction over the Department of the Interior.

Congressman J. Hardin Peterson was Chairman of the Public Lands Committee. He was contacted and there followed a series of discussions and finally several public hearings. I was one of the Conference members to testify; in fact, Congressman Crawford asked me why the Conference was pushing me out in front as the principal witness. The answer, I believe, was that I was a very small concessioner and a returning veteran, and the loss of our facilities at Lassen National Park would be contrary to everything Congress was doing to enable returning veterans to reestablish themselves. In fact the emphasis on my veteran's status was so great that at the close of one hearing, Congressman Crawford proceeded to belittle my testimony, debunking any privileges that I might have as a veteran. He pointed out that I was just one of millions of veterans and was not entitled to any more consideration than any other veteran. All of which I agreed to. I was not sharp enough to respond that I was not asking for special consideration, but that I resented the Department of the Interior taking away from me what Congress had granted. I could have pointed out that even though I had used all my veteran's preference to reestablish the Lassen operations, I would lose this if another concessioner or the government could take over our operations and, as discussed, on more favorable terms than were extended to me as a concessioner. The effect would be to deny me the preferences that

Congress had voted for veterans. Unfortunately, I was too green and not alert enough to make these points.

Congressman D'Ewart said:

I would like to thank Mr. Hummel for appearing before this committee and presenting his case as a veteran who is doing his best to serve the public as a concessioner in a national park under conditions that seem insurmountable. It is not only discouraging to him but to others. How he can proceed from here and give the people who visit his area the services they are entitled to is hard for me to understand. I sincerely hope that this committee will proceed with this investigation and work out a solution that will encourage just such men as Mr. Hummel in the carrying on of their operation and the continuance of their facilities so they will be available to the public over the years.

I think that is something this committee has to undertake right away. In the meantime, I sincerely hope you will not be disturbed in the use of your facilities until this committee can act and write a policy that will be in the interest of the public as a whole.

Then Mr. Engle said:

May I concur, Mr. Chairman, in the statement made by my friend from Montana. I have known Mr. Hummel for several years. The first time he came to my office he was in uniform. Since then I have had rather close contact with him in connection with his operation in my district. I know that he runs a good facility there for the public, and that he is sincerely interested in doing a good job in running his concession. He has also indicated a real interest in the public welfare.

The final hearing on the concessions matters was held in Santa Fe, New Mexico, on November 10, 1949. It was at these hearings that I got to know Trev and Ellie Povah, of Hamilton Stores, Inc., in Yellowstone National Park, and this was the start of a lifelong friendship. Ansel Hall, who was president of the Mesa Verde Company, and one of the witnesses, had brought a bound volume of compliments and complaints he had received on the Mesa Verde operations which he put into the record. As he had been Chief Park Naturalist turned concessioner, he was badly berated by the National Park Service as a turncoat.

After the hearings, Congressman Peterson, of the Public Lands Committee, advised the Conference that there would be no time to enact any legislation. He advised the Conference to negotiate new contract terms, and informed us that he had told the Department of the Interior there would be no money to acquire concession facilities and that they had better make their peace with the concessioners.

Pursuant to the suggestion of Congressman Peterson that the Conference and the National Park Service negotiate new contract terms, four of us were assigned to attempt to get agreement on language for new contracts. There was Harry Edelstein, the assistant solicitor who had read the opinion questioning the concessioner's property rights; Jackson Price, who was the solicitor for the National Park Service, Herman Hoss, the attorney for the Conference, and myself. We were told to go into an office, negotiate a contract, and not to come out until we had agreed.

Herman Hoss, who was normally an unflappable individual and an excellent attorney, had a superior capacity in the use of the English language. He insisted on precise use of words. So much so that the government representatives referred to him as "that technical bastard." A doctor had taken Herman off smoking, as he had a growth on his tongue. Harry Edelstein, realizing Herman's nervousness, started to needle him. This discussion concerned how to express the concessioners' interest in their facilities, since the government had the legal title. Herman suggested "possessory interest." Possessory interest was to be defined as all incidence of ownership except legal title, which remained in the United States. The term was borrowed from California tax law, wherein the State of California taxed buildings that were constructed on public land. The property interest of the owner of the buildings was described as "a possessory interest". After some heated discussion, Harry Edelstein said to Herman, "Well, why don't we just drop the concept?" Whereupon, Herman got up and walked to the window and said, "Oh, hell, what's the use?" Harry said, "Yes, what's the use," and took his papers and walked out of the room. It took Jackson Price and me two hours to get these men back into the office to continue our negotiations to agree upon the standard language for concession contracts.

The new Secretary of the Interior, Oscar Chapman, through his Undersecretary, Dale Doty, issued a statement on May 6, 1950, which, in effect, reestablished the policies that the concessioners had been operating under since the beginning. The Mather/Albright policies had always recognized the right of the concessioners to the security of their investment in the national parks. By this time we had agreed to the new standard language to be used in concession contracts, much to the chagrin of Harry Edelstein, who really wanted to make it as difficult as possible for the concessioners. He was thoroughly imbued with the idea that the government should own and operate the facilities in the national parks. To protect the concessioners, Chairman Peterson advised the National Park Service that any contract that was signed with a concessioner had to be deposited with the Public Lands Committee for 30 days before the Park Service could sign. This was to give the concessioner a chance to complain to Congress if the Park Service or the Department of the Interior did not specifically follow the agreements that had been reached. This was instituted as we often thought we had agreement with the Department of the Interior, but when the written document appeared, it contained a very different conclusion.

In order to give committee approval to the Secretary's policy statement, the Public Lands Committee of the House adopted a resolution on July 18, 1950, stating:

> WHEREAS, the Secretary of the Interior issued a memorandum on May 6, 1950, to the Director of the National Park Service clarifying the concessions policy of such department, and
>
> WHEREAS, the policy announced by the Secretary on May 6 seems to meet many of the problems which had arisen and would enable the concessioners to give good public service and provide adequate facilities; and
>
> WHEREAS, such clarifying policy by the Secretary seems to adopt the principles of proposed legislation being considered by the committee...; and

WHEREAS, the matter relating to security of investment by the concessioners, although not covered in the
memorandum, ...may be covered to the satisfaction of all
parties concerned in new contracts between the concessioners and the Park Service.

RESOLVED: That the policy...under date of May 6, as
attached and made part of this resolution, is approved;
...the Secretary of the Interior and the Director of the
National Park Service are requested to give notice...of
any change in policy...; any breakdown in
negotiations...relative to recognition...of the investment
security (including the possessory interest) of the concessioner.

J. Hardin Peterson, Chairman

The Lassen contract was the first one negotiated and
approved under the reestablished policies. George Hartzog
was an assistant to the Chief of Concessions in the Washington office, and he and I negotiated the new contract. I
am afraid I was too naive or generous, as we subsequently
had to amend the contract. It contained provisions which
were too onerous for a small operation in a little-known
park. I had agreed to a higher franchise fee than the
business could support.

Once having agreed to the new standard language, both
the Park Service and the concessioners rushed to negotiate
new contracts and get on with the business of refurbishing
their concession facilities. They had not only seriously
deteriorated during the war but subsequently during the
contract fights, which postponed financing for repairs and
expansion. Tom Flynn was named as the new Chief of
Concessions in Washington, D.C. Tom had been an assistant to an Assistant Secretary of the Interior. Sometime
thereafter, George Hartzog, who was Assistant Chief of
Concessions, resigned from the National Park Service and
took a job as the director of the project in St. Louis to build
the Arch for the Western Gateway. (The area under the
Arch was rededicated in 1985 as the George B. Hartzog, Jr.
Visitors Center.)

Newton Drury resigned from the directorship of the
National Park Service, a position he had held during the

entire war, and subsequently during contract negotiations. He returned to California to become the Director of the California State Park Systems. He had made his reputation in the drive to "Save the Redwoods." Conrad Wirth became the Director in 1951. He proposed a ten-year program to begin in 1956 and to terminate on the 50th anniversary of the National Park Service, to bring the national parks up to standard. It was called Mission 66.

While the Secretary of the Interior's Policy Statement of May 6, 1950, reestablished the Mather/Albright policies for national park concessioners, the whole question of federal government policies of providing outdoor recreation facilities had not been resolved.

In an attempt to provide basic policies, Congress, by Public Law 85-470 (72 Stat. 238) established the Outdoor Recreation Review Commission to:

1. Inventory the nation's outdoor recreation facilities;
2. Determine how they should be made available for use;
3. Examine the question of government ownership of recreation facilities;
4. Examine concessioners' interest in structures built on government lands (possessory interest);
5. Examine government supervision and changes in government policies and their effect on outdoor recreation in the United States.

The Commission was composed of prominent citizens, members of Congress and was chaired by Laurence Rockefeller. The report took four years and was issued in 1962. The report, written by Henry Diamond as Staff Director of the Commission, concluded that:

> The private sector of the economy (the concession system) is by far the most promising source of potential new funds for recreation facilities. The general health of the concession system is good and has shown great capacity for growth.

It further concluded that:

> The problems of short seasons, high costs of construction and shifting desires of consumers were exacer-

bated by contradictory government attitudes and supervision, occasional introduction of political consideration, changes in public policies, vaguely worded contracts and legal concepts novel to the world of orthodox finance.

The Commission recommended:

A clear statement of federal policy toward the concession system be issued setting forth the role of concessions in a national recreation program; and a revamping of contracts and leases with concessioners that seem unduly weighted on the government side and unnecessarily stringent in light of actual operating conditions. The central goal of public policy should be to reduce these difficulties...

In 1961, I had been elected Chairman of the Conference of National Park Concessioners. The procedure had changed so that a chairman and a secretary were elected by the membership. The chairman was still authorized to make all decisions during the interim between annual meetings. It was still the responsibility of the chairman's company to pay any and all bills incurred by the Conference during the interim period — a practice I found very burdensome for a small company. The company was reimbursed by the membership at the following annual meeting. I was the first chairman of the Conference to be elected who did not represent one of the big three companies. I attempted to introduce some democratic procedures in the Conference by appointing an executive committee to consult with during the interim. I felt that it was poor business to have one man making decisions for the Conference without collaboration with any of the other concessioners (which was the practice prior to 1961).

During this period of time, the cooperation with the National Park Service was excellent; in fact, I, as Chairman, and some other members, were usually invited to the Superintendents' Conferences and given a place on their agendas. This gave us a chance to become acquainted with park problems and to exchange views with many of the park superintendents. Heretofore we had dealt primarily with our own superintendent and the Director and his staff in Washington, D.C. This increased our understanding of

National Park Service problems, and their understanding of the concession system and the difficulties of financing visitor facilities.

It was at the Superintendents' Conference in Yosemite National Park when the new Secretary of the Interior, Stewart Udall, addressed the superintendents. He was preceded by Assistant Secretary of the Interior, John Carver, who had delivered an unfortunate address to the Conference, in effect, belaboring Connie Wirth, the Director of the National Park Service, and some of the park's performances. This did not set well with the superintendents, as Connie was a very popular director.

Secretary Stewart Udall was late in arriving and missed Carver's speech. George Hartzog and I were sent out to meet Stewart and escort him to the Conference. This we did, and in the short span of time it took to walk from the car to the hall, I advised Stewart what had occurred and what a bad reaction had been engendered. He was therefore able to mollify the group when he spoke. At this meeting Secretary Udall announced George Hartzog as the new Director of the National Park Service effective January 1964.

George asked me to take a walk with him that evening in Yosemite. During the walk he stated that Howard Hays, the President of Sequoia and Kings Canyon National Parks Company, and I were his real friends, and he expected us to tell him if he was getting "off the track" during his administration as director. I took this very seriously and often over the years reminded George of our conversation when I objected to some of the policies he was initiating, often on the insistence of environmental organizations. While he always listened, he seldom responded to my suggestions.

The most pernicious and devastating for the park visitor was the start of a program to limit, exclude and remove visitor facilities from the parks. This was and is a prime objective of environmental groups. The record, which follows in later chapters, demonstrates their effectiveness in dominating the National Park Service. But now we must return to the end of World War II and pick up the story of my personal experiences.

9
Return to Lassen

I RETURNED to Lassen around March of 1946, after having been released from active duty with the Air Force. I contacted Fred L. Taber, whom I had authorized to run the operations while I returned to China. He had done a good job under difficult conditions. We had about $15,000 in our account. No maintenance had been done, of course, during the war. Lassen was one of the few operations to continue full services throughout the war.

Soon after my return, I learned that the Public Service Commission had held a hearing and we had lost our bus franchise to operate between Redding, California, and the park. We had received no notice of this and it had taken place while I was still in the service. I knew we had records to establish that we had complied with the obligations under our certificate.

There was still snow on the ground and no way to get into the lodge. I had to snowshoe into Manzanita Lake Lodge. I went up to the attic with a flashlight to try to recover the old records to support our franchise. There was no electricity in the area. It was a cold and dismal experience, particularly as I was looking for records I was not sure existed or in what form. Fortunately, I recovered enough of them to cover the granting of the franchise. It was then necessary to show that we had discharged our obligations under that franchise.

We asked for the case to be reopened. The man who was operating a small bus line and had been given our franchise opposed the reopening. After a hearing, our franchise was reestablished, and the man asked if I wanted to sell. I indicated that I did not. This was a mistake, as we never made any money on this operation. Instead, we lost money. It would really have helped our financial position by selling the franchise, but I did not, reasoning that it would be important to our future operations.

I spent the next several months going to many Army surplus sales. As a veteran, I was entitled to a preference and these sales made it possible to get the facilities that were necessary to bring our operation up to standard. I had arranged a loan from Crocker National Bank in San Francisco.

After the first season, it was obvious we did not have anywhere near the facilities necessary to meet public demand. I wanted to put in additional rooms; however, a law had been passed that all new materials for construction were to be used for building homes for veterans; that no new lumber could be used for any recreational development and this included Lassen.

I also had a demand from the National Park Service that we put in a cafeteria and it had to be in operation the following year. As there were still about three feet of snow on the ground, the superintendent and I snowshoed in to the Manzanita Lake area to agree upon a site for the new cafeteria. This requirement was ill-conceived but I was under command of the Park Service to provide the cafeteria. Jimmy Lloyd was the superintendent. He was a man of contradictions; he could be as nice and pleasant as possible one minute and the next minute, completely obstreperous. He and I agreed on a location for the new cafeteria. I had a sketchy plan with me. I told him that I was going to San Francisco that night, and as time was important, I wanted to present this plan to Regional Director Owen A. Tomlinson so we could expedite approval to proceed. We agreed, and he signed the sketch.

Later I received a letter of approval from the Washington office with the wording, "The plan that you have submitted directly to the Regional Office for the construction of the cafeteria has been approved." When Jimmy Lloyd saw the wording, "submitted directly to the Regional Office," he wanted to show that he knew regulations required submission through his office. He wrote me a two-page letter as to how I had to go through his office and not go directly to the Regional Office. This made me mad and I replied, detailing each step of how we had proceeded and how I had submitted this plan to him and he had personally signed it and I had secured his approval to submit it directly to the Regional Office. I ended by saying, "I note that you have sent a copy of your letter to the Director, so to make certain the record is complete, I am also sending a copy of my reply, showing you actually approved this procedure." He never crossed me again on that kind of situation.

Al Donau, my nephew, joined me at Lassen and became a permanent employee after World War II. Shortly after he arrived, Al left to get married to Mary Frank Warren, who thereafter worked for us at Lassen.

At the close of the first season, we made a profit of $10,000, whereupon I received a letter from Assistant Secretary C. Gerard Davison who said, "Although the amount of your profits are small, you must, regardless of the obstacles to be overcome, arrange for the expansion of your overnight facilities." This was despite the fact that the law prevented me from utilizing any new materials to add to our lodging.

I learned that the Standard Oil Company was dismantling a plant down in the Bay area and was seeking bids for the removal of some old buildings. I bid on and was successful in acquiring these buildings, whereupon I got a crew together, started tearing them down and moving the secondhand lumber to Manzanita Lake.

This was difficult in that I did not have adequate transportation to move the material to the park. I attended another sale of surplus and bid on two big 6x6 Army trucks. I only needed one, but as they were packed two together I had to buy both if I wanted any. I then had the job of getting them unpacked and assembled so I could use them. I hired a mechanic to assemble the trucks.

I moved the secondhand lumber to Manzanita Lake and used the old lumber to make tent platforms and sides for 50 tent units. This provided me with the platforms, but I could not find any tents, so I bid on some Army tent material and had the tents made. It was excellent material, but had been treated to prevent catching on fire. As a result, there was no breathing capacity in the canvas. It made for a very hot tent.

The next job I had was to find beds and, here again, I bid on and bought a number of Army cots which would be used in the new tents. After that I had to find mattresses to fit the cots. I found mattresses, but they were a little larger than the cots, so they hung over the sides. They were, however, mattresses! I then bid on some Army blankets and bought a great number of these, but we were still without pillows. When I finally located pillows at another Army surplus, I had to buy considerably more than needed, because that was the way the Army was selling them, and you either took all or none. We had pillows, pillows and pillows!

This was quite an experience. I think I attended every Army surplus sale in the State of California, and there were many of them, but it did give me an opportunity to acquire facilities at less than market price, although often not of the quality that I would like to have had.

At the end of the next season, the park interceded and I was authorized as a veteran to buy some new construction material. I had plans made to extend the kitchen facilities in the lodge, which were far less than needed and had deteriorated through the war years. We arranged to build a new kitchen and employees' dining room, which was the first time we were to have adequate facilities to feed our enlarged personnel staff.

I hired Herschel Keathley, brother to Charles Keathley, to handle construction. We had lost our old standby, Earl Potter, who was a master carpenter and an excellent construction man. He had gone into business for himself so was no longer available to us. While he was working with me, the following incident took place. Earl was an ardent anti-union man and I had agreed with the unions that I would pay union scale, but I refused to conduct a union shop, stating that whether a person joined the union or not was none of my business; but that I would meet the union hours and wage requirements.

One day a group of union people came up and met Earl Potter. They demanded he join the union and hire only union men. They soon came into my office protesting that Earl had called them "a bunch of damned communists." They said they wanted me to fire him. I told them I was sorry for the language he had used, but he was one of the best carpenters in the country and I refused to fire him. They said, "Well, he is just a guy riding on our backs. We work to get improved working conditions and improved wages and he goes along and gets the advantages, but doesn't do his share." I told them not to talk to me about doing his share, because he did twice as much work as any one of their men and at the same time bossed the job. I called attention to the fact that some of their people who were working on this crew were not pulling their weight, but since I had agreed to pay union scale, I had to pay everybody the same amount. I said if I had a choice, I would pay some of their people more and less to others, but I could not do that. I said, "You know and I know who is carrying their weight and who is not; the rest of you are just subsidizing them, so don't tell me that Earl Potter is riding on your backs."

It was several weeks later on a Saturday payday when the group paid another visit to my office claiming I had shorted their checks. I said I didn't understand. They said wages had gone up at the beginning of the week by 25 cents an hour, and it was not reflected in their checks. I said, "Don't you think it is a little late to be telling me this?" They agreed that it was and I said, "Well, next week I will start the new wage." They said they could not accept this because the union would fine them.

I said, "Well, do you think that it is fair to come in at the end of the week and tell me about this?" They did not think it was fair, but that was the way it was. I said, "Do you realize that room and board went up $2.00 a day this last week?" Their faces sort of fell and they left grumbling.

As they were leaving I said that the tourist season was starting and they would have to move to construction tents and move out of the cabins, as I needed the cabins for guests. This didn't go over very well, but they said nothing further.

I was at the desk Sunday night when some of the crew started returning from Red Bluff and Redding. One man — a carpenter who was obviously about half drunk — came up to me and said, "I've got two nots." I said, "You have what?" He said, "I've got two nots." I tumbled and said, "Okay, what are they?" He said, "I'm not going to sleep in a tent and I'm not going to pay that extra $2.00 per day for board and room." I said, "That's fine, but haven't you forgotten the third not?" He said, "What do you mean?" I replied, "You're NOT working for me." That was the end of that, and the job went on through to completion.

I found a great change had taken place during the war years. It was difficult to get employees, as many facilities were starting up and our access was only to very young people. Many of these had worked in the defense industry. That industry was not particularly concerned about work productivity because they were on a cost-plus basis. I was exasperated and finally called Hil Oehlmann to find out what his experience was at Yosemite. I thought maybe I had been out of the country too long and did not understand the employees. He assured me they were all having the same problem.

Fred L. Taber, our former manager of the facilities (the school principal who had run the business for us during the war years), was invaluable when we were trying to get employees. This was not easy to do, especially to get someone who would take responsibility. I will never forget when he sent a gal who had been a hostess in a cocktail lounge. She arrived in a fancy low-cut dress and had a feather in her hat. She was dressed appropriately for a lounge, but not for a dining room in a national park. She was pretty independent and resented working under such conditions.

At that time, people would gather early and line up at the dining room door to get dinner. All tables would be filled immediately. This put real pressure on the waitresses and also on the kitchen. One evening this gal didn't arrive to serve her tables; each waitress was responsible for four tables. I was embarrassed because people were sitting at her tables with no waitress to wait on them.

I served them water and said the waitress would be down soon, then went upstairs. There she was, lounging and clad only in a bra and pair of panties. I said, "Your tables are full and the people are waiting for you downstairs." She said, "I'll be right down." I went down and tried to placate the guests. When she didn't arrive, I went back up and she was pretty much in the same condition. I told her she should be down in five minutes or she didn't have to come down at all. I went back to our guests and told them I was having trouble with their waitress and I would appreciate it if they would not tip her. She finally came down and finished serving, but she never got a single tip. She exploded. I drove her down to Redding, back to the atmosphere she found more comfortable.

As we now had a vacancy, I offered the waitress job to a young girl on our housekeeping crew. She was an excellent employee, a good worker and very jovial and while we hated to disrupt the housekeeping crew, we felt it only fair to give her the first chance to be a waitress. When I offered her the job, I was amazed when she turned it down, as she surely would have increased her earnings through tips. I asked her why and she said, "Well, when you are cleaning, a toilet doesn't talk back to you." With that explanation, we started looking for another waitress.

We were having particular difficulty on our front desk, where reservations were received and people were assigned to rooms. The desk clerk was also the cashier for the entire operation, including the gift shop. There were two young workers on the front desk from New York. They were capable, but I had a feeling they were helping themselves to money and not really taking care of the company's business. I attempted to check up on them, but found this impractical, in view of the fact that the receipts from the gift shop were intermingled with the dining room receipts and those for lodging.

It was about this time that Alberta Mitchell, her niece, Genee Mitchell, and Martha Jepson arrived. Rooms were at a premium, so they had Martha Jepson ask. Martha was a white- haired lady and they felt they had a better chance of getting one with her asking. Fortunately, we were able to accommodate them but only in a tent; not the quality accommodations they were seeking.

Shortly thereafter, Genee asked if we had a job, stating that she and Lou Ann Large, another teacher, would like to work there for the summer. This was not only a welcome opportunity to get more mature employees, but I was particularly taken with Genee. I assured her that we had jobs for them, and asked how soon they could start. She said she had to return to the Bay area first, then visit her parents in El Paso, Texas, before she could report. I urged speed and was disturbed when she failed to report for several days.

Al tells the story that he was sent to San Francisco to secure some additional cooks in the Bay area and that I was very disappointed when he did not bring Genee and Lou Ann back with him. He says I asked nothing about his success in getting cooks, but was only interested in Genee and Lou Ann. When they did arrive, they were hired and put on the front desk.

We were then able to release the two New York employees, who left without protesting. I was sure they had been well compensated for the time they were on the front desk, albeit without my approval.

I started dating Genee and whenever she had time off, I took time off. On one occasion we took two horses into the Bear Lake back-country. When we had not returned by dusk, Al and Dick Hemstead, the wrangler, came looking for us. This aggravated me as they knew I knew my way around the park, but they protested that they thought maybe something had happened. I said that we had taken steaks and cooked dinner. Al's response was, "If I take bacon and eggs, that doesn't mean I am going to stay all night."

Toward the end of the season, Genee and I went to Redding and called her folks to advise them that we were engaged and wanted to be married on her folks' wedding day, which occurred in November. Genee's dad, Cornelius Mitchell, or Mitch, as he was called, protested on the basis that we had not known each other very long. He told Genee later that he thought being in the park, she had stars in her eyes, and he objected to the quick decision.

In the meantime, Genee had written the school system in Sunnyvale, California, where she was teaching high school, advising them she would not be returning that year. She returned to Palo Alto and informed her parents we still planned to be married. The date was set for December 27, 1947. I was to spend the Christmas vacation in El Paso with her family. I am pleased that after we became acquainted Mitch never objected to our marriage.

My brother Gail came over from Tucson to be best man at the wedding. We were married in the Episcopal church in El Paso. The reception was held at the Mitchell home and then Gail, Genee and I drove back to Tucson. I was scheduled to start work as Assistant United States Attorney on the following Monday.

I had arranged to rent a small one-bedroom apartment in Frontier village. Space in Tucson was very tight and I had to pay six months' rent in advance to secure the quarters. We lived there for the first six months of our married life. During this period of time, we arranged to buy a house on 3rd Street. It was small, but comfortable.

As Assistant U.S. Attorney, I was responsible for all the government's civil litigation. K. Berry Peterson was the other Assistant U.S. Attorney. He handled all the criminal cases. K. Berry was a brilliant attorney but, unfortunately, had a drinking problem and often he was not available when cases were called. On occasion, I filled in for him, but told the U.S. Attorney in Phoenix, Frank Flynn, that I did not want to handle criminal cases. I disliked criminal practice of law and wanted to avoid it as much as possible. We had other difficulties in that a new federal judge had just been appointed. His name was Howard Speakman. He had a heart attack and seldom came into the office to hold court. This made it difficult to carry out the government's business, but was advantageous to me, as I was allowed to take outside practice. This enabled me to start building up my private practice as permitted by the regulations.

It is interesting to note the change of attitude toward drug dealers when I was Assistant U.S. Attorney and now. We had to isolate drug dealers from others awaiting trial for criminal activity as they threatened to kill the drug pushers. It is too bad that feeling does not persist today.

We moved into our new home on East 3rd Street where Donna was born on November 8, 1948. Genee and I were agreed that we wanted several children, so our first announcement of Donna's birth was a poem which read as follows:

> Please send no gifts, my folks implore,
> 'Cause I'm just the first of three or four.
> Donna is my name; 6 pounds, 14 oz. my weight,
> I arrived November 8, nineteen hundred forty-eight.

This turned out to be an accurate prophecy, as we had four children. Diane was born November 10, 1949; Cliff on

August 8, 1951, and Charlene on November 23, 1953.

As I was now married and starting a family and had returned to law practice, I needed assistance at Lassen. Al Donau was made the general manager in charge of operations at Manzanita Lake. We had an ongoing expansion at Lassen.

Here begins the first in a series of Genee's legendary Christmas Letters that will hereafter be interspersed with the narrative.

Genee's Christmas Letter, 1950:

This holiday season finds us settled in our new home at 2360 E. Waverly. We moved in on the 9th of November, the day between Donna's two-year-old and Diane's one-year-old birthdays. We live in Catalina Vista and indeed have a beautiful view of the mountains. We have lots of room, so if you're out Tucson way we'd like to have you visit us.

The fall has passed so quickly for us and we have had such an unusually warm, mild season that we can scarcely believe it's Christmas time again. Don has been busy. He's scarcely caught up with himself. He still holds the Assistant U.S. Attorney's job and has his own personal practice.

We spent two wonderful months at Lassen Volcanic National Park again and returned to Tucson shortly before Labor Day. Genee could not get used to a telephone after the summer's peace and quiet without one. Fall activities began immediately for the Pueblo Jr. Women's Club. The office of program chairman has taken lots of her time, but she likes it. The move entailed showing and selling the old house as well as looking for this one, moving in, and then out of boxes. And now there's Christmas shopping and preparation for the holidays to be done. It's nice that this includes a word to our friends.

Our babies have grown so much, they are babies no longer! Donna is a very domestic, helpful, generous, sympathetic, observant young lady. Her hair is long and very blonde, her eyes somewhat gray-green. She still has her round baby face and pink cheeks, but has suddenly outgrown last season's dresses. She is quite independent and chatters to herself, tries to say almost everything. Diane has been walking since 11 months and walking well since a year. She is our tease and our rascal, our cuddly, affectionate, and sometimes jealous one. Her eyes are almost black, her hair is blonde and curly and 95 percent of the time she's still taken for a boy. She has quite a vocabulary, including "all done," "baby," and "Hummel" in answer to "What's your name?," etc. She has been feeding herself since the 1st of December and really knows what the spoon is for — a messy, but very determined and satisfied young miss. She and Donna laugh and giggle together and have very few differences of opinion.

We have had our minor colds but all in all are well and happy. We hope this greeting finds you the same. Let us hear from you and about your activities during this coming year. Our very best wishes for the nicest holiday you've ever had.

❄ ❄ ❄

I resigned my position as Assistant U. S. Attorney in 1951 and set up my personal law practice in the Valley National Bank building. I was still involved with the operation of Lassen and rotating between summer in Lassen and law practice in Tucson in the wintertime.

Construction program for Lassen: In 1946, we had spent $34,400 for a new employees' dining room and some 50 tents, plus the equipment necessary to furnish them. In 1951, we remodeled some of the older cabins at the cost of $2,500. Two years later, in 1953, we built some additional hotel bungalows and remodeled some of the other cabins at a total cost of $43,400.

During the time Al was managing Lassen, he started a repainting program for the housekeeping cabins we built the first year of our operations.

One morning he was behind the desk checking the reservations when a woman came into the lobby. She said, "I want to see the manager."

Al replied, "I'm the manager." She said, "Follow me," and walked out of the lobby and across the bridge to a housekeeping cabin. Al followed. She said, "I was here frying my eggs..." and she went through the motions over the stove... "and felt something and I looked back, but couldn't see anything. I returned to my eggs and felt it again." She said, "look," and held up her nightgown which was splattered with brown stain. Al heard the patter of the compressor operated by the painter outside. In spraying the cabin, the painter had passed over a knothole, spraying the woman's fanny with brown stain. Needless to say, we bought her a new nightgown.

Genee's Christmas Letter, 1951:

Christmas promises to be more fun than ever this year. Both of the girls have been talking about Santa Claus, although we suspect that as far as Diane is concerned, she is not quite sure of the meaning of it all. Donna has requested a car and a truck but primarily a package with a big bow on it. Santa will start this year to bring our tree on Christmas Eve as the girls begin to change from babies to embryonic young ladies.

We spent 2-1/2 months at Lassen National Park this summer. The girls were old enough to undertake more adventures including wading in the streams and helping to build and cook over their first campfire. Don had to make several trips while we were in the Park but managed to be close at hand as Cliff, our heir presumptive, became more apparent. Cliffy arrived right on schedule (August 8) so there was no last minute dash down the mountain to Redding, the nearest hospital some 50 miles from the Park. Cliff is a blue-eyed, fat and healthy boy who grins at everyone — even the photographer, as you can see.

After unusually busy summer we foolishly anticipated a quiet fall at home. This never materialized as Tucson usually arouses from a lazy summer to an ambitious fall and both Don and Genee found time-consuming activities to keep them busy. Don resigned his Assistant U.S. Attorney's job and will go into private practice full time the first of January. The old Hummel building in Tucson was sold and demolished this summer so in addition to finishing up affairs at the Federal Building he had to find and establish a new office. He's looking forward to his return to private practice.

In spare moments, Genee has been practicing on the newest addition to our household, a spinet Hammond organ. We will have some real Christmas carols this year — provided Genee gets that far along in the instruction book.

Donna started her education this fall, having attended the first session of the nursery school conducted by the University of Arizona. It's contributed no end to her ego and self-reliance. Diane, not to be outdone, announced, "I big girl too," and strives to live up to it. She's still our fireball and sometimes difficult rascal.

All in all we're imbued with our fortunate lot and we welcome this chance to extend an invitation to you to share at least a part of it with us this coming year.

❄ ❄ ❄

In April, 1952, I received a call from Roy Sifford, who was the owner of the operation in the southeastern part of Lassen Volcanic National Park, known as Drakesbad. The winter had been particularly severe and when Roy went in to open the facilities, he found the dining room had been crushed by snow. His doctor advised him not to attempt to rebuild, but to make some other arrangements for the operation. Roy's first thoughts were of the many patrons who had been with him year after year. He called them and canceled their reservations. He then called me and asked if I would take over the operation on a lease basis. I would have preferred having done it the other way, but I agreed.

We went to Drakesbad to evaluate the damage and determine how best to get the operation going. I told Al he should handle the Manzanita Lake operation and I would go to Drakesbad. Al thought I was crazy, because Drakesbad had a capacity of only about 50 people. It was more like a guest ranch operation than the operation we had at Manzanita Lake. The facilities were primitive, to say the least. There was a lodge building which had a lobby and desk for the office in the lobby and five rooms upstairs. There were approximately 12 separate cabins and six tents. There was no electricity. All the lights were coal oil lamps. Coleman lanterns were used for the lobby and the dining room. The only refrigeration was a propane-operated domestic refrigerator, which had minimum capacity. There was a horse corral and, if I recall correctly, 12 horses owned by Roy which would be used in the operation. Roy agreed that he would return to assist us and handle the horses. There was a regular practice of taking rides during the day, and occasionally they would have what they called a "hot dog ride" where all the guests would go to some spot in the park and have hot dogs prepared over an open fire, then return by moonlight.

To understand the operation at Drakesbad, a brief history of its development is appropriate. Located in the southeast portion of Lassen Volcanic National Park was an active volcanic area consisting of a boiling lake, hot springs, fumaroles and steam vents, besides a beautiful meadow bordered by a trout stream. It had been known as Hot Springs Valley. A man by the name of E. R. Drake homesteaded a portion of the valley, which was known as Drakes Place. Alex Sifford, Roy's father, bought Drakes Place and at the seller's request continued the name. Drake had built a small bathhouse made of hand-hewn timbers. The trough to carry the water was scooped-out logs and the tubs were made of wood. Natural hot water supplied the baths and the small swimming pool.

The Sifford family moved to Drakes Place, now called Drakesbad, in 1900. It took them three days to travel the 54 miles from Susanville, as the streams were high and had to be forded. Alex Sifford drove the big wagon, mother and sister Pearl the spring wagon and Roy, age seven, followed, driving the milk cows with the calves tied to the cows' tails to permit them to cross the high water streams.

Drakesbad was built largely by the Sifford family. 1905-1910 were the big camping years, reaching up to 300 people in August. Lassen Peak and Cinder Cove were declared National Monuments in 1907. Philenda Spencer, an often-time visitor and the mother-in-law of Congressman John Raker, proposed that they petition to make this area a national park. John Raker, the congressman, took the petition to Washington in 1911 and introduced the bill to establish Lassen Volcanic National Park. Lassen Peak had a series of eruptions starting May 30, 1914. There followed the big eruption on May 22, 1915. Lassen became a National Park in 1916.

After agreeing to assume the operation of Drakesbad in 1952, we rebuilt the dining room, but found that all the furniture had been crushed and was unusable. Genee was able to buy hickory tables and chairs in Arkansas which fit in very well with this rustic, simple dining room, lighted by Coleman lamps. Some of our employees lived in the loft above the storage room, and our family lived over the dining room, where we shared the space with some of the female employees. Separation was effected by hanging up a blanket partition. We all shared the one tiny upstairs bathroom.

We had about eight employees besides Genee and myself and Roy Sifford. Benny, a Chinese, had cooked for Roy for many years and fortunately he stayed on with us. He was invaluable; a wonderful cook, and a very pleasant person. He was one of the favorites at Drakesbad. All the guests knew him personally. We were able to contact most of the guests who had made reservations and Roy urged them to return, stating that conditions would be much the same as they had been in the past. They were skeptical, but decided to try us. I don't believe they were disappointed, as they continued with us for years.

As all the meat and produce were kept in a cellar dug out of the side of the mountain, and with no refrigeration, we had bear problems, as well as food preservation problems. It was difficult to keep the bears out of the cellar. One particularly difficult problem occurred the following year. We had, unfortunately, put some canned goods, sugar and flour and other non-perishables in the little walk-in box in the kitchen to prevent it from freezing. The box had no refrigeration. The kitchen, of course, was permeated with food odors as there was no fan, and the food odor permeated the walls.

This attracted bears and when we returned the following spring to open the facilities, we found that a bear had entered a second story window, which was about the level of the snow in that area. The bear had caused much damage. It ripped up the beds, and apparently saw itself in the mirror and slapped it and spread glass shards all over the upstairs. Then, instead of going out the way it came in, it made another exit and for some reason or another, had pulled a mattress halfway through the hole in the wall. We found it protruding from a second floor window. In the downstairs area, the bear had broken into the walk-in box. It proceeded to bite into all the canned goods, so the juice of the vegetables and fruit was on the floor. It ripped open the flour and sugar bags, which mixed with the vegetable and fruit juices. We had gooey stuff about eight inches deep all over the floor! It was a terrible job trying to clean up that sticky mess. We never left any food in the kitchen thereafter!

We had to go to Chester three or four times a week to pick up our supplies. We had arranged to get there about 6:00 in the morning and take our dirty linen to the laundry. They would get it washed immediately and by the time we had done the purchasing and run the other errands in Chester, we could pick up the laundry and return to Drakesbad, arriving around noon. This saved a large laundry inventory.

Drakesbad was a wonderful place to raise small children. There was a beautiful meadow with a trout stream running down one side, with hot water coming out of one side of the valley, and practically ice cold springs out of the other side. We needed no ice for water on the tables. In fact, Roy Sifford had put in a constantly running fountain on the porch of the Drakesbad Lodge, where you could get a cold drink at any time. It ran constantly from the day we opened until the day we closed; that is until the Park Service took it out because it was not chlorinated! The children had an opportunity to ride with us on various rides in the park; in fact, Charlene usually rode on the saddle in front of me. This was a marvelous experience for our entire family.

Genee's Christmas Letter, 1952:

We left Tucson earlier this year, about June 5th, as the Lassen National Park Company took over the operation of Drakesbad, a resort on privately owned land in the southeastern section of Lassen Volcanic National Park. Its dining room had been crushed under twenty feet of winter snow and had to be rebuilt before guests could be accommodated. The Lassen Company also expanded their facilities at Manzanita Lake, in addition to adding a new souvenir store in the Sulphur Works area. Don's appearance in work clothes as straw boss of the construction program was the source of many jokes by the employees, in his alternating character as president and rock mason. This with his law practice in Tucson kept him as busy as the proverbial one-armed paper hanger.

The month of June in Lassen was bitterly cold with several unseasonable snowstorms. The Lassen Highway was not open to the public until June 29th, and the last four miles through snowbanks had controlled traffic until July 23rd. Twenty-foot snowbanks in July were quite incomprehensible to our Tucson friends who were suffering in excessive temperature.

The first of September found us turning our reluctant footsteps Tucson way. However, Tucson soon claimed us again as its own. The usual fall activities started immediately. Genee completed an intensive course in tailoring and has been filling a term as first vice president of the Junior Women's Club. She also reviewed for her book club Freeman Tilden's informative and interesting book on "Our National Parks — What They Mean to You and Me." Incidentally, she only has three children to feed, bathe and clothe. We don't know what she does with the rest of her time. Don plunged into his law practice. He's happy to announce a new partnership with Mrs. Anna von Seggern Engel. Mrs. Engel formerly practiced in California.

The girls celebrated their third and fourth birthdays on November 9th, the day between, with their first full-fledged birthday party. Twenty-five of their friends assembled, and what fun they had!

Donna is becoming quite a conversationalist. She's also developed some awkward and self-conscious signs of growing up, but is generally referred to as a "little lady." Di remains our devilish, irresponsible tease and flirt. She's full of zip when she wants to be, and at other times is a most aggravating dawdler.

The devil in her dark brown eyes contrasted with her blonde hair has a modulating effect after arousing your ire to fever pitch. We have just started the "You've been talking, now let me talk" stage.

The girls love a story about a little monkey named "Curious George." We call our smiling, blue-eyed, tow-headed Cliff, Curious George. He has to examine all the drawers, peek into all the recesses of the cupboards and crawl onto tables, and on two occasions we found him on top of the stove. He took his first steps at nine months and three weeks, so there are few places he hasn't conquered at his ripe old age of sixteen months. He's had his first haircut, so now looks as well as acts like a real boy.

Altogether, we join in wishing your house the same Christmas cheer that abides in our household.

❅ ❅ ❅

10
Conference of
National Park Concessioners

I BELIEVE it appropriate at this time to discuss the formation and the modus operandi of the Western Conference of National Park Concessioners. The Conference of National Park Concessioners was originally formed in 1929 when Secretary Ray Lyman Wilbur called a meeting of the concessioners to discuss policy considerations for operations in the National Park System.

At the time of the meeting there were 29 principal operators in the national parks and some 25 sent representatives. On the appointed day of December 6, 1929, park operators gathered in the Secretary's office. The Secretary opened as follows:

> The success of the development of the National Park System depends upon the joint medium of which the government, as represented by the National Park Service, is one part, and individuals or corporations acting under franchise to furnish services to the public is the other. This is the American method of trying to bring together government and business in such a way that private business may be maintained. We must work out a joint program to handle the whole matter on a larger basis: we protecting the parks and their visitors, providing good parks and trails, and generally supervising; you public utility operators providing the machinery for developing peculiar types of accommodations necessary in order to care for the public adequately.

Representative Louis C. Cramton of Michigan, Chairman of the House Appropriations Subcommittee handling Interior Department funds, told the concessioners:

> The operators are, generally speaking, performing a great part in the task of determining and maintaining proper use and essential preservation of these great areas. The Appropriations Committee realizes that the

foundations are now being laid for the great National Park System of the United States and that they and the public utility operators are privileged to be in at the beginning, helping to lay the foundations for a wonderful system which it is hoped for centuries to come will continue to serve and aid in a proper development of our people.

Secretary Wilbur and National Park Director Horace Albright posed a number of questions to the operators for which they wanted answers. These could not be answered without substantial investigation.

Later in the two-day conference, Assistant Secretary John H. Edwards suggested that Secretary Wilbur would be pleased if the concessioners formed a permanent organization to deal with such questions. Something informal, nothing with binding power over individual concessioners. The concessioners agreed.

Horace Albright wrote of this meeting in his Annual Report of the Director of National Parks on June 30, 1930:

> An outstanding accomplishment of this meeting was the formation of an organization of operators to work together for their mutual benefit and for the best interests of the visiting public.

In 1931 the Depression deepened and other problems just as serious arose. One opinion delivered by the Comptroller General of the United States threw the status of concessioners into complete turmoil. The opinion involved contracts. The Secretary of the Interior had routinely authorized temporary four-year contracts to new concessioners with the assurance that if they succeeded in rendering good public service the temporary contract would be canceled in favor of a new 20-year contract. In late 1931 the Comptroller General ruled that the Interior Secretary had no such authority. The only possible interpretation was that all 20-year contracts made under such circumstances were illegal and void. In 1932 the Comptroller was asked for clarification.In this instance, the Solicitor decided that the Interior Secretary could legally cancel old contracts and issue new 20-year contracts within the authority granted him by Congress.

During the life of the Conference, it has been called by four names: National Park Operators Conference, Western National Park Operators Conference (used interchangeably with Western Conference of National Park Operators), Western Conference of National Park Concessioners and, finally, the name it now bears, the Conference of National Park Concessioners.

During the first several years the Conference collaborated closely and had membership not only by the park concessioners, but by the Department of Interior and the National Park Service itself. After some period it became obvious that there were conflicting interests so the Department of Interior and National Park Service representatives dropped out of membership.

The Conference then became the representative of the concessioners to deal with the National Park Service and the Department of the Interior. The Western Conference was dominated by the large parks; in fact, the chairmanship of the Conference rotated between Yosemite, Yellowstone and Grand Canyon. It was not exactly a democratic organization, as the representatives of these three parks decided who was to chair the organization for the following year and what policies would prevail. At that time there was no such thing as an organizational structure or dues.

The company that had chairmanship would pay any expenses incurred on behalf of the Conference, and then they would be divided among the members at the end of the year.

During this period there was a minimum of Park Service regulation of concessions. Many of the concessioners still had leases. Control was almost exclusively through competition, with few regulations. This worked rather poorly, as there were too many concessioners and each wanted to provide the profitable services and no one wanted to provide the less profitable. The lessees wanted to open for July and August and close as soon as travel dropped. This meant that early park visitors in June and late visitors in September usually found few, if any accommodations. This posed a real management problem for the Park Service.

Competition sometimes took bizarre forms. In one instance, at the rail center for Yellowstone, two drivers for competing coach companies grabbed a prospective guest, tearing his coat in half.

Contracts were then substituted for leases to give the Park Service greater control. Franchise fees were based on a percentage of the net profit and were minimal. The concessioner was entitled to make six percent on his investment which was cumulative; in other words, if he did not make six percent that year, he could make six percent the next year, plus any amount he had not made on the prior years before paying a fee. After earning six percent, 37 percent was to go to the government and the balance was retained by the concessioner. The cumulative provision resulted in the concessioner seldom having to pay a fee, as he rarely made a six percent return on his investment. Revenue to the government was not considered important. The Park Service was interested in good services at reasonable rates. Operating conditions and short seasons militated against the earning of substantial profits.

The result was that Steve Mather, National Park Service Director, and Horace Albright, Assistant Director, forced mergers of a number of concessioners in the parks, under threat that no lease or contract would be given to either of them.

One of the best examples of this was the Yosemite Park & Curry Company, which was the merger of the Yosemite Park Company (Desmond Hotel) and the Curry Camps. These two companies were told that if they did not merge, neither of them would be given a contract. When the merger was accomplished in 1925 the Yosemite Park & Curry Company resulted, and was headed by Donald Tresidder, the Curry's son-in-law.

Paralleling this forced merger was the concept of principal concessioners. In other words, to avoid the allocation of too much land and to solve some of the management problems of the Park Service, the contract to a principal concessioner authorized one company to provide many or most of the needed services. This was essential as there was too little business to support several companies.

This new system called for greater government regulations and control. In other words, the Park Service substituted regulations for competition. The concessions were not exactly lucrative operations, to say the least. They were in remote areas, with erratic transportation facilities, short seasons, sporadic patronage, and difficult operations.

The concessioner had to house and feed all his employees and transport his products from the urban centers by rail and wagon. There were few or no facilities for storage and preservation of food, no laundry facilities, nor any of the modern amenities that we rely on today. It made for difficult operations and as the seasons were short, the returns were slim. These were some of the problems the Park Service faced and for which they wanted an organization of concessioners to consult with and establish a concessions policy.

There had been created a National Park Concessions, Inc., company which was a not-for-distribution-of-profit corporation. There were no stockholders. All earnings were reinvested in additional facilities and services. It would provide a model to be used as the vehicle through which the national park visitor facilities were to be operated. This caused considerable consternation among the concessioners. It resulted in extended discussions of ways to meet this threat of government ownership and quasi-government operations.

I joined the Western Conference of National Park Concessioners in February 1936 during the Great Depression. The Conference was meeting in Washington, D.C. The members were quite distraught when the then Secretary of the Interior, Harold L. Ickes, announced that he felt the government should acquire all these companies and operate them.

To be honest, I didn't know that any of these horrendous concessioner policy problems existed. I joined simply because I thought it would help the professionalism of Lassen. My first conversations with fellow concessioners, however, did not do much for my image as a professional.

I could not help overhearing concessioners commiserating with each other over how difficult it was to provide facilities at uniform rates from park to park. Particularly for the Depression-induced, low-cost shelter cabins. Billy Nichols, who ran Yellowstone Park Company, asked Paul Sceva of Rainier National Park Company, "What do you get

for your shelter cabins, Paul?" Sceva said, "I get $2.00."
Nichols said, "What's in them?" Sceva replied, "Well,
there's a table with a washbasin and pitcher, a chair and a
cot with a mattress, and the people bring their own blankets." "Where do they get their water?" asked Nichols.
"There're spigots outside, one for about each ten cabins."
Nichols said, "That's about right."

I foolishly stepped up to Nichols as he walked away
and volunteered, "We're only charging $1.75 at Lassen. We
have hot and cold showers in the cabins and we furnish the
blankets. We're fully equipped." Nichols called, "Hey,
Paul, come listen to this," and he made me repeat my story
to the Rainier concessioner. Sceva listened and asked, "Do
you make any money?" As I learned later, we did not. At
that time, I did not grasp the difference between positive
cash flow and a net profit, which we did not have. I said,
"Yeah, we made some money."

Nichols then called all concessioners around the room
over to our corner. "Hey, you guys, come listen to this." A
little intimidated by now, I again repeated my story. I could
tell that everybody thought I was underpricing myself out
of business. Nichols, perhaps the biggest of the big three
concessioners, then told his peers: "I suggest we all go
home before the Park Service puts a gold medal around this
guy's neck and makes us out a bunch of sons-of-bitches."
Welcome to the Western Conference of National Park Operators, Don Hummel.

Adolph A. Aszmann, General Manager of Glacier Park
Operations of the Great Northern, had the good grace to
take me aside and say confidentially, "Now, look, these
guys are supposed to be working for everybody, but
they're very sensitive to their own interests. Don't be
deterred if they razz you a little. And if you ever need any
assistance just give me a call."

11

My First Experience in Politics

In 1952, shortly after Christmas, I received a call from John Molloy, who said that he was representing a group who wanted to know if I would run for Mayor of the City of Tucson. I said, "What's the joke?" He replied, "It's no joke — we are interested in coming out and talking with you about running for mayor." A group of about 10 arrived at our home and asked if I would declare candidacy for Mayor of Tucson. I said I could hardly afford it, as I was just getting reestablished in my law practice, having served four years as Assistant United States Attorney, and recently opening my private office. Their argument was that we all talk about good government, but when it comes to doing our share, we say we can't afford it. I agreed to run for mayor.

While they did not tell me the number of individuals they had asked before they came to me, I know they had talked with a number of prospective candidates. The problem was that with the Eisenhower landslide and Richard Nixon's talk about 20 years of treason, referring to the democratic national administration, many did not want to run on the Democratic ticket. In fact, many did not want to admit they were democrats. The Tucson Charter calls for a partisan government, contrary to many city governments which have nonpartisan elections.

Then came the scurrying around to get three councilmen to run with me. We were able to get two, but unable to get the third for the first ward when time ran out for submitting the petitions. This meant that, if elected, we would have two councilmen, with four councilmen opposed to us. This did not deter us and we started campaigning. I enlisted the help of many of the democratic officeholders who controlled county government, including Lambert Kautenburger, the Chairman of the Board of Supervisors. Lambert had quite a political machine. He agreed to use his organization and put up a number of signs announcing my candidacy. I went to see Bill Matthews, publisher of the *Arizona Daily Star*, and a dominant force in the Democratic party. Bill Matthews indicated that he intended to support my opponent, the incumbent, Fred Emery, and was very negative toward my candidacy.

My campaign got some momentum and it appeared as though we were going toward victory, when Bill Matthews interceded behind my back, calling Lambert Kautenburger and the other Democratic officeholders in the Court House, advising them that he would oppose anyone who supported my candidacy. I learned, to my dismay, three days before the election, that Kautenberger had ordered his men to take down all my political signs. Fortunately, we were defeated by a small number of votes.

I say fortunately, because we would have been in a minority position and it would have been a hassle with no opportunity to institute our own programs.

Genee's Christmas Letter, 1953:

This year we'll have to start with the first of January instead of the usual summer at Lassen, as this was one of the busiest winter-and-springs on record for the Hummels. On January 1, a group of Tucson citizens prevailed upon Don to run for Mayor. As a result he gave up much of his private life for numerous meetings, speeches and radio talks, culminating with the whole family on television. Cliff at the age of 18 months stole the show. Don was the Democratic nominee, but lost by a small margin to the Republican incumbent. The experience was enlightening, although I doubt that he'd recommend it. The buffeting one takes in politics from some elements makes you understand why so many shun political office.

In the meantime, and on the same day that Don lost, Genee was elected president of the Junior Women's Club. We're all wondering — particularly the family — whether this was a victory, as Genee is now the captive of one community obligation after another. There's argument in our household as to which one should be consoled.

Lassen looked pretty good to us when we arrived in mid-June even if it was cold and the heavy snows delayed opening the Park highway until June 27th. Snow was 24 feet deep in some stretches, but melted rapidly in the July and August sunshine. Don was again the executive in work clothes as the construction program continued. Sixteen more bungalow rental units were completed and a brand new service station. The latter of modern style promises to be the forerunner of similar construction for other areas due to its fine functional design. Lassen for Genee was as supervisor of the constant picnics, swimming and outing events that the children engage in.

Early September found the Hummels back home. En route the family enjoyed a memorable day at the California State Fair as guests of one of the Directors, and also had time for a very brief look at beautiful Sequoia and King's Canyon National Park.

Don has converted a portion of the garage into another bedroom, and the two of us wielded roller and brush there, and in the three bedrooms, and did some redecorating. We managed to finish our household projects the day before our Charlene was born (November 23, 1953). She weighed 7 lbs 14 oz., and is a healthy, contented baby. Looks like a Hummel. The other three are so excited about her they can scarcely wait until she is old enough to play with them. Our young lady, Donna, five now, is in kindergarten. She counts Saturday and Sunday until Monday comes again as she loves it so. Diane is still our crackerjack, affectionate and full of bounce. Cliff, now two, is in the "own self, me do" stage, but with a happy disposition and a ready smile. He is all boy and will certainly hold his own, even if he is outnumbered by three sisters.

So much for 1953. It's been a wonderful year, and now for 1954. We wish you each health, happiness and good living.

❄ ❄ ❄

In 1954 the election of three councilmen was scheduled. The Charter called for the mayor and council to be elected one year for a two-year term, and the following year, three members of the council for a two-year term. Pancho Gonzales, Everett Drescher and Dick Summers were nominated and elected on the Democratic ticket. The year was uneventful, in view of the fact that we did not control the council and could not advance a program of our own, being in the minority.

Genee's Christmas Letter, 1954:

Springtime was Convention time in the Hummel household. Don is still Secretary of the Executive Committee of the Western Conference of National Park Concessioners. Early February found him in San Francisco attending that annual meeting. While Don's oldest children, Genee and baby Charlene — then nine weeks — went along. Charlene proved such a good traveler that it was a pleasure to take her on the Conventions that were on Genee's "must" list. Before completing her year as President of the Pueblo Junior Women's Club, Genee and Charlene attended the Arizona Federation of Women's Clubs Convention in Yuma. Genee's Mother extended a visit to Tucson to enable the trio to attend the Municipal League Convention in Flagstaff.

Genee couldn't pass up the opportunity to combine the General Federation of Women's Clubs convention in Denver with a long overdue visit with the Grecos. Thus it was that Charlene, who had to go where Mama went, came to have an enviable early exposure to civic-mindedness.

Lassen Park always offers a welcome change from the whirl of business, social and civic activities of Tucson. The change was even nicer last summer, as Don managed the Resort at Drakesbad in the south-eastern section of the Park.

This is a perfect spot for a family vacation: At the end of the road — no transient traffic — located in a beautiful mountain meadow with a rushing trout stream down one side, with clear, cold drinking water cascading from the canyon walls — a small place, accommodating only 50 guests — a chance to get acquainted, ride, hike, fish, swim in a plunge warmed by natural hot springs, or just sleep. Quite a contrast to bustling Manzanita, where 260,000 people passed through last season and gave the Lassen company the best season of its history.

September meant turning footsteps Tucson way and starting formal entrance to school for three of our four children. Donna began first grade, Diane started kindergarten, Cliff, now three, joined the procession by going to the nursery school conducted by the University of Arizona for its education majors.

At first Donna had her doubts about the big school, but is happy now and thrilled about learning to read. Diane took to kindergarten like a duck to water and was completely in stride the first day.

At first Cliff missed the girls, as his "school" did not start until later. He is now trying to decide whether to be a doctor or a baseball player. Charlene's career is beginning early. At seven months she kicked and splashed and thoroughly enjoyed her swimming lessons at Drakesbad. She took her first steps at 9-1/2 months, walked well by 11 months. Now a year, she is climbing, too, having climbed up and fallen into the bathtub before her first birthday. (Luckily no injuries.) The children adore her, but she is into everything and already the cry is going up, "Mother, Mother, come get Charlene — she is getting into our things."

Fall always enlivens the activities in Tucson. Genee is still serving her Junior Women's Club and has added committee responsibilities on the P.T.A. board.

Don's interests range from the Tucson Festival Board and the University to the ever fascinating and time-consuming field of politics. But it's all fun and finds the Hummel household bustling and happy. ❋ ❋ ❋

Mayor of Tucson

In 1955, I again sought election as mayor, together with Bill Wisdom, Limey Gibbings and John Hardwicke, who was the only Democrat defeated. We were sworn into office in April. Shortly after the election, but before being inaugurated, Luther Davis, who had been city manager, resigned his position to take over the presidency of Tucson Gas, Electric Light and Power Company.

Upon assuming office, we appointed Phil Martin as the acting city manager. Phil had been head of the Water Department for a great many years and had occasionally acted in the capacity of city manager. We were immediately criticized and challenged by the *Tucson Daily Citizen* for appointing Phil, suggesting that we had no real desire to get a professional city manager for the position as we had stated in our campaign. We assured them we intended to do just that and were making a nationwide search for the best possible person. This took a considerable length of time and the *Citizen* was certain we were dragging our feet and making no concerted effort.

On August 3, 1953, the *Tucson Daily Citizen* had editorialized under the caption, "What About it, Mr. Mayor?" Mayor Fred Emery had campaigned on the pledge to appoint a professional city manager. Nine months went by before Donald P. Wolfer was hired but the mayor continued to intrude in city management; trouble ensued, and Mr. Wolfer was fired. The mayor had promised a professional replacement, but hired Luther Davis, a 29-year-old assistant city attorney with no prior business or management experience.

This was the background when I campaigned for mayor and pledged to provide an experienced and competent city manager. The *Citizen* launched a series of editorials starting on our swearing in day of April 15, followed by editorials on June 2 and June 8 on the city manager's vacancy. Despite assurances that we were searching for the right man, the editorial on July 28, 1955 was captioned, "Quest for City Manager Moving Slowly If At All." The editorial stated that

almost four months had passed and the mayor had acknowledged that he had more than 85 applications for the
$12,000 a year position.
It said:

> The Mayor himself has been most outspoken to the
> effect that the entire program of the administration to be
> basically sound depends on the selection of a profession-
> ally trained and experienced city manager.

The editorial also commented on my refusal to appoint
members of the council to be responsible for city departments. Though this had been the practice over many years,
I refused to follow suit as I believed that it resulted in
councilmen dabbling in administration which is the province of the city manager. It also tended to divide city policy
into competing councilmen the way a ward system does.

We finally decided on three candidates for the city
manager's job, and asked them to come to Tucson incog-
nito, as we did not want the newspaper bandying their
names about. Those applying also did not want their
names published, as they were employed in other city
government positions. We interviewed Porter Homer and
agreed that he was to have the position. He had been
Director of Research and Budget for Kansas City, Missouri.
Harry Ackerman, who was active in democratic politics,
was having a party that night and we took Porter with us,
never indicating that he was a candidate for the city
manager's position. The secret was kept and no one knew
who the city manager was to be until we announced it at a
city council meeting. The fact that Porter was just 32 years
of age was the subject of criticism by the labor paper, who
headlined, "Thirty-Two-Year-Old to Run the City."
On September 22, 1955, the *Citizen* stated in an editorial:

> The Mayor and Council selected 32-year-old Porter
> Homer for the past six years assistant to city manger of
> Kansas City, Missouri.
>
> In making the appointment, the Mayor and Council
> lived up to avowals that they wanted a man of training,
> experience and good personal qualifications. Back-
> ground information indicates the new appointee has all
> three.

The editorial also commented that Porter Homer had a sense of humor. When presented to the City Hall group, Homer said, "This is a great day for Homer; time will tell if it is a great day for Tucson."

Time and performance demonstrated that it was truly a great day for Tucson. Porter Homer provided the expertise that we lacked. We had great plans for Tucson and were willing to implement them.Porter showed us how.

Our first function, after adopting the operating budget that had been approved by the previous administration, was to start a reorganization program of the city departments. Each department was almost a unit unto itself. The city manager had little or no control over the various departments and each one operated almost independently. They were also staffed by individuals who had been in city employment for years and had drifted along without much change of direction or help from the city council. This program of reorganization proceeded but as you might guess, took a considerable length of time to accomplish.

In addition to strengthening the role of the city manager over the city departments, we reorganized the departments and created a parks and recreation department, headed by a director. We also changed the financial organization by creating a director of finance. We established a separate post auditor position to give greater security in the handling of city funds.

We combined a number of functions under a Department of Public Works and hired Herman Danforth as its director. We streamlined the City Inspection Office, which had been the source of many complaints by contractors and homebuilders. In fact, our annexation program was opposed by the Homebuilders Association primarily because of their opposition to our Inspection Department.

Genee's Christmas Letter, 1955:

This year has been a most eventful one for the Hummel family. When we thought we were busy before, we didn't know how busy we could be.

Last January Don entered the Tucson mayoralty race. January, February and March was campaign time, and an arduous time it was. We expected some respite between election day on April 5th and the oath of office on May 2nd, but instead Don found himself on the banquet and speech-making circuit as soon as a tally of the votes showed him to be the victor.

The whole family was on hand to witness the inauguration. We all showed our pride at the occasion except Charlene, then 17 months, who began crying very lustily just as Don raised his hand to take the oath of office. We might refer to the affair as a howling success.

Early June again found the family heading toward Lassen National Park and Drakesbad. Don had planned to commute between the Park and Tucson for Council Meetings during the summer, but a strike in the local transit company soon changed that. In the role of mediator and go-between, Don's work kept him in Tucson, with the family at Drakesbad.

Genee became in fact and name, Drakesbad's manager. This was a new experience for her — responsibility for 50 guests and four children — but after a couple of sleepless nights and days of ordering groceries, supplies and overseeing a crew of ten with the multitudinous details of a Guest Ranch in the mountain area, she responded to the challenge of the job to the great satisfaction of her family.

We returned to Tucson the first of September, and to the busy life of a Mayor's family. Many and varied are the experiences of a Mayor. Never did Don expect to enter a milking contest — but he did, and won. Never did Genee expect to see him driving around a race track in a micro-midget racer, but she did. Never have we been so hospitably entertained nor seen such festivity as guests of our Mexican neighbors in Sonora, Mexico. Don says it's easy to make an after-dinner speech but it taxes one's ingenuity to give a welcoming address thirty times a month and not say the same thing twice.

Annexation has been the most vexatious problem facing Tucson. Upon assuming office, this problem was attacked with vigor, and as this letter is written, Don is announcing the successful conclusion of the largest annexation program in Arizona history. It has increased the area of the City by 50 percent, the assessed valuation by 30 percent and the population by 35 percent.

Our children, still our primary interest, are rapidly growing up. Donna, now seven, is in the second grade and a first-class student. She's a regular patron of the library and a proud member of the Brownies. Diane, six, feels real grown up as a first grader. She is showing good progress and enjoying the thrill of learning to read. Cliff is four now and still "Mr. Sunshine." He's a husky, active boy, still wears his Davy Crockett hat, but has a predisposition to be a Beau Brummel with his love of his gray suit. Charlene's our clown — a real talker, strong willed and mature for her age — our baby, two on November 23rd, she's growing up too fast.

❋ ❋ ❋

In October 1956 three police captains filed 23 charges against Police Chief Don Hays and resigned. The *Arizona Daily Star* editorialized under the caption, "Cry-Baby Police Captains," and stated that the charges dealt solely with internal administration and discipline; stating that there was not even a whisper of graft or corruption. Bill Matthews, publisher of the *Star* continued his support of Chief Hays, stating that he had the task of building a department in a growing city and had kept it "clean."

The *Tucson Daily Citizen* editorialized in a more balanced way and commended Porter Homer, the city manager, for handling the dispute in a prudent and competent manner. They pointed out that one relatively minor complaint is insignificant but when there are multiple accusations and grievances by three veteran police captains, a full investigation is warranted.

Don Hays requested a leave of absence and then asked for medical retirement, which was granted. Thus was resolved a continuing battle between the chief and his department. The first question Bill Matthews asked me when I announced my candidacy for mayor and solicited his support was, "How do you stand on Chief Hays?"

After a nationwide search, Barney Garmier, from Eau Claire, Wisconsin, was selected as new chief. This was generally accepted and emphasized his handling of police work as we almost doubled the size of the city through annexation and needed time to expand the number of policemen. He performed admirably.

We never regretted our selection of Porter Homer as city manager. He was not only well versed in city government, but contrary to some professional managers, recognized the political realities and needs of the elected officials. An example is the appointment of Chief of Police Garmier. The appointment (contrary to good city procedures) was vested by the Charter in the city manager. While Porter interviewed the candidates, he recommended Garmier, but left the actual selection to the mayor and council.

We made several changes in the City Charter. It had

been put together in 1919 by the City of Tucson which took provisions often lacking in coordination from many other city charters and incorporated them into Tucson's Charter without bothering to harmonize them. The Tucson Charter is still a hobgoblin of disparate and obsolete provisions, but our attempts to do a major overhaul were put off for more demanding changes, as any change, regardless of how inconsequential, raises political objections. We had more important battles to fight.

As annexation had been avoided for many years because of the political cost of bringing reluctant groups and areas under city regulations and taxes, predecessor administrations had let the outskirts grow, whereby there were five persons claiming Tucson as their residence for every one actually living within the boundaries of the city. We knew this had to be changed, but with the city tax rate being $3.20 per hundred, no individual or business wanted to voluntarily assume this extra burden. Our annexation laws required that we designate an area for annexation and then secure signatures of the owners of over 50 percent of the assessed valuation of the property in the area to be annexed and then annex by ordinance.

The city had relied almost exclusively on property taxes. They were too high to sell an annexation program. As annexation was one of our principal goals, we knew that property taxes had to be reduced.

On May 4, 1954, Bill Matthews had editorialized condemning the suggestion that the previous Republican city administration was toying with a city sales tax. The *Star* said the revenue would be offset by losses in city business. He also said:

> To imagine that the money raised by 1/2 of one percent sales tax would go to the reduction of property taxes is wishful thinking.
>
> In addition, it imposes another set of brakes on the already slowed up annexation program which is in the last analysis just about the best way of broadening the tax base.

Despite these dire predictions and with knowledge that if Bill Matthews fought our tax proposal we would have great difficulty in passing a Charter change to permit the city to levy a sales tax, we proposed a levy of 1/2 of one percent sales tax. We simultaneously agreed to put a cap of $1.75 per hundred on the property tax rate. This was a reduction from the $3.20 per hundred. This disarmed Bill Matthews and the opposition and our Charter change was approved.

Genee's Christmas Letter. 1956:

Don finds that being the mayor of a mushrooming city like Tucson (from 60 to 103 thousand since he's become mayor) demands increasingly more of his time. The mayor's job is part time — which means 14 to 16 hours out of each 24. He has found the problems interesting, varied and challenging. Providing services for 40,000 new residents, acquiring private water companies, and expanding administrative service within the archaic law of budget limitation requires ingenuity and gymnastics.

Between times and while earning his living at law practice, he has sandwiched in duties as State President of the League of Arizona Cities and Towns, and just last month he was one of six elected to the executive committee of the American Municipal Association (the national organization of the cities of the United States).

The pace has been fast, but, except for the absence from his family, he seems to thrive on it. In fact, he's just announced that he will seek another two-year term to complete his program.

The family has enjoyed some experiences directly connected with his official duties. We all had an exciting ride in the mid-winter Rodeo in a horse-drawn carriage. One of the horses was not temperamentally suited to a parade. He was frantic and fought until one rein broke and Don finally put the family out of the carriage. Shortly thereafter, the horse reared and fell and had to be taken out of the parade. We all enjoyed tooting the horn of the 1904 Oldsmobile that set the cross-country record in that year, and then having our pictures taken in the Car of the Future at GM's Parade of Progress. The children were close observers when Genee christened a new air flagship with a "Cloud Gun" — and lipstick! It seems the "Star of Tucson" was laid up for repairs, and a substitute ship arrived with the wrong name. The occasion was the inauguration of TWA service into Tucson. The plane left Tucson with the proper name and Genee minus a lipstick.

Summer saw us once again on our way to Lassen Park. We stopped en route for a few days at Yosemite for the opening of their beautiful new Yosemite Lodge. Later in the summer we had our own official dedication of our new Public Service Center at Manzanita Lake. Long a dream, it is now a reality. Genee found herself in the manager's shoes during most of the summer at Drakesbad, as Don commuted between the Park and his Tucson duties. The warm swimming pool at Drakesbad was the children's center of interest. Donna, Diane, and Cliff all learned to swim the length of the pool. Charlene was a fearless and energetic diver and paddler. Except for the lack of a tail, she's a mermaid in every sense of the word. All of the children started their horseback instructions, accompanying the grownups on day rides. The "hot dog" trips to Willow Lake complete with campfires were highlights for Donna and Di. Charlene at 2-1/2 had to be content with having her horse led on short meadow trips. It was a grand summer for all of us.

Now Donna and Di are in 3rd and 2nd grade and beginning ballet lessons... both becoming young ladies. Cliff's in kindergarten and his own happy self. Charlene feels she is a big girl, too, going to nursery school. They all had measles last spring, but have been full of pep and in good health since. They all miss their busy daddy and hope he will make an appointment with them each week so they can enjoy playing with him. They have such fun together and would like to join us in saying Merry Christmas and Happy New Year to you.

❇ ❇ ❇

Protecting Tucson's Water Supply

We also purchased quite a number of water sites in the Altar Avra Valley, which were to be held in reserve for future water development. When the council at a later date attempted to develop this water, they were restrained by a court action on the basis that they could not take the water off the land and transport it for city use. This required the city to buy a considerable amount of land which they did not need, but which was required if the city was to transport the water for city use. This is a typical example of how the state legislature favored the rural areas and failed to recognize urban needs.

As a result of our annexation programs, we now had expanded the city boundaries to incorporate 72 square miles to bring 220,000 people within the boundaries. This enabled Tucson residents and businesses to get financing from insurance companies and other financial agencies, who had previously declined to provide money for investment in the community, as it was too small to justify supervision of their loans. As the census is the basis for determining how large a city is, Tucson had been at a great disadvantage since it was listed in the census as having only 50,000 people. Now that we were 220,000 in the Tucson community, we asked for a special census to improve our access to loan capital. It also helped to improve our access to television programs, as programs are sold and distributed on the basis of population to justify advertising fees.

We promoted Bill Bray to purchasing agent for the city. Bill subsequently got into trouble and had to be released. I do not know exactly what happened, except that we were paying more for some material purchased for the city than could be bought for retail on the open market. Bill was forced to resign and took a job with the Horizon Land Company. We put Tom Price in control of the Sanitation Department, which had greatly expanded as a result of our annexation programs.

Water franchises were not the only problem the city had with the Corporation Commission. The commission had the authority to compel railroads to install flashing signals at grade crossings if they were determined to be hazardous. Demands had been made on the Southern Pacific Railroad for signals at South Park and South Cherry avenues. The Southern Pacific wanted the city to contribute to the costs. The *Star* demanded that the Corporation Commission order the railroad to install the flashing signals without contribution from the city. The commission delayed and evaded taking definite action.

On November 23, 1955, the *Tucson Daily Citizen* had editorialized that the railroad warning signals for South Park and South Cherry were back on the top of the city's agenda; that Mayor Don Hummel found encouragement in a recent hearing of the Arizona Supreme Court that railroads must install and pay for signals at hazardous crossings if ordered to do so by the Corporation Commission. The city manager was ordered to study the possibility of submitting Tucson's request to the Corporation Commission.

Southern Pacific sponsored a bill in the legislature to require participation by the local authority. I, together with other Tucson officials, opposed this bill before the House

Bridges Committee of the State Legislature, on March 3, 1956.

The controversy was complicated by the Pima County Board of Supervisors who, on the recommendation of County Engineer Burg, agreed to pay the $8,000 cost of installation of flasher signals at a railroad crossing in Pima County on Irvington Road. The *Star* condemned this and sought a reversal of the sharing of costs. The State Attorney General ruled that it would be illegal for any political subdivision to enter into a contract with the railroad to share the costs as this was exclusively the railroad's responsibility.

A bill was passed in the State Legislature which would have permitted the railroad to charge half of the costs of installation of wigwag signals at grade crossings. Governor Ernest McFarland vetoed the bill.

The City of Tucson sued to bar payment for the signals at Cherry Avenue crossing from being installed. The court in Maricopa County, where the suit was tried, ruled in favor of the City of Tucson. The railroad appealed to the United States Supreme Court but the city's position was affirmed.

Southern Pacific again introduced a bill to have the state and local governments pay a portion of the costs. It was passed and despite my strong protests to Governor Paul Fannin, he signed the signal bill into law.

Under the new law the railroad paid half and the state paid half. If a city or county thoroughfare was involved, the city or county must pay 35 percent. This did not affect Cherry Avenue and Southern Pacific paid the entire cost of construction.

On March 16, 1956, I called for the town of South Tucson to disincorporate and become part of the City of Tucson. I pointed out that this cut off Tucson's southern expansion and that the joining of forces would make for a stronger overall community. The comments were made following a flood control meeting which pointed up the problems of dealing with two incorporated communities in attempting to solve a joint problem. John Merrill, mayor of South Tucson, was present.

Tucson Councilman Phelps agreed, saying that he felt the people of South Tucson would be better off as part of the city. He said he would like to see the whole metropolitan area as one big City of Tucson.

Roger O'Mara, reporter for the *Arizona Daily Star*, was assigned and prepared a series of articles on South Tucson as a result of numerous complaints from citizens. South Tucson had doubled its size by annexations in 1949 and 1953 which resulted in mass protests. When requests were made to examine the petitions on which annexation was based, they could not be found. In one instance, when a group of citizens protested that they did not want to be annexed, the mayor said we will "unannex you" and passed a resolution leaving out that particular area. Rather irregular! Eventually, both annexations were withdrawn. Some petitions were discovered but were sloppily drawn and of doubtful validity.

Other problems developed as adequate financial records had not been maintained to document what tax collections had been made and how the money was spent. Expenditures had not been made in accordance with budget procedures and town money had been loaned out. The mayor, councilmen and town clerk were charged with concealing documents and lending public money. Raul Castro, the county attorney, seized the town's records. Kenneth Hammes, a public accountant, was hired to audit the accounts. He testified in court that there were inadequate records to perform an accounting. In the meantime, the county tax collector made a mistake and distributed to South Tucson $8,000 more than they were entitled to which the town promptly spent without regard to its budget.

A trial was held in Maricopa County before Judge H. S. Stevens, who was heard on two occasions to say that "the case was mis labeled and should have been "William R. Matthews vs. the Town of South Tucson." Twice during the trial the state requested a motion for a mistrial charging misconduct on the part of Judge Stevens. This he refused and directed a verdict of not guilty.

On May 29, 1956, the South Tucson Lion's Club polled 6 to 2 in favor of South Tucson joining the City of Tucson. On June 1, Soleng Tom, a prominent South Tucson merchant, sponsored the passing of petitions to have the town disincorporated. Tom stated, "We have a city incapable of giving us the services we need and want. We buy our water from Tucson, rely on Tucson for our sewerage disposal and garbage disposal. South Tucson relies on the county for our jail, our fire protection is inadequate and our police department too small."

A mass meeting was called by the South Tucson mayor and in a steering session they determined that most wanted to maintain their town identity pointing to the low taxes. Mayor Merrill and town attorney William I. Martin, who conducted the meeting, blamed their problems on Bill Matthews and the *Arizona Daily Star*. No further action was taken and the town continues to the detriment of all.

Urban Renewal

Another big project for the City of Tucson was the attempt to replan part of the areas that had degenerated and could be classed as slums. This was primarily the original part of the city in the southwestern section, along the railroad tracks on the west and the main central city on the east. As a result, we proposed an urban renewal project, which consisted of some 417 acres of land, occupied in many instances by dilapidated and rundown structures with little or no street improvements; in fact, the streets were narrow and winding and sometimes not even paved. Utilities, such as sewer and water systems, were substandard. The amount of taxes collected was minimal.

The urban renewal program was designed to take such rundown areas, clear the sites, widen and replace the streets, put in new utilities and then after clearing and improving, sell the land back to the private sector for development in accordance with an established plan. We held innumerable neighborhood sessions pertaining to the urban renewal program with residents who lived in the affected areas. We got good support from them, on assurances that they would have an opportunity to get improved housing after the land was cleared and redeveloped. Downtown business people were thoroughly behind us on this project as their area was dying and unless we were able to rejuvenate sites adjacent to the central city, the downtown area would degenerate and be scattered to other locations in the city.

We put Bill Bray in charge of the urban renewal program, in addition to his duties as the city purchasing agent. The principal objection to the area was raised by Bill Matthews, who did not like a lot of these newfangled approaches to city government. It was like walking on eggs trying to keep Bill from undermining the program.

When I finally decided that I was not going to run at the end of my third term, and the new candidates for mayor and city council were belittling the urban renewal program, Mundy Johnson, who was the Valley National Bank representative in Tucson and very active in community affairs, particularly in the downtown businesses, asked if I would postpone, or rather vacate, the notice of hearing to adopt this urban renewal program for submission to the national government for funding. I told Mundy I did not like what I was hearing about the urban renewal program by the candidates running for city office. He said, "Well, we are fearful — the business people are fearful — that the new administration will come in and say, `This is a Hummel project — why should we continue it?'" I said I would agree to vacate the hearing so that it could be held by the new administration, provided they would publicly make assurances that they would continue the program. This was done and we vacated the hearing.

Shortly after the new administration came in, the public hearing was held, but they promptly vetoed the plan. This was a great disappointment to me.

Shortly after going into office, the Arizona Municipal League met in Phoenix and I was elected President of the League. The League was in disrepute in that the director, an attorney in Phoenix who, on a part-time basis, was extremely interested in the League's activities, was also very much a procrastinator. As a result, the League did not have much standing within the state. It was not too long after I took over as President of the League that the director was disbarred for failure to properly handle a law client's business. He neglected to respond to a complaint and a default judgment was entered against his client. When this happened, we asked for his resignation and started looking for a League director. Through municipal channels all over the country, we indicated that we were interested in hiring a person to head up the League, which we had just reorganized and renamed The League of Arizona Cities and Towns.

Jack Debolske, Assistant League Director from Colorado, was hired. Jack was young, but looked exceptionally younger than his years, and some people were skeptical as to how he would act or be accepted by the state's legislators. Hiring Jack was one of the best things we did for the League. He was knowledgeable, politically astute and aggressively protected the cities' and towns' interests. Jack, after 30 years, is still heading up the League's activities.

Because of my services to the League in reorganizing and revitalizing it, I was made the first Life Member, a position I still value. The League is a most respected and effective organization, representing the urban interests of our cities and towns.

In reorganizing the League, we agreed that contributions by cities should be on a per capita basis. This meant that Phoenix and Tucson would pay about 75 percent of the dues. The problem we encountered in the state was that small towns dominated all municipal legislation which came before the State Legislature. Each county had two senators and a representative, patterned after the national government. Representatives of small towns and their legislators had very little interest in the problems that the fast-growing cities of Phoenix and Tucson were having, and would not support bills before the State Legislature which the larger cities required. By assessing the big cities and then putting the mayors of small cities out in front, we were able to build an effective political organization which soon earned the support and respect of the State Legislature. Jack Debolske worked assiduously on these problems and the League gave him complete support. He turned the League of Arizona Cities and Towns from an organization that was snubbed into one of the most effective political organizations on behalf of city government in the State of Arizona.

Genee's Christmas Letter, 1957:

January ushered in the beginning of another political race as Don and three Councilmen came up for reelection. Although the Mayor's position is supposed to be a part-time job, the principal issue was "year around leadership," a reference to Don's obligations in Lassen Park. The favorable majority this time was two to one, so we were gratified with the voters' answer.

June found us back at Drakesbad. An unusually light snowfall and early spring made the opening pleasant. With Don attending to his Tucson duties, Genee again had the responsibility of managing Drakesbad. It was easier this year with the children older and Genee's mother there to help with them.

The children enjoyed hiking, horseback riding and swimming. We were all proud to have Charlene join the ranks of the swimmers. At the age of three and a half, she was diving in and swimming the width of the pool. Cliff received a fishing pole on his sixth birthday and the very next day caught a seven inch rainbow. His grin was as broad as the fish was long.

Fall brought the family back to Tucson and into the swing of events. Genee's back on the Board with the Junior Women's Club, Vice President of the Girl Scouts, member of the two Brownie Troop committees, a worker in the United Community Fund Campaign and, to top it all, she was called and is on the Superior Court jury panel.

Donna, nine now, is in the 4th grade. She lives for school, is a first-class student and real bookworm. Di is in 3rd grade. She was eight in November. She's still our effervescent one, but she's beginning to seem more grown up and is doing well is school. Cliff is an enthusiastic first grader. Doing well, but his Dad suspects him of smiling his way through some situations. Charlene's main interest is Mittens, her pet cat. Charlene is especially gregarious, inclined to be boisterous and alert to all that goes on.

Don's activities revolve around his duties as Mayor in one of the fastest growing cities of the United States. Tucson has increased 450 percent in the last fifteen years. To meet the problems of rapid growth, the City has projected a ten-year capitalization program which, if passed, will provide 41-1/2 million dollars' worth of needed improvements. As Don is president of the League of Arizona Cities and Towns and was elected as one of twelve in the United States to the Executive Committee of the American Municipal Association and has also been active with the American Council to Improve Our neighborhoods (ACTION), he's found too little time to be an active member of our family. This has been our one regret.

A real vacation was enjoyed by Genee, Donna and Di when they accompanied Don to Yellowstone National Park and the Grand Tetons where Don served as the Director of National Parks' Committee to advise on development of our National Parks. While Don attended meetings, Genee and the two girls had a first-class tour of these two beautiful parks.

❄ ❄ ❄

Our largest annexation program was 23 square miles on the north and east side of Tucson. We proposed the city boundaries to be extended to the Rillito River. The size of the program aroused great opposition and there were threats of separate incorporations and threats to take us into court. Annexation laws in Arizona were fairly strict. The number of people in the area was not an important factor; it was the amount of the assessed valuation of the property. If you secured signatures representing more than 50 percent of the assessed valuation, you could then have the city council incorporate the area by ordinance. The problem was, of course, to get enough people to sign the petitions to be sure you had 50 percent or more of the assessed valuation.

In this connection, we had an interesting development. Both the Tucson Gas, Electric Light and Power Company and the Bell Telephone Company had tremendous properties assessed with large valuations. They did not want to take a lead and in fact, secretly did not want the areas incorporated, as their taxes probably would go up and they would not profit as much as individuals. They would take no position for or against, but when we had 50 percent of the value of property other than theirs, they would sign the petition and would not attempt to hold up our annexation program. This became ludicrous in our big annexation program, in that neither Luther Davis of the electric utility, nor John Albright of the telephone company, wanted to sign first. I finally went to Tucson Gas, Electric Light and Power Company and invited John Albright to sit across the desk from Luther Davis. I handed each a pen and said, "Now, both of you sign at the same time." This was accomplished and our biggest single annexation program of 23 square miles became a fact.

As opposition developed on the large annexation programs, our practice was to have public meetings to discuss annexation. We attempted to show that it was not going to cost the tax payers much more to have their property in the city than outside. The difference in cost was minimal as we promised immediate police protection, which they had not had before, and fire protection, which was to be instituted as soon as annexation took place. This would reduce their insurance premiums. We showed that such things as library tax, which they had to pay when living in the county, was assumed by the city. Also, and they would receive cheaper water rates. All of these facts were presented either to small neighborhood groups or in fairly large groups at public meetings.

We had a large meeting at Doolen Junior High School on Grant Road and Country Club. Fred Finney, who was the public relations representative for Tucson Gas, Electric Light and Power Company, and a silent supporter of annexation, told me I should do some thing to put a little humor in the presentation when I spoke at the school, because the public was enraged at the size of the annexation program. He suggested I wear an armor when I appeared on the platform and tell the people that I was ready for anything.

I contacted Peter Marrony, head of the Drama Department of the University of Arizona, and secured a suit of armor. Unfortunately, people in the audience did not see the humor; it only intensified their anger. I was never allowed to forget this incident, as my political opponents often used it against me whenever they were opposed to some program my administration had instituted. They ridiculed me by reproducing photographs of me in armor.

During the large annexation program, I had a visit from Lewis Douglas, a banker and former Director of the Budget under President Roosevelt. He had also been ambassador to the Court of St. James in England. He said, "Don, I'm getting a little disturbed with you politicians — you are moving too fast and too far, and I'm just a little bit upset about it." I said, "Lew, do you know exactly where our boundaries are?" (I knew he was disturbed in that he had an unimproved 10-acre tract of land in the north eastern section of Tucson and did not want it incorporated into the city.) I said, "Let me show you on the map here." As I traced the boundary it showed that we did not go out quite far enough to take in his land. He had an immediate change of heart. He praised me for my vision and my willingness to take on controversial positions in the city.

During this 23 square mile annexation program I received a visit from an old schoolmate from Safford School.

Arthur Felix had purchased a home in a development which had been owned by Howard Hughes. When Howard Hughes came in to build the Hughes Missile Plant, he had Roy Drachman secure options on hundreds and hundreds of acres of land which were then to be developed and would make Howard Hughes a lot of money. This section of land was just northeast of the old town of South Tucson. The development stagnated as too few people wanted to live in this area. As a result, the promoters, six men living in Dallas, Texas, decided they would give up their program and turn it over to the Federal Housing Administration who had issued the mortgages.

Arthur Felix said South Tucson was secretly taking out petitions and was going to incorporate this large area into South Tucson; people did not want to reside in South Tucson, but wanted to join the City of Tucson. I gave Arthur Felix a petition with instructions to get the names of all the people in this subdivision and have them sign to join the City of Tucson. I instructed him not to disclose that he had had any contact with a city official; he was to present it on his own initiative. I was having enough problems with the north side annexation without starting another battle. After Arthur presented me with all the names of those living in that development, I contacted the owners living in Dallas, Texas, and asked if they would sign these petitions to include all the houses they had built but had not been able to sell. They agreed, and I secured their signatures. This was all done without letting anybody on the city council know of the plan.

As these were new houses, the assessed valuations were high and this could incorporate a lot of the area adjacent to South Tucson, where the houses were old, small and with little assessed valuation.

With the help of the city manager, we circumscribed an area to completely surround the City of South Tucson. I then called a special meeting of the city council and presented this with the request that they adopt the ordinance and incorporate the area next to South Tucson into the city, thereby cutting off South Tucson from expanding its boundaries.

You can imagine the publicity and consternation of some when headlines showed that we had annexed this area south of Tucson while we were in a bitter battle for the large area northeast of Tucson. This annexation was likened by the *Los Angeles Times* to a military maneuver, which stated that while all the attention and infighting was occurring in the northeast area of town, the city council, with a diversionary force, had incorporated a considerable amount of area south of the city. Needless to say, my political opponents did not like this at all!

We promised residents of all annexed areas that we would buy private water systems and provide them with city water rates.The city water system had been limited to areas within the boundaries of the city. There were some 33 small independent water systems surrounding the Tucson area. We immediately started a program of purchasing these systems and were quite successful.We bought on the basis of so much per water service, based on the quality of the system we were buying.

One day I received a call from Bill Matthews. He said he was writing an editorial about our purchase of the water systems, and that we were paying too much. I said, "Bill, before you write that editorial, let me give you the facts, because we have documented them pretty well." He said, "I've already written it."

I said, "Well, please don't publish it then until I have given you the figures." I immediately took over a stack of papers about 12 or 14 inches high listing the water service companies that we had purchased and presented them to him in his office.He looked a little nonplused when I handed him this volume of paper. To make a long story short, he held onto these for about six weeks, and he never did publish the editorial.

Corporation Commission Opposition

Another problem we encountered in the expansion of the water system was the animosity of the Corporation Commission, which controlled private water companies, but had no control over municipal water systems. They saw their power slipping away as we purchased one water company after another, and we heard rumors of money being paid under the table. Porter Homer came to me and said that he was meeting with a water commissioner and that he understood a bribe was to be offered to him to participate in the purchase of water franchises. I agreed that he should go through with the meeting and that he was to carry a "bug" on his body so as to record the conversation.

The numerous private water companies that had sprung up as building flourished outside the city limits were subject to Corporation Commission franchises. The commission did little to keep these water rates down but were generous in giving franchises for water companies despite the city's objection.

On November 12, 1959, Bill Matthews ran an editorial entitled, "The City and the Corporation Commission." It stated:

> Mayor Don Hummel performed a necessary service to the community when he protested against the free and easy way in which the Arizona Corporation Commission has granted domestic water franchises within the past few years covering as much as 16 square miles, much of it uninhabited, to individuals in face of opposition from the City of Tucson.
>
> Today the situation has changed. Under Mayor Hummel's leadership the city has voted and sold $5 million of water revenue bonds. It has the money and the determination to provide domestic water for any legitimate housing development. Yet in the face of this obvious willingness of the city to shoulder the responsibility, the Corporation Commission in its open sessions has treated the city like an intruder. This treatment would not be so bad if it were not for the fact that within weeks after granting of some franchises, one of the Corporation's own employees has approached the mayor and the city manager suggesting that they buy these franchises at ridiculously high prices.

It was the last paragraph that tipped off the Corporation Commissioner (referred to as an employee in the editorial), that the attempted bribe of the city manager was known. The failure of the recorder prevented us from proceeding with charges against the Commissioner.

I had confided our plan to record this conversation with the Corporation Commissioner to Bill Matthews to protect the city manager in case the Commissioner attempted to say Porter Homer solicited the bribe.

Water Politics

The city council was in the process of examining a possible increase in water rates which were far below surrounding cities.During the discussion Councilman Kirk proposed a cheaper rate for motel owners. I promptly squelched this proposal. The *Star* criticized Councilman Kirk, who was motel owner. In the "Voice of the People" on January 26, 1959 the following exchange appeared:

VOICE OF THE PEOPLE
Statement Criticized

Editor the Star:

Why do you continue to misrepresent and falsify the record of Councilman Kirk's speaking on behalf of the Tucson Motor Hotel Association's request for consideration of a different method of calculating water bills for users outside the city? You were told your first editorial was untrue and you grudgingly admitted it in part but then in "Arizona Politics" you repeat the former falsifications. Have you no concern for the truth? Are your personal political objectives (sic) so paramount that they justify the use of any means at your disposal to obtain your goal?

LAWRENCE N. MANROSS
Owner, Mobile Motel
2315 Oracle Rd.

Editor's Note: The objectionable quotation appeared in "Politics in Arizona" Monday, Jan. 12, as follows:

Opponents of annexation have been the first organized groups to take after Mayor Don Hummel in his race for nomination in February and election in April. One group is the Motel Owners Assn. that resents the lead that the Mayor took in rejecting Republican Councilman Kirk's plea to give them special water rates.

The *Star* insists that every word printed above pertaining to Mayor Hummel and Councilman Kirk is true, and not "false." It has a copy of the minutes of the council meeting furnished by Councilman Kirk to confirm the truth. The *Star* will be glad to show Mr. Manross the copy of these minutes if he is really interested in learning the truth.

Shortly before final approval of the large annexation program, I had a call about two o'clock in the morning from a man who opened the conversation by saying, "Why don't you mind your own damned business?" I said, "What have I done now?" I knew this was just another objection to annexation. He said, "This annexation program." I said, "What's wrong with it?" He answered, "You're making this city too big." I said, "I'm not making the city too big; I'm just trying to expand the boundaries to give some uniformity to the streets and regulations in the area."

He said, "I have moved three times and every time I've moved, you have expanded the city limits to incorporate me." I said, "Well, if you want to live in isolation, go up to Mt. Lemmon, because we have no intention of going up on the mountain." His response was, "Well, I just don't like it." I said, "Wait a minute now — how long have you lived here?" He said, "Three years." I said, "Well, I have lived here 50 years and we liked it before you came." I said, "As old-timers, we are accused of trying to dominate the situation in Tucson. All I'm trying to do is expand our boundaries to accommodate people like you who have moved here to the Tucson community and give you a voice in the city government." To my amazement, the man said, "I think you are right; I apologize, and I'm sorry I called." Then he hung up. In my almost seven years as mayor, I think that is the only time anyone ever said I was right!

In order to preserve the water for the future growth of Tucson, we got a bond issue passed so that we could buy water sites surrounding Tucson. When the bond issue was passed we engaged the services of John Carrola, a hydrologist, and his partner, a retired geological surveyor whose name I do not recall. We asked them to determine where the water sites were and to give a report to the city. After some search, John Carrola came to the city council and stated that they had accomplished their work, but there was one report they wanted to give us in a confidential manner, separate from the others, because if they included it in the major report, we would never be able to buy these water-bearing sites.

He stated that the San Pedro area had a medium sized gravel area which was cut off at the lower end by the igneous dike that cut across the canyon, and while this didn't hold a lot of water, it was rapidly recharged and could give the city another good source of water. We authorized him to give us the special and confidential report on the San Pedro area. The other report was delivered as a public document and accepted by the city council. Upon publication of this document, I was stopped on the street by Carlos Ronstadt, who advised me that he represented the Chamber of Commerce on their water commission and that if he could be of any assistance I should call on him.

Sometime thereafter, Porter Homer said, "Can we trust Carlos Ronstadt? I would like to see about buying that San Pedro water area, but once we disclose this, we are vulnerable if the information gets out." I said I had known Carlos a long time and that he had been a very responsible citizen, that he was serving as a director of the Tucson Gas, Electric Light and Power Company; had been the head of the Cattlemen's Association for the State of Arizona, and that as far as I knew, he was trustworthy. About three weeks later, Porter called me and said, "Can you have a special meeting of the council? I want to present a proposal to purchase the San Pedro water area." He said, "It has to be right away, because our option runs out in three days." I said, "Why in the world did you wait so long?" He said, "I didn't want to buy this or propose it to the council unless we had it checked by Carrola and his partner to be sure of its value. They have just reported the results of their check and it looks as though it is in an excellent source of water."

I called a city council meeting and presented this proposal to buy 2,000 acres of water-bearing land in the San Pedro. The price quoted was $600,000.

The council approved the contract of sale and the matter was headlined in our daily newspapers. The following day I reported to Davis Monthan Air Force Base, as I was still in the standby Air Reserve and was fulfilling my required duty of a half-day duty on the base. I received a call about 11:00 a.m. from Jack Weadock, Associate Publisher of *The Arizona Daily Star*. He asked me who sold us this land. I said, "It's funny, but I just called Porter about an hour ago and asked who owned the land."

I knew we had bought it from a trust, but I asked Porter who actually owned it, and Porter said he didn't know. I told Jack that I would find out and let him know as soon as

I got off duty. Jack said, "Well, the `old man' [referring to Bill Matthews] asked me about it this morning and I told him that I was going to deal with you as I always had and just ask you outright who it was purchased from."   I assured him that I would find out and let him know.

When I got off duty at noon I went down to City Hall and attempted to call Carlos Ronstadt a number of times, but could get no answer. I finally called Norman Hull, who was representing Ronstadt, and asked him where Carlos was. Hull said Carlos was in Mexico but would be back that afternoon. I said I had had an inquiry as to who owned the land that the city had purchased. Norman said, "Well, I haven't any idea, as we dealt with a trust." I said, "Well, how can I find out who we purchased this land from and who were the people in the trust?" Norman said, "Come over and I will give you the files."

I immediately went to Norman Hull's office and he handed me a file about three inches thick. I started going through it. When I came to a description of the property I said, "My God! This is only 2,000 acres of a 6,000 acre tract, plus a lot of state-leased land." I asked how much they had paid for it and Norman said he really didn't know. I said "Well, who were the owners of this?" He said, "I really don't know." I said, "Well, what happened to the balance of the land?" He said, "That I don't know either." I said, "Tell Carlos I am going to have a council meeting and I expect him to be there." He said, "What's wrong?" I replied, "Carlos was supposedly representing the city; not someone else."

I immediately called a special meeting of the council and disclosed the information acquired at Norman Hull's office. I said, "I am going to call for an abrogation of this contract because I think the city has been taken." Porter Homer, the city manager, remonstrated with me and said, "Now wait a minute — this is important water land and you're not just buying land, you are buying water, and it seems to me that the price is reasonable." Just then the telephone rang and Carlos Ronstadt was on the phone. He said, "I understand you're questioning this water deal." I said, "Yes, Carlos, and I have the council here and I want you to come over to answer some questions." He said, "I won't come without my lawyer." I said, "I don't give a damn — bring your lawyer." He replied, "Well, he can't come until later because he is tied up." I said, "There will be a special council meeting at 7:30 tonight and you be there to answer some questions."

I immediately called all the news media and said there would be a special council meeting that night at 7:30 to discuss the purchase of the San Pedro water. When the meeting opened Bill Matthews was sitting in the front row. I told what I had discovered and said that I was now calling on the council to abrogate the contract, as the information was given to Carlos Ronstadt for the purpose of representing the city and that this did not appear to be the case. I then asked Carlos to make a statement before the city council and the assembled press. I said, "Did you make a profit on this?" Carlos got up before the microphone and said, "Yes, I made a profit. This is not Russia and I expect to make a profit." There was considerable exchange and Porter Homer interceded in the discussions, defending the agreement saying it was for the benefit of the city. This really antagonized Bill Matthews and Bill set out to get rid of Porter Homer from that time on.

A Mr. Golder had been the owner of the land and an option had been taken from him through a trust. The trust consisted of Harry V. Cameron and his wife. He was the President of the Arizona Land Title & Trust Company, with Carlos Ronstadt and his wife, Betty, as beneficiaries of the trust. When Golder found out the value of the area he had sold, he refused to go through with the contract and after a great deal of pressure and adverse publicity, Carlos Ronstadt and Fleming agreed to assign the total contract to the City of Tucson. We had to sue Golder to compel him to go through with the sale. The result was that the City of Tucson acquired not only the 2,000 acres that they had originally purchased, but about 4,000 other acres of land, plus several thousand acres of state leasehold land for $357,125.

There was a sequel to this San Pedro water deal. Several months later, Jim Kirk, the councilman who was desirous of running for mayor, brought the matter before the city council. He stated it was his understanding that the mayor and city manager had more knowledge about the San Pedro

property than had been admitted at the previous city council hearings, and that he proposed the city turn this whole
matter over to the County Grand Jury which was meeting
at that time for inquiry.

I demanded that if Kirk had information concerning
mine and the city manager's activities, he give it to the
council immediately. He refused. I asked Harold "Whitey"
Neubauer, the city attorney, whether we could compel
Councilman Kirk to provide this information since it was a
matter concerning the official conduct of the mayor and the
city manager in which the council had made the decision to
purchase this water-bearing land. The city attorney advised that we could convene the city council as an investigative body and subpoena Mr. Kirk to compel him to provide
such information as he had concerning these activities. For
our protection it was essential that all facts be made
public.Information turned over to the Grand Jury is secret
and cannot be divulged to the public. This would protect
Kirk if the inquiry disclosed no wrongdoing but would
leave a shadow over the city manager and me.

I convened the city council as an investigative body and
we hired a special prosecutor to bring all relevant information before the council for their action. We selected Jack
Johnson, a former chief justice of the State Supreme Court,
as the investigator.When the session was called several
days later, Mr. Kirk was subpoenaed and asked to divulge
the information he had. He could produce no facts. You
can imagine the amount of adverse publicity we had received following Kirk's charges. When Kirk admitted that
he had no facts to support the charges, the *Tucson Daily
Citizen*, who normally supported Kirk in his political aspi-
rations, stated:

> ...when Councilman Kirk opened his little box to
> divulge information, it was empty.

In the meantime, during an exchange between Kirk and
myself, he threatened to fight me and started taking his coat
off. After it was disclosed that Kirk could not support his
charges, the city council officially censured Councilman
Kirk.

On July 15, 1959, *The Tucson Daily Citizen* editorialized:

Property Tax Rate Down Sharply in Two Years.

Major reason for the big drop...is the city's adoption of a sales tax along with a property tax ceiling of $1.75. This major shift of city tax policy resulted in a drop of the city's property tax rate from a $3.10 figure in 1957-58.

The improved county tax picture resulted from among other things the relief of county expenses as a result of the City of Tucson's 21 square mile annexation.

12

Democratic Politics in Arizona

DICK JENKINS was active in Arizona Democratic circles in 1956. He owned the La Osa Ranch with his twin sister Nellie Jenkins — the ranch lay on the Mexican border about 70 miles south of Tucson. When it came time to elect the Chairman for the Democratic Central Committee of Pima County, Dick Jenkins was one of the candidates. He was also a personal friend of Adlai Stevenson, who was scheduled to run for the presidency. Adlai Stevenson often spent some of his vacation at the La Osa Ranch.

Another candidate for Chairman of the Democratic Central Committee was Frank Minerik who had been a classmate of Senator Estes Kefauver. Senator Kefauver, from Tennessee, had been campaigning for over a year, traveling across the country and shaking hands with everyone. Frank Minerik also became a candidate for the Chairman of the Democratic Central Committee of Pima County. The competition was rigorous and got to be rather personal, as each one had a personal interest in a candidate for the Presidency of the United States. Dick Jenkins won and when it came to appointing or designating the delegates from Pima County to the Democratic Convention to be held in Chicago, Illinois, in 1956, Dick refused to name Frank Minerik as one of the delegates. This left Frank without portfolio, but as he was representing Kefauver's candidacy, he attended the convention.

The opening of the convention was a stimulating affair, with all kinds of negotiations going on between the various committees from all of the states. Adlai Stevenson, of course, had a large percentage pledged to him, as did Estes Kefauver. As the delegates are called by state in alphabetical order, this put Arizona close to the head of the list. We agreed with the Adlai Stevenson forces to defer to the State of Illinois when Arizona was called, so that Stevenson's name could be placed in nomination by Illinois. This we did, and Adlai Stevenson was selected as the Democratic presidential nominee over Estes Kefauver.

When this occurred, Frank Minerik came to me and asked if I would sponsor Estes Kefauver in the Arizona delegation for Vice President of the United States. This occurred after Adlai Stevenson threw open the nomination to the floor, rather than designating his running mate, as had been the custom in the past. I agreed, and after considerable discussion, the Arizona delegation decided that Estes Kefauver would be a good running mate with Adlai Stevenson. Stevenson was known as an "egghead," an intellectual, who often spoke over the heads of the electorate. Estes Kefauver, on the other hand, was a down-to-earth politician who had already gone around the country. We thought this would be a good balance and would be helpful in our campaign. The Republican nominee was Dwight D. Eisenhower, a national hero. After Stevenson was nominated, Jack Kennedy was nominated for vice president. Arizona yielded to Tennessee for the nomination of Senator Kefauver as vice president. A considerable battle and great maneuvering took place between these two forces, with Kefauver winning out as Jack Kennedy lost support and removed his name from nomination.

During this period of time, or just prior to opening the convention, Averill Harriman had made a strong bid to be the presidential nominee. During preliminary maneuvering, outgoing President Harry Truman came out in favor of Harriman. This caused consternation among the supporters of Adlai Stevenson. There was a great confusion in the Stevenson quarters. Amid much pandemonium, I finally got up on the table and tried to quiet the Stevenson supporters, pointing out that this was just one man's preference even though he was an outgoing president, and that this probably would not swing enough votes to nominate Mr. Harriman, who was a dark horse candidate. As I stated, the nominations took place and Adlai Stevenson was nominated as the presidential candidate, with Estes Kefauver as his running mate.

The campaign that followed for the election was heated. It seemed to swing back and forth, but it was apparent that Stevenson was running behind General Eisenhower during most of the campaign. There were a number of rallies and at one, Lyndon B. Johnson came out as principal speaker on behalf of Adlai Stevenson. This was the first time I met Lyndon Johnson, then a senator. A tragic event took place toward the end of the campaign. Stevenson forces had set up closed circuit television for Adlai to address and thank all the Democratic workers on his behalf. This was shortly before the election date. The meeting in Arizona was set up in Phoenix and the Governor of Pennsylvania was to be the principal speaker.

I joined Dick Jenkins, who was the host, and scheduled to introduce the Governor. We all had dinner together and then went to the convention hall to hear Adlai and also to be addressed by the Governor of Pennsylvania. Dick had a heart attack and was supposed to conserve his energy. This he would not do. Despite all our urging and remonstrating, he was obviously living too active a life and drinking too much. When we arrived at the hall with about 1,000 assembled Democrats to listen to Adlai Stevenson's talk, Dick took his place on the platform with the microphone. He had a tremendous sense of humor and opened with a repertoire of political jokes. He then said, "Now take Tricky Dick Nixon..." I saw him sway and then fall to the platform. It took me a fraction of a second or more to realize what had happened, and as I was in the front row, I jumped to the platform and was one of the first to get to reach him. A number of others crowded around, but he was dead from a heart attack.

The governor never did give his speech and the meeting broke up without further activity. It was a tragic end for one of the most popular Democratic politicians in the State of Arizona.

Some time later, just before the election, Adlai Stevenson made a trip to Phoenix and read a eulogy for Dick Jenkins. I remember he clearly stated that Dick's philosophy had always been dictated by the adage, "It's not the years in your life, but the life in your years" that counted, and that Dick epitomized this philosophy.

While he had been warned many times to slacken his pace, he lived life to the fullest, enjoying what he was doing each day of his life. We buried Dick Jenkins on the La Osa Ranch in a little cemetery on the Mexican border.

Another incident I remember clearly during this period of time was the visit to Arizona by Jack Kennedy, who was scheduled to speak at our Sunday Evening Forum. I received a call from Jack Greenway, the son of Isabella Greenway King, former congresswoman from this state, and owner of the Arizona Inn. Jack said Kennedy would be staying with them and that Kennedy wanted to have dinner with me before he appeared at the Sunday Evening Forum.

Arrangements were made and we met for dinner at the Arizona Inn. Jack's purpose for asking for the interview was that he wanted to know why the Arizona delegation had been against him as the vice presidential nominee at the convention. He knew, of course, that I had led the delegation, urging the nomination of Estes Kefauver. I told him we had nothing against Jack Kennedy, but that we knew nothing about him and our primary interest was in electing Adlai Stevenson. Estes Kefauver had made a very extensive campaign for president around the United States and was well-known in the West. I explained that his, Jack Kennedy's, name was not well-known in the West and we thought that Kefauver would add greater weight to Stevenson's campaign. This satisfied Jack and we became friends. After this initial meeting, I became a supporter of Kennedy for president following the Eisenhower administration.

Former President Harry H. Truman was the main speaker at a Democratic rally in Phoenix. His close friend, a former councilman from Kansas City, Missouri, was traveling with him. Our City Manager, Porter Homer, had been the head of research and budget in Kansas City government. He gave me an introduction to the city councilman. When I delivered it, he said "Would you like to meet the boss?" I said, "Yes," and was introduced to President Truman. He had just been handed a glass of bourbon as it was recess time. President Truman invited me to join him on the couch. I said, "I understand this is your rest hour." He said, "Rest hour, hell, that's their idea, not mine!"

Truman called to a couple of young Phoenix officers who had been assigned as an honorary bodyguard and told them to join us. One officer said his brother had served in the armed services in the South Pacific Theater. That started Truman talking. He said, "I'll never forget putting the Medal of Honor on General 'Skinny' Wainwright." Truman said, "Tears as big as your thumbnail were running down Wainwright's face." The General had responded with, "Mr. President, I thought you would be court martialing me, not honoring me."

The President continued, "General Macarthur thought I'd honor him but I fired the son-of-a-bitch. When we were scheduled to meet on a small island in the Pacific, he arrived before I did and continued to fly in circles waiting for me to land. He wanted me to receive him, not him receive me. We finally got together and General Macarthur said, 'Mr. President, I'll stake my military career that the Chinese will never get involved in the Korean War.'" President Truman said, "That was a mistake. I've made lots of them myself but when he went behind my back and started playing politics with the Republicans, I fired the bastard. After all, I was the Commander in Chief." That ended our conversation on the war.

Jack Greenway took over the chairmanship of the Pima County Democratic Central Committee upon Dick Jenkin's death. He held this position until a later date when he was defeated by Frank Minerik.

At the close of the Eisenhower administration, or rather right after the election of President Eisenhower, Jack Kennedy started his campaign to be the Democratic nominee at the next election, some four years in the future. He spent a considerable amount of time gathering support among Democrats and others. He visited us on several occasions and on his first visit I gave him the key to the City of Tucson. Several years after his death this key was auctioned off as one of the Kennedy mementos.

During my second term as mayor, I was urged by Judge Ernest MacFarland, who was running for governor, to run for attorney general of the State of Arizona. I made some inquiries and as the climate appeared to be favorable, I took out nomination petitions.

Shortly thereafter, Wade Church, a labor attorney in Phoenix, also filed in the Democratic primary. MacFarland immediately distanced himself from me, as he did not want to be involved in a contest in the Democratic primary; particularly with Wade Church's labor support.

Wade was not particularly popular and I was considered the front-runner. My campaign was haphazard. I never did like to campaign and the attorney general's office did not offer any policy opportunities. I found myself talking about running a good legal office for the state. It was less than exhilarating, but I was, by all consensus, the front-runner, until big labor from all over the United States sent in 50 men to defeat Barry Goldwater in his reelection bid for U.S. Senator.

These labor representatives had nothing to do, as Barry had no primary opposition. As Wade Church was a labor lawyer, they were assigned to support him in the primary election.

I started getting calls from my supporters advising me that these labor representatives were contacting all labor organizations and visiting the mines to urge the selection of Wade Church. This turned the tide and I was defeated. I often wonder how winning might have changed my life, as I would not have been selected President of the American Municipal Association (National League of Cities), the Advisory Commission on Intergovernmental Relations, Assistant Secretary of HUD, and all those activities related to my municipal service. I believe the defeat was in my interest, but whether it was or not, that's how the ball bounced. Politics has its vagaries.

Prior to the next Democratic convention in 1960, I was visiting in Washington, D.C., and dropped in to see Stewart Udall, our congressman. Stewart had taken Porque Patton's place when the latter resigned because of the salary scale, which was about $12,000 a year. Porque thought he had to entertain every Arizonan who came to Washington, and he was greatly in debt. Those campaigning for president were Lyndon Baines Johnson and Jack Kennedy. Jack was not popular with his fellow congressmen. He had a poor record in Congress with frequent absenteeism. The only congressman I recall who had publicly come out in support of Kennedy's candidacy was Abraham Ribicoff, the senator from Connecticut. During my visit with Stewart, I asked who he was going to support.

He said "Adlai Stevenson." I said, "I do not understand how you can support Adlai when he is not running."

Stewart's reply was that he was the only one worth supporting. I said, "If that's the way you feel, you ought to go over and see Jack Kennedy, and support him." I said, "If Jack Kennedy does not have sufficient pledges to nominate himself, he has enough to determine who the nominee will be; and he would undoubtedly throw his support to someone other than Johnson, his principal opponent. That person could be Adlai Stevenson."

About 10 days later in Tucson, I received a call from Stewart Udall who said he had been thinking about our discussion and he thought my analysis of the situation was sound. He was going over that afternoon to see Jack Kennedy and pledge his support. As a result of this, Stewart Udall went on the campaign trail for Jack Kennedy.

When Kennedy was elected, Stewart was very anxious to get an appointment to the Cabinet. Jack had promised the Secretary of the Interior job to my friend, Rex Nicholson, but when Nicholson was indicted, along with a number of business leaders, for anti trust activities, Nicholson asked that his name be removed. I heard that Jack Kennedy then offered the appointment to Senator Moss from Utah, who declined. It was at this time that Stewart Udall was considered for Secretary of the Interior.

Next, I received a call from Horace Albright who wanted to know what Stewart Udall's attitude was toward preservation and how strong an environmentalist he was. I assured Horace that I thought he would be an extremely strong environmentalist and that I believed they would find him acceptable. Stewart was appointed Secretary of the Interior. He never acknowledged my role in getting him on the campaign trail for Jack Kennedy.

When Stewart was named Secretary of the Interior, he had to vacate his congressional seat. As I had deferred to Stewart's candidacy when I decided to run for mayor of Tucson rather than for Porque Patton's seat, I was promised to have the Udall family support when the next congressional seat opened in the second district of Arizona.

Mo Udall, who was the Pima County Attorney, ran for Judge of the Superior Court. There were two or three vacancies and Mo was believed to lead the ticket for Judge. It was a shock when he came in last. The ballots were printed with Udall at the top, but this was for Stewart and the congressional seat. Mo Udall, as a candidate for Judge, was on the bottom of the list, as the names were placed alphabetically. It appears that many thought they had already voted for Mo when they voted for Stewart. This left Mo without a position.

Jack Marks was my city attorney and a close friend of Mo's. I was asked to attend a luncheon with Mo and Jack Marks. The subject was a release from me of the Udall pledge to support me, and allow Mo Udall to run for Stewart's seat. I agreed, and Mo went on to win the second district congressional seat. The rest is history. Mo still occupies this seat in Congress.

As the next Democratic convention neared, Stewart Udall became the dominant force in Democratic politics in the State of Arizona. Though we had been friends, Stewart never really included me in the inner circle as Dick Jenkins had in the past. Frank Minerik was not as popular a Democratic leader as Dick Jenkins had been, and with the predominance of voters in Maricopa County, the power was shifted entirely to Phoenix and the Tucson people became an appendage, having much less influence on state Democratic politics. This, of course, had been true for many, many years and only through the leadership of Dick Jenkins and his friendship with Adlai Stevenson had Pima County had a major role in dominating the Democratic politics of the state during his tenure.

The U.S. senator from Arizona was Ernest MacFarland. MacFarland had been the governor of the state, and was elected to the United States Senate. During the Truman administration, he was the majority leader of the Senate. President Truman was a controversial President and subject to ridicule. While history shows him as a great President, his popularity during his administration after the war was thin. Senator Lyndon Johnson had selected Senator MacFarland as his representative in the State of Arizona to espouse Johnson's candidacy for president. This was a great mistake, as Senator MacFarland, while not in ill repute, was certainly unpopular among the Democrats who had arisen to positions of power since MacFarland had gone to the United States Senate. As a result, Johnson got very poor representation.

In one instance, Johnson sent Mayor Teyes, the mayor of El Paso, Texas, to see me about getting support for Johnson's candidacy. Teyes was imbued with the power of the then Texas Senator, and attempted to put pressure on me with threats. This did not go over very well and I told the mayor flatly that I was going to support Kennedy and that threats of retaliation were ill-advised. I told him to get out of my office. Teyes was used as a "hatchet man" by Senator Johnson during the campaign. I could never understand why Teyes had the power he had. He was certainly not a polished politician.

During the Kennedy administration, Rex Nicholson, who had given up his opportunity to become Secretary of the Interior, decided that Arizona was a good place to invest money. Rex had made a considerable amount of money right after the war, when rationing was discontinued. He was a representative of the Fordson tractor in the Western states. Being an important agricultural instrument, control was minimal. Rex made a lot of money selling tractors throughout the United States. He contacted me in Tucson and said he would like to become associated with me, as he wanted to invest in Tucson. I was still pretty busy with my own affairs and did not take an active role, but maintained close touch with Rex during his purchase of supermarkets and other places, such as the El Dorado property, including the El Dorado mansion, which was owned by Miss Pond, the heir of a railroad fortune. I do not know exactly what Rex paid for it, but he got a real bargain at something over a million dollars. This was the property my brother, Gail, had held an option on several years before for $200,000, but his financial backer got scared and checked out. With the mansion went something over 200 acres of prime land and resulted in a fortune during its development.

During this period of time, President Kennedy was urging Rex Nicholson to go to South America and find out what had happened to the Alliance for Progress. The Alliance had been greatly ballyhooed as the forefront of our relationship with the Central and South American countries, but with few apparent results. This was part of the AID program. Rex had run a large corporate structure in

South America; he spoke Spanish fluently, and was a very aggressive businessman in that area. He came to me one day and showed me a wire he had just received from President Kennedy urging him to take some time and go down and evaluate the program. Rex said he had enough of government and he wanted to spend his efforts in the private sector. I told him I thought he was wrong. I pointed out that this was not an indefinite assignment, but that the United States had a problem, the President was asking for his assistance, and he had an obligation to respond. "I'll go," he said, "provided you go with me." This put me in a position where I could not refuse and I agreed.

Shortly thereafter, I received a wire from President Kennedy designating me as the Consultant on Municipal Affairs for the Alliance for Progress. We went to Jamaica and a number of the Central American countries and to Venezuela in South America.

During the trip we saw what had obviously happened. The political powers had diverted funds from the program that was designed to improve the lot of the ordinary citizen and had utilized these funds to enlarge their own authority and to provide them opportunities for making money.

For example, we found highways developed at great expense which served only the haciendas of local politicians. We found housing that had been built for so-called poor people which included all the amenities such as running water and flush toilets, but no development of the water source to make them usable, e.g., toilet bowls were being used to store wheat, as they obviously could not be utilized for their principal purpose without water. To sum up matters, it was a political boondoggle by the Central American countries for the benefit of their politicians.

On my return, I left Rex Nicholson at Mexico City. He flew back to Washington, D.C., while I came to Tucson. I had just taken over the operation's in Glacier National Park, Montana, and I had all the organizing to do for the opening of the season. If I recall correctly, this was during the month of April 1962.

It was some time before I heard from Rex, and my attempts to contact him were fruitless. I learned later, when I returned to Tucson, what had happened. He arrived in Washington, D.C., and President Kennedy asked him to come over immediately for an oral briefing on the findings before the submission of a written report. This Rex proceeded to do and the President said he should write his report, but give it directly to him, not through the AID department. This Rex agreed to do, and on returning to his office at the State Department, there was a copy of his resignation on his desk. He looked at it, picked up the resignation, tore it up, and left Washington, D.C.

What had happened was that Robert Kennedy, who was the Attorney General, had opposed Rex representing the President in South America because of his previous indictment for antitrust violations, to which Rex had pleaded "nolo contendere," or no-contest. The judge fined him $500 saying, "I know you weren't really involved in too much of this, but you are an able and smart man, and should have known what was going on." The result was that Nicholson left Washington, D.C., and returned to Tucson.

Rex never submitted a written report on our findings. I remonstrated with him, stating that the fact that Robert Kennedy had intervened was no reason for him to leave the President in the lurch; that he was just playing into his opponents' hands. Rex agreed later that he had handled this matter badly, but as a result the report of the chaos that existed in the Alliance for Progress was never conveyed except orally to the President. The President never followed up and that was the end of our mission to Central and South America.

Nicholson continued his investments in Tucson, but as I was fully involved in my new enterprise in Glacier National Park I did not participate with him further. He subsequently left the Tucson area and died, but it was some time before I was informed of his death, as we had not maintained contact.

13

American Municipal Association
(National League of Cities)

IN 1956 I had been elected to the Board of Directors of the American Municipal Association. There are two associations of mayors and councilmen representing local government. They are the Conference of Mayors and the National League of Cities, formerly called the American Municipal Association. The latter also has state leagues as members.

On my election to Mayor of Tucson in 1955, I was elected to the Executive Committee of the National League of Cities. I also attended one meeting of the Conference of Mayors, but did not return as I found little substance in their agenda which I felt would be of benefit to Tucson.

In 1960 I was elected Vice President of the National League of Cities. Mayor Ray Tucker of St. Louis, Missouri, had been elected President at the convention in Denver, Colorado, in February 1960. 1960 was also the year the International Association of Local Authorities was to meet in Tel Aviv, Israel. This association meets on the biannual basis and represents local governments worldwide. As President Tucker was ill, I was designated as the Chairman of the U.S. Delegation. The Canadian Delegation joined with us and I also spoke for them. We flew to Rome, Italy, where we boarded El Al, the Israeli airline, for Tel Aviv. We had been advised that if we wanted any spiritous liquors, they should be purchased before we arrived in Israel.

I bought a pack which was contained in a cardboard case designed to carry four bottles. I had opened one bottle to give some visiting mayors a drink and then recorked the bottle. It was checked along with my other luggage. Unfortunately, the baggage compartment was not pressurized and the cork came out of the bottle, saturating the cardboard carton to the point of collapse. I must have smelled like a brewery. No one commented. I do not know whether or not they thought I was a real boozer.

The previous meeting had been held in Berlin, Germany. Protocol was for the mayor of the city hosting the previous convention to deliver its national flag to the new host city, where the flag would be flown. This created some apprehension. It would be the first time the German flag would fly in Israel after World War II.

Willi Brandt, as Mayor of Berlin, delivered the German flag. He started his talk with, "I know the burdens I bear as I come to Israel." This released a lot of tension and he was well received. Despite this fact, the German delegation left immediately after the opening ceremony.

The Israeli government rolled out the red carpet for our delegation. We were shown a good part of Israel. They took us to the Negev Desert, showed us a number of kibbutzes. We visited Haifa and other cities. We were impressed with the ingenuity and development that was demonstrated by the Israelis.

King Hussein of Jordan allowed us to pass through the Mendenhall Gate — the first time it was opened for transit from Israel and just for us. It was closed immediately. Tensions grew as we passed through the gate guarded by troops manning machine guns. It was particularly trying for the Jewish members of our delegation. We visited Jerusalem and stood at the Wailing Wall. We also went to the Garden of Gethsemane and the sepulcher where Jesus was buried.

The Association's meetings were simple, designed for those countries that had little or no independent local governments. It was boring for the U.S. and Canadian delegations.

We returned through Istanbul, Turkey; Paris, France; and London, England.

On arrival in the United States, I was informed that I should hurry as we were to meet with the press for a TV appearance followed by cocktails and dinner.

I had purchased an antique necklace in the Thieves Market in Istanbul for Genee's anniversary present and did not want her to know about it. As we were going through customs, Genee insisted on watching the search of our baggage. I was attempting to get the customs agent to acknowledge that the necklace was antique and free of duty, but Genee's close inspection got in the way.

I finally said, "Genee, go over and sit down." It worked but she was dismayed as to why I was provoked with her. I was successful and got through customs without revealing the necklace to her.

The TV appearance and the dinner party was a real ordeal. It was eleven p.m. before we sat down, but it was four a.m. on Paris time. I never sat through a worse dinner. I think I slept through about half of it. Someone would talk to me and I'd finally awaken enough to respond.

As President Ray Tucker was still ill, I was asked to preside at the conference the next morning in New York City. Genee was called upon to welcome the delegates' wives as Susan Wagner, the New York Mayor's wife, was too nervous to make the welcoming address.

All presidents of the National League of Cities were invited to be introduced on the Ed Sullivan Show. We were told to be there an hour early to be sure there was no slip-up. Genee and I dutifully arrived at the theater, but there was no one present. We were seated in the eighth row. Just before the introduction, the other mayors arrived. They were all introduced except me. This was the slip-up that was supposed to be avoided. Besides, it was a lousy show and we had spent an hour waiting for it to start. As the introductions were broadcast nationwide on television and I was shown along with the other mayors, many of my friends back home asked why I was not introduced. I think they were as mad as I was at having Tucson omitted, at least they expressed their dismay.

The meetings of the American Municipal Association dealt in large measure with the struggle the cities, particularly the larger ones, were having with problems encountered by the vast expansion of suburbs at the expense of the central cities. The state legislators, who were controlled by rural interests, failed to recognize these problems and refused to redistrict the states to reflect these changes in voting patterns.

In his speeches, Ben West, Mayor of Nashville, Tennessee, and former president of the Association, often highlighted this problem by saying the pigs and chickens had more voting power in his state than the urban dwellers. It was this imbalance that forced the cities to seek help directly from the federal government.

While partially successful through federal programs designed for the cities, many municipal officials felt that it would not be adequate until they had a representative at the federal cabinet level to represent municipal interests.

This approach was controversial. There were many who felt this approach was a forerunner of the loss of independence by municipal government. The history of this conflict goes back to 1912.

The creation of the Department of Urban Affairs was first presented by Philip Kates in an article for the *American City* in 1912. "Municipal government has been our national failure" and he urged Congress to create a department that would study municipal conditions in the United States.

Thomas P. Coogan, former President of the National Association of Home Builders in 1953, called for the elevation of the Housing and Home Finance Administration to cabinet status.

Mayors did not get into the act until 1955 when Richardson Dilworth, Mayor of Philadelphia and newly elected President of the American Municipal Association, urged the delegates to endorse the idea of a Department of Urban Affairs. They refused. In 1957 the President's Advisory Commission on Intergovernmental Relations reported that a Department of Urban Affairs was greatly needed and suggested that HHFA be the basis for it. Congressman Albert Rains of Alabama introduced a bill to accomplish this. The Eisenhower administration was not receptive.

I had completed my term as President of the National League of Cities in December 1961 when my term as Mayor of Tucson expired.

Genee's Christmas Letter, 1960:

It was fun for us to host the 20 mayors, wives and directors of State Leagues who were here in February for the Executive Committee Meeting of the American Municipal Association, and then, the League of Arizona Cities and Towns Convention in April. It was fun for Don and Genee to attend the executive committee meeting of the Alaska Travel Promotion Association in April, too. What a wonderful meeting traveling up the Inland Passage from Juneau to Skagway, Sitka and Ketchican — delicious meals, good company, deck-side meetings, no telephone.

The summer Park season had its ups and downs. Sporadic travel, construction dislocations, a disappointing management, a fire which burned down one cabin balanced out the new duplexes built at Drakesbad and the ten new housekeeping units at Manzanita Lake. For the children, though, it was a good summer with swimming, horseback riding, and lots of visiting.

The earlier school year was not greeted with enthusiasm. Donna, a young lady of 5 feet 3-1/2 inches, is in an accelerated program at Junior High and still brings home an almost perfect report. Diane is all girl, dressing up and primping. Her feet not quite on the ground, she is still a "B" average student. We wish we could say the same for Cliff — a happy fourth grader who is thrilled to be playing school football (runnerup in city championship). He's been served notice — better grades or no football. Charlene is our self-reliant second grader — delightfully matter of fact, observant, and logical. Her prize remark came when Don announced he was working out the financial arrangements to take over the Glacier National Park operation: "I'll help you, Daddy. You can have my dollar and thirty cents"! We're all happy about this.

Fall was busy with Don attending the Inter-American Congress in San Diego as chairman of the U.S. delegation, with working on the successful passage of six Tucson Charter Changes and our electioneering for Kennedy (Don was asked to serve on his Urban Affairs Committee). Tucson's grown from 45,000 in 1950 to 212,000 in 1960 and we're keeping our fingers crossed as its being considered for the All American City Award.

On November 30, Don and Genee left to attend the International Congress of Local Authorities in Tel Aviv, Israel, Don as chairman of the U.S. delegation.

We were greeted, wined, dined, toured and shown so much. It was a wonderful trip. We returned to New York in time for the American Municipal Association Conference. In the absence of the President, Don presided at the sessions and at the close of the convention was elected president for the coming year.

All this makes us realize we have been particularly fortunate with all the privileges of an American family.

❋ ❋ ❋

14

Mount McKinley National Park Company

As IF I was not busy enough, the National Park Service requested that I take over the concession operations in Mt. McKinley National Park, Alaska.

George Collins, whom I met at Grand Canyon, reported as a permanent ranger and was subsequently promoted to the Washington office. He was then sent to Alaska to plan the development of a park which would enable them to provide for visitors to Alaska. During Secretary of the Interior Harold L. Ickes' regime, he insisted that the National Park Service provide hotel facilities in Mt. McKinley National Park to serve visitors on the Alaska Railway, a wholly owned subsidiary of the Department of the Interior.

Pursuant to this request, Tom Vint, National Park Service, was sent to Alaska with instructions to build a hotel and have it available for the summer season. It was to be a rush job. Tom was told not to return until the hotel was completed. As a result, he found some old blueprints for another hotel which he took to McKinley Park and had the hotel built in accordance with these plans. It was obvious the plans had not been designed specifically for Alaska, but they did provide overnight facilities for visitors to the park, most of whom arrived by Alaska Railroad.

George Collins wrote me a number of times trying to entice me to come to Alaska to be the concessioner. My concept of Alaska was sled dogs and year-round snow, and as I had no money, I declined.

In 1957 I received a letter from Duane Jacobs, superintendent of the park. He said he understood I was to attend the Superintendents' Conference in Yellowstone and that he would like to present some figures to me for the purpose of encouraging me to take over the concessions in Mt. McKinley National Park. It appeared that a man named Lawson had been the concessioner but had gone into bankruptcy. I agreed to meet with the superintendent in Yellowstone after the conference.

Genee and I went to Yellowstone, taking our two daughters, Donna and Diane, with us. Because I was involved in a number of affairs, representing the Conference of National Park Concessioners at the Superintendents' Conference, Daggett Harvey and his wife, Jean, took the two girls under their care. They had a wonderful time. I do not know exactly how it came about, but Daggett was called "Dagwood" and Jean was called "Blondie" by the two children. They all seemed to thoroughly enjoy each other's company.

I met with Duane Jacobs, who showed me that the traffic to Mt. McKinley National Park had increased very substantially to a total of 25,000 for the season since the opening of the Richardson Highway. The superintendent convinced me that I should come to Alaska and look over the operation, as they were very anxious to get a regular concessioner. After Lawson went into bankruptcy, the Park Service had engaged National Park Concessions, Inc. as the operator. National Park Concessions did not have a contract except to operate the existing facilities on a temporary basis until a regular concessioner could be located.

The operation was losing about $50,000 a year. The government was paying National Park Concessions for their services and picking up the tab for the losses.

Upon my return to Tucson, I called Al Donau, who was in Lassen, and told him to get ready to go to Alaska with me. Al did not question what for; when his wife Frankie asked him why he was going, he said didn't know, but I had asked him and that was enough for him. We secured tickets on Alaska Airlines and started for McKinley.

Alaska Airlines at that time carried very few passengers; in fact, they had taken out all the seats from the aircraft and we sat on, or for the most part slept on, the cargo in the ship.

When we arrived in Alaska, we were met by Sam King, who informed us that Superintendent Jacobs had been transferred and that he, Sam, was the acting superintendent. He took us in a four-wheel-drive vehicle to see a portion of the park. As I recall, this was around November and there were about six inches of snow on the ground. We were intrigued with the wildlife which abounded, mostly caribou. Sam showed us the hotel and the facilities, which included a dormitory for employees and a powerhouse that generated all the electricity used by the hotel.

We then took the Alaska Railroad back to Anchorage. There we learned an the Alaska Airline flight would be leaving in a few hours and that there would not be another trip to the lower 48 states until two days later. We immediately went to the airfield where the flight was in the process of departing. The girl who sold the tickets also helped with the loading and we had difficulty finding her. We finally located her, but she refused to sell us tickets on the basis that it was too late and she did not have time. This would have meant a three-day delay. Al went out onto the runway and stood in front of the aircraft, signaling to the pilot that we wanted to board. The pilot called the girl and told her to issue us tickets, so we finally caught the plane back to Seattle.

Several days later we went to the Regional Office in San Francisco to negotiate a contract for the concession. All the facilities to continue operation were in place, but the financial record was a miserable one.

Lawrence C. Merriam was the Regional Director and conducted most of the negotiations. I do not recall who exactly was there from the Washington office to participate in negotiations with Al and me. We finally came to agreement on terms, but only after my refusal to take over the expense of running the powerhouse to heat the hotel during the winter. This was a source of most of the losses of the operation. Because the hotel had been erected hastily and without regard to a method of draining the facilities, it had to be kept heated to avoid frozen pipes. In fact, one year they did not drain it and it cost about $50,000 to break into the walls and repair all the broken pipes in order to get the operation going again.

I told them I would not agree to pay the cost of heating the hotel for a three-year period. The Park Service could not understand this reservation and wanted to know why I wanted to postpone it. I explained I wanted enough time to determine what could be done to cut down the heating bills. They did not see that I could save where they had not been able to. I told them that was the basis on which I would take the concession operations, and so they agreed.

That summer I made inquiries and talked with the power plant operator as to the method for heating the hotel. It soon developed that there had been no attempt to control the circulation system, and that one part of the hotel would be down to 50 degrees and another up to 80 degrees. As the wind came primarily out of the north, the north wing was the one in which the temperature dropped so low. I contacted the 3M Company in Minneapolis and secured temperature gauges with high and low recordings. I put one of these on each floor in each wing of the hotel to ascertain where the temperature loss was serious and where we were unnecessarily heating the hotel.

When I had this information, I made arrangements to change the circulation so that those areas that had reasonable temperatures would not call for any heat, while those that were dropping rapidly would call for heat in that section of the hotel. In this manner, I was over several years able to reduce the cost to one-third of what the government had been paying. I did this slowly by dropping the temperature five degrees at a time. When I got down to 55 degrees, the Park Service objected to me going any lower on the basis that if they had a breakdown in the powerhouse they would not have enough time to make repairs and to prevent damage to the hotel. I informed the Park Service that if they were going to participate in the decisions, then they would have to participate in the winter cost. We finally agreed that each would pay half of the winter cost of heating and as we had already reduced it by two-thirds, the government did not find this objectionable.

We had an operation that had just gone through bankruptcy and we found credit hard to establish. People did not differentiate between the previous bankrupt concessioner and ourselves. This became critical when we wanted to erect a new service station and store. We finally solved the problem by going to Standard Oil Company of California. It had been the practice of Standard Oil to advance money for service station operations in the parks in exchange for agreement to utilize their products.

We built a new service station and then took what

should have been the grease rack and turned it into a grocery store. This was a very handy unit, in that many people who were camping came by truck or car and as they stopped for gasoline, they were also able to purchase any needed supplies.

Our contract included transportation facilities to take the visitors into the park on sightseeing tours. The equipment was deplorable, so we had the job of financing new buses. Regular buses were out of the question, as they were running about $65,000 to $75,000 each, and we needed three of them. We solved the problem by getting in touch with the Bluebird Bus Company in Phoenix, Arizona. This is the company that builds a great number of school buses. We had three bus bodies built and bought Chevrolet chassis to provide our transportation services. These operated very well. Each bus would hold about 22 passengers.

Our sightseeing trip went into the park approximately 65 miles to Point Eilsen where the government had built a visitor center. The tours had to be coordinated with Alaska Railroad. The train would leave Anchorage at 8:00 o'clock in the morning and arrive at noontime at McKinley Park. The people would then be taken to the hotel, where they would spend the night. The following morning they would take the tour bus trip into the park, returning in time to pick up the train which left McKinley Park Hotel shortly after noon to go to Fairbanks, Alaska.

If the people were to get an opportunity to see the wildlife in this park, they had to get out early. This was also important in that the clouds started generating around Mount Denali (McKinley) early in the day and if one did not get out early enough, the mountain would be obscured. As a result, we would get the people up at 3:30 a.m. and the bus tour would start at 4:30 a.m., after a full Alaskan breakfast of sourdough pancakes, bacon, eggs and coffee, returning to the hotel in time to catch the noon train.

This sounds like a terrible schedule, and to some people it was, but the fact that there were 24 hours of daylight in Alaska during the summertime, made it seem less objectionable. I was always uneasy about our transportation services as the road was extremely narrow, particularly Polychrome Pass, where a mishap could take a bus down 1,000 feet into the riverbed. We never had a serious accident, although there was one when a bus driver went to sleep and ran off the road. The bus turned on its side and injured a few people, none of them seriously. Fortunately, in our 15 years of operation, this was the only accident we had, although I was always apprehensive with our young drivers.

Al and I would rotate going to Alaska to check the operations, each of us making from two to three trips during the summer. This was minimal at best in that we were attempting to operate the facilities from some 2,000 miles away. We had a number of managers; the one who spent the most time with us was Wally Cole. On one occasion we had manager problems and sent Ken and Mary Tibbet up to be the managers. Ken Tibbet had been our maintenance man at Lassen and operated the ski tow during the off-season, which included a small lunch counter at the Ski Chalet. This turned out to be a mistake, as Ken never really wanted to go back to work after he had a taste of management. After that he thought he should only supervise and never do any physical work himself. Years later we were to hire Ken again as head of maintenance for Glacier Park, Inc. and the tragedy that resulted therefrom is detailed under the Glacier operation.

Chuck West, an experienced Alaskan bush pilot, dropped out of flying to set up Westours in order to sell Alaska. Chuck was a very progressive individual with a tremendous amount of drive. He was often rather arrogant in his approach and indicated to us that if we would not agree to pay Westours 15 percent (the normal was 10 percent) on our tours, he would not handle them, nor would he put McKinley Park in his tour brochure. Chuck also controlled some of the accommodations in Fairbanks and Anchorage, two terminal points in Alaska. He had difficulty getting accommodations for his tours and so arranged to provide his own by building a couple of large motels. This posed a problem for us, but we decided to see the thing through and in the Alaska Travel Association brochure we had a big picture of Mt McKinley. We took a double spread in the center section with the heading at the top:

**IF YOU HAVEN'T SEEN McKINLEY PARK,
YOU HAVEN'T SEEN ALASKA**

Mt. McKinley National Park was one of the main attractions in Alaska. This brought Chuck around and we began working together. In fact, I was elected to the Alaska Travel Promotion Association Board of Directors. Al Donau followed me on the board. Chuck West, of course, was also a member of the board, and this gave us an opportunity to exchange views. We had a number of interesting trips in which we laid plans for the promotion of Alaska in the following years. The most memorable one was on the Glacier Star, which was a ship owned by Chuck. We took the Inland Passage up to Glacier Bay and returned, holding our meetings aboard the ship. It was a very pleasant experience and we ironed out a lot of difficulties that we had encountered with Chuck and some of the old-timers in Alaska.

In 1970, along with a wave of employee discontent throughout the country, the employees of Mt. McKinley National Park Company reached a peak of criticism of the National Park Service and of the McKinley Park Company, writing an extensive report which they distributed to travel agents and others. Among other things, their principal concern was the danger posed by a frame hotel, which did not have many of the modern devices for control of fire.

There was an alarm system established in the hotel, which sounded throughout the building if and when temperatures raised to a dangerous degree. It was pointed out that the building was not only isolated, but empty during long Alaska winters, which had a drying effect on the lumber in the building. The employees took it upon themselves to write an extensive report condemning both the National Park Service and the McKinley Park concessioner.

They said they had been alerted to the danger through meetings with management calling attention to their responsibility not only in preventing fires, but in arranging for evacuation of the building in the event of fire.

Employees were critical of the number of people housed in the hotel and the fact that they were mostly elderly people, which would make evacuation difficult. They were extremely critical of the Mt. McKinley Park Service, saying that they were morally negligent. They took their complaints to the Park Service, who advised them that there was a lack of appropriate funds to make all of the recommended improvements and that they felt nothing could be done without providing for a totally new building. This did not satisfy the employees and they embarked upon a program of vilification and charges of negligence.

The criticisms were not only directed to the hazards that were entailed with a possible fire in the hotel, but the Park Service's arrangements for the disposal of sewage as well. Employees claimed this was an ecological disaster and that great dangers existed.

The result was an investigation by the National Park Service, with some recommendations for rectifying those conditions that could be accomplished under the circumstances. This did not satisfy the employees and the more radical ones recommended that they put cement in the toilet bowls and slash the tires on the buses, cut the fire-fighting hoses, etc. Fortunately, a saner group of employees took control and prevented the vandalism that the more radical group had contemplated. There is no question that there was a fire hazard in the hotel, but nothing more dangerous than existed in many public buildings in Alaska. While this does not justify it, the problem facing the Park Service was the lack of appropriated funds to provide a new structure. The structure, of course, was owned by the National Park Service and it was the government's responsibility to take what action was necessary to provide a safe building.

There were also numerous piddling types of complaints, such as that female employees had access to a telephone in the hall of their housing facilities and men did not; that the contracts were vague, referring to the fact that we required orderly conduct in the dormitories and that men had to be clean-shaven; that waitresses were provided a complete uniform, while the waiters were only supplied shirts and jackets and had to supply their own trousers; that the company required a $25.00 deposit with their application as insurance that employees would report for work, and if they were a no-show, the deposit was forfeited (deposits would be refunded in the event of a 30-day notice, which allowed us time to secure a replacement).

The Park Service sent a couple of rangers to make an

investigation and their report was so sloppy that I made a 15-page report to John Rutter, the Regional Director of the National Park Service, Northwest Region. My report was accepted and that was the last I heard of the numerous complaints.

It turned out that a few agitators wrote the complaint and then submitted it to the employees as a whole for endorsement. Some of the employees refused to endorse it while others endorsed parts of it, and the nonagitators finally prevailed.

As we were getting short of space to house the improved visitation to Alaska, I arranged for the addition of a prefabricated 50-room unit and a lobby to the hotel. Our contract prevented us from adding to the building, since we could receive no possessory interest in the structure. We made arrangements to build the addition separately, and it was joined only by a long closed passageway to the original building.

Construction in Alaska is difficult at best, and most expensive. I contacted Gene Zanck in Spokane, Washington, as I was told he was an excellent builder of prebuilt structures. Gene Zanck had worked for Boise Cascade Company but had decided to go out on his own. He was anxious to get started and welcomed the opportunity to build these units for Alaska. Each room was built separately and then joined together with an aisleway down the middle and a roof over the top. The fact that they were built individually meant that each room had a double wall, which made for a very solid structure.

The next problem was how we were to get them to Alaska and erect them in motel-type form. We solved this by shipping the units by train to Seattle, then loading them on barges to go to the rail head at Seward, Alaska. We then put these units on the Alaska Railroad to take into Mckinley Park. We purchased all the furniture to furnish each room and put them in the units so that the entire structure could be sent in one shipment.

In order to prepare for the arrival of these units, we had to get a contractor to do the foundation. This was rather difficult to arrange, as there was a considerable amount of permafrost in the area and we had to be sure that we could get in a place where the permafrost would not crush the foundation during the wintertime. This had occurred during construction of the McKinley Park Hotel and the building had to be supported by huge timbers to hold the foundations in place.

We built the units, or rather assembled them, in McKinley Park and put the roof on.

They were attractive units and solidly built so that they were better than the units we were renting in the McKinley Park Hotel. We assembled and erected these units $5,000 per room, which had been shipped up completely furnished. This was unheard of in Alaska.

In the meantime, George Fleharty had contacted me for the purpose of merging the Alaska/Lassen and Glacier units with U.S. Natural Resources, an organization that was interested in expanding into the recreational field.

We had met George through his association with the Redding Chamber of Commerce, where he was the staff director. George introduced me to Robert Katz, the head of U.S. Natural Resources, and we started negotiations.

U.S. Natural Resources had been expanding rather rapidly and, as I was to learn to my sorrow later, was not equipped to handle all the recreational facilities they were attempting to acquire. They had acquired 38 percent of the stock of Yosemite Park & Curry Company from George Fleharty. Fleharty, who had owned the Ice Follies and a hockey club in Canada, had sold out and had four million dollars in cash. George then tendered for stock to the owners of Yosemite Park & Curry Company, but had acquired only 38 percent of the stock when his money ran out. He then took U.S. Natural Resources stock in exchange for his Yosemite stock.

At the same time, I had come to agreement with Bob Katz on the exchange of stock on Lassen National Park Company and Mt. McKinley National Park Company. The exchange was made on the basis of $30.00 per share for U.S. Natural Resources stock. The agreement was that I was to head up the Recreational Division of U.S. Natural Resources and, as part of the assignment, was to reorganize Yosemite Park & Curry Company as they were slipping financially.

When the exchange of Lassen and McKinley parks was consummated, I moved to Menlo Park, California, which was the headquarters of U.S. Natural Resources. In the interim U.S. Natural Resources had been attempting to get some changes made in the Yosemite Park & Curry Company, but the existing board of directors was adamant that they were not going to give up direction and control of the company to U.S. Natural Resources.

As U.S. Natural Resources succeeded to George Fleharty's 38-percent position, control remained in the old board.

While I had turned over control of Mt. McKinley National Park Company through the transfer of stock to U.S. Natural Resources, I was still responsible for the operations in Alaska, as I held the position of vice president in charge of national park activities.

As U.S. Natural Resources' fortunes began to deteriorate, it was apparent to most of us in the operation that there was trouble ahead. George Fleharty was particularly disgruntled and convinced the Shasta Telecasting Company to buy the McKinley Park operation. The head of Shasta Telecasting had been given his first job by George Fleharty. A deal was made whereby U.S. Natural Resources sold the McKinley Park operation for a million dollars and assumed a debt of $300,000. I will never quite understand this deal, as I cannot see how the National Park Service agreed to this sale since practically all of the physical structures were owned by the government.

This sale was a sore point with Al Donau, as he had a third interest, and to have received some stock from U.S. Natural Resources only to have the facilities sold for $1,300,000 really aggravated him. It disturbed him to the extent that he threatened to sue U.S. Natural Resources, so I arranged a meeting between John Del Favero, who had taken Bob Katz's position as president. The meeting was held at Rex Ranch with Al, Frankie, John Del Favero and myself. At that time Del Favero agreed to pay Al $25,000 a year for five years to avoid any litigation. I think Del Favero felt that U.S. Natural Resources was on shaky ground and if one suit was started there would be a series of suits.

I did not join in this as I had elected to work with U.S. Natural Resources and to reestablish their national park operations, particularly the Yosemite Park & Curry Company, to a profitable status. As I look back, this was probably a mistake, as we had made the deal with U.S. Natural Resources for Lassen and McKinley stock on the basis of $30.00 value for U.S. Natural Resources stock. The final result was that we settled for an average of $5.00 per share. This was the most disastrous financial decision I have ever made and the effect was to lose the two companies: Lassen and McKinley.

My justification for the exchange of stock was that this would give my heirs some security with the opportunity to sell stock to pay my estate taxes in the event that anything happened to me. As I was the major stockholder in three national parks, my death could have created havoc, in that those were not liquid assets and if my heirs wanted to convert to cash, they would have needed the cooperation of the National Park Service to sell. I could visualize that the family would be left without anything after a sale to pay the estate taxes. My error was that I did not look more closely into the real status of U.S. Natural Resources.

The organization was adept at putting together, through mergers, a potentially profitable conglomerate; however, they were short on operational experience and had expanded the corporation prematurely on debt. When the government clamped down on mergers at the same time interest rates began to skyrocket, U.S. Natural Resources's future was destined. The company was finally bought out by another company through a tender for the stock, which they acquired for $8.00 per share. I had sold most of my shares prior to that time at $3.50 per share, so came out with about an average of $5.00 per share; a disastrous result.

15

My Experience in City Government

Genee's Christmas Letter, 1958:

EXPERIENCE AND the growth of our children have taught us that time is fleeting. Even then we could not believe that the winter holiday season was upon us, had it not been for the unseasonable and unprecedented six inches of snow that blanketed us in Tucson in November. We had not yet forgotten the 110 degree temperatures of July. Hot or cold, the seasons are busy ones for us, and we're delighted to say happy ones.

Don's activities usually start with a morning breakfast meeting on taxes, aviation, or some municipal problem, followed by a welcoming talk to some convention group, appointments until noon, a luncheon talk, conferences, endless and persistent telephone calls, a legal matter or two, a banquet and ball in the evening with the usual requisite, "a few words from the mayor." He says it's real hard to say welcome twenty different ways in a week.

The City took its next step toward meeting its growth problem by voting a $15 million bond issue. Don had no more than completed his term as president of the League of Arizona Cities than he filed for the Attorney General's race. Many of the voters must have felt the same as our son Cliff, who said he wouldn't vote for his daddy if we had to leave Tucson, as Don got the experience and one of the other candidates got the nomination. During the campaign he took time to travel to and address the Washington, California and the Utah Municipal Leagues.

Genee's spring involved a stint on Superior Court jury duty where she had the fascinating but frustrating experience of serving on two hung juries (one civil, one criminal). In addition to her regular civic and child activities she especially enjoyed giving a report on a wonderful book about the sky, weather and flight named "Song of the Sky" by Guy Murchie. It must have been good as she was asked to repeat it at a session sponsored by the Y.W.C.A.

Summer found her and the children at beloved Drakesbad. A manager and his wife shared some of the burden she shouldered alone last year. Separation of our family during the summer was our greatest sacrifice. Each year Drakesbad takes on a greater meaning for the children. Cliff, now seven, fishes, swims and rides with a greater degree of freedom. Donna, ten, Diane, nine, enjoyed the experienced of sleeping in tents with their cousins, the start of a real enjoyment of the great out-of-doors. Charlene, five, swims like a fish and is still our pixie, independent, not-much-longer baby. All the children are looking forward to a trip to Mt. McKinley National Park, Alaska. Don organized a company and signed a contract with the National Park Service to conduct the concession operations in Mt. McKinley.

Right after the election we left for Alaska. Genee's mother stayed with the children as all are in school now (5th, 4th, 2nd and kindergarten). We were thrilled with Alaska's magnificent fall coloring and we marveled until we ran out of superlatives. The MckInley Park Hotel is a large, flat roofed wooden structure, surprisingly modern with its self-sustaining power plant, dining room, laundry, and with rail service only a quarter of a mile away. There is more of a feeling of wilderness at Drakesbad than at the hotel site in McKinley.

Once out of sight of the hotel, the wilderness is apparent. The sweep of the mountain ranges, the large, broad valleys, the grayish movement of the glacial streams, moderated and heightened by a vast expanse of the brilliant colors of the tundra, makes Alaska a place of beauty in the fall.

As this is written, we are looking forward to a trip to historic Boston and the annual meeting of the American Municipal Association. We hope to return via Sarasota, Florida to visit the Dorts, partners in the Lassen venture.

Once again Don is faced with a decision: to run for a third term as mayor, or to step out. The prospect of more time for private and family affairs was enticing, but a visit by sixteen civic leaders turned the scales and he's in the race for another two year term.

❊ ❊ ❊

When we went into office, the city boundaries encompassed only 14 square miles and about 50,000 people. At the close of my administration, Tucson had increased from 261st to the 54th largest city in the United States. Our assessed valuation had increased from $46 million to $183.8 million; the per capita cost for services decreased from $70 to $60. The area had increased to 72 square miles and the population to 220,000 people. The city boundaries when we took office were Speedway on the north and Country Club on the east. We encountered considerable opposition to annexation, particularly from the Homebuilders Association. They had great animosity for the city inspection staff and did not want to have to go through city inspections for approval of their housing programs. This opposition lasted for several years of our term, but we finally convinced them that we were responsible in responding by modernizing our Inspection Department and consequently finally had their support for annexation.

I am afraid I had too many irons in the fire at one time. I had been elected Mayor of Tucson in 1955, while trying to expand my law practice. The mayor's position was considered part-time, and the position only paid $200 per month. It turned out to be the fullest full-time job I ever experienced! In 1956 I was elected President of the League of Arizona Cities and Towns and to the National Board of the American Municipal Association, subsequently named the National League of Cities.

Simultaneously I was trying to keep up with the Lassen development and manage the Drakesbad operation. My family had grown to four children; ages two to seven, without my income expanding proportionally. Had I not participated in buying and selling real estate, I could not have made it.

If I neglected any of these activities, I am ashamed to say, it was probably my family. The only compensating factor was my opportunity to be with them parts of the summers in the national parks.

I paid a big price for this neglect, as I never established the rapport I should have with my son, Cliff, during his impressionable years. By the time he was in his teens and away at school, the opportunity had been lost. I feel that this contributed to his untimely death — too big a price to pay for public service.

My administration of the city government, which lasted from my election as mayor in 1955 through December of 1961, was a period of great change. It marked the greatest growth in the history of the City of Tucson. The net effect was to convert a village to a city. This put great pressure on both the administrative structure of the city, which had to be reorganized, and the need to finance these changes. The expansion of the city boundaries increased the requirements for new buildings and expanded services for this larger city. Most importantly, it took political courage by the city council as people resist change, and changes are accomplished over opposition and often with political retribution.

The mayor and council worked very closely together and it was through this cooperation that so much was accomplished for the city. There was one exception and that was James Kirk, a councilman whose ambition to be mayor often overruled his judgment. He was a constant source of irritation and discord. Many of the programs we had planned for the city manager were delayed through his opposition and pressure on city management. He attempted to profit politically on the discontent and problems that arose out of the changes.

One of these was the purchase of the San Pedro water sites when he claimed the mayor and city manager had withheld information. He was censured for this by the council. This was only the tip of the iceberg and did not reveal the loss of time and effort that occurred as a result of his destructive tactics designed to give him publicity and enhance his chances to be mayor of the City of Tucson.

While there were occasional intrusions of partisan politics, for the most part all the council members cooperated to advance the city's welfare. One man I want to mention particularly because he was from the Republican contingent and the Democrats controlled the council. Ray Weaver showed real statesmanship and was often the swing vote in politically sensitive situations. Ray always managed to vote for and support those programs he felt were in the best interests of the city. He should be given great credit. He paid a price, as he was often under pressure from members of his own party to play a political role.

A measure of credit must go to Porter Homer, our city manager, who not only was well grounded in city organization and structure, but was a tireless worker and cooperated fully with the council. Through his long association with city government, he brought to the mayor and council an insight and understanding that many of us did not possess. We were also blessed with having selected some outstanding attorneys to serve as city attorney for Tucson. Whitey Neubauer, who came to the West for health reasons, suffering badly from asthma and emphysema, was a fine attorney and provided excellent service in revamping city ordinances to respond to areas of change. After Whitey's death, Jack Marks was made the city attorney. As anyone familiar with activities in Tucson knows, Jack Marks was an exceptional attorney, possessing good legal training and judgment. He went on to become a Superior Court Judge in Tucson, after leaving our administration.

It would not be a complete picture if we did not outline some of the major changes we made as the city grew from a small village status of 14 square miles and 50,000 people to 72 square miles and 220,000 people. This expansion was accomplished in roughly four years. We solidified our expansion in the next two and a half years, but had to leave some projects uncompleted. Such rapid growth and the necessity to provide first class services for the expanded areas not only put pressure on each of the city departments, but required a great capital program. In our annexation program, we promised the new citizens in the incorporated areas full city services. I believe in large measure we accomplished this.

We adopted a major capital improvement program. This had many ramifications. As an example, we had only a main library, which was built in 1916. There were no branch libraries in the city and as the city grew, it became more and more difficult for people who wished to patronize the library to have access to it. We expanded the downtown library and proposed three branches. Bill Matthews threatened to oppose our entire improvement program if we did not reduce the number of branch libraries to one. As a result, we dropped two of them and constructed only the Himmel Park Branch.

Another necessary requirement for a growing city, if it is to provide the essential space and recreational facilities in a first class city, is to acquire large tracts of land for future parks and other public buildings. We did this in Tucson in our capital improvement program. The first requirement, of course, was to expand and improve the existing parks. We expanded a regional park on the south side. We called it a regional park as it would serve several areas and was larger than a neighborhood park, with more diverse opportunities. We also added swimming pools to two existing parks; one at Del Norte Park and one at Menlo Park.

A major effort was made to improve and expand the facilities at Randolph Park, which is the city's major park. We planned and started construction of an additional 18-hole golf course. This would provide a total of 36 holes of golf. In order to make better use of the facilities, we also erected a club house on the property on Alvernon. We then leased the facility to the private sector for operation.

It is essential that fire stations be appropriately located. In fact, the locations of fire stations have a tremendous bearing on insurance rates. The basic rate is established by an agency that represents the insurance companies. If you do not comply exactly with their standard, all the homes and businesses pay a premium rate. During our administration we built four new fire stations, in addition to renting facilities for temporary stations in some of the newly annexed areas. This, of course, required the addition of equipment and we added four new fire trucks and accepted bids on two more. Fire equipment is an expensive initial capital outlay, but the equipment can be used for years.

The enlarged city required additional sewage plant capacity. In order to respond we built a new plant. As as soon as it was in operation we closed the old one, modernized it, and put it back into service. When the new plant went into operation, a truck went off the road, breaking down a power line that served it.

The result was that raw sewage was going into the Santa Cruz River. One woman became irate and started calling me at home at one o'clock in the morning. She called me every half hour complaining about the stench and asking what I was going to do about it. I explained that it was a temporary situation which had occurred, not as a result of our negligence, but because a truck had knocked over the power pole which supplied the plant with electricity. She did not accept this, and after about five calls, I finally took the telephone off the receiver. She obviously intended to harass me for the entire night. This kind of experience exemplifies the problems local authorities are subjected to. The people you are serving can reach you at any time of the day or night and are not at all bashful about complaining.

We felt that the public should have access to their representatives so we refused to have an unlisted number.

City Hall, which we occupied, was built in 1916, and except for our improvement and expansion of the second floor, nothing had been done prior to our administration. Even with the expanded facilities, we were having difficulty, due to the enlarged city. We held a competition for architects to submit plans for a new City Hall. The council approved the plans submitted by the architectural firm of Friedman and Jobusch. We then approved and provided the funds for the first stage of construction. We didn't have the money to build the total structure. We built the basement and the first two floors and the building was completed under subsequent administrations. The city jail was in the basement of the old building and this soon became over-crowded, so we built a new farm jail, where we could retain inmates who were not considered dangerous. We erected a minimum security building, surrounded by a security fence.

All of these expansions strained our communication facilities, so we had to establish and erect a central communications system. These new buildings to house the facilities vastly improved our ability to administer the various programs in the city.

The communications system gave us the opportunity to communicate, but did not solve the problem of getting to and from various facilities. That required opening, widening and improving streets. We started with the downtown area. At this time, we enforced an old agreement the Tucson Gas and Electric Power Company had made with the city to take down all the electric power lines and put their facilities underground so as to improve the esthetics of the downtown area. Though agreed to many years before, nothing had ever been done. We insisted on compliance with the previous agreement.

Another facet of the improvement of the streets was a new sign ordinance, which was essential if we were to enhance our beautification program. All this had an impact on zoning and we found ourselves faced with the problem of revising the zoning regulations for the entire city. This was accomplished but with considerable controversy.

In addition to a capital improvement program and improvement of existing facilities, we wanted to define a program to accommodate the future of our city. We adopted a general land use plan, attempting to anticipate where the development would be and the nature of use to be made of the land. A master plan was adopted designating the location of future schools, recreational and park areas, fire stations, community buildings and so forth. This was our contribution to the future — an attempt to guide orderly expansion of our fast-growing city.

One facet was a road plan for future streets and particularly to assure that they were wide enough to respond to the growth that we knew would come. Developers were establishing residential and commercial developments that did not provide for adequate rights of way. We insisted that before plans for construction would be approved, adequate rights of way would be deeded to the city or the county. We had excellent cooperation from the County Board of Supervisors in insisting on the need of developers to recognize public requirements. In this way we saved the future city government millions of dollars that would have been required to acquire rights of way to expand the streets or provide neighbor hood parks, in accordance with a modern city.

We also attempted to lay out a plan for arterial ways within the city which would take most of the arterial traffic out of the neighborhoods. We proposed a freeway which would parallel the Southern Pacific Railroad along the old Butterfield Route which the pioneers used in the early days of Tucson. Intercepting this freeway would be a beltway which would be in the nature of a parkway adjacent and paralleling the Pantano and Rillito Rivers.

It is a matter of tremendous disappointment that subsequent administrations did not follow through with this plan and, as of 1987, the community is still fighting over whether or not the freeway and parkways should be constructed. Through this delay, the city streets are bearing a disproportionate share of the traffic, which should be served by freeways which would give access to the eastern and northern parts of the city. The cost of doing those now will have increased many thousands of percent because the city councils have permitted construction adjacent to the railroad and to the riverways. These areas are flood-prone and will result in untold damage in the future. We are paying a big price for the timidity of our city fathers.

Another major construction program was the design and widening of Broadway to six lanes, with a center median which we beautified by planting grass, palm trees and other plants. Councilman Phelps referred to Broadway as Hummel's Folly. He thought it was too large a street for Tucson. I do not know what he thinks of it now! Broadway was bottlenecked downtown by an underpass which was one lane each way, and it was so extensive and without proper ventilation, that if a car got stalled, carbon monoxide gas endangered the lives of anybody stuck in the underpass.

The problem arose out of the fact that the railroad had some 18 tracks above the underpass. I met with Southern Pacific people on a number of occasions. They were most difficult to deal with. They took the position that street improvement was totally the responsibility of the city and imposed no obligations on them. In a session with Southern Pacific Railroad President, D. J. Russell, I pointed out that the long tunnel imposed a safety problem in that the number of tracks the railroad company maintained prevented us from building a more open underpass. I asked for their cooperation in reducing the number of tracks to enable us to modernize the underpass. President Russell said he did not think safety was the railway's responsibility. I pointed out that they erected crossing signs in the countryside where roads crossed over the railroad. I said, "Don't you believe that this is a recognition of your responsibility to help insure safety?" He said, "Those crossing signs were put there so as not to frighten the horses as they approached the railroad." They did finally agree to reduce the number of tracks when it was pointed out that this would make available some very valuable land for lease or sale to the private sector. The 18 tracks were reduced to four, which enabled us to modernize and open up the Broadway subway which was essential if Broadway was to become a major thoroughfare. We planned it and the subsequent administrations constructed it.

Speedway was another major problem. It had been erected with federal funds as a farm-to-market road. In those days they required that a hump be erected in the middle. Even though this had long ceased to be a farm-to-market road, we encountered great difficulty in attempting to modernize this street. We finally succeeded by taking out the central hump and putting in a modern divider. The businessmen along Speedway were very desirous of improving the facilities and appearance of the street. They approved a street lighting program wherein the cost of the lights would be assessed against the property owners. Cecil Gaver was a property owner on Speedway and spent hours of his time in getting the cooperation of other owners for the beautification and improvement program. The improvements were finally made; the hump was removed, the dividers installed and lights erected. We had an official opening and at the same time changed the name Speedway Street to Speedway Boulevard. It was a happy day for the property owners on Speedway. But time marches on and there is a new plan to widen Speedway at great cost.

I have previously discussed the problem of the acquisition of private water companies and expansion of the city water system. One day I received a phone call from the head of the Central Arizona Project Committee, asking me and the city council to meet with them in Phoenix for a briefing on the Central Arizona Project. During the briefing they indicated that they planned to reestablish this project, which had been turned down as too expensive for agricultural support, by changing the financial support base from agricultural to urban. In other words, they could not justify the great cost of building the Project on the basis of fees coming from agricultural use. It would have to be changed to water fees for urban use, which brings a much higher rate. During the discussion it was apparent that there was nothing planned in the revised project to bring water to Tucson, although Tucson was included in the financial support.

I questioned this and was informed that this was designated by the government as a "Central" Arizona project. By bringing Southern Arizona into it, the federal government might take the position that this was an entirely new project which could cause them to lose the opportunity to reestablish and take advantage of all the work that had been done. I said, "Does this mean Tucson is not to be included as a part of this project?" The answer was yes, we would have to rely on the "good faith" of the people who were erecting the Central Arizona Project. We could not become a part of the original program.

I stood up and, speaking to the Tucson council and city manager, said, "Gentlemen, we have heard enough. Let's go home." The committee chairman said, "Sit down, sit down — and we will talk about it." They urged us to stay and discuss the matter further, so we did. We were adamant that they could not use Tucson to support their program unless we were included in the original project. They subsequently agreed that Tucson would be included, with a canal to bring water into this area. Our allocation would be 100,000 acre feet of water per year. With that, Tucson was designated as a part of the Central Arizona Project.

It was sometime later, when I was serving in Washington, D.C., as Assistant Secretary of HUD, that I got a telephone call from Tom Chandler, who was the attorney for some big mining companies. He stated that they were disturbed that the then city council was reluctant to sign a Letter of Intent agreeing to take the 100,000 acre feet of water. They felt the water would be too expensive. Tom asked if I could come out and, if not, at least prepare a statement to be read at the hearing, as the mining community and other organizations were alarmed with the city council's stand. I prepared such a statement and I understand it was presented at the hearing. The council signed the Letter of Intent, saving Tucson's interest in the Central Arizona Project. Now I understand that I am among those who are to be honored for their participation in bringing the Central Arizona Project to fruition.

It was evident that if Tucson was to discharge its obligations of making available what facilities we had in the community, they had to provide an agency through which such information could be disseminated. We established the Tucson Information Center. We also set up an Industrial Development Board as a vehicle to encourage companies to move to Tucson and invest in our community.

This was essential if we were to provide jobs for the people who were moving to the City of Tucson in ever increasing numbers. We had Booz, Allen and Hamilton prepare a plan to help direct Tucson's future.

During this same period of time there was a clamor throughout the United States to protect the rights of minorities. Many businesses discriminated against Blacks, Hispanics and others, but particularly Blacks. They were not allowed to eat in restaurants and at certain lunch counters or get accommodations at hotels or motels. It is difficult now to think that at that late stage, many of the businesses were actively discriminating against Black Americans. They were. In fact, the Woolworth lunch counter would not permit a Black to eat there and many of our hotels and motels denied accommodations to Blacks.

Even though there was discrimination here, we were far in advance of many of the other cities in the United States and particularly those in the south. Sam R. Kaufman, a local haberdasher, was particularly interested in getting a commission created to attempt to rectify these problems of discrimination. Previous mayors and councils declined to act. I was reluctant at first, as we had so many projects going and so many political fights, that I did not want to take on one which I felt would be hard fought with great emotion on both sides. Sam convinced me and I set up the first Human Relations Commission in the State of Arizona.

This committee was very active in attempting to eradicate all forms of racial discrimination. I believe we were quite successful. We had a number of prominent individuals take an active role in the committee urging the mayor and council to take legislative action to eradicate discrimination in our community. One recommendation was that we pass an ordinance which would make it illegal to discriminate by denying accommodations at hotels and motels, refusing to serve food to any individual because of race, creed, color or national origin. The lodging and food industries were up in arms at the prospect of adopting a city ordinance and a committee was formed to represent those interests. Jim Durbin, the manager of the Pioneer Hotel, was the chairman of this committee to fight the adoption of this ordinance. I called him and said I would like to discuss the matter with him and he advised me that a meeting was to be held of the committee representing the accommodation and food services that night at the hotel.

I asked if I could attend and he said he would be pleased if I would.

I attended this meeting and told these individuals I thought it was nearsighted for them to be planning to oppose the eradication of discriminatory activities in the City of Tucson in the conduct of their businesses. They agreed, but stated that they did not want it made a matter of legislation through the city adopting an ordinance. I said I was not wedded to an ordinance, all I wanted to do was accomplish the results of stopping discrimination in our city and particularly in these basic industries. We came to an agreement. If I would withhold the adoption of the ordinance, they promised to get commitments from 100 percent of the owners of all accommodations and food service facilities in Tucson that they would not discriminate. They would need one month to do this. I assured them I would be glad to give them the time, but questioned whether they could get 100 percent, which we reduced to 97 percent, of their people. They said they didn't believe that would be a problem and so I agreed to delay the adoption of the ordinance.

When I announced I was withdrawing the ordinance to give these people a chance to come in with voluntary compliance with the antidiscrimination objectives, I was visited by a great many representatives of minority interests, including many of the people I had appointed to the Human Relations Commission. They held a meeting, which I attended, and tempers were high. They said that this was a mistake, a delaying tactic, and that I was naive in accepting the assurances of compliance by 97 percent.

I stated that we could afford a month for them to prove them selves. Since I was the one who had prepared the ordinance, I intended to be the one to withdraw it to give these people a chance to show that they could get compliance. I said I thought voluntary acceptance was far better than trying to enforce it by law, with all the enforcement problems and the means that could be employed to circumvent the terms of the ordinance. It was a hot meeting!

The following morning I viewed from the window of the mayor's office picket lines around City Hall deploring my withdrawal of the ordinance. I walked out to the picket line and, as I did, all of the pickets surrounded me. I stated that I couldn't understand their objections, as we were going to get voluntary compliance, so why should we go through the process of adopting an ordinance; that this was a much healthier way for a community to stop discrimination practices. We had quite a discussion about whether it was better to get voluntary compliance or by legal enforcement. Finally I said, "Some of you have decided to picket and I recognize that you have a right under the law, as this is an expression of free speech." I added, "This includes the right to make damn fools out of yourselves." I turned and walked away and the picket line broke up and that was the end of the demonstration.

The Food and Lodging Association fulfilled their promise. They got agreement from all but one restaurant. We had accomplished our objective by voluntary compliance.

Another area of great concern was to modernize our rules, regulations and our relations with our employees, to insure that their rights were recognized and protected. This was long overdue, as the growth of the city had left recognition of the responsibilities of our employees far behind. We adopted a group insurance plan, giving the employees protection against the vagaries of unemployment. We also reduced the hours of work for the Fire and Police Departments and equalized a pay scale for similar jobs.

In this modernization we attempted to reduce our expenses by making arrangements with Pima County to take over all the Health Department programs. The city had a Health Department and the county had a Health Department. The merger avoided double taxation for the city residents who were paying for these services through the county and again through the city tax roles. We also joined with the county in a cooperative extension of streets that went beyond the city limits and particularly in the construction of an underpass under the railroad on west Speedway.

Many of these changes required revisions in the City Charter, which did not adequately cover a number of problems we were facing. The first, of course, was the right to levy a one-half of one percent sales tax and the reduction in the property tax rate.

We also consolidated departments by merging many of the functions and clarifying the lines of communication and authority. My administration time was coming to a close, as I had chosen not to run for mayor again so I proposed, and we passed, a City Charter change that would move the election date from April to November and the terms of office from two to four years. This meant that there would be a city election every two years instead of every year and the four-year terms gave some stability to the opera tions of city government. I did not propose this earlier, even though it would have solved a considerable number of problems, as I felt that I would be accused of trying to perpetuate myself in office. By changing the election time from spring to fall, we had to extend our term of office to coordinate with the new elections. As a result, I served as mayor an additional seven months beyond my sixth year.

My recommendation, as we came to the end of our administration in December 1961, was to urge the City of Tucson to include and expand its Municipal Airport so as to respond to the demands of the expanded air age. I also urged the redevelopment of the urban renewal area as a must, if we were to solve the problems of the downtown area and improve the living conditions of those in the nearby-slum areas. I stated that the completion of the Broadway underpass was a most important step to be taken, if the downtown area were to survive. I urged that another important program was to follow up on the water area we had staked out through the purchase of water sites; that it was essential for the life and growth of Tucson that we secure adequate resources for both domestic and industrial use. We also recommended, although it did not occur, that a metropolitan sewage system be operated not by a sanitary district, but by the City of Tucson.

While my service as mayor was ending, the problems and developing of Lassen were continuing.

Lassen was having growing pains and requirements. It was obvious that the small store building at Manzanita Lake which we had in the basement under the dining room, was inadequate and we proposed to the Park Service that we build a store building, which was completed in 1955 at a cost of $90,000. In that same year, we added additional cabins at a cost of $30,000. Two years later, we built a manager's house at a cost of $23,000.

The manager, Al Donau, and his wife Frankie, up to this stage and this time, had been living in one of the housekeeping cabins; not exactly a homelike atmosphere. Then, in 1960 we added some additional cabins and built a repair shop for the maintenance staff. The expansion of the facilities required considerable more attention to the maintenance than the man we had working out of his truck, which was not efficient enough, could supply.

The next year we remodeled the remaining number of cabins at a cost of $5,000. Two years later we built a duplex, and had to provide these new facilities for employees. This cost $10,800. The next year we built a dormitory — our most expensive building, as it cost $105,000. With additional employees requiring to be housed and fed, additional quarters which no longer could be provided in a haphazard manner had to be built. The following year we built new cabins, which cost $68,400. A new service facility was erected in the campgrounds to accommodate those occupying the government campgrounds. It included a small store, showers for the campers and laundry service. In substance, we had, without government request, except for the cafeteria which was never built during the 22 years of service in the park, expended $540,000.

In an attempt to provide himself year-round gainful employment and to retain his position as general manager of the Lassen operation, Al Donau had secured a job as manager of the Rex Guest Ranch in Amado, Arizona. When Rex Hamacker decided he wanted to sell the ranch, we made arrangements to purchase it through the Mt. McKinley operation, and operate it to retain Al's services. This necessitated making arrangements for the operation of the Sulphur Works Ski Operation in Lassen, which Al had managed during the winter off-season. We solved the problem by leasing it to a subconcessioner.

Genee's Christmas Letter, 1959:

The first of the year and the beginning of another Tucson winter season opened with conventions, the Fiesta de los Vaqueros Rodeo, the opening of Rex Guest Ranch just south of Tucson at Amado, and a full scale calendar of meetings at teas, schools, clubs, and organizational gatherings. The reason was twofold: Election time was again at hand and a full scale annexation program was under way.

This was the most ambitious expansion program that had ever been attempted for Tucson. Both projects were successful as Don was reelected Mayor on April 6 for his third term and the annexation was accomplished on March 26th. While successful, both projects were not without opposition. The election had its personal invective and the Annexation is still being fought in the courts. It was not enough to comply with the law, we are having to sustain our position in the courts.

Lassen National Park occupied our summer attention with an extension of cabin facilities at Manzanita Lake and a new kitchen, some cottages, and a new pool schedule for Drakesbad. A new manager at Drakesbad gave Genee relief from managerial duties and time for swimming, riding and picknicking with the children. Practically all meals were eaten outside complicated only by a super-abundance of bees brought out by the warmest, driest summer in 80 years. The stimulation of travel with statehood gave us our best season at McKinley Park. Don made three trips to Alaska during the season taking Donna and Di with him on one of the trips. This was something less than successful as both girls came down with high temperatures and flu with the result that one or the other of them was in bed four days out of the seven day trip. Di didn't even get to see the sled dogs perform. They did pick enough wild cranberries to provide berries for Thanksgiving and Christmas without the necessity for an official governmental clearance!

All of the children are attending the same school. Charlene, a white-thatched, brown-eyed, independent little girl, is our first grader. Charlene's propensity to go visiting after school without permission causes us to question the wisdom of honoring her request for a bicycle for Christmas. Cliff, a solidly built blonde, blue-eyed boy is a third grader and a cub scout with a sunshiny disposition. If he grows up to his two front teeth, he'll be quite a man. Di's in the 5th grade, a girl scout and taking organ lessons. She knows the words of every commercial and popular song on TV. She has a thoughtful and generous disposition. Donna is growing up. She's a 6th grader and our dependable one. She's on the student patrol, a girl scout and, when we can get her nose out of a book, she takes dancing and flute lessons.

Genee's in the chauffeuring stage with dental appointments, music and dance lessons, club meetings, and girl scout activities. She's reviewing for the second time a book on Alaska. The highlight of the year came when on the same night that a testimonial dinner was being given for Don, she won first prize in a sewing contest on a velveteen suit she made for Donna.

Don's speaking engagements have expanded as he's been called on to speak on Urban Renewals and city problems in California, Utah, Nevada, and Oregon. His crowning achievement came just last week when he was elected Vice President of the American Municipal Association which represents the mayors and councils of the United States on the very same day he received a call from the White House notifying him of his appointment as one of four mayors to the President's Advisory Commission on Intergovernmental Relations just established by Congress. If this wasn't enough for one day, Genee was elected vice president of the Girl Scout Council for Southern Arizona.

❊ ❊ ❊

16

Glacier National Park

DURING THE year 1960 I was contacted by James Kenady who was in charge of property for the Great Northern Railway Company. He had been advised that I might be interested in acquiring the operation in Glacier National Park and the adjacent Prince of Wales Hotel in Waterton Lakes National Park, Canada. He advised me that Great Northern had notified the National Park Service that they were no longer interested in carrying on the operation in Glacier National Park and had terminated their contract. I advised Mr. Kenady that I would be interested and asked him to send me some information concerning the operation.

I do not recall how long after our conversation it was, but some time later I received a minimum of information and did nothing toward contacting Great Northern. Again, I got a call from Jim Kenady, asking me if I was really interested, as they intended to dispose of the property. I advised him that I was interested, but that I had received so little information, I had almost nothing to go on. I asked for five years' of financial reports. Upon receipt of these reports I realized why they had not sent me this information earlier. The operations did not show any profit during the previous five years and showed losses up to $535,000 in a single season. I learned later that the operation had accumulated a deficit and had not made a profit for the years 1940 to 1960.

At this time, my brother Gail was going to Montana to look at an operation at Swan Lake, so I asked him to go to Glacier National Park and look at the facilities. Upon his return, he informed me that I should check into it thoroughly, because there was a tremendous number of facilities in the park and he thought the opportunity would be excellent.

Shortly after that I received another call from Jim Kenady advising that they were telling their employees that Great Northern would not operate the park facilities the following year. He felt Great Northern had many good employees we would want to retain, but that they would have to have assurance of being hired, or would be applying elsewhere for summer jobs.

I met Jim in Great Falls, Montana, in early September and we drove to Glacier National Park. We examined all the facilities in one day except the Prince of Wales Hotel. Time did not allow us to take a trip into Canada. At each of the various locations they gathered the staff and introduced me as the prospective purchaser and operator for the coming season. I then assured the employees that we would be interested in having them continue in their jobs, as it was essential that we have a crew conversant with the operations.

Shortly thereafter, Kenady came to Tucson and Gail and I met with him to discuss the purchase of the facilities. Great Northern had set a cash purchase price of $1,300,000 and wanted considerably more for the installment purchase. Gail suggested that we purchase the facilities for $1,300,000 with $250,000 down and the balance over a period of 10 years. Upon Mr. Kenady's return to the Great Northern offices in St. Paul, he advised that the terms we had suggested would be satisfactory.

During the negotiations we learned that Glacier Park Transport Company, which was operated as a separate corporation, had $100,000 in cash in the account. I asked Great Northern Railway to leave this cash in as part of the assets and add $100,000 to the purchase price, making it $1,400,000. I pointed out that instead of paying taxes on the $100,000 to be taken out as dividends, they would be transferring the cash on a capital gain basis. They accepted my proposal.

The Great Northern balance sheet, furnished to us after the purchase, showed the facilities in the United States were constructed or acquired over the years at a total cost of $3,558,683 with a remaining book value as of December 31, 1960, of $1,527,869. This did not include the Prince of Wales Hotel or auxiliary property in Canada, nor the Glacier Park Transport Company. The construction cost of Glacier Park Lodge was $1,545,796 (1914-15), while Many Glacier Hotel was constructed with timber cut in the park at a cost of $893,313 in 1915-16.

It is interesting to note that the land and buildings at Lake McDonald were acquired from the Lewis estate for $266,896. The government paid $133,448 while Great Northern paid $310,485 including the improvements to the property. The government received the title without recognition of any interest by the Great Northern!

After receipt of notice that the purchase could be made on the installment basis, Don Ford attempted to secure money through people who had the Mercedes Benz dealership in Hollywood, California. A proposal was made to us, but they wanted control of the operation. This I refused to grant. Gail was contacted by a group who had just sold a motel in Nogales, Arizona, and had $150,000 in cash. They agreed to come into the company, but demanded management control. This I also refused to do and turned down their offer.

A short time later I was advised that Dudley Tower, the President of Union Oil Company, was attending a meeting of the Board of Directors of Pima Mines, and that he wanted to talk with me. The Union Oil Company had a refinery outside Cut Bank, Montana, but had neglected the sale of their product in the State of Montana. They wanted to get back into the sale of Union Oil products in the state and to establish their stations in the park. When I received the call, I was busy with my duties as Mayor of Tucson and advised that I would not be able to meet with the President of Union Oil until some time later in the afternoon. The President was also in a board meeting until later that day, so arrangements were made to meet at a motel lounge on Miracle Mile at 4:00 o'clock in the afternoon.

We had a pleasant meeting and the Union Oil representatives verified that they were interested in selling Union Oil products in Glacier National Park. Shortly before the meeting broke up, the President said to me, "Is there anything I can do for you?" I said, "Yes, I need $250,000." I offered to give Union Oil preferred stock representing the $250,000 which would enable them to get their money back, and a 25 percent equity interest in the company. I agreed to establish their services in the park and sell their products. Without hesitation Tower said, "We'll do it." We shook hands to seal the deal. This is how I secured the initial down payment for purchase of the Glacier operations in Montana.

I immediately contacted Jim Kenady and advised him that we were ready to sign the contract for the purchase of the premises. Great Northern's assistant chief counsel, Terry Slattery, drew up the contract for the sale of the facilities to a company which I had incorporated as Glacier Park, Inc. Since Gail and Don Ford had raised money, which I declined to accept, I gave them each a seven percent interest in the corporation.

At that time, I was totally involved with the responsibilities of being Mayor of Tucson and President of the National League of Cities, which required considerable travel and speaking engagements around the United States. I would not be able to serve as the general manager of the Glacier operation for the 1961 season. I had to search for someone else.

I learned that George Golsworthy, who had worked in executive positions at Yosemite Park & Curry Company for almost 30 years, was available, as he was handling the hotel operations for the Winter Olympics in Squaw Valley. I contacted Hil Oehlmann and asked him to provide me with some information and recommendations on George Golsworthy. He gave Golsworthy his approval, but failed to mention that Mr. Golsworthy had a drinking problem.

Arrangements had been made to take possession of the Glacier premises at the end of December, 1960, which meant that we would be saddled with the winter expenses without any income.

There were a number of permanent employees on the payroll which we continued to employ. Some were Cy Stevenson, the long-time maintenance engineer; Lyle McMullin, the supervisor of the Transport Company; and Ian Tippet, who was manager of Lake McDonald Lodge, whom I advised would be moved to the position of manager of Many Glacier Hotel, the largest hotel in the operation.

We also continued to employ William Carlson as director of public relations and "Hi" Olson, who was purchasing agent and in control of the warehouse.

The facilities acquired under this purchase plan were extensive. At East Glacier, Montana, which was outside the boundaries of the park, was Glacier Park Lodge, a beautiful 157-room hotel. This was the center of the operations and included all extra facilities such as warehouse, garage, maintenance center, general laundry and powerhouse, general offices and reservation facilities. This was on 630 acres of land, which was to be transferred in fee. It was located on ground surrounded by the Blackfeet Indian Reservation. The largest center was at Many Glacier Hotel, which was a 220-room facility with auxiliary buildings for employee dormitories. Across the lake a mile and one-half distant, was Swiftcurrent Motor Lodge, consisting of a general store, coffee shop and a number of cottages which contained almost 100 rooms. Many of these facilities at Swiftcurrent were substandard and without individual bathrooms, except for the motel units containing 52 modern rooms. There was a central shower and bathroom which was available for cabin guests and campers, as well as for our employees.

On the Going-To-The-Sun Highway, was the Rising Sun Lodge, which consisted of a store, coffee shop, two motel units and a number of cottages along with employee dormitories. These were in better condition than those at Swiftcurrent, but lacked modern facilities as there were no showers in the cabins.

On the west side was Lake McDonald Lodge, a unit containing 33 rooms plus 14 cottages; each unit contained four rooms, but only one bathroom for each cottage unit. They were heated by wood stoves and the hot water was a central coal-fired system, which required the night watchman to tend the fire on his rounds. This often resulted either in steam or ice water. There was a general store at Lake McDonald which contained a soda fountain; also there was a small counter service in the old theater-like building which was used for lectures, interpretive programs and a place for the employees to gather. The Lodge had a small dining room which was the principal food operation. There were three small dormitories and Cobb Cottage, which was used to house the older employees. Cobb Cottage had been the home of Irving S Cobb, the author. At the lower end of the lake, there was the Village

Inn Motel, a new unit which had been built by the owner of the land and subsequently sold to the National Park Service, when the contract exceeded the amount of money they had available to pay for it. It was an excellent facility, located on the lakeshore overlooking Lake McDonald.

Two Medicine, which had been an overnight facility, had deteriorated to such extent during World War II that the lodging facilities were destroyed, leaving the lodge dining room, which had been converted into a camp store to serve the campground. It had a very large fireplace and had been used by President Franklin D. Roosevelt for one of his fireside chats.

In addition to these facilities was the Prince of Wales Hotel, in Waterton Lake, Alberta, Canada, a unit with 84 usable rooms, three dormitories and a year-around facility for the caretaker, plus a powerhouse and water system.

The first year of operation was a trying one. I was not able to stay in the park during the summer and made periodic trips about every two weeks for the weekends. I had taken over one cabin at Lake McDonald for the summer, and put the family in there for the season. The weather was perfect and the family enjoyed a wonderful time, particularly as they were on the lakefront and could spend the days swimming and in the sun. Genee's mother, Ruth Mitchell, accompanied them that summer.

On my periodic visits that summer, I was disturbed to see the lack of organization and control, the failure to control costs and the overabundance of employees for the amount of business we were doing. Had I been free to stay, I would have discharged quite a number of employees as a result of the things I observed, but knowing that I would be leaving in a day or two, and that word of any discharge would spread through the entire operation, I bit my tongue and allowed the conditions to exist. Had I discharged anyone, I am afraid that I would have lost control of the employees. There was one exception to this.

I was staying at Glacier Park Lodge when I heard a tremendous racket in the lobby. It was 2:00 o'clock in the morning. I got up, dressed and went to the lobby. The bar stayed open until 2:00 a.m. and the band was just disbanding. When I addressed the night clerk about what was going on, he said he didn't understand what I meant. I said, "This terrible racket — do they do this all the time? There are people sleeping in this place." He said, "Well, the band is just breaking up." I asked who the man was sitting over in the lobby reading the newspaper. He said, "Oh, that's the night security officer." I called the security officer over and told him to meet me at 8:00 in the morning. Needless to say, he was the exception and was dismissed the following day.

I tried to exercise tight financial control and every expenditure other than the normal course of providing products had to be submitted to me for approval. We also had an obligation to pay $52,000 per month for a four-month period to pay for the gift shop inventory, which was not included in the original purchase price. In order to have the cash to make these payments, I immediately put everything in the gift shop on sale. The predecessor company, the Don Knutson Hotel company, had spared no opportunity to buy for the gift shops. I believe the exorbitant amount in inventory came from the fact that they expected to take over the operation and this would have been a nest egg for their first season. As a result of the unusual discounts we gave, we were able to sell out a lot of the inventory, which provided us with cash to pay the $52,000 per month we owed Great Northern.

I believe that a few words are appropriate about the Knutson Hotel and Construction Company. It seems as though the Knutson Construction Company had a contract to build a new hotel or motel complex in Minot, North Dakota. The contract ran considerably over the cash available by the owner and, as a result, the construction company took over completion of the hotel complex and its operation. As this was one of the first new lodging facilities in that area west of the Mississippi, it was an immediate success. This prompted Great Northern Railway to contact them to take over remodeling and refurbishing the Glacier operations for the purpose of putting the facilities in condi tion to sell. I have heard, but do not confirm, that this company spent some three million dollars of Great Northern Railway's money in improving the facilities in Glacier National Park. The principal money was put into modernizing the kitchens and putting on new roofs and to some degree, refurbishing the rooms and modernizing some of the bathrooms. The understanding was that when the four-year contract ran out, the construction company was to have first right to purchase the facilities.

I was told by former employees who were there that there was little effort to conserve any money; in fact, many employees of the company they could not keep employed in Minneapolis were placed on the payroll in Glacier National Park.

Theft of facilities at Glacier was rampant. Many construction workers loaded their cars at the end of each week with construction material to take home with them. Protests were made by Cy Stevenson, chief engineer, to Great Northern Railway officials in St. Paul to no avail. The theft of equipment and materials continued and costs were completely out of control.

When the Don Knutson contract terminated in 1960, the railroad offered to sell the premises to him, but with the knowledge they had acquired during their operating and remodeling period, they offered to take over only if the railroad would subsidize them for a period of five years. This was not exactly the type of deal the railroad had in mind and they notified the Knutson Company that they would seek other purchasers. They did, and contacted a number of firms in New York, but as each firm looked at the financial condition of the company, the railroad received no offers until I was approached and made my proposal.

At the close of the 1961 season, as a result of our control of costs, we had accumulated some $200,000 in cash. This on a total season income of $1,400,000. As the Union Oil people had expressed dissatisfaction with the deal that was made with them, I called Don Ford, who had contact with their legal department, stating that I would be willing to return their $250,000 if they would release their interest in the company and their preferred stock. This was accepted. I needed additional funds to consummate the deal and still have some funds to carry us over the winter during the time that we had no income, so I went to the First National Bank in Great Falls and asked to borrow $100,000. They indicated that they needed some security for the money.

I then contacted Great Northern Railway and asked if they would allow me to mortgage some of the facilities outside the park, primarily those around Glacier Park Lodge. They agreed, stating that they would not sign the note, but would approve my mortgage. As a result First National Bank of Great Falls extended me $100,000 in credit, but insisted that I take out an insurance policy on my life which would pay off the debt to them in the event that I were to die before the debt was discharged. This was arranged and I bought back my 25 percent interest I had previously transferred to Union Oil Company. This meant I had an additional 25 percent interest, of which I apportioned 10 percent to Don Ford and 10 percent to my brother, Gail, and added five percent to my interests.

Genee's Christmas Letter, 1961:

We started the New Year of 1961 by attending the Inauguration of President Kennedy. For Don this was the beginning of a heavy travel itinerary. He has crossed and recrossed the United States, not to mention nine trips to Washington, D.C. (twice to see President Kennedy concerning the proposed Department of Urban Affairs, and three times for meetings of the Advisory Commission on Inter governmental Relations), plus trips to Glacier National Park, Lassen and McKinley. Most of his traveling was to address municipal officials for the American Municipal Association, an experience he found demanding and challenging.

Genee's usual quota of P.T.A., school, church, Girl Scouts, civic and child-related activities was varied this year with ribbon cutting and speeches. When the year ended, she had given eleven talks on Israel, which she and Don visited while attending the International Union of Local Authorities Congress in Tel Aviv. Certainly the most interest ing experience was substituting for Don to address an all-male kick-off dinner of the Combined Jewish Appeal. In the spring she reviewed Walter Lord's "The Good Years" — America from 1900 to 1914, and on December 6th she was elected President of the Sahuaro Girl Scout Council. Don received his share of honors, being Man of the Year for the Conference of Christians and Jews, and also for the City of Hope. He was honored by the Advisory Commission for his municipal work. As he did not run for mayor, his last official act was to dedicate the new City Hall. He questions the family coordination, with Genee just taking office as he leaves his official duties.

Our summer at Glacier was wonderful. Don and Cliff even

had a three-day pack trip into the magnificent wilderness area. We stayed in a quiet cottage on Lake McDonald in West Glacier. The scenery is fabulous — breathtaking, the beautiful hotels each have a distinctive charm. The summer went all too fast.

This fall finds Donna and Diane both in Junior High. Donna is 5 feet 6-1/2 inches. She is blossoming out as our first teenager and has an A average in an accelerated program which includes High School Algebra and Spanish. Di is her same sweet, lovable and exasperating self, so anxious to grow up. She's a B+ student. Both take organ and dancing lessons, have had ice skating and first aid in their Girl Scout troop. Cliff has kept his sunny disposition and is developing as a conscientious hard-working boy. His scholastic record has improved and he is now janitoring at Don's new Glacier-Lassen-McKinley office. Charlene, in 3rd grade, is a happy girl with her eyes open and her mind clicking. She is practical and independent, but still climbs into her Mother and Daddy's bed early in the morning.

The time finds us looking forward to moving to our new home at 40 Calle Encanto. The house will give us more room and has very attractive grounds.

❋ ❋ ❋

1962 was the first year I could spend full time at the park to direct its operations. It was also the year of the World's Fair in Seattle, Washington. This materially increased the travel to and through Glacier by people who were headed primarily to visit the World's Fair in Seattle. I was still a member of the Advisory Commission on Intergovernmental Relations and in the early part of the year, I drove to Great Falls to catch a morning flight to Washington, D.C., to attend a meeting. I was late in arriving, as I did not leave the park until about 10:30 p.m. At 1:30 a.m., I was awakened by a telephone call at the hotel. Coming out of a sound sleep, I had difficulty locating the telephone. When I did, a voice on the other end of the line said, "Hummel?" I said, "Yes."

And he said, "You're out of business. They just blew up the power plant." It was Cy Stevenson, in his blunt way informing me that there had been an explosion at the power plant at East Glacier. The power plant provided all of the hot water for the bathrooms and kitchens and all the space heat for the entire hotel, as well as water for the central laundry.

I immediately arose, checked out of the hotel and

started back to East Glacier. On the way I was trying to evolve some solution to the problem we were facing. We had a full house at East Glacier, and now there was no hot water for the kitchen, the bathrooms or the space water heaters that heated the hotel. I speculated that perhaps we could get the Great Northern Railway Company to put a steam engine on a siding to substitute for our boiler plant at East Glacier.

When I arrived at East Glacier, Cy Stevenson and his assistant, Howard Olson, were already busy attempting to shift the steam system from a small boiler that provided hot water to the dormitories to the kitchen in the Lodge. The boiler room was a total disaster, with the roof raised some three feet and all of the sides pushed out, except the one in front of the boiler. Fortunately, this was the place where the boiler engineer stood and he was uninjured. The man on duty was a professor who had every type of certificate for boilers that you could get, but he did not have much common sense. An electrical storm had cut off the igniting flame and the warning in the boiler that the fire was out was a large Klaxon sound. Instead of following procedure of shutting off the fuel and starting the exhaust fans, this professor put a torch down into the boiler and promptly blew up the entire system.

I immediately got on the telephone to Great Northern Railway headquarters in St. Paul, as Cy Stevenson had advised me that the railroad still had specialist crews to repair boilers which were carried over from the old days of the steam engine. I talked with John Budd, President of the Great Northern Railway, and he assured me that he would have a crew on the train for East Glacier within a couple of hours. When they arrived, we put them on a 24-hour basis, with instructions to spare no expense to get the boilers back in operation. In the meantime the dormitory boilers allowed us to provide a minimum of hot water to the kitchens so guests could be fed.

As all of our linen service was handled at the laundry at East Glacier for all locations except the Prince of Wales Hotel in Canada, I started telephoning the laundry companies to see if I could get temporary linen service. One laundry service in Kalispell saw an opportunity and immediately called all the laundry companies adjacent to Glacier, indicating that if they would stick together, they could demand their price for providing services while we reestablished our laundry. The price was exorbitant and I refused to accept their proposal. I finally made a deal with Quality Cleaners in Cut Bank, Montana. They agreed to rent their entire plant to us from nightfall to the following morning, if I handled the operations and provided the crew to service the laundry. This we did, and had a van take our crew down to Cut Bank each evening and return in the morning. That was how we worked out our linen problems.

Cy Stevenson advised that some of the oil fields had small steam-operated plants. We rented one and installed it outside the boiler room and were able to reestablish, on a limited basis, the services to Glacier Park Lodge. This was of course not adequate to operate the laundry, but it did put us back in business.

On the seventh day, the specialized crew furnished us by Great Northern Railway had the boiler room back in service so we could continue a normal operation. I do not know what we would have done had it not been for the cooperation and support of the Great Northern Railway. In this connection, I have never dealt with a higher-class company. Although they had no legal obligation to me, they went completely overboard in attempting to be supportive.

They, of course, were familiar with operations in Glacier National Park and, I believe, had sympathy for the problems I was encountering. We ended with a good season, despite the problems we had faced.

Genee's Christmas Letter, 1962:

With Don out of the Mayor's office for the first year in seven, this year found us enjoying a far more normal and quiet family life in our comfortable new home. It's only new to us as it's 23 years old with beautiful grounds and spacious rooms for our growing family. Genee has had fun painting, decorating and furnishing.

Don and Genee attended the Western Conference of National Park Concessioners' meeting in San Francisco in February, and once again in Washington, D.C., in November to discuss the perennial problems of private investments on public lands. Don is chairman of the association. They also attended an American Municipal Association Meeting in Miami Beach as Don is serving as adviser on program and structure. He still meets a travel schedule and has given talks in Seattle, West Virginia, New York, Chicago and Detroit. He was appointed to the Advisory Commission on Intergovernmental Relations and was designated Vice Chairman by President Kennedy. He was also named as a consultant on Municipal Affairs to the Alliance for Progress and had an interesting trip to Jamaica, Venezuela, Peru, Bolivia, and Mexico.

Genee's travel has largely been confined to Southern Arizona as that is the area of jurisdiction for her Girl Scout Council. She finds being President a time-consuming, but satisfying experience. She has another year to serve before joining Don in their agreement to give up some political and civic duties.

Summer found us all back at beautiful Glacier Park. We were located at Glacier Park Lodge in order to be close to the administrative offices as Don was active as general manager. Glacier enjoyed its best season. Practically all the family worked — Genee where needed, Donna at the gift shop, Di in the warehouse, Cliff at the golf course. We even had a two-day pack trip from Two Medicine to Walton into a spectacular, remote area of the Park.

A change of homes meant a change of schools. A few years ago we had everyone in one school; we are now faced with four P.T.A.s! The children are adjusting.

Donna, a freshman in high school, is an inch taller than Genee, and developing into a young lady. Di's very happy about her new junior high and is doing well. Both teenagers now, they belong to the same Girl Scout troop, enjoy after-school activities. Cliff combines after-school football and Boy Scouts with ballroom dancing and weekend hunting. His 6th grade report — his best. Charlene's a slim nine-year-old, still boisterous and lovable. It's hard to believe "our baby" is so self-reliant.

While the tempo slowed for the Hummel family in 1962, it still reflects more than enough activities — fewer politics but a rising tide of family affairs. Don and Genee brace themselves for the years to come with the prospect of four teenagers in the household. "Our cup runneth over."

❆ ❆ ❆

The 1963 season was not particularly eventful except for the threatened railroad strike between the unions and the railroad. They kept postponing the date for agreement and determination as to whether the strike would be called for the rest of the summer. In the interim, about one-third of our tours canceled as the great majority of our tours arrived by rail. They were uncertain as to whether or not they would be stranded by a strike. This drastically hurt our financial operating season, although we adjusted to these problems.

It was obvious to me that if we were to be successful in improving patronage to our hotel and lodge units, we had to improve access by air. Automobile travelers largely used our motel and cabin accommodations. Railroad traffic was declining and there were talks of eliminating the Western Star, leaving only the Empire Builder to serve us at Glacier National Park. The threatened railroad strike exacerbated this problem.

I decided that we needed an airport comparable to Yellowstone if we were to attract foreign travelers. Japanese tours were rapidly expanding into Yellowstone but bypassing Glacier, as the 140-mile bus trip from Great Falls discouraged foreign travel.

I contacted people from surrounding communities as far away as Kalispell on the west side of the divide. We set up an informal organization, established a small bank account, and I proposed that the Park Service acquire some land about three miles from East Glacier.

The F.A.A. was contacted on September 11, 1963, and proposed a 6,300 foot runway. The Park Service started acquisition of the land. This was difficult as the land was owned by some thirty Indians. The slow pace of the Park Service in contacting the Indians did not help the situation. On April 25, 1967, the Montana Aeronautical Commission proposed the strip and approach pattern be extended to 9,000 feet.

In the interim, Kalispell Airport attempted to grab the money set aside for East Glacier Airport, but the Montana congressional delegation refused to allow this raid on our funds. The Kalispell Airport then issued bonds, extended their runways and changed their name to Glacier Park International Airport, usurping our proposed name. The Park Service purchased the balance of the land, but as they took five years, the funds for construction were no longer available. I had convinced Alaska Airlines to agree to service this airport, but it was too late. Recently the Park Service gave the land to the Blackfoot Tribal Council. That ended our attempt to provide an airport.

The Montana Power Company established a gas line to make Canadian gas available. This enabled us to convert our oil-burning unit in our laundry at East Glacier to gas. The conversion cost $12,250, but we recouped this cost in two seasons, as gas was cheaper and we no longer needed engineers for three shifts. I also converted our permanent employee housing to gas at great savings.

In an attempt to improve the attractiveness of our Glacier Park Lodge, which was outside the park, I contracted for a swimming pool. Unfortunately, my contract was with a crook who was short changing us on cement mix. I closed down the operation and was sued, but we won the case. I had the pool finished. The total cost was $9,850. This was a great outlet for our employees' free time, as well as for our guests.

Genee's Christmas Letter, 1963:

Holidays are happy days but these days this year must be shared with our Nation's tragedy. No rejoicing can completely escape the somber note of this hour. A family tragedy earlier in November took the lives of Don's nephew, wife, and two-year-old daughter, leaving orphaned 3-1/2 and 5-1/2 year old boys. The boys are darling and have helped to brighten our days as they have been spending some time with us. Our children's response to their lively activities is a joy for all.

A review of this year's calendar shows the usual full days of the last few years. Genee's schedule includes P.T.A.s, Tucson Community Council, United Fund, church, symphony, a book review club, but mostly girl scouting as she winds up her second year as president of the Sahuaro Area Council. This included the national Girl Scout Conference in Miami Beach. Don's year finds him traveling more than he or his family expected — a combination of service as Vice Chairman of the Advisory Commission on Intergovernmental Relations, Chairman of the Western Conference of national Park Concessioners, Chairman of a study committee for American Municipal Association, but mostly in connection with his own operations in the national parks. One of these was a trip to Alaska in which he and Genee joined the Ed Hummels, the new Park Service Regional Director (no relation) who was surveying Alaska's parks and monuments. After Mt. McKinley National Park, Don and Genee enjoyed a brief but marvelous trip with the Bill Sneddens of Fairbanks, Alaska, at beautiful Valdez Harbor where they caught their first salmon. Another trip took them to Yosemite National Park to attend a meeting of the national Park Superintendents.

The highlight of the year is always our summer at Glacier National Park. The family moved to East Glacier immediately after the close of school stopping en route for a delightful visit with the Halls of Mesa Verde National park. The days at Glacier were full with swimming, hiking, riding, picknicking and, of course, work, too. Donna clerked at the gift shop, Diane sorted and marked at the gift warehouse, and Cliff washed dishes at the Tipi Grill. Charlene looks forward to the day when she can join the labor force. Our business at Glacier was marred by the threat of the railroad strike; otherwise business was good in Lassen, and McKinley reported its best year to date. We held Lassen facilities open for a visit by our late President. Al Donau's house was the White House on September 27th.

The emblematic white telephone is still there — reminiscent of the event.

Our home though spacious is filled to overflowing with our children and their friends. We will have three teenagers next year when Cliff joins Donna and Diane. Three years from now will round it out with four. Donna and Di are in high school, Cliff in junior high, Char in 5th grade.

All of us are looking forward to our first family vacation together which will be in Hawaii during the Christmas Holidays.

❄ ❄ ❄

1964 was a memorable year. On June 8, at about 4:00 a.m., Cy Stevenson pounded on my door, stating that there was a terrific torrent of water coming down Midvale Creek and that he had to see what he could do about getting across to rescue his daughter, Kathy, and the children. Kathy's house was located fairly close to Midvale Stream. Midvale is the stream that provides all the water for the system in the hotel, the laundry and for many of the local residents of East Glacier, who had, with or without permission, attached to our water system. We almost lost Cy that night, as he tried to cross a side stream and was caught by the swift waters, but fortunately he grabbed hold of a willow tree branch and was able to get out of the stream. A little later that morning Civil Defense sent a chopper over and we were able to airlift Kathy and family across the stream.

It was about this time that we began to learn how widespread and drastic the flooding conditions were. We had lost our water system for East Glacier. The dam and several hundred feet of water flume were completely gone. All communications with other units of the park had been cut off, including the National Park Service headquarters at West Glacier. We subsequently set up a temporary system by car radio and agreed upon times during the day the Park Service would go to their automobile and I would communicate what information I had on the conditions on the east side of the park.

Secretary Stewart Udall, of the Interior Department, was scheduled to speak at a meeting at the Blackfeet Indian Reservation in Browning. As a result he had an army helicopter and invited me to accompany him over the route to Many Glacier Hotel to determine what damage had occurred there. We landed in the parking lot above the hotel. I found that Swiftcurrent Lake had risen to such a level that it put one and one-half feet of water in the lower floor of Many Glacier Hotel. Ian Tippet, the manager, had banquet tables put up and most of the furniture moved to the table tops, which saved a lot of money and a lot of damage. The Many Glacier water system was out, as was the sewer system. This required the hotel staff to dig trenches to serve as temporary latrines until the sewer system could be put back into operation.

The Swiftcurrent Motor Lodge area was completely flooded and had no power of any kind. The big electrical transformers were in the basement under the dining room and coffee shop. They were completely flooded and nonoperational.

I reported to the Park Service that the road to Many Glacier was out in five or six different places and would take a considerable amount of construction to make them even passable for vehicles. I then followed, by helicopter, the railroad tracks from East Glacier to West Glacier. Some 14 miles of railroad roadbed were gone, including many miles of tracks. In some instances the water had washed out under the tracks, leaving the rails suspended many feet in the air. Intermittent parts of U.S. Highway 2, for a distance of 15 miles were destroyed, making it impossible for any form of ground transportation to use this federal highway.

The major bridge leading into the park from the west side over the Middle Fork of the Flathead River was condemned. The trees brought down by the flood had become stuck in the bridge and formed a dam with the result that it almost washed out the entire bridge. The underfitting and the pilings had been undermined. This was the only access there was to the park from the west side.

I helicoptered into the Village Inn and discussed the matter of damage to that facility with the manager. He informed me that they could have moved the furniture to the second floor, but were assured by a ranger that it would be foolish; that they would never have water that high. The ten-mile Lake McDonald had risen six feet in eight hours. I walked through the rooms in the Village Inn with water actually up to my thighs and all the furniture floating around. Some 13 large plate glass windows had been broken out and the place was filled with silt and debris. We had to dismantle all of the furniture in the motel, sand it, refinish and reglue the chairs, beds, etc. The entire floor had to be removed and new carpet laid. For weeks afterwards, we would have small explosions in the electric stoves, due to water having been trapped in some part of the stove, and as it got hot, the steam caused minor explosions. This caused some concern for our guests.

I then helicoptered to Lake McDonald Lodge. Lake McDonald Lodge suffered the greatest damage, as the water came down Snyder Creek and undermined the large cedar trees, which formed a dam that diverted the water into the hotel. About half the kitchen was gone and about one-third of the dining room. The dining room floor was lying at the bottom of the creek. The big stone fire place at the end of the dining room was completely gone. The roof and logs extending from the building were without support. The elk and goat heads were still intact, but suspended over the stream in what remained of that part of the dining room.

The theater-like building that was used for an employees' gathering place and for the Park Service's interpretative talks was filled with nearly four feet of silt. It was so hard-packed that they took out the end of the building and brought a Caterpillar tractor in to break up and push the silt out of the end of the building. The floor had to be completely replaced and, of course, the end of the building had to be reinstalled.

When I arrived I found Ralph Erickson, the manager, had established a place for the cooks to prepare food for the employees who had already reported for work. They cooked outside over a campfire for about two weeks before we could get enough of the kitchen back in operation to reestablish service in the employees dining room.

The flood came on June 8, 1964, shortly before we were to open for business, so most of the employees had reported or were en route to the park. As facilities were disrupted for miles, we did not know where many of our employees were, or even if they were alive. Emily Moke, my secretary, spent practically all of her time on the telephone, with a list before her of employees who had reported. Parents called, alarmed by reports of the flood and Emily could only say, "They are here—they are safe; no I can't give you anymore information, as there are others waiting." When a parent called and the employee had not reported, alarm was of course expressed by the parent, but there was nothing we could do at that stage to ascertain whether or not the employee was safe.

The Montana Junior Chamber of Commerce was scheduled to have a convention at Many Glacier Hotel, however, it was impossible to get to that hotel, so we arranged to transfer it to Glacier Park Lodge. We could not afford to lose the business so we arranged for a temporary water system to be established and went forward with the convention. The JayCees have a reputation of having pretty wild drinking parties and as we could not get water to the fourth floor, and as conventioneers were constantly pacing the halls, I placed four spotters on each floor to survey the activities to be sure no fire was started during the night. If a fire had started, it would have been impossible for us to extinguish, for we had only a minimum of water in the hotel.

The manager of Glacier Park Lodge was seen to be wandering up and down the lobby saying, "Gee, what a beautiful hotel." He apparently had a small stroke and did not know that he was the manager of the hotel, nor was he able to provide any organizational services. We had to send him home. At that stage of the game, I called on Ken Gelston, who had for a number of years been the chief clerk, or assistant manager, at Rising Sun. I brought him to East

Glacier to set up the front desk and function as acting manager until I could secure another manager.

Speaking of Rising Sun, Roes Creek had gone completely out of its banks and water ran through the lobby, dining room and store. Most of the trees between Rising Sun store and the road were washed downstream. The manager there was new, but pitched in immediately to try to get it back into operation, once the road through the park was open.

The sequel to this was the refusal of Ken Gelston to stay at East Glacier, stating that he liked Rising Sun because it was a good hiking area and he wanted to return. Unfortunately, he did return and, while hiking, slipped and went over St. Mary Falls. His body was never recovered.

We had a similar casualty at Two Medicine Camp Store. The road and bridge to Two Medicine had been washed out and access was available only by helicopter. I removed several of the employees, but Mr. Sweet, the manager, said he wanted to stay in. When enough of the road was repaired so he could take his automobile out, he started for East Glacier and about halfway out he died of a heart attack while driving his car. Fortunately, the car stayed on the road, but we buried Mr. Sweet in a cemetery near Glacier Park Lodge, where a headstone was also erected for Ken Gelston.

I was in a real quandary in that no hotel except Glacier Park Lodge could be reached except by helicopter. We already had 600 employees on the job and not a single guest. It was my practice each evening to gather all the employees who reported to Glacier Park Lodge, as this was the point from which distribution was made, and advise them of the conditions that exited. After the third day I told them that I would be unable to pay them until I could get the facilities open, but that I would provide them room and board without charge. I also stated that anyone who wished to do so was free to leave, without any reflection on his or her employment record. I was delighted that not a single employee left. All decided to stick with the operation.

In my attempts to keep up with what was happening in the way of reconstruction of roads, railroads, buildings, etc., I made frequent trips around the park by helicopter. The main bridge over the Middle Fork of the Flathead River had been condemned, however, there was an old, small bridge downstream with the cement arch still in place, but no deck for the bridge. A contract had been let for the reconstruction work and I noticed that the crew was taking long coffee breaks, while everyone else was breaking their necks trying to get back into operation. This exasperated me. While serving as President of the National League of Cities, I was a member of a mayor's committee that met with the state engineers around the United States to discuss mutual problems. As a result I knew Rex Whitten, Chairman of the Bureau of Public Roads. I called him — it was about 1:00 a.m. Washington time — got him out of bed and told him of my disgust at the waste of time the contractor was permitting in restoring a deck on the bridge and that this had to be completed before we could open the park again. That afternoon, on the train out of Portland, Oregon, a supervising agent from the Bureau of Public Roads arrived, and we had no problem thereafter in expediting completion of the work. The park was opened for traffic on June 29, just three weeks after the flood.

I think it is important to make a few observations resulting from the flood destruction in and adjacent to Glacier National Park. There were some 114 bridges out in Glacier County, together with miles of roads that could not be traveled. The interesting part was that the various agencies who normally compete with one another got together to form a reconstruction program. There were the Bureau of Public Roads, the National Park Service, Glacier County Road Crew, the Corps of Engineers and the Montana State Highway Department. They all worked together. If a contractor or equipment owner had a piece of equipment to rent, the Association of General Contractors assigned him to the job he was to work and then paid an hourly scale of wages which was authorized. This prevented any attempt by contractors and equipment owners to go from one job to another to see where they could get the best price. It was an outstanding example of complete cooperation.

Another comment is on the attitude of the press. We had numerous reporters who came and their first question was: "How many people died?" When you said that no one except off the Blackfoot Reservation had died, they were not interested in any other aspect of the flood. Two dams had broken, and 17 Indians had been caught by the walls of water and were drowned. These were the only losses of lives directly caused by the flood water.

There was one notable exception. Mel Ruder, publisher of the *Hungry Horse News*, a weekly newspaper, covered every aspect of the flood and, as an outstanding photographer, gave the public a vivid portrayal of the flood and damages. Mel was recognized by being awarded a Pulitzer Prize for his reporting.

The Great Northern Railway moved three-quarters of a million yards of dirt in 21 days and reestablished their railroad from East Glacier to West Glacier, although 14 miles had been completely eradicated by the flood. In the interim, the Great Northern ran a shuttle out of Minneapolis to the east side of the park and out of Seattle to the west side. They also sent their passenger agent, Kent Van Wyck, to East Glacier and each morning he and I would make a report to all the travel agencies and others who had reservations to come to the park to provide them up-to-date information. In this way, we were able to salvage a great number of our reservations, particularly the tour groups which were essential, if we were to stay in business. The cooperation with us by Great Northern was fantastic.

The Air Force sent in three helicopters in case we had an emergency evacuation or to help move those of us who had to go to different parts of the park and were unable to do so by roads. In one instance, Cy Stevenson was flown by helicopter to our Many Glacier Hotel and when he did not return by 6:00 p.m., I got worried because the Air Force was not supposed to fly after 6:00 p.m. After stewing a bit, I finally got a call from Many Glacier. I said, "Cy, where are you?" He said, "Many Glacier."

And I replied, "Cy, what in the world are you doing there? They are not supposed to be flying after six o'clock." He said, "We crashed." And I said, "What?" He said, "Yes, something happened to the helicopter and we crashed in a tree about 30 feet up. I climbed out of the tree and got the lieutenant out and we walked back to Many Glacier." This was Cy's matter of fact report, and second close call.

The destruction at Waterton Lakes, Canada, was enormous. Fortunately, the Prince of Wales Hotel is high on a moraine and did not suffer direct damage, but it became the rescue site for the entire village and our hotel was filled with non-paying refugees. We did lose our pumping station and our power plant was put out of operation. The skipper of our ship, Launch International, which was a 73 foot twin diesel-powered sightseeing vessel with a capacity for 250 people, had the presence of mind to park the Launch and tie up to the trees in the picnic area. That is how high the water was in that location. He saved our ship. The dock was destroyed and the structure to house the International during the wintertime was almost completely obliterated.

Due to the tremendous cooperation from all sources, we got the park open on June 29. That was the date the deck was completed over the Middle Fork of the Flathead River at West Glacier. We opened the facilities one by one as we were able to reach them by road.

A great part of the credit goes to the Great Northern Railway, who made it possible to hold on to many of our tours through their shuttles to provide us interim service from each side of the park.

I could not help but be apprehensive about the problems we faced. I realized that even if we got into operation, there was a good chance we would lose most of our reservations. On Good Friday of that year, an earthquake had occurred near Anchorage and while our facilities at Mt. McKinley National Park had suffered no damage, the wide notoriety of the earthquake in Alaska served to drastically reduce the patronage for the season. We would receive 30 reservations and 90 cancellations in the same mail. I could just imagine the same thing happening to us in Glacier National Park where we had received such tremendous publicity on the amount of damage to our facilities and the inability to get to or through the park. The outstanding cooperation of the Great Northern prevented this result and we retained most of our reservations.

The flood in Glacier National Park had come without warning. We had some late snows and colder than normal weather for June. June is a variable weather month, so the late snows caused no undue concern. What was not anticipated was the warm rain that followed. The new-fallen snow melted in record time, causing a literal cascade of water down the mountainsides. The streams and valleys could not accommodate this rushing torrent of water and the dams that had been erected for storage gave way, inundating not only the water channels, but the mesas above them. Not even the "old-timers" could recall such a flood.

After restoration and with prospect of reasonable business for the season, we expanded our building program to put in 18 much needed showers and 18 toilets in the Lake McDonald cabins. We also put in electric heaters in the dormitories at Many Glacier and improved their living conditions. It is remarkable what a little sunshine will do to bolster the spirits and expand confidence!

Genee's Christmas Letter, 1964:

It is hard to believe it will be a year ago that we spent two wonderful weeks in Hawaii. We plan to vary the climate and have a white Christmas this year in Glacier National Park. The children have never experienced a Christmas in the snow.

This year has been another busy, active one, marked with unforgettable events. We offered to provide a home for Don's two small nephews who were orphaned through an airplane accident, who we took to Hawaii with us last Christmas, but a quarrel has ensued and we were not allowed to take them to the Park this summer. The matter is before the court and the final decision has not been reached. Our own children have really grown this last year. Only Charlene remains in grade school. The other three are teenagers who keep the household buzzing with friends and activities. Donna and Cliff worked most of last summer season at Glacier. Genee's calendar is dotted with their band practice, Tri-Hi-Y meetings, dentists' appointments, etc.; P.T.A., Girl Scouts, as well as United Community Campaign, Youth Board, Tucson Community Council, symphony and book club activities. Added to her usual list was some active campaigning in a lively School Board election and the general election, particularly the gubematorial race. Don served as Sam Goddard's campaign manager for Pima County. We were elated with his success. It was a real victory.

Don has continued to make numerous trips, mostly in connection with the National Parks, and on various phases of government and recreation. He was in Anchorage, Alaska, a few weeks after the earthquake and was shocked by the extensive and erratic damage it wrought, particularly in the residential area. McKinley Park Hotel felt the jolt, but received no physical damage. The devastation was confined to a short, narrow area along the coast. Although summer travel to Alaska dropped considerably, we were fortunate in that our operations in Mt. McKinley National Park faired well, and our operations in Lassen were the best ever.

Don flew back from Alaska in early June to drive the rest of us to Glacier Park. We had not even unpacked when the unbelievable floods came. A steady 48 hour rain on a heavy spring snow pack melted the snow, breaking two conservation dams, and destroying more than 20 miles of roads and railroad lines, washing out 114 bridges in Glacier County alone. Employee morale remained remarkably high through the crises and throughout the rest of the season. All facilities and the East-West Highway through the Park were opened June 29th, the result of a mammoth and determined effort by all levels of government and individual initiative. It was heartening to experience the spirit of cooperation and demonstrated how well people, government agencies, and individuals can put aside their usual differences and cooperate with each other when the need arises.

In all, we felt fortunate not to have lost any lives, nor to have irreparable damage, but it was an experience we will never forget, and it was a summer we never want repeated.

We are now looking to the New Year for new beginnings and renewed enthusiasm for all the opportunities and challenges it will bring.

❆ ❆ ❆

My concern for Glacier was justified as our financial report for the off-season from January through May 1966 showed a loss in excess of $200,000. This required us to borrow money to defray expenses. Our receipts for the season, starting June 1, 1966, reached $2,209,715, and we closed the year with a net profit after taxes of $82,315. While not large, it was reassuring.

We had encountered difficulty in serving our guests at Rising Sun since the destruction in the flood of 1964. The flood had wiped out most of the trees between the lodge and the road. This exposed the lodge to car traffic on the highway and swamped our coffee shop. Before, the lodge was so obscured, traffic mostly passed us by and entreaties to the Park Service to allow more signs had regularly been denied. The flood caused a good view from the highway.

In 1966 we erected a new coffee shop which provided a new kitchen, 40 tables and 135 chairs, a registration desk for our motels and cabins, a small gift shop and a dining and recreation room for our employees. The cost of construction was $101,000.

This freed up the space for the old kitchen, which was converted into employee quarters. The coffee shop and lobby were converted into 12 new motel rooms, giving us a total of 40 motel rooms plus the 30 cabins.

In 1966 I accompanied Director Hartzog to the Horace Albright Training Center in Grand Canyon National Park, as I had been scheduled to conduct a program on concessions for incoming rangers. While there, word was sent in that the Secretary was on the telephone and wanted to talk to me. The Director was a little put out, thinking it was the Secretary of the Interior. It was Secretary Robert Weaver of the Department of Housing and Urban Development.

Secretary Weaver offered me the position of Assistant Secretary for Renewal and Housing, a position in charge of the department's housing program and urban renewal for the United States. I hesitated about accepting since involvement with the Glacier operation demanded close attention. On returning to Tucson, Genee urged me to accept. My nephew, Al Donau, who was running our Lassen operations, offered to take my place in Glacier. His wife, Mary Frank Donau, would manage the Lassen business. It was agreed and I notified Secretary Weaver of my acceptance.

I reported to H.U.D. in Washington, D.C., in May 1966 for this new challenge (see the chapter on H.U.D.). This was the department that I had urged President Jack Kennedy to establish when I was President of the American Municipal Association, now named the National League of Cities.

1967 in Glacier was plagued by a series of lightning fires. There were 35 fires going at one time being fought by over 350 men. What caused us the most concern was a small snag fire on Heavens Peak. In 1936, a similar fire had jumped the continental divide, wiping out most of the Swiftcurrent cabins and would have destroyed the Many Glacier Hotel had the Forest Service and company employees not manned the roof with buckets of water to put out sparks that landed on the roof.

While we complained to the Park Service about the

neglect of this fire, it was never fought until the wind picked it up and spread it over the Going-To-The-Sun road up to the Garden Wall. This effectively closed the park two weeks early, limiting our season and the financial results.

I learned of our real tragedy being awakened at our home in Bethesda, Maryland, by a call from Al Donau on August 13, 1967, notifying me that Julie Helgeson, an employee of ours at East Glacier, had been killed at Granite Park by a grizzly. I refused to believe the second call a few hours later that Michelle Koons, an employee at Lake McDonald Lodge, had also been killed by a grizzly bear at Trout Lake. I argued that this was just a mix-up of reports stemming from the same accident. Unfortunately, I was wrong. We lost two beautiful girls in one night, 20 miles apart, by two separate grizzly attacks. Speculation, arguments and so-called scientific reasons still prevail. There is, in my opinion, an overriding cause. Bears in national parks are protected and have lost the fear of man. The so-called Glacier Bear Management policy would be more aptly described as a "People Exclusion Policy." When a bear is sighted on a trail, the trail is closed. Campgrounds have been closed when bears venture into the vicinity. Visitors have traveled thousands of miles, only to be denied an opportunity to explore Glacier through this exclusion policy.

This need not be, if the Park Service would adopt a policy of "teaching" bears to fear and avoid humans. A program to shoot near — not to kill or injure — would soon make bears keep their distance. How often have you heard of a mauling in the forest areas where bears are hunted and shot at? This generation of bears in Glacier have never heard a shot fired.

I have attempted to advance this proposal at public hearings on bear management, but have been limited to five minutes. The so-called experts and those making a living on studying bears dominate the proposals.

The facts demonstrate the failure of the present policy. Although thousands of visitors went into the back country in Glacier in the early days, there was never a fatality for 57 years preceding 1967, until our two employees were killed. Bears were shot at then, and avoided humans. Since establishing this policy, a period of 18 years has expired. There have been several maulings and five fatalities, including two more of our own employees: Jane A. Ammerman and Kim R. Eberly were killed on July 5, 1980. Jane and Kim had been hiking and camped along Divide Creek, just two hundred yards from St. Marys Lodge — not a place one would consider grizzly territory. Both their sleeping bags had been dragged and the bodies mutilated. Kim's body was still partially within his sleeping bag, but badly mutilated.

Isn't it about time to try something new and return the parks to the people for their enjoyment? The parks were set aside for this purpose but the bears appear to have preference. If you doubt this, read "The Night of the Grizzlys" by Jack Olson.

At the close of the 1967 season, Laura Stuart, who owned the Lake McDonald Motel adjacent to our store at Lake McDonald, died. I had talked with Laura about buying her motel; we were woefully short of rooms, having only 71 rooms in our complex at Lake McDonald. Increased traffic, particularly in group tours, required us to backtrack our guests to the east side for lodging, where we had 541 rooms, including Glacier Park Lodge outside the park, plus the Prince of Wales Hotel. Guests resented backtracking and this complicated our scheduling.

Backtracking also further congested the Going-To-The-Sun Road. The acquisition of this motel would give us some respite for a few years.

After considerable negotiation with her son, who was executor of her estate, I purchased the motel and adjacent cottages. The one unit of the motel had only five rooms for employees and a gift shop. I immediately converted the gift shop and remodeled the employees' rooms to guest rooms. This gave me a total of 30 more rooms, with a capacity of 120 pillows as each room was equipped with two double beds.

In order to make this purchase and pay for the new coffee shop at Rising Sun, I borrowed $230,000 from the First National Bank of Great Falls. I gave them a mortgage on Glacier Park Lodge.

17

Challenges to Concessions Policy

ON THE convening of the Conference meeting in November 1962, I reviewed the Secretary's policy statement of May 6, 1950. I pointed out that prior to this time our problems had come from the Department of the Interior, but now they were coming from government operations and appropriation congressional committees. The criticism by the congressional committees was directed not only at the concessioners, but at the National Park Service. The essence of the problem was who would best provide the facilities in the national parks.

It was obvious that if the private sector was to continue to assume these obligations, there had to be a strong policy statement supported by congressional action. The lack of security and poor economic climate plus the rising political harassment made our position untenable. Secretary of the Interior Stewart Udall and Solicitor Frank Barry had both reaffirmed their support of the May 6, 1950 statement by Secretary Chapman, but we were experiencing a rising tide of congressional criticism. Assistant Secretary Carver was particularly supportive as he felt strongly that the private sector was the proper source for funds to provide visitor facilities in the national parks.

The concessions contract is, of course, the legal basis of the concessioners' rights and obligations. The contract language was developed to implement the Mather/Albright policies which were designed to encourage private investment in visitor facilities in the parks. Government ownership of this type of facility had not been considered as Congress had never seriously regarded public funds as appropriate for this type of investment. This was acknowledged to be the province of the private sector.

Some of the most important policies and provisions which were reflected in the standard language contracts were:

1) granting of a property right described as a possessory interest in structures erected on government land with private capital with the approval of the secretary;

2) payment of just compensation for this investment, if taken for public use;

3) administration of government policies giving the concessioner a reasonable opportunity to make a profit on his investment as a whole;

4) granting of a long-term contract, if a substantial investment is required;

5) a preferential right to renewal of the concessioner's contract, if his services have been considered satisfactory by the secretary;

6) approval of rates, to be based primarily on comparison with rates for similar services under similar conditions prevailing outside park jurisdiction;

7) administration of policies designed to encourage and enable private investments in the parks with continuity of operations, including the cancellation of unexpired contracts and issuance of a new one for a longer term, if major investments were required.

8) preferential right to provide additional services of similar kind was permitted, but not required.

These policies, which had been developed over the years and which had nurtured the concession system, were supported by the Secretary of the Interior in his statement on May 6, 1950, and confirmed by the appropriate congressional committees. The provisions were incorporated in the standard language worked out between the solicitors and concessioners in that memorable meeting heretofore discussed.

While the policy was designed to encourage private investment, I learned to my sorrow that a good policy is not enough for a banker or investment firm to provide the money. As Mr. Frisbee, our Lassen banker in Redding, California, advised me when I sought a loan to expand the facilities in Lassen Volcanic National Park:

It's a good policy, but a policy can be changed at any time and does not provide security for me to loan you bank funds.

I decided in 1962 that we would have to stabilize the policy by legislative enactment. As I was Chairman of the Conference, I informally took up the subject with the other concessioners. I received a rather cool reception from some of the larger concessioners. This was understandable, as they were fearful of losing some of the favorable provisions in the policy. Also, they were able to successfully finance their operations, as they had long records of borrowing and repayment with their banks. Some concessions such as Lassen had good relations, but with the increase in facilities needed and the increased cost of construction, required sums of money far in excess of previous loans. The standard was a commercial loan that had to be repaid in five years. This was no longer adequate for the funds required. After considerable discussion agreement was ultimately reached with the Conference. When finally agreed to, there was no half hearted support. All supported a proposal to have the policies enacted into law; that is, all but the Utah Parks Company, a subsidiary of the Union Pacific Railroad, which had signed a 20-year contract despite the Solicitor's opinion, and were losing money. They saw no advantage in participating.

Congressman Michael K. Kirwan of the Appropriations Committee had initiated an investigation into concessions policies. The Committee was particularly critical of the concept of possessory interest, the preferential right of renewal and the preferential right to provide new facilities. Pursuant to this investigation, a number of the concessioners were contacted and questioned as to these terms, asking particularly how the investment would be completely amortized so that some other concessioner could come into the park. Hil Oehlmann, at Yosemite, reported that he advised the investigators that most of the concession operations were for sale but there were no buyers, so that the criticism that these contracts were exceptionally favorable for concessioners was not borne out in the facts. Hil also pointed out that there was constant need for reinvestment in the parks so that it was highly unlikely that investment could be completely amortized at any given time. These inquiries and criticisms made long-term lenders dubious of the security of the investment particularly as the political climate in the parks did not support the Secretary's policy statement.

The question of franchise fees paid by the concessions was also being questioned. There were those who felt that the government should get the maximum amount possible, while the Park Service wanted good services at reasonable rates rather than revenue to the government. This concept had not been accepted by the Appropriations Subcommittee for Parks. Following the lead of the Appropriations Committee, the Park Service began talking about collecting fees on the basis of the type of business that you were engaged in, irrespective of the profit situation.

As a result of this congressional pressure on the Park Service, the question of franchise fees resulted in a growing dispute between the National Park Service and the concessioners. The Appropriations Committee and others thought the franchise fees were too low for the privileges granted. This criticism grew out of the fact that the concession operations were not particularly profitable and that every dollar taken out for franchise fees went into the general treasury.

This was the reason that the policy provided that revenue to the government was to be subordinate to good services at reasonable rates. There was a whole series of proposals by the National Park Service designed to increase fees and make them uniform. The Conference made it very clear that this was not a practical approach, as fees were related to profits and rates and an attempt to uniformly apply them to all concessioners was not a reasonable approach. This conflict continued without resolution.

On February 27, 1964, Director Hartzog submitted a memorandum to the Secretary of the Interior pertaining to established guide lines for concessioners' franchise fees. There were two parts to the proposal. Operations which served to provide housing (high capital investment) were to be charged at the rate of three-fourths of one percent of gross receipts.

Operations concerning sales in stores, transportation services, guide services, lunch rooms, boat rentals and sales of fishing and similar services, were to be charged at the rate of one and one-half percent; thirdly, operations whose primary purpose was the sale of souvenirs, curios and photographic shops were to be charged at the rate of three percent. These were to be consolidated into one fee based on the concessioner's primary business. If the business was to provide housing and feeding, the fee would be three-fourths of one percent plus an addition for the total operations, including all sales. The Director advised the Secretary that this franchise fee schedule had not been put into effect even though there had been long protracted discussions with concessioners without agreement.

As the Western Conference was to meet with him again, he said he would like to have the Secretary's approval to urge these proposed changes on the Conference. His proposal was presented to the Conference and the Chairman responded by stating that, "In the last analysis, franchise fees were a matter for individual negotiation."   The Conference's position was that fees were a poor method of raising revenue for the government, and should be, as stated in the policy, subordinate to the goal of better accommodations and good services; and that any proposal to take as much as three percent of the gross receipts of the concessioners would raise only a million and a half dollars and force government ownership in the operation of many concessions.   The records showed that most concessioners would not be in a position to pay this high a fee. Earnings were minimal.

In a meeting with Assistant Secretary Carver, the Conference's position was restated.   The Secretary acknowledged that franchise fees were a poor regulatory tool and inadequate means of raising revenue for the government. He stated that they were in no hurry for an answer. The Conference never did approve these guidelines, but the Park Service used them in negotiating contracts without Conference approval.

It was apparent that the policy statement issued on May 6, 1950, reestablishing the Mather/Albright policies recognizing the concessioners property rights was not adequate to provide the security necessary for the concessioners to secure adequate financing to provide the facilities that the public was demanding which had been exacerbated by increased travel to the national parks. The Conference then turned to ways and means by which they could improve the situation which would enable them to discharge their obligations.

In 1950, at the height of the problems with the Department of the Interior, Herman Hoss had drafted proposed legislation which supported the terms of the existing contracts. This had been dropped when Chairman Peterson advised the Conference that there was no time for legislation and recommended getting together with the department on contract language.

In 1962, when I proposed that we again seek legislation as the policy statement was inadequate, the Hoss legislation was proposed to provide the basis for stabilizing legislation.

There was also proposed a loan guarantee plan. This had been drafted primarily by Hugh Galusha, the accountant for Hamilton Stores Inc. and Yellowstone Park Company. Questions were raised as to whether the loan guarantee program should be included with the policy legislation. Hil Oehlmann said he felt it might prejudice the possibility of enactment of the policy bill. The question was raised as to what the attitude of the National Park Service would be to the Conference initiating legislation. The Chairman was instructed to explore this problem with the National Park Service and a meeting took place later that day.

The Conference met with Director Conrad Wirth, Chief of Concessions Tom Flynn and Park Service Solicitor Jackson Price. Director Wirth questioned whether private enterprise was still able to do the job, remarking that he was not certain in his own mind, but knew that better service was being demanded than was being provided in the national parks. I responded that the Conference shared the Director's concern of the criticism being directed at both of us, but that I felt it was unjust and unfair, in that we were being requested to provide services, but that our hands were tied by lack of stable policies which would permit access to adequate financing.

I stated that we had felt the concession system offered the best chance of solving the problem in the parks and that any shift to government ownership to solve the problems would only change the source of them. I said that while the policies were adequate, we needed legislation to remove many of the uncertainties and difficulties and the possibility of the retraction of the present policies. I said I thought this was consistent with the recommendations of the Outdoor Recreation Review Commission Report, which had just been released. I asked for Director Wirth's blessing in exploring with the Department of Interior the possibility of seeking legislation to enact the policy statement into law.

Director Wirth was hesitant about the legislative approach, stating that we might lose some of our policy and advantages, pointing out that we had semi-legislative approval with the submission of each contract to the Interior and Insular Committee where it remained for 60 days before the Park Service was authorized to sign the contract.

Director Wirth seemed to favor the loan guarantee bill rather than legislation enacting the policies which were in effect. I pointed out that recognition of possessory interest and the concessioners' right to compensation, if that interest was terminated, was vitally important to us and this would not be covered in the loan guarantee bill. To this Assistant Secretary Carver agreed. Herman Hoss, the Conference attorney, added that as well as guaranteeing the loan, we needed a guarantee of the policy for the expected life of the loan, as changes in policies could have disastrous effects on the concessioners' businesses. Director Wirth seemed concerned about protecting the administrative responsibility of the Department of the Interior and the National Park Service. Dale Doty, former assistant secretary and now Conference representative, pointed out that the policy statement was not in conflict with the Park Service and the concessioners but that our problem was with the constant review of policy by other interested parties, such as the Kirwan Appropriations Committee.

Later in the day, as Chairman, I met with Assistant Secretary Carver and Director Wirth. Assistant Secretary Carver opened the discussion by stating that he had gone over the agenda of the Western Conference and he wished to state that it completely paralleled his thinking. He stated that his position was in favor of private enterprise in the national parks, and that he recognized the need for security of investment made on public lands. He asked the chairman if private enterprise could do the job. I replied that it certainly could, if concessioners were given access to the money markets through proper security of their investments at proper rates.

Assistant Carver stated that he was bothered by the preferential right to provide new services. He said he did not understand why there should not be competition in the parks. I replied that competition in the parks had been proven to be impractical, as the conditions for competition in the parks did not exist. If you were to have competition you had to at least double the facilities in the park and that the system of the Park Service control of rates, services to be performed, opening and closing dates and prices, was preferential to the previous experience of the parks when competition did exist.

Assistant Secretary Carver disagreed with Director Wirth and recommended that we proceed at once to secure legislation and not wait for the results of the current Kirwan investigation. He stated that he would support the Conference in its attempts to secure passage of the law supporting the policy statement.

I stated that if the Department of the Interior was to do its job, existing policy needed to be clarified and strengthened, that legislative security for the property interest of the concessioner's tenure, their preferential rights must be reaffirmed by legislation. He indicated his full support for this approach.

Les Scott, Grand Canyon, suggested that the Chairman and the Committee investigate the possibility of enactment. Trev Povah and George Mauger expressed agreement with this proposal. I then appointed an executive committee composed of Les Scott, Hil Oehlmann, Trev Povah, Ray Lillie, George Mauger, Hugh Galusha, Gerry Bemiss, Herman Hoss and Dale Doty as the committee to prepare legislation for submission to the Park Service and the Interior and Insular Affairs Committee of the House of Representatives.

There was considerable discussion as to who should present the bill. It was suggested that if the concessioners presented it, it would look like specialized legislation for their selfish interests. On the other hand, if the Park Service was to present the bill, it would have to go through the normal process of getting approval of the Department of the Interior and a long delay would follow. Daggett Harvey of Grand Canyon asked what would happen if the bill was defeated or it was not acted upon. It was felt that if the bill was not acted upon the present policies would continue, but if we faced the possibilities of actual defeat, we should probably not introduce the bill at all. The matter was turned over to the Chairman and the executive committee for examination and decision.

After a joint session of the executive committee and the Park Service, it was agreed that the Conference would proceed with the legislation as had been agreed upon between the parties. The proposed government guarantee bill was to be presented but emphasis was on the policy bill. The chairman was instructed to proceed.

It is obvious, in view of the serious questions that were facing the Conference and its expanded responsibilities, that we should reexamine the Conference structure and determine what form it should take and how we should proceed in the future.

It was impractical to await the annual meetings of the Conference to make decisions. I appointed Ray Lillie, Grand Teton Lodge Company; George Beal, Yellowstone Park Company; Stewart Cross, Yosemite Park & Curry Company; Paul Sceva, Rainier National Park Company; A. S. Donau, Lassen National Park Company; and Daggett Harvey of the Fred Harvey Co., who was to act as Chairman, to make recommendations concerning the revamping of the structure of the Conference. The committee was to render a report to the meeting of the Conference in March of 1963.

Daggett Harvey reported at that March Conference that it was agreed that the Conference should not have formal trappings and should largely follow its present informal basis; that if Bylaws were to be adopted, they should be confined to setting up the basic structure of the organization and provide for a chairman and executive committee.

The committee confirmed that the present requirements for membership should not be changed; that membership should be open to anyone who had a contract or permit who asked for membership, but that no drive be conducted to enlarge the group. The committee also recommended that there be no formal standing committee; that the executive committee and legislative committee should be appointed by the Chairman. The executive committee would be empowered, with the Chairman, to make decisions in the interim between Conference meetings.

It was also agreed that one meeting a year was adequate, with the right of the Chairman to call other meetings, if conditions required. The proposal that the Conference act as an employment clearinghouse was voted down. It was agreed that there would be advantages if there were more general public relations under the auspices of the Conferences, and that this matter should be thoroughly explored. The committee recommended against the Conference attempting to police its members' activities.

18

Growing Restrictions

OVER THE next two decades, the guarantees we had achieved were methodically reduced through policy and contract changes as the National Park Service responded to the escalating potency of environmental organizations, whose objectives were to reduce visitor facilities in the national parks.

Wilderness Areas
(Public Law 88-577) September 3, 1964

We in the Conference had not been diligent in following the proposed application of the Wilderness Act to the national parks. The Park Service had, we believed, administered their park areas so as to leave them "unimpaired for future generations." We did not fully realize that the environmental organizations did not share our views and wanted to protect them from the National Park Service; i.e., to remove as many areas as possible from encroachment by visitor use. The environmentalists did not trust the National Park Service and worked to have as much of the parks restricted to any development, including roads and trails. They loaded the wilderness hearings with their members.

Under the terms of the Wilderness Act, as enacted, the Secretary of the Interior was required to review every roadless area of 5,000 contiguous acres or more in the national parks, monuments and other units of the National Park System, including wildlife refuges and game ranges, and report to the President his recommendations as to the suitability or nonsuitability of each area for preservation as wilderness. Final determination for designation of Wilderness Areas was vested in Congress.

Pursuant to this act, large portions of the parks, in some instances equal to 97 percent of the area, were designated as wilderness, and thus unavailable for roads or any man-made structure to serve the park visitor. The concessioners expressed their concern, as this effectively cut off most areas for expansion needed to provide visitor services, while avoiding concentration and the protection of the quality of the experience.

Chairman Cross had reported to the Conference at a meeting in March 1967 that Director Hartzog had stated he expected the concessioners to participate in the designation of wilderness areas and master plans, as the Park Service team made its survey. The Director advised his staff that the concessioners were to be brought in at the beginning and not after the plan had been adopted. It had been reported that the superintendent at Mammoth Cave had recommended tearing down the concessioner's hotel, and building a new one about 40 miles away, without prior consultation with the concessioner involved, who owned the building.

It was obvious that the Director's instructions were not being followed. The Director had stated that the concessioner should be allowed to write his own views on the master plan and the wilderness survey and that this report should become part of the permanent record. This did not materialize.

Director Hartzog reported that "at all hearings for the national parks, the wilderness groups were present en masse and made presentations, but the hearings lacked other interested organizations such as the Hotel Association, the automobile clubs, chambers of commerce and other interested parties who represent the majority of visitors to the national parks. The wilderness groups were after entire areas of the national parks and actually other groups were needed to begin expressing just how much of these areas should be devoted to wilderness needs and how much should be devoted to the average visitor to the national park."

At the meeting of the Conference in Williamsburg in March 1972, I was reelected Chairman of the Conference. There followed a meeting with Park Service representatives, Director George Hartzog and Associate Deputy Director T. F. Flynn, Jr.

The Director advised that they were developing new vistas and that great pressure would be put on us all. He informed us that he considered environmental policies one of the concessioner's responsibilities and that we should handle them with pride. Some of the items in this program were implementation of the Secretary's directives, which included the limiting of the use of areas in the parks, reduction of automobiles in the parks, improvement in the quality of the park experience. This was the first admission by the Park Service to the Conference that they were pursuing a policy of "limiting visitor use of the national parks" as the policy of the Department of the Interior and the National Park Service.

I responded that we concurred with the Director's remark that change was the order of the day and that this doubled the importance of keeping open lines of communication. I said that private investment, once made, loses some of the flexibility to change and change can alter services and cause losses. I further commented that crowding on specific days and in specific locations was often translated to total over-crowding, but that I did not believe this was so. I thought the exclusion of visitors was not the answer. I suggested, as other approaches, extensions of the season, more entrances to the parks to avoid back-tracking, the opening of new areas in the parks, the Park Service's emphasis on less visited parks and recognition of the impact of these policies. I requested that the concessioners be given an opportunity to participate in decisions being made by the National Park Service which affected the concessioners' responsibilities.

Director Hartzog responded that he recognized that there was not over-crowding in the parks, but that he had received very little agreement upon this view. He said he received great pressure from the wilderness groups, ever since the enactment of the Wilderness Act in 1964. He said the definition of "wilderness" had bothered him, first as to legal definition, and secondly as to the physical condition and allocation of use.

Master Plans

Master plans were another device used to further restrict concession expansion and the ability to provide visitor services. The application of the "wilderness" designation removed large areas from any development for visitor use. Now, through the master plan, the remaining areas would further be reduced for facilities for the accommodation of park visitors. I examined twelve of the principal master plans and every one provided for reduced or limitation of visitor facilities. This, despite the fact of the parks' increasing popularity and visitation.

The goal of the environmentalists was the removal of visitor facilities regardless of who provided them. The concessioners took the brunt of their tirade as Congress had decided that the private sector was the preferred method of providing for visitor services.

If the environmentalists were to be successful, they had to rid the parks of the concessioners. This was pursued in various ways. One was to claim over-commercialization and too much emphasis on profits. Another was to question the right to use a national park to make a profit. As a result, proposals were urged to encourage the use of non-profit organizations or government ownership and/or operations. It would be easier to reduce or remove facilities if the private profit entrepreneur was first discredited and then removed. All of these alternatives were urged with the merging of the concept to remove visitor facilities to areas outside park boundaries. For this approach, the environmental organizations encountered support from the National Park Service. Master plans were an effective means of eliminating expansion of visitor facilities. Reduction of investment safeguards by contract provisions was another. Both were vigorously pursued.

The environmental organizations were getting bolder and more direct in their pressure on Park Service policies. This reached new heights as the centennial of the national parks was approached.

19
Controversy Over Souvenirs

THERE HAD been controversy from time to time about the character and worth of the items sold in concessionaires' gift shops. The contract provisions being included in concessionaires' contracts were as follows:

> The merchandise authorized to be sold under terms of this contract will include only that which is approved by the Secretary or his authorized representative and its sale will be in accord with standards to be established from time to time by the National Park Service.

On December 16, 1944, the following guidelines were proposed after present stocks were depleted:

> 1. Any article not manufactured in the United States, its territories or insular possession unless expressly authorized.

This was objected to by Hilmer Oehlmann calling attention to the fact that our government was committed to a policy of enlarging international trade and combating isolationism.

Hill indicated that the Ahwahnee gift shop offered articles of art from Persia, India, Russia, Finland, England, Belgium, Norway, Sweden, Mexico and China.

George Mauger of Sequoia and Kings Canyon National Parks also objected as running counter to most other United States agencies who are seeking a friendly and reciprocal economic relationship with other countries. He pointed out that sales from their gift shops permitted them to maintain reasonable rates for room and food services stating that the profits from gift shop operations often were the only profits their company experienced. He said he agreed with control of rates for necessities such as food and lodging but saw no reason that concessionaires should be singled out for control of voluntary purchases such as souvenir and gift items.

The Conference members agreed that articles from materials indigenous to the area unless plainly marked as not acquired in the park were objectionable. We also agreed that trophies, skins, mounted heads, etc., should not be sold. Imitation Native American handicraft must be plainly marked when sold.

The regulation also prohibited articles which were neither useful nor durable such as keys, whistles, toy balloons, good luck charms and carnival-type articles.

This prohibition was objected to as to its propriety and difficulty of administration and subject to wide differences of opinion.

Jack Verkamp of Verkamps of Grand Canyon stated that his superintendent objected to souvenirs that they were not indigenous to the area and had nothing to do with the park. He pointed out that the sale of handicrafts and similar articles were often more than the visitor wanted to pay and alone produced insufficient profits for him to stay in business.

The policy of prohibiting the sale of foreign made souvenirs was repealed by Acting Director Hillory A. Tolson.

As the policy continued to pose controversy through different interpretations by superintendents in the various parks, Director Conrad Wirth appointed a souvenir committee in each of the regions consisting of a regional representative as chairman, a superintendent and a concessionaire. I was the concessionaires representative for Region IV in San Francisco.

The policy at this time was as follows:

It shall be the policy of the Department to encourage (1) the sale of appropriate souvenirs, jewelry and the like, which are authentic handicraft and labeled as to origin; and (2) the sale of articles associated with or interpretive of the areas administered by the National Park Service.

Trev Povah listed his thoughts on souvenir policies:

1. Though the idea of selling products related to the area is a sound one, in practice it is impractical for the reason that most areas do not produce sufficient volume of products to meet demands. This will get worse as travel increases.

2. Since foreign made articles are admitted to the United States under import regulations, there is no rea-

son why the Park Service should discriminate against such products.

3. The supply of genuine Indian handicraft is welcomed by concessionaires in all National Parks but the supply is dwindling.

4. As regard this task: who is to judge? In America we believe in educating not dictating. Items the public regards as in bad taste, they do not buy.

5. The law of supply and demand has always been the determining factor as to what a retail establishment offers for sale.

6. The average pocketbook does not allow the purchase of costly souvenirs. Most families desire a memento for a neighbor child or a friend. These dictate inexpensive souvenirs.

7. The volume of dry goods, groceries or fountains would not of themselves justify a concessionaire operating in a National Park.

8. As long as the merchandise a concessionaire sells is not harmful or morally objectionable, he should be authorized to sell what retailers sell outside the park.

Hil Oehlmann, as Chairman of the Conference, responded to Trev agreeing with his analysis and stating that I had paralleled his thinking with the report we sent from Region IV.

The National Parks Association by letter dated June 25, 1959, to Hil Oehlmann advised that they were requesting statements on the subject of national parks concessions and requested one from Hil. The letter contained the following quote:

The souvenir concessions of many of our national parks are the butt of increasing criticism by serious-minded people in the United States. Visitors do want souvenirs. This being true, it would seem that the finer sort of concession proper to the park environment and purposes could replace the carnival-type shops. The Service has proven on the Blue Ridge Parkway that this high class of concession can be instituted (the government built these buildings). The cheap souvenir with its common factory junk, decorated with trick sayings, attracts the kind of tourist whose values are not geared to appreciating national park areas. It seems that some of the expense of maintaining clean parks might be reduced by eliminating such cheap concessions.

Hil Oehlmann's reply follows in full copy:

Mr. Bruce M. Kilgore, Editor
National Parks Magazine

Dear Mr. Kilgore:
   I have received your letter of June 25 on the subject of souvenirs in the national parks and have noted the quotation from a manuscript you have received. Your proposal to present several viewpoints is eminently fair, and I am glad of the opportunity to give you my own considered judgment. Without presuming to qualify myself as an expert I only mention that I have been in close touch with the sale of souvenirs in Yosemite National Park for 33 years, and for half that period was in direct charge of this field of our company's activities.
   I begin my remarks with the frank avowal that I do not consider it a responsibility of the national Park Service and its supporting organizations to improve the public taste, and certainly no such duty devolves upon the concessioners in the parks. The appropriate media for achieving this objective are the homes and schools.
   If "serious-minded" people are distressed by the merchandise they see in souvenir shops, I should think they would find the apparel of the customers even more disturbing. Stout women in slacks and hairy men in shorts surely must offend the fastidious more acutely than the "common factory junk" which these (I almost added "common") people are admiring. I am afraid we come to another facet of that snobbishness which subconsciously persuades the elite that the very fabric of their appreciation is of finer texture than that of the mass of men.
   It is time for the critics to reflect that approval and distaste are subjective qualities. Tourists the world over seek and purchase the same type of souvenirs which appear cheap and tawdry to persons of discrimination. In my earliest experience with our own shops I used to wonder at the choices made. Longer exposure to the scene changed my attitude. I observed that selection of mementos for themselves and gifts for friends and relatives was an important activity of visitors to the park, and the purchase of a felt pennant, an Indian doll, or a terra cotta bear appeared to give as much pleasure to one person as the choice of a book or picture to another.
   In some areas handicrafts are available, and where

this occurs their sale generally is encouraged. In most places such articles either do not exist or are on their way out. In my time there has been a total disappearance of Yosemite basketry and beadworking. Jewelry, pottery, and rugs are declining in the southwest, both in quantity and quality. Parenthetically, an example of maladroit federal intervention occurred when Secretary Ickes prohibited concessioners from handling imitation jewelry at a time when the Indians weren't making the genuine article because they were on the rolls of WPA.

The whole question had best be left to the judgment of the Americans who visit our parks. Restriction of choice amounts to regimentation, of which the world already has seen too much. I suspect that by the time park visitors have learned not to discard beer cans and tissues on the roadside they will be looking for more tasteful souvenirs. Assuredly, then the concessioners will be happy to supply them.

Very Sincerely,
H. Oehlmann

In December, 1964, the subject of concession souvenirs was again raised by Director Hartzog by letter to the Conference requesting the subject be placed on the Conference agenda.

The annual meeting of the Conference was held in March 1965. The Director advised that he had been instructed by Secretary Udall to tighten the policy on selling souvenirs in concessions shops. The Director requested that the Conference appoint a committee and make recommendations. The Chairman appointed Trevor Povah as chairman and Kay Burgess of Mount Rushmore and J. D. Hubbard of Carlsbad Caverns as members.

Kay Valdes made a report of her efforts to secure Indian-made handicraft which included visits to various Indian reservations and letters to the governors of all the states requesting assistance to contact Indian groups in their state for the purpose of securing Indian handicrafts.

In response to our request that the Park Service provide a definition of native handicraft, Jackson Price, Assistant Director, by letter of May 28, 1965, responded as follows:

Native Handicraft items are articles or products of high intrinsic value which are predominantly hand made and which are individually produced under conditions not resembling an assemblyline or factory system and with only the help of such devices or machines as allow the manual skill of the maker to condition the shape and design of each individual product. Native handicraft must also be a regional product or article, designed, produced, fashioned and decorated by a native inhabitant of a particular region using traditional materials and designs of that region.

At the request of the Director, each concessionaire made a report for the Director specifying the handicraft sold in his shop and outlining the segregation of handicrafted items.

The committee I appointed met in Mount Rushmore. In addition to our committee members, Mr. Robert Hart, Chief Arts and Crafts Board, Bureau of Indian Affairs; Mr. James Wilson, Business Analyst, Industrial Development Board, Bureau of Indian Affairs; Tom Flynn, Chief of Concessions, National Park Service; and I, as Chairman, met to discuss our problems. The reason for the meeting was to more clearly define and identify merchandise designated as "hand made." This was made even more apparent with the presentation by a representative of Turtle Mountain Authentic Reproductions, Inc., that we needed to classify "Indian Made Merchandise."

We were encountering difficulty in identifying the native handicraft which would conform to the Park Service definition. In an attempt to comply we proposed classifications with symbols to identify the product.

Indian Handicrafted - Blue Buffalo One.

Products of Indian created design handicrafted by an American Indian will be classified Number One, Indian Handicrafted. Indian handicrafted products which are of repetitive design and produced primarily for the commercial channels of trade would also be so classified. The handicrafter may be invited to add his name or mark if his production technique utilizes sufficient handwork to merit it.

Indian Reproductions - Red Buffalo Two.

Products of authentic design, manufactured an/or hand finished by American Indians will be classified by Number Two, Indian Reproductions. It should be the responsibility of the Indian Arts and Crafts Board to certify the authenticity of design. It should be the responsibility of the Branch of Industrial Development, Bureau of Indian Affairs, to certify that production is achieved by a labor force consisting of at least 50 percent American Indians.

American Indian Souvenirs - Yellow Buffalo Three

Products mass-produced for the tourist or premium markets are classified Number Three, American Souvenir. It should be the responsibility of the Branch of Industrial Development, Bureau of Indian Affairs, to certify that production is achieved by a labor force consisting of at least 51 percent American Indians.

American Indian Manufactured - Green Buffalo Four

All other types of products manufactured on or near Indian reservations will be classified Number Four, American Indian Manufactured, when the labor force used in production consists of at least 51 percent American Indian. It should be the responsibility of the Branch of Industrial Development, Bureau of Indian Affairs, to certify that such Indian employment is achieved.

It was the consensus of opinion of the group that to further enhance the quality of the gift and souvenir shop, that there should be a general classifications for native handicraft other than Indian handicraft.

(1) U.S. Native Handicraft (Other than Indian)
The definition of handicraft heretofore discussed would apply with equal validity to U.S. Native Handicraft and would enjoy the same incentives of freedom from franchise fees. It would be the responsibility of some governmental agency to certify the authenticity of design and manufacture. No attempt was made at this meeting to establish classifications or symbols for the general field of Native Handicraft.
(2) Foreign Handicraft
Articles of handicraft as herein defined but made in countries other than the United States are sold in National Park areas and help to raise the quality of the shops.

It was also the recommendation that concessioners give further emphasis to the display of arts and crafts. All concessioners present felt that the concessioners as a group were probably leaders in the field of sale of native handicraft, but were derelict in proper segregation and presentation of these wares to the public and in making known to the National Park Service and the Department of the Interior the quality and quantity actually being displayed and sold.

In order to correct this situation, it is recommended that concessioners plan their displays of native handicraft articles, and particularly Indian made handicraft, in a manner which leaves no possibility of confusion in the visitors' minds. In this connection, consideration might be given to separate departments for handicraft items and where this is impractical, separate areas of display, plainly identifying the areas of native handicraft. Where for any reason a sufficient quantity of native handicraft is not available, the concessioner might consider putting all handicraft in one shop rather than attempting to display it in all the shops.

Recommendations

The Western Conference, National Park Concessioners, makes the following recommendations to the National Park Service and the Secretary of the Interior:

(1) Define "Native Handicraft" items as articles or products which are predominantly hand-made with the help of only such devices or machines as allow the manual skill of the worker or workers to condition the shape and design of each product.

(2) Adopt and promote the classifications herein submitted for Indian made articles, together with the symbols representing such classifications.

(3) Charge the Indian Arts and Crafts Board of the Bureau of Indian Affairs with the responsibility of certifying articles included in the first two classifications; i.e., Indian Handicrafted and Indian reproductions.

(4) Hold the Bureau of Industrial Development, Bureau of Indian Affairs, responsible to certify that the labor force used in the manufacture of the product is the proper proportion of Indian labor for Classifications Nos. 3 and 4; i.e., American Indian souvenirs and American Indian manufactured.

(5) Have the Bureau of Indian Affairs and the National Park Service sponsor an annual native arts and

crafts show to which the concessioners would be invited for the purpose of focalizing the sources through which the supply of handicraft are available to the concessioners. This would parallel the gift show now held annually for the ordinary commercial souvenirs.

(6) Require concessioners to put increased emphasis on the proper segregation and display of native handicraft as herein discussed.

(7) Request concessioners to consider the advisability of reducing the variety of commercial souvenirs in a particular price range and emphasize the sale of those souvenirs in that price range that have, in his opinion, the most merit in maintaining a quality shop.

(8) Request the Western Conference members to collaborate to stimulate the production of commercial souvenirs which would be available for sale exclusively in National Park areas.

(9) Prohibit the display or offer for sale of any product or article that is risque or borders on the vulgar or obscene.

(10) Exempt all revenues derived from the sale of United States native handicraft — Indian or other — from the application of the franchise fees.

Despite these recommendations and the urging of the National Park Service to emphasize and enlarge our handicraft supplies and to identify Indian handicrafts, the Bureau of Indian affairs and Arts and Crafts refused to participate in certifying Indian handicraft. In fact they never commented on our proposals to assure the authenticity of their handicrafts.

Despite these efforts I received a critical letter from Director Hartzog dated October 20, 1965, stating:

1. The report does not suggest acceptable standards for display of Indian or other handicrafts. I think suggestions along these lines would be helpful. In far too many instances, handicrafts are now jumbled together with inferior merchandise. They are not segregated and are not clearly marked.

The Director did not support his complaint with specificity even though our committee had visited numerous concession gift shops. It should be noted that there is a wide variation in the parks on the space available and the type of merchandise offered which militates against anything but general guidelines.

2. The report ignored one of the major points made by both the Secretary and me, namely, the formulation of standards or guidelines for upgrading the general quality of souvenirs in the national parks.

It was obvious that the Director was playing to the Secretary.

I was not involved further with souvenir problems of the National Parks until I returned from my tour of duty as Assistant Secretary of the Department of Housing and Urban Development. By now the problem had involved the Secretary's Advisory Committee. Steven Rose as Chairman asked me to brief him on the problem.

My letter of October 17, 1972, to him provides a brief history of the problem and the efforts at solution.

Copies of the letters follow:

October 17, 1972
Mr. Steven Rose
Biltmore Galleries

Dear Steve:

During our informal discussion in Los Angeles, the question of souvenir policy was raised. This has been the source of misunderstanding and confusion for a number of years. There is merit on both sides of the question. I would like to generally outline inquiries that have been made in the past and, if you need specific documentation, I will provide dates and times.

There was a citizen committee established to explore the question of appropriateness of souvenirs sold in the national parks in the 1950's. In 1967 the Secretary of the Interior established a souvenir committee that spent two years investigating this problem. A report was made on October 24, 1969, and adopted by Secretary Udall January 15, 1969 (copy attached). Note the members of that committee: Hilmer Oehlmann, Y.P.C.; Ed Hummel, Deputy N.P.S. Director; Mike Frome, Environmental Columnist; Bill Everhardt, N.P.S.; Harthon Bill, Associate Director, N.P.S.; Tom Flynn Assistant Director, N.P.S.; Frank Harrison, N.P.S.; Dr. Stanley Cain, Assistant Secretary, Department of the Interior; Citizens Rowan, New, and Eames I do not know personally.

Some time prior to the establishment of this committee, the Conference of National Park Concessioners appointed a souvenir committee which has been active continuously for the last seven or eight years. They have made checks of various concessioners during the last several operating seasons and made recommendations in ways that the concessioner could improve the quality of his merchandise and display. Compliance, of course, was up to the individual concessioner.

The lack of quality and availability of good products is the major problem facing the concessioners. Concessioners have explored every recommended source of crafts only to find that there was a limited and erratic supply.

In the case of Indian goods, we actually devised and proposed a certification system which would enable the concessioner to assure himself that the article being bought was genuine. The Secretary's Indian Arts and Crafts Board and the Bureau of Indian Affairs were asked to cooperate in finding sources of Indian crafts and to certify their authenticity. We received absolutely no assistance and no cooperation from either, although we were responding to the Park Service criticism.

Attached hereto is the latest example of the problem. Note the exchange between Kay Valdes of Mount Rushmore and the Park Service. Note the recommendation by the Park which turns out to be a sales gimmick by those wanting to cash in on the idea of Indian crafts and the gullibility of some Park Service people. This was the problem we were trying to avoid when we asked the Indian Arts and Crafts Board to certify the genuineness of the articles we sold.

We had been advised that the Smithsonian Institute handles only quality products and would be a source of supply. Our committee visited with them and obtained the same type of merchandise and the same sources that the concessioners were presently using, including those which are often referred to as "junk." Quite a number of concessioners send their buyers to the Indian reservations and buy directly from the Indians. This is an expensive procedure and yields only a minimum of the yearly supply.

We have offered every agency who advised us that they had a source of handicraft that we would buy all that was available. This has produced practically no items. We are constantly beset with the statement that appropriate products are available, but no one can provide us the source. Two weeks ago I discussed this with Inga Garrison and promised her full cooperation as she indicated she has a source.

Before any drastic limitations are imposed on the concessioners, I suggest that the Secretary and those advising him make a thorough inquiry to ascertain the financial contribution made by the gift shop operations in the parks. If these were to be removed, you may have a number of insolvent concessioners. It should also be borne in mind that the general public wants a souvenir of their visit that is inexpensive either as a keepsake or to remember somebody back home. The Conference will be glad to cooperate in any way it can to help solve this troublesome problem.

Sincerely,
Don Hummel
Chairman of the Board

3 enclosures follow.

October 3, 1972:
Superintendent Wallace McCaw
Mount Rushmore National Memorial
Keystone, South Dakota 57751
Dear Superintendent McCaw:

I regret the delay in answering Mr. Ashley's correspondence of August 29th, however, we had planned to be in the Tetons and Yellowstone the second week in September, so decided to wait until I had the opportunity to see the Wind River Native Crafts, Inc. Indian products before answering. I am very glad that I did just this as I was very disappointed to see a sales area at the new Indian Museum in the Colter Bay Visitor's Center taken up by bead work from the Wind River Crafts, Inc. Practically in its entirety this is loomed bead work — what we call "Boy Scout bead work," and a product that is available in practically every souvenir shop in the country. The bead work from Hong Kong and Japan is all loomed bead work. Nearly every Hobby Shop in America sells these small looms and the beads to work with, and the reason I referred to it as "Boy Scout bead work" is that practically every Boy Scout troop at some time in their tenure, does have a loomed bead work project. This is not a native Indian craft.

I tried to contact Superintendent Everhardt in the Grand Tetons, but it was such a busy time for everyone with the World Conference in session, I thought it not the time to take up the matter of the sale of loomed bead work in the overnight Visitor's Center. I do feel that it is a very serious matter and one that should be aired. We made ourselves acquainted with the young man in charge whose name was Alfred and he gave us his mother's name, Leona St. Clair, as the person who operated the shop. We asked him what consideration they made to dealers and he informed us that there was 20% off the retail price. This is a completely unrealistic figure for anyone in private enterprise.

I have purposely pointed up the above objections in order for you to inform Mr. Ashley that although Superintendent Everhardt undoubtedly advised our Regional Office of "Availability of Indian-Made Products" in good faith, there is very definitely a need for someone in Concessions in our Regional Office to investigate this whole concept.

I am sending a copy of this correspondence to both the Chairman of our National Conference of Concessioners and Mr. Robert Hart, Director of the Arts and Crafts Board of the Bureau of Indian Affairs.

Most sincerely,
Kay Valdes, President
Mountain Co., Inc.

January 15, 1969
(to Hil Oehlmann)
Dear Hil:

I wish to express my appreciation for the time and effort you have contributed as chairman of the special souvenir committee to provide guidance to the National Park Service and park concessioners.

The recommendations contained in the report by the committee are to be adopted as the souvenir policy for areas administered by the National Park Service. The guidelines will aid the National Park Service in its continuing program to enhance and upgrade concessioners' offerings of souvenirs.

I also wish to acknowledge your personal comments which supplemented the committee report. These were of particular significance to me in light of your past experience in this field.

Sincerely yours,
Stewart L. Udall
Secretary of the Interior

October 24, 1968

Report and Recommendations of the Souvenir Committee

The Souvenir Committee takes note and Public Law 89-249 provides that:

"...the preservation of park values requires that such public accommodations, facilities, and services as have to be provided" within areas administered by the National Park Service "should be provided only under carefully controlled safeguards against unregulated and indiscriminate use, so that the heavy visitation will not unduly impair those values and so that development of such facilities can best be limited to locations where the least damage to park values will be caused. It is the policy of the Congress that such development be limited to those that are necessary and appropriate for public use and enjoyment of the national park area in which they are located and that are consistent to the highest practicable degree with the preservation and conservation of the areas."

The selection and sale of souvenirs in areas administered by the National Park Service must be in accordance with the policies enunciated by that law.

Toward the achievement of that objective the Division of Interpretation should assume a high degree of responsibility for cooperation with the administrative officials of the Park Service and with the concessioners in seeking out appropriate souvenirs for sale in national park areas.

The Director and his staff should instill in Park Superintendents and their staffs a conviction that the park experience to visitors can extend to the selection of souvenirs, and that these officials recognize their responsibility and authority to enforce the declared policies affecting the sale of these articles.

The Souvenir Committee recommends that the proposed statement to be included in the "Handbook" on Concessions Management read as follows:

PART I - MERCHANDISE
Need for Merchandise Service

The visitors' need for merchandise varies from park to park. In the larger relatively isolated parks with large campgrounds and a large number of resident employees, a wide range of merchandise — groceries, clothes, gifts, souvenirs, photographic and art supplies, etc., may be necessary to satisfy the needs. Gift, curio, and souvenir shops, as well as general stores and other shops may be needed to provide such merchandise. The visitors may expect to be able to purchase articles or items which are associated with or interpretive of the park, its geographic region, or the national park system. The visitors' need for merchandise may be satisfied in these general ways:

(1) By commercial establishments outside the park,

(2) By National Park Service Cooperating Associations which operate under agreement with the Service; and

(3) By concessioners who operate under contract with the Service.

Policies

1. *Souvenirs*: The sale of souvenirs shall be limited to those items which serve the mission of the Park Service and are appropriate for the public use and appreciation of the park.

2. *Native Handcraft and Artifacts*: The sale of appropriate handcraft articles associated with or interpretive of an area is to be especially encouraged and there should be a continuing effort to enlarge the scope and supply of local handicrafts where these exist and to establish them where they do not.

Archaeological specimens or objects of American Indian origin over 100 years old may not be sold regardless of their origin.

Guidelines

To carry out these policies the superintendents should apply the following guidelines in their regulation of concessioners' shops:

1. *Items which are promoted*: Superintendents should encourage concessioners to give preferred treatment to the selection, display, and sale of handcraft articles which meet the following production standards:

(a) That the articles are predominantly handmade;

(b) That they are predominantly individually produced under conditions not resembling an assembly line or factory system;

(c) That they are produced by using only such devices or machines as allow the manual skill of the maker or makers to condition the overall shape and design of each individual.

Producers (or associations of producers) of handcraft articles must certify to the concessioners that their products are produced according to the product standards. This may be done as a part of the normal billing procedure through an invoice certification which states: "The merchandise covered in this invoice meets the National Park Service production standards for genuine Native and/or Indian Handcraft."

The Superintendent, the concessioner, or producers should call upon the Regional Arts and Crafts Specialists of the Secretary's Indian Arts and Crafts Board concerning the sources, availability, or genuineness of Indian handcrafts. (We tried this without success.) Whenever possible, Superintendents and concessioners should co-operate with Craft Guilds. In addition to handcrafts as described above, emphasis should be placed upon the sale of pictures, books, and other publications pertinent to the area, the national park system, and the conservation movement.

2. *Items which may not be sold*: If the Superintendent finds any articles in the following categories offered for sale he should order them removed:

(a) Articles which persons of normal sensitivity might consider obscene, suggestive, indecent, blasphemous, profane vulgar, or in ridicule of established institutions or customs.

(b) Articles which contain "gag" sayings or depict humor of an earthy type.

(c) Tawdry articles common to a carnival midway, but not including unobjectionable merchandise suitable for children's toys or apparel.

(d) Animal skins and taxidermal specimens.

(e) Articles which are mislabeled as to character or origin, or otherwise misrepresented.

3. *Appearance of shops*: Shops should be clean, well lighted, and ventilated. Display fixtures should be of good quality and sufficiently separated to allow freedom of movement. Massive displays and large quantities of suspended merchandise should be avoided. Displays of preferred items should be clearly visible. Overall the shops should have an uncluttered appearance.

After all the years of controversy, we ended with some improvement in Park Service requirements, but with the same vague and subjective language. The Park Service dropped its critical pressure on concessionaires without materially changing the articles sold in the gift shops and providing no answers to the problems of supply of handicraft.

20

Public Law 89-249 - Concessions Policy

MORRIS K. UDALL was a member of the Interior and Insular Affairs Committee and my congressman from Tucson, Arizona. I asked Mo to sponsor the bill before the committee. H.R. 4886 (H.R. 5872) — identical bills — related to the establishment of concession policies in areas administered by the National Park Service. This was to emerge as Public Law 89-249. H.R. 5887 and H.R. 5873 concerned the loan guarantee bill. It was never enacted, although the Park Service still favored it over the policy bill.

Hearings were scheduled before the Interior and Insular Affairs Committee of the House of Representatives of the 88th Congress on February 27, 1964, on both the policy bill and the loan guarantee bill. An impressive group of witnesses appeared in support. Senator Lee Metcalf of Montana, an avowed conservationist, cosponsored Udall's bill in the Senate (S-1376), and testified in support of the concessions bill. John Carver, Assistant Secretary of the Interior, and George Hartzog, Director of the National Park Service, appeared to provide Department and Service support.

John Carver submitted a letter to the Chairman of the Interior and Insular Affairs Committee of the House of Representatives dated September 24, 1963. Mr. Carver offered a substitute bill, stating:

> The only reason we are considering a substitute bill, instead of commenting point-by-point on the introduced bill, is to provide the Congress with a more succinct presentation of the provisions we have heretofore regarded as having congressional approval.

Assistant Secretary Carver then went on to discuss the policies and practices. He stated that in the early history of the national parks, it was difficult to attract private capital. This capital had to be relied upon to provide visitor accommodations in view of the statutes relating to concessions, which had been enacted. He stated that in several instances the railroads, such as the Northern Pacific to Yellowstone, the Great Northern to Glacier, the Santa Fe to Grand Canyon and the Union Pacific to Zion, Bryce and the North Rim of the Grand Canyon, developed facilities for the visiting public in an effort to stimulate railroad passenger traffic. In Mt. Rainier National Park, Stephen Mather, the Park Service Director, prevailed upon businessmen and national park supporters to invest in the facilities that were needed to provide accommodations to the public.In order to induce this, the contracts provided preferential right to provide additional services, if and when required, and recognized the concessioner's equity, which has more recently been defined as "possessory interest" in the facilities; also the right to be reimbursed for the facilities if someone else was granted the privilege; and the contract provided the opportunity to earn a reasonable profit on overall operation. The franchise fee provision allowed that the concessioners would be entitled to earn net profits equal to six percent on their investment before they would pay any franchise fee.

Secretary Carver advised that when World War II occurred, drastic curtailment in the scope of the concession operations resulted; that on existing contracts where concessioners were entitled to six percent per year, which was cumulative, a great many accumulated rights had built up and that the Park Service had to continue contracts where they had little or no opportunity to receive any franchise fees. This brought criticism from some government agencies. He stated that some of the contracts had expired during the war and that in the case of Sequoia and Kings Canyon National Park Company, the solicitor released an opinion stating that the Sequoia Company retained no interest in the facilities in the park; that they were entitled only to a right of reimbursement at current market value if a successor took over the operation.

Commenting on the post-World War II period, Secretary Carver cited the appointment of the Concessioners Advisory Group stating that among other things, the advisory group recommended that national parks should not be regarded as revenue producers, and that franchise fees should be abolished, so far as practical.

The group recommended that private capital was preferable to government-ownership, and that contracts should provide for the concessioners to have an equitable title to all property acquired through the investment of their funds. They recommended that contracts should be awarded to known operators with satisfactory records and known reliability. Upon their performing satisfactorily, their contracts should be renewed. The group stated that public interest would be served best by giving preferential contracts to concessioners, and concessioners should be entitled to earn a minimum return on their investment, with the further right to additional earnings to compensate for the risks assumed and to provide an incentive for good operations.

Carver further advised that the General Accounting Office, by Decision B-80362, of October 28, 1948, had ruled that government should give recognition to the capital investment of the concessioners in the facilities that had been developed by them. He reported the conflicts that existed between the government and the concessioners, which resulted in the memorandum of May 6, 1950, directing the National Park Service to follow certain practices; that this was approved by the Public Lands Committee and subsequently by the Interior and Insular Affairs Committee.

Assistant Secretary Carver advised that pursuant to the act of July 14, 1956 (70 Stat 543), all contracts in excess of five-year terms, or which had a gross income of more than $100,000, were required to be submitted to Congress 60 days before the award was made. He stated that they were under the impression that such clearances by the Interior Committee afforded assurance of congressional guidance and approval. He stated he was concerned, however, by recommendation of other congressional committees which indicated conflict in Congress over the policy. He named the House Appropriations Committee and the House Committee on Government Operations as two that raised conflicting statements.

Mr. Carver further stated that existing policy recognizes that adequate service to the public at reasonable rates is more important than the amount of franchise fees paid to the government. The House Appropriations Committee wanted the fees increased, while the House Government Operations Committee advised that there was a disproportion in the franchise fees in the type of operations conducted, and that fees for some concessioners appeared unreasonably low.

Assistant Secretary Carver also pointed out that it was the policy that the concessioner should have a preferential opportunity to conduct more operations of like character in the same park and should have a preferential opportunity to negotiate a new contract, providing his services have been satisfactory. The House Appropriations Committee objected to this and suggested that competitive bidding should be required in lieu of preferential opportunity in the issuance of a new contract. He also pointed out that the Controller General reported to Congress in June 1963 that some concessioners providing new facilities were granted reductions in franchise fees in violation of the Economy Act and without adequate evaluation of need.

As Chairman of the Conference, I was the lead-off witness to outline the provisions in the bill and why they were needed. As my statement is a resume of the record substantiating the need for legislation, excerpts follow:

> My name is Don Hummel. I am President of Glacier Park, Inc. and Chairman of the Western Conference of National Park Concessioners.
>
> The report of the Department on the proposed legislation relates the history of concessions policy. I will not try to repeat it other than to point up some of the important facts which I believe emphasize and explain the need for legislation.
>
> When Stephen T. Mather, and subsequently Horace M. Albright, assumed the role of Director of the National Park Service, they recognized the need to improve facilities for the use of visitors to the national parks.
>
> In order to accomplish this, several important policies were adopted.
>
> 1) The policy of giving a contract to one responsible concessioner who would be required to provide a balanced service, even if some services were provided at a loss. When you had competition, each concessioner wanted to provide the profitable service and avoid the unprofitable ones. To avoid this, the Director forced consolidations of competing concessioners and elimi-

nated unsatisfactory ones. To those who provided satisfactory service they gave preferential rights to provide any new services that were required. It should be noted that this was a first right only — not a monopolistic right. If the concessioner did not provide the new facilities, others could be given the contract to provide them.

2) Another preferential right was the right to a new contract, if satisfactory services had been rendered. This could come at the end of the contract, or, if new and heavy investments were required and too little time remained on the contract, the contract could be canceled and a new contract for the full statutory term granted. This gave continuity to the operations.

3) A third policy was a cumulative priority of earnings before payment of franchise fees. This entitled the concessioner to earn six percent of his investment cumulatively before he paid the government anything. This was based on the government's preference for good facilities at reasonable rates, rather than additional revenue to the government.

The policy of cumulative earnings went by the board in 1950 when the franchise fees were based upon a percentage of the gross revenues; however, the policy of good services at reasonable rates in preference to revenue to the government was continued.

These policies worked reasonably well as the investments made in the parks, other than the so-called "Railroad Parks," consisted primarily of personal earnings, reinvestment of profits and depreciation accounts by the individuals who operated in and knew the parks.

Even with these policies, it was a struggle as the demand for facilities exceeded the capital available. Bankers were skeptical of resort businesses of three months duration, and particularly since they were built on government-owned land and subject to regulation and control. Commercial loans repayable in three to five years were usually the best terms that could be secured. This rapid payoff made adequate financing most difficult. The problem was further complicated in 1934 when Secretary Ickes announced that the long-range objective of the Department would be government ownership and operation. The financing problem that had been difficult before was now almost impossible.

During the depression, however, there was little need for major construction and none, of course, during the war years. Right after the war, the need for new and expanded facilities skyrocketed, but a solicitor's opinion which in effect said the concessioners did not own their facilities and could not be compensated unless they sold to a successor concessioner, caused a complete breakdown. The Mather-Albright policies were repudiated and new contracts offered on terms which were completely unacceptable. Concessioners refused to sign the new contracts and new concessioners could not be found.

At this point, we took our troubles to Congress. It was before a predecessor of this committee that the policies were examined. It resulted in complete rejection of government ownership and a reaffirmation of the Mather-Albright policies. These policies were restated by the Secretary of the Interior on May 6, 1950, and approved by resolution of the House Public Lands Committee on July 18, 1950, and reaffirmed by this committee on August 30, 1960.

We thought the idea of government ownership had been repudiated, but we are again confronted with statements which raise our suspicions. On July 19, 1963, the Comptroller General wrote Chairman Aspinall as follows:

When additional visitor accommodations are needed, the Park Service should promptly take the necessary action to provide the facilities (p.29).

And, on p. 35, there is the statement that the alternative to finding private purchasers of concessioners' possessory interest:

would be for the Park Service to request appropriations to permit direct acquisition.

We have always taken the position that we believe private ownership is preferable, but that it is for the Congress to determine the policy. We say only that if the issue is government ownership vs. private investment, the issue should be frankly and openly debated and not arrived at by policies designed to establish it through the back door.

We believe that the Mather-Albright policies supporting private investment have been good.

We believe that private enterprise not only can do the job, but offers the best solution provided that policies supporting private enterprise are continued and given stability.

We are here to support H.R. 5886 and H.R. 5872 as furthering this objective.

The question sometimes posed is: "Why is legislation necessary now, as it would appear that the pressure of enormously increased travel to the parks should attract sufficient capital to provide the necessary investment?

The answer is found in these facts: The lag in providing adequate facilities that took place during the depression and then the war, which was further delayed by the threat of government ownership and operation, when coupled with the effect of Mission 66 which rejuvenated government facilities and stimulated greater travel to the parks, almost engulfed the concession system.

Facilities that had been accepted before the war were no longer acceptable to the traveling public. They now demanded better facilities and services. The shelter cabin gave way to deluxe motels; service was expected to be comparable to those found in metropolitan areas built for year-round use and occupancy. The investment per rental unit skyrocketed.

The concessioner now had to interest not just his local banker in three- or five-year commercial loans — he had to get long-term capital and here the reception was even more icy than that of his local banker. With the many investment opportunities, the insurance company, the banker, or the investment trust are not interested in risks of an investment in a one-purpose business, built on public lands catering to the vagaries of summer travelers and subject to changing government policies.

Even those investment company representatives that could be sold on the economic ability to repay from a three months' operation, demurred when the policy was challenged and demands were made for better accommodations, cheaper rates, and higher fees simultaneously without regard for the economics involved.

The Outdoor Recreation Resources Review Commission established by the Congress in 1958 to examine the problems of adequate recreational resources and facilities thoroughly examined this problem and made, among others, these recommendations:

In ORRRC Study Report 12, "Summary and Suggestions":

The private sector of the economy (the concession system) is by far the most promising source of potential new funds for recreation facilities. The general health of the concession system is good, and it has shown great capacity for growth the past 10 years. But capital requirements are mounting rapidly. Unless specific steps are taken ranging over a wide variety of government policies, the concession system may not be equal to the new burdens being placed on it.

The climate is made all the more troublesome by contradictory government attitudes, the supervision of public agencies, the occasional intrusion of political considerations, changes in public policies, vaguely worded contracts, and legal concepts that are novel to the world of orthodox finance.

The central goal of public policy should be to reduce these difficulties as much as possible, while still protecting the paramount interests of the public.

And the report makes these further recommendations:

Consideration for policy makers: A clear statement of federal policy toward the concession system is badly needed. Such a system should set forth the role of concessioners in a national recreational program as precisely and forthrightly as possible.

The goal should be to rewrite the agreements in terms that would fully protect the public interest but which would be more reassuring to prospective investors and lenders.

As a direct means of aiding the concession system, government insurance of loans made to concessioners should be considered.

The Guarantee Bill H.R. 5873 and H.R. 5887 was intended to implement this ORRRC recommendation.

The provisions of the Policy Bills (H.R. 5886 and H.R. 5872) are intended to be a statement and clarification of the Mather-Albright policies under which we have operated and which have endured the test of time. These policies are reflected in the language of our present contracts. This has been the policy of the National Park Service. It has had the informal approval of this committee. What we need now is a statement by the whole Congress that this is their policy. This will give those of us who have acceptable records of earnings access to the long-term financing that is necessary for us to do our job.

For those areas that do not have a record of earnings, the Guarantee Bill (H.R. 5887, H.R. 5873) will permit private investment to provide facilities after the Secretary of the Interior decides they are necessary and are economically feasible.

The case for these two legislative proposals can best be stated — not by my words — but by the summation in the ORRRC Report:

Outdoor Recreation for America, p. 166:

A congressional review of the concession situation would be most helpful. There are actions which could be taken to ease the difficulty of concessioners in obtaining capital. These include a strong statement of policy at a high level to create confidence in the system; a government loan-guarantee program; contracts of long duration and on favorable terms; and tax incentives. Some aspects of these actions amount to a subsidization of the concession system.

Herman Hoss, the Conference attorney, had the principal burden of explaining and justifying the principal provisions in the law that explained and paralleled the contract provisions. He proposed much of the language that formed the basis for the contract provisions. Hugh Galusha presented the terms and justification for the Guarantee Bill. The Bureau of the Budget opposed enactment of the Guarantee Bill.

The hearings were scheduled to cover both the policy bill and the loan guarantee bill. As a practical matter, there was very little information on the loan guarantee bill and it was largely ignored by the Interior and Insular Affairs Committee. This was somewhat of a disappointment to the National Park Service.

Joseph Campbell, Comptroller General of the United States, submitted a statement which was largely critical of the National Park Service's administration of the concession system, and generally opposed to the provisions of the bill being submitted for enactment. He was particularly critical of the provision of granting concessioners possessory interest in their facilities at the current fair market value, or in capital additions or improvements, stating that when coupled with the concessioners preferential rights to construct additional facilities determined to be required by the Park Service, placed the government in an unfavorable bargaining position.

He asserted that the concessioners had offered to sell their possessory interest at prices so high as to discourage prospective purchasers, and that the Park Service had difficulties upon expiration of termination of a concessioner's operation reaching agreement with a concessioner on the value of the possessory interest.

He proposed that future contracts require the concessioner to amortize the cost of the concessioner-constructed facilities over the realistically useful life of the facilities. He proposed that the contract should provide that if the concessioner's right to operate is terminated for any reason during the contract period, the government or a third party acceptable to the secretary could purchase the concessioner's existing possessory interest at the unamortized balance of the cost of the facilities. He also recommended that Congress adopt a long-range program for acquisition of existing possessory interests, if the concessioners did not desire at the time of contract renewal to continue their operations under this new policy as recommended.He generally objected to most of the provisions in the policy statement and the proposed legislation which was deemed necessary to encourage private investment in the National Parks. He was one of the few dissenting voices.

The policy bill, that had been designated as Public Law 89-249, was passed in large measure in accordance with the proposals that had been made to the Interior and Insular Affairs Committee. I was asked at the last hearing by Chairman Aspinall why I was disturbed by Congressman Marsh's (D-West Virginia) amendment in that he insisted, and the committee accepted, a statement that when a contract was to be renewed, public notice was to be provided and other proposals would be evaluated. Aspinall asked me why I objected to the public notice. I said that I did not object to the notice, but I thought that it put the Park Service on the spot, when the law said that we would have a preferential right of renewal.

For the Park Service to evaluate others and inform them that we had preferential rights seemed to me to introduce needless confusion. We had been told that this provision had inadvertently been left in the bill, but that it was Congressman Udall's intention to have this removed at some point in the legislative process. This was never done. The record will show that this continues to cause a great deal of confusion throughout the renewal process.

Another problem that developed in the final hours of the adoption of the law was another amendment by Congressman Marsh. We had discussed for hours on end that there were not a sufficient number of sales of concession interests in the parks to establish a market value. In the absence of a market value, the law provided that:

> Just compensation shall be an amount equal to the sound value of such structure, fixture or improvement at the time of taking by the United States, determined on the basis of reconstruction cost, less depreciation evidenced by its condition and prospective serviceability in comparison with a new unit of like kind.

Congressman Marsh's amendment added the words, "but not to exceed fair market value." I pointed out that it would be just as difficult to establish market value at that time as it would at the beginning of the process, and that this introduced a great deal of contradiction and confusion into the law, but the amendment was passed and I was overruled. Subsequent experiences demonstrated that this introduced all kinds of questions, as it largely contradicted the previous provisions concerning compensation.

Wayne Aspinall, the Chairman of the House Committee of Interior and Insular Affairs, was the floor manager of the bill. After two days of debate, and over the objections of Jack Brooks, Chairman of the Government Operations Committee, the bill passed by a comfortable majority. It then went to the Senate, where it was passed without debate on the consent calendar.

Henry (Scoop) Jackson, Chairman of the Senate Interior and Insular Affairs Committee, who had been kept informed of the progress in the House, had promised me that he would support the legislation. He did when it came before the Senate.

Jack Brooks, who opposed the legislation, took the matter up with his friend and fellow Texan, President Lyndon B. Johnson, who was convalescing from a gallbladder operation in Bethesda Naval Hospital. President Johnson refused Congressman Brooks' request to veto the bill, but in deference to his friend, issued instructions to the National Park Service not to implement its provisions until the Bureau of the Budget Office explored its terms and determined whether they should have general application to other federal agencies with recreational lands. The President then signed the bill as public law on October 9, 1965.

The Park Service was under the restrictions imposed by the President on the renewal of all contracts to one year terms. The concessioners were encountering difficulties in their attempts to upgrade their facilities and to respond to some of the provisions that were being incorporated in the one-year contract. It had been agreed with the Conference that any change in the standard language would be discussed and changes made in accordance with the agreement with the Conference. The Park Service appeared to be departing from this by inserting terms that ran counter to the law, which had been held in suspension, and this caused considerable antagonism. Major contracts were delayed and solutions to problems postponed because of this problem.

In addition, Chairman Brooks continued to harass the National Park Service. His principal point seemed to concern the full amortization of investment over the contract's life, and competitive bidding for contract renewal. These demands run counter to the law. Congressman Brooks objected to the granting of a five-year contract to Mt. Rainier. It was his opinion that the term was too long, considering the magnitude of the new investment, and secondly, he felt that the National Park Service should negotiate between bidders to secure the highest possible return to the government. This, despite the provisions of Public Law 89-249. It was pointed out that the nature of auctioning contracts was absolutely contrary to law and would completely invalidate the preferential right of renewal, and was contrary to the entire history of concession management, which enabled the Park Service to choose the best qualified concessioner. Congressman Brooks was not deterred and demanded that the Park Service adopt procedures which were contrary to the law.

A meeting was set up with Secretary Stewart Udall, Assistant Secretary John Carver, Director George Hartzog and members of his staff. The director opened the meeting by commenting on the presidential instructions on the limiting of terms of contracts to one year. He stated that the Bureau of the Budget had developed four tests for exception to the presidential policy of one-year extensions. These tests were:

> 1) The projection of a substantial long-term building contract, for which an extension of the contract was essential;
> 2) The circumstance in which the concession was to be sold and a long-term contract was required in order to attract a purchaser;
> 3) The necessity for long-term contract in order to attract an operator for government-owned facilities; and
> 4) The issuance of long-term, irrevocable permits.

He said he thought that it could be shown that one-year extensions in these situations were completely impractical. Mr. Hartzog stated that he had pointed out to Congressman Brooks, the relationship of rates and profits to franchise fees under the terms of both the law and the contract, but that the congressman was not convinced and felt that the Park Service should pursue and effect an auction method of letting contracts.

Genee's Christmas Letter, 1965:

The year started out with a gala Governor's Inauguration in Phoenix. Sam Goddard is the first Governor of Arizona ever elected from Tucson. The event was complete with civic chorus, stirring inaugural address and a formal ball. Don had served as Sam's campaign manager for Pima County.

Don is in for a new experience as he has been appointed a member of the Arizona Power Authority. He's learning there is more to power than turning on a switch. He was also appointed a delegate to and attended the White House Conference on Natural Beauty.

Genee's year continued with board positions on Girl Scouts, Tucson Community Council, Youth Board, plus P.T.A., symphony, United Community Campaign, and Tucson Nursery School. She's just finished programming a delegate conference for the Tucson Community Council and giving a book review (Betty Friedan's provocative "Feminine Mystique"). Now she is busily preparing for a Christmas at home, something she hasn't done for two years.

Our summer proved a wonderful one, with good business, and good friends visiting us. This summer brought the first real change in our family. Donna's friend, Pam, stayed with us all summer. She and Donna worked different schedules and were índustrious companions. Diane and Cliff flew to Lassen National Park in California in mid-July. They were to visit, then Cliff was to attend Stanford University's coaching camp. As Diane had the opportunity to work at Drakesbad, she spent the rest of the summer there as an employee. Only Char was left to accompany us on the many short trips in Glacier. We now realize our children are growing up and growing away.

McKinley park Hotel had a fine season too. Don made several trips, the nicest being a ten-day Alaska survey at the invitation of the Director of the National Park Service, George Hartzog, and the Park Service Advisory Council. He and Genee have made some short but wonderful trips this fall; to the Superintendents' Conference in Gatlinburg, on the edge of the Great Smoky's National Park, with a marvelous weekend in the back hill country of Hazel Creek; to Souvenir Policy Concessioners' meeting in Mt. Rushmore, with an extra day to explore the magnificent Black Hills; then to San Francisco for the Western Conference of National Park Concessioners meeting. Now we have just returned from a fabulous visit to Jamaica and Miami with Don's brother, Gail, and Helen, and the Don Fords. Gail designed a revolutionary beverage transport truck which was displayed for the first time at the Coca Cola convention.

After a spring semester at Orme Ranch School, north of Phoenix, Donna elected to spend her senior year at Tucson High. She has been in a flurry of activities revolving around the Symphony Cotillion in which she was a Junior Patroness. She and her daddy performed in a waltz chorus for the event. Diane joined the table of friends and family for a gay and festive evening. Di and Char are interested in tennis, and Di is in Tri-Hi-Y and modern dance. Cliff, now in high school, made first string guard on the unbeaten freshman football team. Tucson High's varsity team won the State Championship (12 wins, no losses). Despite their activities, all the children's grades keep them on the Honor Roll for which we are thankful.

❊ ❊ ❊

21

Study of Concessions on Federal Lands

In October 1966, the report requested by the President from the Bureau of the Budget was released. This survey was to ascertain whether the granting of a possessory interest and other terms contained in Public Law 89-249 should be extended to other federal agencies providing recreational services on federal lands.

The report discloses that other federal agencies either expressed an interest in providing for or were already recognizing the concessioners' rights (possessory interest) in buildings and structures built on federal lands under their jurisdiction. This was accomplished by contracts which had never been challenged except in the case of the National Park Service.

Possessory Interest

Bureau of Land Management

The Bureau believes that the most satisfactory arrangement for the construction and operation of facilities requiring high capital investment would be through the development of concessioner contracts. The Bureau has no present authority to enter into such contracts.

Bureau of Reclamation

Possessory Rights: The Bureau notes that in recent years the need for the recognition of the concessioner's possessory rights has become more apparent. Earlier concession operations did not require large financial investments and, therefore, could be removed from federal property as the need for removal developed. The Bureau notices that the recent development of large concession operations requires increased investments and the recent agreements entered into by the managing agencies have provided for consideration of the concessioner's possessory interest.

Bureau of Sport Fisheries and Wildlife

Possessory rights. The Bureau recognizes the concessioner's possessory rights to facilities which he contracts or develops, and this recognition is reflected in contract provisions. These rights are the concessioner's to sell, transfer or assign as approved by the Bureau.

Corps of Engineers

Possessory rights. Corps policy regarding possessory rights of concessioners to the facilities they construct is reflected in the standard concessioner contract document. Structures or equipment erected or furnished by the concessioner "remain the property of the lessee."

Forest Service

Possessory rights. The Forest Service holds that the improvements made to federal lands are the property of the permittee and that they may be sold on permit termination or be renewed by the permittees. Many Forest Service permits have experienced a change of ownership and in nearly all transfer cases, a permit was issued to the new owner.

Tennessee Valley Authority

Transfer and lease to state and local governments and the sale of land to private enterprise. Before said land is sold, transferred or leased, TVA requires submission of evidence of ability to discharge responsibilities of development, management and operation of the properties in a manner which will preserve and enhance regional values in the public interest and will further TVA program objectives.

TVA policy regarding possessory rights of the concessioner states that improvements which can be removed from federal land at lease termination remain the property of lessee.

Defense Department

Corps policy regarding the possessory rights of concessioners to the facilities they construct is reflected in the standard concessioners contract document. Structures and equipment erected or furnished by the concessioner "remain the property of the lessee."

The report concludes that:

As a result of the lack of specific guidelines on use of concessioners, the agencies have gone diverse ways. In part, this flexibility has been useful and desirable and has permitted agencies to adopt policies and procedures suited to their particular objectives and to meet specific situations.

Privileges and benefits offered concessioners:

Most of the criticism concerning various agency concession policies relates to the granting of privileges and benefits not normally given in a free competition environment or in normal governmental contractual relationships. Justified on (a) conditions under which required to function, (b) short seasons, (c) prices controlled, (d) no title to the land, (e) federal agencies free to change policies, (f) concessioners required to remain open when volume of business does not justify, and (g) help the concessioner obtain and retain qualified help.

Privileges granted include:

(1) Possessory interests, (2) relatively long-term contracts, (3) monopoly locations, (4) opportunity for additional facilities, and (5) low fee payments.

The report also verified that:

Congress gave careful consideration to the granting of possessory interest and the payment of just compensation if discontinued.

We have found that the incorporation of the possessory interest concept in Public Law 89-249 has already added significant credibility to previous administrative interpretations of the value of possessory interest.

We believe that while there are problems associated with the granting of possessory interest...there is no useful way to change the policy without seriously disrupting future investments in the national parks.

...it is generally agreed that the use of concessioners offers the best means of providing the bulk of needed recreation facilities and services on federal lands.

...It would be contrary to general federal policy to have the federal government directly engage in such operations which private enterprise is willing to provide on reasonable terms.

Concessioners should be selected on their ability to provide the necessary facilities and services to the public rather than on the amount they are willing to pay the government.

Duration of Contract

Relative to the length of term of contract, the Bureau of the budget reported:

Uniform federal policies for granting of concession contracts for periods of time up to 30 years shall be developed. Agencies should have authority to make contracts for longer periods up to 30 years to encourage concession investment and allow a reasonable length of time to repay loans.

The Corps of Engineers grants concessioners contracts for periods up to 10 years where investment capital is under $25,000 and up to 25 years when the investment is over $25,000. If the concessioner performs satisfactorily, he is always given a renewal contract if he so desires. There has never been any criticism of these liberal terms.

Forest Service grants permit up to 30 years. Where long-term need is not evident, investment is small and the land may be needed for another purpose, shorter-term permits are issued.

Bureau of Sport Fisheries and Wildlife. The Bureau makes a distinction between minor concessions, facilities of seasonal or temporary nature, and major concessions, more permanent privileges and facilities. Major investments call for terms from 5 to 20 years.

It had been the policy of the National Park Service to give 20-year terms when a substantial investment was required. They were authorized by law to give 30-year contracts when extra ordinary investments involving multimillions of dollars are required. Duration of contracts in the parks are being drastically reduced as part of the program to reduce facilities in the national parks.

On October 6, 1966, President Lyndon Johnson approved this report with the following language:

> The recommendations made in the report are consistent with the intent of Congress in passing Public Law 89-249 which established concessions policies for the National Park Service. Implementation of these recommendations does not require changes in that law. Therefore, I rescind the constraint which I placed on the terms of concession contracts granted by the National Park Service in my signing statement of October 9, 1965.

The concessioners had finally achieved the stability required by the financial community to approve funds to provide visitor facilities desired by the National Park Service to serve the park visitor.

We were to learn however that congressional policy is only as effective as the administering agency agrees with the policy. While other federal agencies administered their concessions policies, the National Park Service, under pressure of environmental extremists, were sabotaging the intent of the law; and the people's right to use and enjoy their national parks was put in jeopardy.

22

Department of Housing
and Urban Development

DURING MY service as a board member, vice president and subsequently president of the American Municipal Association (National League of Cities), mayors and councilmen complained of the lack of support by the state to respond to city problems. Most of the state legislatures were rurally dominated and unresponsive to urban problems. As the cities were in great need of help, they turned to the federal government for assistance. The cities felt that they needed a strong voice at the federal level.

As representatives of city government, we urged the creation of a federal department, with cabinet status, where the problems of urban affairs could be heard. We had a number of hearings before congressional committees designed to create such a department. The most responsive committee was the one chaired by Senator Edwin Muskie of Maine. The cities' problems grew out of the fact that people were flocking to urban centers to secure a better education for their children, or a better job, or better living conditions. The population was being concentrated in the urban centers, but most state constitutions which called for redistricting to respond to this change of voter concentration, were being ignored. State legislators resisted redistricting as no representative wanted to give up his district or risk loss of his membership.

As a result, the voters were concentrated in the urban centers but were being disenfranchised, as their voting strength was being diminished. Appeals to the court had been unsuccessful. The courts took the position that this was a political problem which had to be handled by the legislatures rather than by the judiciary. This led to an impasse until, finally, in the case of Baker vs. Carr, a judge stated that failure to redistrict was a repudiation of the state's constitution. He reversed the process by ordering a redistricting of the political boundaries so as to balance the voting strength between rural and urban centers. In the interim, the cities were experiencing some very difficult problems. There was a continuing migration from city centers to the suburbs, leaving mostly poor people in the central cities with no tax-paying capacity. This resulted in deterioration into what we call the Urban Ghetto.

Along with the deterioration of the city plant, new construction representing tax resources went to the suburbs, leaving the central city without capacity to meet its problems. Added to this was the fact that the poor, who were concentrated in the cities, were disproportionately on relief. The city had no source of funds to respond to the rising demand for welfare.

After President-elect Kennedy was elected, but not yet inaugurated, he called me to meet with him in New York City to discuss city problems. Richardson Dilworth, who was the president of the Conference of Mayors was also invited. We met with Jack Kennedy at a hotel in New York in December 1960. Dilworth suggested that I make the presentation, as I represented the strongest Municipal Association. This we proceeded to do, with the understanding that President Kennedy, after inauguration, would submit legislation to the Congress to establish a new Department of Urban Affairs headed by a secretary with cabinet status. When this did not occur after several months, I contacted the President. Richardson Dilworth had resigned as mayor of Philadelphia and was running for governor of Pennsylvania.

Dick Lee, the mayor of New Haven, Connecticut, succeeded Dilworth as president of the Conference of Mayors, and he and I met with President Kennedy in the Oval Office in June 1961. At that time we pressed him for action, in accordance with his promise to establish a new department. He promised to do so and later submitted a proposal to Congress to establish a Department of Housing and Urban Development. Time passed and then an article appeared in the *Washington Post* indicating that President Kennedy planned to appoint a Negro to head the new department when it was created. This immediately lost him the support of many of the southern democratic congressmen. They had been the strongest supporters for an urban department.

It was not until after Kennedy's assassination and the elevation of Lyndon B. Johnson to the presidency that the bill was pushed and finally passed, creating a new department, headed by a secretary and called the Department of Housing and Urban Development. I left the office of Mayor of Tucson in December 1961. The Department of Housing and Urban Development was not created until several years after I was no longer associated with municipal government.

In 1966 I was at Grand Canyon with Director George Hartzog, to attend the Horace M. Albright Training Academy. I was to speak on the problems facing the concessioners in the national parks. While there, a message came to me that the secretary was trying to reach me. George Hartzog was quite upset. He did not under stand why the secretary was trying to reach me instead of him. It turned out that it was not the Secretary of the Interior, but the Secretary of Housing and Urban Development (HUD), so he was appeased. I returned the call and was advised that they would like to appoint me as Assistant Secretary of HUD to handle the housing programs and the urban renewal program. I was hesitant, as I was pretty much involved with concession operations in Glacier, Lassen and McKinley National Parks. Upon arriving in Tucson, Genee convinced me I should make some arrangements for the supervision of Glacier Park, Inc. and that I should take this position. Al Donau, my nephew, interceded and offered to take over the direction of Glacier, while his wife, Mary Frank Donau, managed Lassen. We had a hired manager for McKinley. This would allow me to take the position in Washington, D.C., which I did and reported in May 1966.

Genee's Christmas Letter, 1966:

1966 brought more changes to the Hummel family. In the spring all of us joined Don who attended a Park Service meeting at the Horace M. Albright Training Center on the south rim of the Grand Canyon. While Don and George Hartzog attended the sessions, Helen and Genee, with their children, hiked and picnicked. During the meeting Don was told he had a phone call from the Secretary. George wondered why the call was for Don and not him, but it wasn't the Secretary of the Interior, it was the new

Secretary of Housing and Urban Affairs. He offered Don the job of Assistant Secretary, to be in charge of all housing programs (except F.H.A. and V.A. mortgage programs) and the entire urban renewal program for the country. What an exciting proposal. We talked it over and decided it was too good an opportunity to pass up. There was the problem of Glacier Park. When approached, Al Donau agreed to take over the Glacier operation and said Frankie could manage the Manzanita Lake operation. Thus, it was set.

The children had mixed feelings. Donna would be a freshman at Irvine College, but it would be Diane's senior year. She had made yearbook staff and cheer leader. We all went back to Washington, D.C., for Don's swearing in. The children were impressed when Vice President Hubert Humphrey attended the reception and they could have a photo taken with him. We saw the wax museum, took the F.B.I. tour, visited the Smithsonian buildings and the capitol. Genee had a Stanford friend living there with children the same age. We got together and the children went off to all the schools the Cary children had attended and find out what it was like to live there. Diane felt better about making the move.

Don took office in May. Genee and the children flew back to Tucson. Don was able to get back to Tucson in June to drive the family to East Glacier. We were able to take our beloved cat, Mittens, with us. Over the 4th of July weekend, Genee flew to D.C. to house hunt. Emily Moke moved into our house to be there with the children. In four days Genee looked at some 65 houses. Only on the last day did she find four possibilities, so it was easy to agree on our favorite at 8404 Beechtree Road, Bethesda, MD 20024. Don was able to get to Glacier for a few days every other week. So the summer passed. Genee flew to Tucson in August to get ready for the move.

Our move to D.C. went smoothly. Don had unpacked everything during his long lonely evenings. Diane and Cliff went to the same high school they had seen with the Cary's children; Charlene to a nearby junior high. Our neighborhood was friendly. Diane and Cliff found good friends next door. Di joined a rock climbing group and helped with cheerleading. Cliff played on the football team. Genee painted one of the rooms and the rusted back steps, and made some bedroom curtains. Weekends we made a point of seeing something of D.C. and its environs, even getting a fall trip into the Shenandoahs.

Donna was able to join us for a wonderful Christmas trip to Eden and Buffalo to be with Don's niece, Aline Larkin, and her family.

❆ ❆ ❆

Assistant Secretary Designate Ralph Taylor and I appeared before the Senate Committee for Approval, since this was an appointment which required the approval of the United States Senate. Assistant Secretary is considered a subcabinet position of the presidency. Senator Douglas, from Illinois, a very well respected senator and active in affairs concerning state and local government, chaired the meeting. He broke in after my statement of my record, as Ralph Taylor outlined his record. The senator said, "I don't understand Mr. Taylor being designated as Assistant Secretary for Demonstration Cities." The name Demonstration Cities was subsequently dropped and changed to Model Cities as there were a number of demonstrations in the cities and they thought this name could be misinterpreted.

Mr. Douglas said, "Here is Mr. Hummel, who has had lots of local government experience with his service as mayor and as the vice chairman of the Commission on Intergovernmental Relations, while Mr. Taylor has been contracting urban renewal projects." He said, "I believe these appointments have been mixed up. It appears to me that Mr. Taylor should be in housing and renewal and Mr. Hummel should be in the demonstration cities program." There was considerable discussion, but finally we were approved as designated. I would not have accepted the position of Assistant Secretary for Model Cities, as it was only a nebulous concept, with practically no program responsibility. It was too theoretical for me. I was fortunate that my appointment gave me responsibility for all the housing programs except the insurance programs of V.A. and F.H.A. I had the responsibility for college housing, public housing, housing for the elderly, urban renewal, and a variety of other responsibilities; in fact, I had 61 percent of the entire departmental program responsibility, with an annual budget of $1.9 billion.

I inherited quite a staff from previous independent agencies. The Urban Renewal Administration was an independent agency attached to no department. Public Housing was also an independent agency. Secretary Robert Weaver had been appointed as the administrator for Housing and Home Finance Administration which embraced these two agencies. He found them almost impossible to administer, as each one had independent status. They were reluctant to coordinate their activities with each other. It was because of this prior experience that Secretary Weaver insisted that when the Department of Housing and Urban Development was formed these two agencies, which had been assigned to the new department, be placed under one assistant secretary. This was a wise decision, as the coordination of their functions go hand-in-hand. As I assumed responsibility, even though both were answer able to me, I encountered considerable conflict. It took some head knocking to get them to coordinate their functions.

The first thing I did was have staff meetings with the heads of each of these agencies. In the case of Public Housing, it was headed by Mrs. Marie Maguire from San Antonio, Texas. She was a great administrator, although too responsive to her staff. Unfortunately, the attorney for this agency, Joe Burstein, had pretty much consolidated all the power of the agency into his office, through the device of requiring legal clearance before any project could be released. This agency was always complaining that they did not have sufficient staff to perform the expanded functions of the Housing Program, which was now designated the Housing Assistance Program. Even though they complained about lack of personnel, when I called a meeting of the staff, they would bring 30 people to my office. After the second staff meeting, I told them I wanted certain decisions implemented right away. About a week later I realized nothing had happened, so I called Deputy Administrator Maguire and was advised that this matter was being cleared by the Legal Department. I immediately called Joe Burstein and asked him what he was doing. He said this was always the procedure and he just had not gotten to it. I told him then that I had made a decision and I had given instructions that this was to be implemented immediately; and that the next time I heard he was holding up something I had ordered, he could find himself another desk. I made it very clear that if I needed legal advice, I would ask for it, and that the old procedure of him passing on everything was no longer in effect.

At my next staff meeting with this group, I asked them to provide me with certain information. They brought a stack of papers about three inches high, with the usual complement of 30 people. I asked what this was and they said I had asked for it. I said, "I asked for specific information." I expected them to provide the information "in not over two pages and the next time you hand me a bunch of papers like this, we are going to make some changes." I said, "I see you think I have never worked in government before, but let me tell you — I know I can't fire you, but I can make it damned uncomfortable for any of you who stand in the way of getting this department going and when I ask for something, I want it in readable form. Don't try to bulldoze me with a bunch of papers because I will not tolerate it." I continued, "By the way, you are always complaining that you don't have enough personnel to conduct the responsibilities of your department but you have 30 people here away from their desks. The next time I want the administrator and the deputy administrator, and if I want anybody else, I will advise you. Now I want you to get back to your desks and do your jobs." After that, I had very little problem with this group.

Urban Renewal

Dealing with the Urban Renewal staff was a little different. The man who headed up the Urban Renewal Administration as an independent agency was not hired; in fact, he had pulled every string possible to get to be assistant secretary for Urban Renewal, but Secretary Weaver would have none of him. As a result, the top position was vacant and being held by Mr. Howard Wharton. He had been Deputy to the Administrator. He wanted the job as Deputy in Charge of Urban Renewal, but I selected him as my staff deputy, much to his disappointment. He was thoroughly versed in the program, knew all the personnel, and was a loyal bureaucrat. I did not feel that with the program I had in mind he was best suited to head up the agency.

Robert McCabe had a supervisory position in the department. He impressed me as being an intelligent and stable person with lots of energy and drive. When I finally offered him the position, he said he was pleased, but somewhat apprehensive in that it had taken me so long to select him. I advised him that there were political implications, as I had decided after my first interview that he was to be appointed, but I had to clear the political decks before I could proceed. He responded very well and was a loyal employee. In fact, I planned to reorganize the entire Urban Renewal Program, as I found it steeped in regulations and too cumbersome to get programs under way. The process called for all the planning to be completed before any housing could be started or any redevelopment program initiated. As planning sometimes took several years, the plan was often obsolete before it was implemented. Urban Renewal was approved on a project basis. This often did not fit in with the programs of the local government, whose job it was to implement them in accordance with our rules and regulations. The law did not permit the flexibility I thought was essential for the proper development of the Urban Renewal Program.

My principal responsibilities, as the title implied, concerned housing and urban renewal programs. I was sworn in and took over responsibility as Assistant Secretary for Renewal and Housing Assistance on May 25, 1966.

At that time I found an ongoing renewal program with reservations of funds of about $725 million. That sounds like a sizable program, but, as I discovered when I analyzed its past administration, the reservation system used to allocate funds for communities for urban renewal resulted in a very inefficient utilization of these funds. Take as an example: There had been authorized about $7 billion since the Urban Renewal Program started in 1950. During that time only $2.2 billion had been disbursed by local communities. It should be noted that this is not a completely accurate index as the communities were advanced operating funds from the sale of temporary treasury notes which were guaranteed by the federal government, so that in addition to the actual disbursal of funds, there were a great many millions of dollars that were being actively used and advanced by the federal government.

Part 1 was federal approval of the program, following the federal government's advance of planning funds. The communities thought they were fully funded when we reserved the funds, but found that they were as much as 74 percent short when they came in with a more definitive plan. In addition to this, we found that through normal escalation of costs and changes which accompanied the program, such requirements for condemnation of property or purchase by negotiation, added about 34 percent. As most urban renewal programs of any size took 10 years from initiation to completion, you can see that the costs originally established were highly speculative. The result was that the funds we set aside usually represented less than 50 percent of the actual cost of the project.

Another thing I discovered as I learned about the program was that communities were, in effect, banking projects. Because of the long delay in starting the project and final funding, the communities would start several projects. I found quite a number communities that had six, seven or eight projects with reservations, and some of them had not even started their planning. To control this, I issued instructions through regulations that if a project, after funding had been reserved for it, was not ready to go into execution at the end of three years, the funds would automatically lapse and return to the Federal Treasury. The normal time of planning had been about 26 months.

The reservation of funds had other negative consequences for renewal projects. When the community announced the project, all normal activity ceased, including private investments. It was not unreasonable for an individual in the urban renewal area to not want to spend money to fix up his house or improve his business, knowing that the area was going to be cleared and all the housing torn down for a new development program. These deterrences to the program were called "the deadening hand of renewal."

After my first inquiry, I took back $150 million and reallocated the funds to other communities. During the second year of my administration, I received $750 million for urban renewal; ostensibly for new programs. I then learned that $400 million of these monies had to go to fund the increased costs of existing projects. This reduced our funds for new projects to $350 million. The problem was exacerbated by Congress constantly adding other responsibilities, such as picking up additional relocation payments, or code enforcement or community renewal plans and rehabilitation of existing facilities, without providing the money to discharge these additional responsibilities. If continued, the urban renewal program would soon have no forward motion whatsoever.

One of the pressing problems that faced me was the critical shortage of housing for low and moderate income families. Having these facilities available was a prerequisite and essential to the solution of most of the urban problems. We attempted to solve part of this by establishing national goals for urban renewal programs and redirecting the renewal process. Most of the urban renewal programs called for complete clearance programs, designed to completely redevelop an area from scratch. These projects usually started in the central business district. The need to rehabilitate and revitalize the central business area was often necessary so as to build the local tax base. This caused problems, but it was essential for the community. It had a drastic effect on the people living in the area. Without adequate housing to move these people to, the entire process was slowed. You must remember that in the old cities particularly, many of the poor people were living in old converted commercial buildings or old residences that had been abandoned as the more affluent people moved to the suburbs. Unless you provided housing for the displaced to turn to, you had rising objection from the community.

Many of the poor people in these areas were Blacks and so you began to hear the term "Negro Removal." While it was not directed on the basis of race, the impact often appeared to be racial discrimination.

It might be appropriate here to discuss the concept and the need for a government subsidized urban renewal program. It is often said that if left alone, the private sector would renew the area. This is true to a limited extent. The problem of private sector investment in a ghetto or a slum area is the reluctance of lending institutions or, for that matter, equity money, going into new facilities only to be surrounded by slum conditions. This is not considered good investment judgment and those who were willing to take the risk found banks and other lending institutions reluctant to provide the money. There is the additional problem, in that many of the areas' properties were on small acreage plots or lots. This complicated their ability to accumulate enough land to build in accordance with the growing marketing trend of larger institutions, such as supermarkets. If the local developer found a place he thought was suitable, but was unable to buy one or two of the lots he thought were essential to put together a tract for development, he was stymied. This often occurred after having spent a considerable amount of money on plans to start a new development.

There was also the need to expand the utilities for this enlarged business; and often even the alignment of the streets had to be changed. Streets in the old days were much narrower than they are in a modern city, and the private developer had no authority to enlarge the streets, nor was he able to afford the repaving and redevelopment of them. Neither could he change utilities such as the water system, sewer system, electric system, etc.

The urban renewal concept was designed to advance government funds to acquire land and buildings in an area that had been defined by the community as needing up-grading or redevelopment. The government would pur-chase the land. If someone refused to sell, it could be condemned by paying the full value of that property and relocating the resident in new housing. The government program then demolished all the existing structures, rea-ligned the streets and replaced the utilities.

After the government had acquired the land and re-planned it to resell, it was put on the market on a competi-tive bid basis to the private sector for redevelopment in accordance with the approved general plan. There was criticism of the program in that this enriched real estate people. If properly administered, it did provide opportuni-ties for real estate developers to acquire land in desirable locations, but if the system operated properly in the com-petitive bid system, the government should get a goodly portion of its investment back. It would never get the full amount, as the government had to buy buildings which they demolished and there remained only bare land to sell. In my opinion, the concept was sound, and if properly pursued, provided a real opportunity to rejuvenate ailing cities and ailing areas.

The harshness of the program on those people who

were living in the area and were displaced was alleviated at least to some degree by these other programs. The payment of relocation costs, providing facilities and better housing to move to, was accomplished by requiring the community to provide a service to help displaced persons find suitable quarters before being evicted from blighted areas. The federal government paid moving costs. Often additional problems occurred when the area and facilities of the relocation site cost more than the person had received from the condemnation of his old facility in a slum area. This was rectified to a degree by the law permitting the payment of up to $5,000 over and above the economic value of the facilities that had been acquired. There were other ramifications that were particularly hard on the elderly, who had no real earnings or a minimum of earnings. They were living in an old house which was debt-free but when they were moved into a new and better structure, there was usually a mortgage to pay. Often the individual did not have the wherewithal to continue the mortgage payments. The additional $5,000 often did not resolve the problem.

After becoming acquainted with the urban renewal program and encountering the problems it entailed, I established some national goals to control the direction of the program. The first one was to give priority to those urban renewal programs which either preserved or expanded the supply of housing for low or modern income families. We gave priority to those projects that had an extensive rehabilitation program rather than an all new housing program. This spread the amount of money available to a larger number of low and moderate income families.

The second goal was to give priority to projects that provided job opportunities for people in the areas, for the unemployed or the underemployed. In other words, those projects which in their development provided job opportunities for unskilled and semi-skilled people. It is one thing to put a roof over a man's head; it is another that he has the financial resources to maintain himself under that roof.

The third goal gave priority to those areas of urgent and critical need; those areas where deterioration had gone so far that we could not delay the eradication of the slum conditions any longer. We permitted some flexibility in the implementation of these goals in that we did not discriminate against communities that were attempting to meet the goals but now had other pressing needs which would give them a balanced renewal program. We permitted approval of some projects, even though they did not fit the three categories of the national goals, if there were other extenuating circumstances. Another exemption from strict application of these goals was extended to communities that had never had an urban renewal program and had in good faith already established a program and needed federal funds to complete it.

I also established policies and issued instructions which recognized that, as part of the urban renewal program, we would acknowledge those programs that provided additional services to people living in the areas. We found communities had a tendency to reduce or slow down normal services to the areas as soon as a project was proposed. This made it difficult for people living there, as they were denied services normally received. For example, the refusal of the local community to continue to repair sidewalks, maintain parks or provide recreational and sanitation services that normally had been provided before urban renewal was common. We instructed the communities to maintain normal services and authorized additional funds to enable them to continue with these services in areas pending the prosecution of the project.

Many of the problems we encountered in the administration of these programs grew out of inadequacies in the law, and could not be rectified without changes in the law.

Genee's Christmas Letter, 1967:

This year in Washington has been an interesting one. Don finds his job directing urban renewal and housing ever more challenging and demanding. He has been concentrating on new and accelerated approaches. His progress was temporarily slowed when the President tapped the man he had selected to run housing to be the deputy commissioner of the newly formed District Government. But it's not all work. Recently Secretary Rusk invited us both to attend a state luncheon for visiting President Ordaz of Mexico. This and other invitations along with trips highlight Genee's activities. The most stimulating, educational and fun was a two-week sojourn in October to visit seven major cities in Germany on an urban exchange.

Our family at home is reduced to two children. Cliff, a junior in high school, played tackle on the football team. Charlene, a freshman, has just been selected cheerleader. She learned how to handle a sailboat last spring. Diane graduated from high school in June, spent her summer as a waitress in Lassen Park and now is an enthusiastic freshman at Colorado College. Donna transferred happily from UofC, Irvine, to Oregon State. She chose the variety duty job of relief girl at McDonald last summer. Genee entertained and kept house in our delightful cabin on Lake McDonald while Cliff bell-hopped at the lodge, Charlene held her first job on a short shift basis at the fountain counter and Don batched in the nation's capitol.

The season at Glacier with beautiful clear weather held promise for a perfect summer only to climax with tragedy in mid-August. A devastating lightning storm ignited 34 fires and some raged for weeks. On a single night in two isolated areas two of our lovely young employees were mauled and killed by grizzly bears in acts unprecedented in historical account. The events of 1967 will not soon be forgotten.

❄ ❄ ❄

There was a political development which largely killed the urban renewal program. It was called Neighborhood Participation. Someone had the idea that the people in the neighborhood should make the decisions as to how the program should be implemented, as it was their neighborhood. This sounds good and had great public appeal, but it was contrary to the whole concept of planning; in fact, planning should be done not just on a municipal boundary basis, but on an area basis, as artificial city boundaries often conflict with the best utilization and development of an area. Instead of enlarging our scope of planning, we were restricting it to the neighborhood. This produced all kinds of problems.

One instance I remember in particular was when the head of the urban renewal program in the District of Columbia came to my office with the District of Columbia's top political representative stating that they had run out of planning money. They wanted $600,000 added so that they could build up their staff. I said I did not understand, because we had a complete planning staff. The political representative said our staff represented the project, but did not represent the neighborhood. They wanted their own planners and their own staff. I said I thought that was a ridiculous approach and after two hours of discussion, I advised them flatly that had I known they were spending money the way they were, I would have stopped the project long before. I told them I would not authorize another dime for the project. This, of course, did not make me popular with the political forces directing activities in the District of Columbia.

From the date of the institution of the Neighborhood Assistance program by the department, which had the support of the Secretary of HUD, the urban renewal program got mired down. It slowed down an already cumbersome and slow program. This was most unfortunate, because the urban renewal program had great merit, if it were administered properly. This was a badly needed device whereby rundown areas could be redeveloped. Urban renewal combined government authority and the resources to permit replanning on a modern scale.

The taxpayer had in effect been subsidizing obsolete buildings and facilities because they paid little if any taxes but required services such as police, sanitation, etc. When the area was newly developed, taxes were dramatically increased for these new facilities. In the long run, the urban renewal program would pay for itself with new and efficient buildings and improved facilities, but it required public authority and advancement of public funds to start functioning. When the program got involved with local neighborhood politics, it came to a halt. This was a real tragedy.

There were instances of abuse of the urban renewal program. One that stands out vividly occurred in Bethlehem, Pennsylvania. The Bethlehem Steel Corporation wanted to expand its facilities and as the residential areas adjacent to the plant had deteriorated, the steel company, operating through city government, established an urban renewal program. While ostensibly this was a community program, the city government was fronting for the steel company to acquire the land adjacent to the steel company which they wanted for expansion purposes. The program would have been legitimate, had they followed the regulations for the purpose of putting back into circulation land and buildings which had badly deteriorated and should have been torn down to be rehabilitated. The steel company made a deal for the city government to acquire the land through urban renewal. In this way, the government paid for the land and buildings and then would sell the land to the steel company after it was cleared and redeveloped.

It caught my attention when my deputy, Howard Wharton, pointed out that there was only one appraisal of the land being required by the urban development officials, and it appeared to be far below the value that the land should return to the project. I told Howard to hold up the project and call for another appraisal, so that we would have facts on which to determine whether or not there had been collusion. Shortly after ordering this, I had a visit from Congressman Rooney, who was the representative of the district including Bethlehem, Pennsylvania. When I did not give him satisfaction, he went to the secretary to complain. A meeting was set up with the executive vice president of Bethlehem Steel Corporation, his public relations representative, Congressman Rooney, Secretary Weaver and Undersecretary Robert Wood.

I attended the meeting along with Howard Wharton. When it opened, Congressman Rooney made the statement that someone "had it in" for the Bethlehem Steel Company, as they were getting a raw deal; that the ordering of the new appraisal of land to be sold was far in excess of its real value and a direct affront to the Bethlehem Steel Corporation. The new appraisal increased the value of the land by $1.5 million. I responded to Mr. Rooney by stating the facts as I knew them. The facts were: urban renewal was not moving rapidly enough and many of the land owners, knowing their land and buildings were to be taken by the urban renewal program, contacted the steel company. The steel company was buying up this land at bargain prices, taking title to it in the name of their attorney's secretary. This, of course, evaded all the urban renewal procedures. The land titles to properties in the urban renewal area were already vested in the steel company, who intended to acquire them at a later date, after they had been torn down at government expense and resold as vacant land. The true titles to the land were not disclosed. The urban renewal program would then buy these properties at appraised prices, not knowing that the title had already changed and was in the hands of the steel company representative.

I informed the meeting, including Congressman Rooney, in response to his statement, that no one had it in for the Bethlehem Steel company, that this was the first time I had met anyone from that Corporation, but I was appalled to learn that this company would engage in illegal activities to save a few dollars, when they had a multimillion dollar expansion program.

I told the congressman and those assembled that I assumed some congressional committee would one of these days be examining the urban renewal program in view of the vast sums of money being expended, and that I was the person responsible to sign off on the funds. When I signed I was assuring the government that the program was on a legal basis and when I discovered what the urban renewal personnel in Bethlehem, Pennsylvania, were doing in collaboration with the Bethlehem Steel Corporation, I ordered a stop to it. I said I would never sign off on this project until it had been established that the government would get its fair share of return for the sale of the land. I pointed out that this authority was delegated to me by Secretary Weaver, who was sitting in the room. I said, "The Secretary can sign, though I doubt that he will, but I can assure you that you will never see Don Hummel's name on this project until this action is rectified."

That stopped the meeting and there were no further proceedings. We insisted on the steel company retaining the land it had already bought, which was in its attorney's secretary's name, and that the government would not include these plots of land so the Bethlehem Steel Corporation would not get the write-down that they had intended to get through their manipulations.

Other instances that come to mind concern the attitude on the part of the local government setting up one project after another to get it approved and the money allocated, and then sitting on the program, which tied up millions of dollars. I made a survey of both housing and urban renewal programs and noted that some of them had approval of funds as long as seven years, but no progress had been made in implementing the programs. I immediately sent notice to all housing and urban renewal program directors at the local level, advising them that they had three months to show some progress, or we would reexamine the program and determine whether it should be abrogated. This caused tremendous consternation. It was absolutely essential, as I had some $2 billion worth of new projects that were awaiting appropriations so we could fund them. There were some $2 billion in projects approved which had received no further action, but had the monies tied up. At the close of three months, we reexamined these projects and I recaptured about $2 billion worth of funds for reallocation to other projects that were awaiting approval. This did not make me very popular with the local agencies. I was the subject of considerable condemnation. I was considered a traitor to local government.

This condemnation came to a head in a meeting of the National Association of Housing and Renewal Officials (NAHRO). This was an association of local officials who were responsible for the housing and urban renewal projects. The format at this meeting was to have three speakers on a panel. I represented the federal level, Mayor Carl Stokes of Cleveland, Ohio, represented the city level, and Ed Louge from Boston represented the local organizations which actually implemented these programs.

I made my statement and was followed by Mayor Stokes. When Ed Louge got up, he started his talk by saying, "Give us the money and get the `feds' out of the way and we will get something done." He got quite a round of applause from the local officials at the conference. Upon his closing I asked for a two-minute rebuttal. I told the assembled group that I noticed the applause given to Mr. Louge's statement about "getting the feds out of the way and get on with the program"; that I didn't want to argue the issue, but just wanted to give them some figures. I reiterated that I had had to take back some $2 billion worth of funding which had been approved by the federal government for local projects, but which had never started their programs. I closed by saying that in the case of Boston, I took back $800,000 dollars from the Boston Housing Program and I sat down. Ed Louge had been the administrator of the Boston Housing Program. The chairman said, "I'm not going to give Ed Louge time to respond, but if I know Ed, he will have something to say." When Ed Louge got up he said, "You wouldn't have gotten the money back if I had still been there," whereupon the audience booed him.

The disappointment I experienced in Tucson's Urban Renewal Plan which could have been corrected when I was Assistant Secretary in charge of Urban Renewal in the Department of Housing and Urban Development. After being in office for some time the Tucson City Council realized the error of their ways and reestablished the urban renewal project in Tucson, but drastically cut it from 417 acres to 92 acres. The result was that there was no housing left in the plan. All of the land was utilized for the Civic Center. This was not in accordance with the spirit of urban renewal. The program was to redevelop rundown areas and rejuvenate them by building new housing, along with necessary public buildings and other commercial development. When the program was submitted to me in Washington, D.C., I was responsible to allocate the funds or the project would never have been given federal assistance. In hindsight, I should have vetoed the program and sent it back for inclusion of some housing, but knowing Bill Matthews' attitude toward urban renewal, I thought that half a loaf was better than no project at all. I believe this was a mistake, and I believe they would have expanded the program to include housing. The result is that we achieved a nice attractive Civic Center, but as no housing was developed in the area, the area dies when the businesses close at five or six o'clock in the evening. Subsequent attempts to correct this error to have failed. As a result, Tucson received less than they should have, partly because of my failure to veto and demand that they expand the program to be consistent with the purposes of urban renewal.

It was not until 1968, however, when we got the law changed to provide flexibility and put urban renewal on a program basis as distinguished from a single project basis. This also enabled us to proceed with the housing programs at the planning stage which would be necessary before it could be redeveloped. This required close coordination with the Housing Assistance Agency.

It includes, in addition to clearance and redevelopment, rehabilitation, etc., such things as concentrated code enforcement programs and grants of funds for demolition of buildings that have been declared unsafe and must be removed. It covered area rehabilitation, including loans and grants to make it effective. I might state that code enforcement in any locality is good in theory, but highly questionable in practice. It is important how you administer it. Many of the areas that need services have deteriorated and are occupied by people who have the least resources to provide improvements. A city government is faced with the fact that if they have a building code to enforce and if the individual occupying the house does not have the resources to bring it up to the code, the local official faces a dilemma. The city cannot just throw the occupants out on the street because the house is substandard; it is better to have a tenant occupying a substandard home than no home at all.

This problem was partially resolved by the Rehabilitation and Improvement Loans Program. These funds were available to assist in the code enforcement program. The loan program, in substance, provided for low interest loans of three percent to bring a house up to urban renewal or code standards. There was also a grant program for those people who couldn't afford a loan. Most people in these slum areas already had one, two or three mortgages on their premises. If you required another lien, the practical effect would be an eviction. Congress provided that if a person had income of $3,000 or less per year and was required by law to rehabilitate his home facilities, the federal government would make an outright grant of up to $1,500 to bring the house up to standard. Later this was increased to $3,000 as $1,500 did not meet the requirements.

Another program for which I had responsibility was the Community Renewal Program. This was a grant program to local communities to survey their problem areas, and to ascertain what resources they had to respond to meet them; to determine their priorities for these particular areas so as to use the renewal process most effectively.

I was also responsible for the neighborhood Facilities Grant Program. This provided for a grant to the city of up to 50 percent of the cost to provide a multipurpose neighborhood center. The purpose of this program was to make funds available at the neighborhood level. This was to be a center to make poor people aware of the resources available through federal/state and private resources. Many poor people do not realize that these services exist and therefore do not take advantage of them. They are unfamiliar with the means necessary to operate through the bureaucracy of the city government; nor are they conversant with the organization of city hall. This program was designed to bring those services to the neighborhood level.

Another program that paralleled this was called the Open Space Program. I was responsible for the program to enable a community to establish urban parks in the central city. Most of the older and larger cities have developed without adequate recognition of the need to maintain some open space with the result that no space was available to provide a park in the inner city. This program was designed to correct that situation. Included in this was a program which provided funds for the beautification of these central city areas.

Housing Assistance

Another housing program which was a major responsibility to administer and direct was the Housing Assistance Administration. This is a new name for the old Public Housing Program. This called for the construction of facilities for low income people, or the acquisition and rehabilitation of existing facilities and the leasing of these facilities through local housing authorities for use by low income families.

Another housing program under housing assistance was the College Housing Program. This was a $300 million a year program which provided loans to colleges to keep dormitory rents low so that a greater number of students could afford to go to college. These funds were to be used by colleges to construct dormitory-type structures for occupancy by college students. They were supposed to be self-liquidating programs, but were subsidized to the extent that the direct loans from the federal government were three percent interest loans.

Still another housing program was Housing for the Elderly. This also was a self-liquidating program, designed to provide housing facilities for elderly people, who were identified as people 62 years of age or older. This program was directed at people with incomes that were above the Public Housing Program, but below their ability to pay market rents in the community. Still another program was the Alaska Housing Program. This was a statewide program designed to provide housing in remote areas for Alaska natives.

In order to qualify for many of these programs, there was a requirement that communities have what we called a Workable Program. This was established so the community would not call on the federal government for funds to eradicate slums and blight, while at the same time doing nothing to prevent the establishment of future slums. The Workable Program was required for most of the other programs administered by other assistant secretaries in the department. I had departmentwide responsibility for its administration. This included improvement of urban design in cities and the responsibility for the establishment and enforcement of social goals. Most cities had been in existence long before these programs started. They had established their own goals and designs, although in most instances, they were haphazard at best. As a result, we could only make piecemeal contribution. The fact that a city had grown without basic established plans was no reason to continue that forever. Cities develop, grow, decay and die by segments of their community. By establishing some planning concepts and some rules for the community, you can help make a contribution toward retarding decay. It takes a long time to see the results.

The last area that I had departmentwide responsibility for was in the area of relocation of people disturbed by various programs which included not only housing and urban renewal, but highway construction and other neighborhood changes. I had to set the terms and policies for implementing relocation facilities for all programs for all of our departments.

The original housing program was established in 1937 as an independent agency. Unfortunately, it was a program that never had full public support. It was started to stimulate and provide housing during the depression, but had considerable resistance at the local, as well as federal, levels despite the fact that there is a tremendous need for low cost housing; and despite the fact that there was great opposition to it, the people who were administering the program believed in and were loyal to the program. Many of them stayed in it to make a career of it, but with constant opposition. They grew defensive in their attitudes and banded together to support each other, so when I became assistant secretary for Housing Assistance, I found a true bureaucracy. They were spiritless, engrossed with the process to the extent that they had almost forgotten what their objectives were, which was to put poor people into housing. The process had become so complicated that it was divided into a one-step-at-a-time process.

They were measuring their progress on how far they had gone on a particular stage of the process rather than how many people they had put under roofs. The result was production had dropped to around 30 to 35 thousand units a year. I thought this was shameful, particularly when the commitment had been to "provide a decent house and a suitable living environment for every American."

That pledge had been made in the year 1949. When the Act was first passed, Congress had talked in terms of 800,000 units in a five-year period. Here it was, 30 years later, and they had produced the magnificent sum of 640,000 units in the 30 years.

It was obvious that drastic action had to be taken if the program was to accomplish its purpose. First, we had to reorganize the department, as it needed new blood, new vitality and enthusiasm, if the program was to succeed. This was delayed to some extent because I was too cautious. I didn't want to move too rapidly, as this was a field in which Secretary Weaver had spent a good part of his life and was vitally interested.

I had no real experience in the housing field. I felt reluctant to make too rapid and too radical changes. It took me some time to convince Secretary Weaver that what I needed was not a person who knew housing, because he could learn the program, but what I really needed was an administrator. I was also delayed because I knew that Secretary Weaver, while he never put any pressure on me, wanted Walter Washington as the deputy secretary in charge of Housing Assistance.

Walter Washington was a wonderful person. He subsequently became the first mayor of the District of Columbia, but he was not a good administrator. Finally, after several abortive attempts, I appointed Tom Fletcher, who had been the city manager of San Diego, California, to be deputy administrator for Housing Assistance. I tried to get Tom some eight or nine months earlier, but he had made a commitment to go into the private sector. It was not until several months later that I learned that this commitment had not worked out to his satisfaction. I got in touch with Tom and hired him as my assistant to reorganize and handle the housing assistant program. The only trouble was that the President had heard of Tom Fletcher too and I had him only four weeks before the President reached down and picked him out from under me and made him deputy mayor to Walter Washington, in the District of Columbia. I had to start all over again.

I think the move to take Tom away from HUD merits a recitation of the events. After Tom had been with me about two weeks, he returned to California to pick up his family to bring them to Washington, D.C. Tom was driving back and was in Rapid City, South Dakota, at a stoplight when a car drew up alongside of him and the driver asked, "Are you Tom Fletcher?" He said, "Yes," and the man in the other car said, "I am with the FBI — please pull over." Tom pulled over and the FBI man advised him that the White House was attempting to get in touch with him and that he should immediately call Joe Califano. Tom followed instructions and Joe asked him how quickly he could return to Washington.

Tom said that he was driving and it would take two or three days. Joe said, "Find out how quickly you can fly here." Tom checked and there was no flight for some time, so he called back and was told to put his family in a motel and that an Air Force plane would pick him up and take him to Washington. This was accomplished and Tom reported to Joe Califano at the executive office in Washington.

After waiting for some time, he was taken up to President Johnson's office. The President offered Tom the position of deputy mayor of the District. Johnson asked him, "Can you run the District of Columbia? Do you want this job as deputy mayor, and do you have any concerns?" Tom said he could do the job, wanted the job, but that he did have some concerns. President Johnson asked him what concern he had and Tom told him that Don Hummel had just hired him less than a month before to head up the Housing Assistance Program in the Department of Housing and Urban Development. The President said, "Don Hummel works for me, too, so don't let that worry you." By that time it was late in the day and the President said, "Have you eaten?" Tom said, "No," and the President said, "Well, come with me." So he took Tom up to his private quarters and they had had a late dinner. Lady Bird Johnson came in and visited with them a short time and then left. Then the President said, "By the way, where are you staying?" Tom said, "I think they have a room for me at the Madison Hotel." The President said, "Oh, you don't want to stay there — stay here. I will get a room for you here."

Shortly thereafter, Califano came in with a stack of papers. The President gave Tom a local paper to read and then moved over to another part of the room. Tom said he knew something was happening, but he didn't know what, and he didn't dare turn around. Finally, out walks the President of the United States, stark naked, and lays down on a massage table. Joe Califano sat on the floor in front of him, and a masseur gave the President a massage. Joe Califano briefed the President and received instructions on the responses to make, then the President fell asleep. Joe Califano left and Tom Fletcher went to bed in the White House.

During this entire period of time, no one had bothered to advise me or Secretary Weaver of the President's action. Secretary Weaver was pretty mad when he learned about the way it was handled, but he did not have much recourse against the President of the United States. I was now back where I had started, having lost valuable reorganization time. I needed a new deputy assistant to handle the housing programs.

I hired another deputy assistant secretary for housing, but he didn't work out so I appointed Arthur Rosfeld as acting deputy assistant. He had been a special assistant to Marie Maguire. He did an excellent job and continued on for a while under the Nixon administration.

The housing organization that I took over when I went to Washington was a bureaucratic nightmare and the delays incurred in getting a new deputy assistant secretary for housing did not contribute to a solution. The fact that it was taking 41 months between the community's application for a housing project and the start of construction was completely unacceptable if we were to have a housing program. This not only delayed the availability of housing but tied up our funds for years.

In order to expedite the development of housing, I instituted a program which would parallel the procedure that would be followed if a private individual were to build a housing project. In other words, we advised the local agency of the number of housing units we would approve. The local housing authority could then advertise for contractors to bid on the housing project. The contractors were to provide the land, the building plans and the delivery price. If agreed to, they built the house according to the approved plans. Heretofore, the local government would find a piece of land; then they would go out and find an architect; the architect would prepare the plans; the plans would be submitted to the council at a public hearing, and, if the council approved, the plans would be sent to us for funding; then if we approved, a contract would be let. This was a most cumbersome and expensive method of building housing. I realized that the procedure I inaugurated was fraught with many dangers, because we would be presented with an accomplished fact and our only decision would be whether or not to fund it. This opened the door to fraud, to conniving and collusion, but I reduced the time application to construction from 41 months to 17 weeks. After I had this program established, I began to retrench by establishing certain safeguards as more and more evidence of collusion and fraud between local officials and contractors began to materialize as we had the new program operating. In fact, I was amused to have contractors come to my office with big diamond stickpins in their ties and shirts that would be worn only by a gambler. The new regulations were designed to protect us against this collusion and fraud.

I set up a task force to reorganize the Housing Administration. We decided on two principal divisions. One was the Production Division and the other was called Tenant Services. Under the Production Division we had attempted to streamline the process for achieving housing units. We were hopeful that with this new approach we could get into a position to provide 50,000 to 100,000 new units each year. This was necessary if we were ever going to solve the housing problem for low and moderate income families.

In an effort to emphasize production, I used what we called the turnkey process. The name was borrowed from real estate parlance of having a house ready to turn the key and move in. Joe Burstein, the attorney, had proposed this for government housing, but it had never been implemented. In substance, it was a process which enabled the local housing authority to make a contract with a local developer, just as any private citizen or corporation might do.

After perfecting the turnkey process, we held a number of forum field discussions across the country with home builders, real estate agents, locally interested citizens and community representatives. We got a tremendous response, but the trouble was that at this stage of the game, we ran out of appropriation authority, so had to slow down the process. This did not help our creditability with the private sector. We also had asked for authority to accelerate the expenditure of some $37 million that was not to become available until the following fiscal year. It died in committee and we were unable to pursue this objective.

The turnkey process speeded up the time of application to start of construction. It put much further reliance on the private sector and it brought the profit motive to bear on the problems. I thought this was essential, if we were ever to produce enough housing. Simultaneously, with the request of President Johnson to increase production, we made a public pledge to him that we would produce 70,000 units to be available for occupancy during the next 12-month period. This was met with considerable consternation within the Housing Assistant Administration. They did not believe it could be done and they were not too sure it should be done. Many were betting we could not double the number produced the previous year. Adding to their consternation was the fact that we agreed to provide 70,000 units "available for occupancy." The criteria they had been using to measure their progress was the number of housing starts. A start was a lot simpler to achieve, but it did not provide housing for the people. We did have some advantage in that we started a leasing program by acquiring units we could lease for extended periods of time and then convert them to housing immediately. The department had resisted this for some time. I thought the leasing program was important, as it contributed a solution to the social problems we were faced with by avoiding concentration of too many people of one income level in one building or area. The program also permitted the leasing of units in existing apartments and thereby integrated some of these poor families with others that were not on relief.

We kept our commitment to the President by making over 74,879 units available for occupancy within the 12-month period. We exceeded our goal.

The housing authorities, in their publication *Journal of Housing*, portrayed this accomplishment on the cover as an arrow hitting the target of 74,859 units. A copy of it was framed and presented to me at their convention.

The concentration of the poor in one building or one area had created all kinds of social problems and did not help our public image. On the other hand, this process was shorter, quicker and brought into availability, facilities in smaller numbers so that we could disperse lower income families among more affluent people. This we found encouraged low income families by example of what they could do if they put forth the effort. It was accepted and made a contribution toward the very objective we sought.

It worked in this manner: The local housing authority could go to an apartment building owner and say, "We would like to rent 10 percent of the dwelling units in your apartment. We will make a contract with you and you can select the tenants at the economic level that is eligible for public housing. These tenants will pay 20 percent of their income to you as rent, and we will make up the difference with an annual contribution." Another way to accomplish the same result was to go to the owner of a deteriorated facility and agree to lease the facility, if the owner would bring it up to standard. The authority then assigned low income people to it. There were many ramifications, but these are two examples.

Another major problem I discovered when taking over this program was the rather deplorable living conditions which had been developed over the years in the existing housing projects. Many of these units had been built years before and had not had adequate maintenance. Nothing had been done to upgrade them and nothing had been done to solve the tenants' problems. This was one of the real tragedies of the program. There had been a cavalier assumption that if you put a person in a better house, he automatically knew how to take care of that house and this would automatically solve his problems. No effort had been made to ascertain the basic or root causes of why this person was in need of low cost housing or why he needed public assistance. I hoped that we could rectify this omission, at least in part. I wanted to bring to bear through all the agencies of the federal government, the local government, private sector, etc., to try to solve the basic problems so the tenant could expand his economic capacity and get back into mainstream society.

We called the second principal division of our reorganization effort Tenant Services. We had several goals. One was to find out what the root problem was which required public assistance and try to bring to bear the services that were available to correct it. The second major goal was to make the person feel that this was his home while he was living there, and by having him participate in the decision-making policies of running the project, encourage better care of the unit. In other words, instead of setting up rules as you would with your children, sit down and tell him what you are trying to do.

This was done by having the housing authorities organize tenant councils. The councils were to sit down with management and try to decide what should be done to correct such problems as vandalism; what should be done in eviction cases, and how to redress tenant grievances; all the kinds of things that arise when you require a group of people to live together. We called for an organizational structure that would give attention and opportunity to solve these problems.

The parallel to this was the issuance of what we called the Essential Goals of the Department. There had been an influx of social scientists into the department, but most often they were highly theoretical. They talked in high flowing terms of general objectives, but in no way could they get down to the hard facts of how to implement social goals, or what kind of instructions should be issued to achieve a social component into the low rent housing program.

As these social scientists complained about the absence of social goals, I asked them to propose social goals for the program. I asked on several occasions and finally ended up having to write them myself, with the assistance of my new staff.   The social scientists were not able to identify and cope with basic components. I laid down two objectives. One was to improve the living conditions of the people while they were tenants of local housing projects; and the second was that I wanted to improve their opportunities of getting out of public housing. In summary, these were our two principal objectives: How to break the cycle of poverty and how to improve conditions while living under public housing.

Subsequently, we had prepared a treatise of the housing program. I was called into a meeting with Secretary Weaver, Undersecretary Wood and the department's social scientists. The social scientists complained bitterly that I did not have a chapter on social goals. This irritated me but I attended the meeting to discuss the treatise we had prepared. I said that I was getting sick and tired of people talking about social goals and not knowing how to define or implement them. Just having a chapter called Social Goals would not accomplish anything; that social goals had to be written into the fabric of everything we were doing. I pointed out 37 references in our treatise which concerned the implementation of social goals. I was angry and perhaps over-aggressive, as I objected to people asking for something when they did not know what they wanted and could not recognize them when they were presented. This was the last time I was ever criticized for not having a chapter on social goals in our program.

An interesting byproduct to this was that some 20 years later I was at a municipal meeting in Nogales, Arizona. A lady come up to me and said, "We are still using the social goals that you put into the program some 20 years ago." In addition to changing management concepts and involving the tenants in management responsibility, we also went before Congress and asked for money to implement the Tenant Services Concept. We were given authority to do so, but were never given any money to help implement it. The Appropriations Committee felt that we were trying to supplement the welfare program.

They never did give us a real opportunity to explain what we were trying to do. We did get started however. As I indicated, many of the housing projects were aging, and had inadequate maintenance. Many of them had been built as temporary facilities during wartime and were inadequately built or did not have proper amenities, so I took $10 million a year that had been authorized and instead of building additional units, I authorized contracts to improve existing units. In other words, we said to the locality: "You come up with a program of what you want to do to modernize and at the same time tell us how much you plan to spend and how you expect to accomplish the program, and we will approve a reasonable project of modernization."

We required them to specify that they had set up tenant councils and would utilize them. We required them to advise us what provisions had been made in child care in the housing projects, particularly for working mothers. We asked them if they had provided instructions to achieve acceptable house-keeping standards for tenants; whether or not they were insisting on complying with these house-keeping standards; whether or not they were insisting on acceptable sanitation standards; whether they had assisted these people in preparation of budgets so they could get a balanced diet for the family. These were the kinds of management functions we thought were essential if housing authorities were to do a proper job. If they had not implemented these conditions, we would not approve their modernization program.

This is how we started our social goals and social services program. It has been very well accepted and hopefully will provide an example to Congress that this is not a boondoggle. It is a genuine effort to help people get out of subsidized housing and break some of the habits of poverty.

I want to mention a few obstacles that must be overcome if the housing program was to go forward on the scale that was required to properly house people. We found

community opposition. Every one says they want a housing program, but do not want it built in their neighborhood.
They agreed with the concept of government spending
money to provide decent housing for people who cannot
provide it for themselves, but they did not want it next door
to them. This arises out of the fear of undermining the
economic value of the investment in their home — a most
difficult problem to overcome.

Another problem is the escalating cost of land. While
costs of construction were going up more than five percent
a year, land in critical areas had been escalating at a far
greater rate. It could drive the low rent housing industry
out of the market.

The high cost of construction was exacerbated by the
inflexible administration of building codes, many of which
were archaic, obsolete and not based on performance standards, in that they did not permit the use of new materials
or new technology.

Along with the problems of restrictive codes, were restrictive labor practices, which had broken down the function of labor into the guild, or craft approach, instead of
taking advantage of the general project approach. Another
deterrent was a lack of initiative at the local level. The
federal government can respond to requests, but cannot
initiate the project. If the local government ignores its
responsibility in the housing field, no new housing will be
started. Still another obstacle to mass production was the
lack of competition among the builders and the fact that
home builders in large measure are a group of small contractors, so you often did not have the well financed, highly
industrial group of people in the home building industry.

A workable program stipulated by Congress as a requirement for federal assistance, in effect said to the local
community, "If you want federal assistance, then you have
to set up and show that you plan to help eradicate blight,
remove slums and start to plan your community." The
general statutory enactment was quite general, but over the
period of its implementation, a workable program became a
precise, almost obstacle-jumping arrangement. It became a
bureaucratic requirement of the federal government which
was imposed on communities regardless of the degree of a

community's advancement and regardless of their needs. It had become more restrictive each year. It had become a source of great resentment by the local community as they were required to have this program recertified each year.

I ordered our staff to reexamine the requirements and get a new approach. The new approach would, in brief, have this thrust: first, each community would set up its own program; not what we said it should have, but its own program; they would analyze the problems in their own community in the light of their state of development, their state of growth, and their particular obstacles; they would then establish their goals for the next four-, five- or 10-year period, and then show us how they expected to reach those goals. They would establish a schedule and a program of what they expected to do the following year and the year after. After they had established their goals and programs, and we had approved them as reasonable, we would say to that community, "We will judge you by your goals and your accomplishments, on the basis of your objectives and what you say your goals are and how you expect to reach them."

Four areas were specified as being important to any well balanced community in the process of eradicating slums. First of all, what they were going to do about building and housing codes. This was a statutory enactment and could not be waived without a change in the law. We asked them to approve a model code and to limit restrictions which would prevent the use of new technology or new materials in building and housing programs. Another request was for them to specify their planning process. The old requirement was the adoption of a general plan. This more often than not was a graphic plat that went on a shelf and that was the last anyone heard of it. We asked, "What is your planning process?" (Note the word "process.") "How do you expect to implement it? How do you connect your planning process with your decision making authority so that you are not just planning, but you are implementing these plans? Show us how you propose to do it."

And next, we stipulated that housing was essential to solving urban problems. We asked, "Have you made a housing inventory, and does this include an inventory of the availability of housing for the low and moderate income family? If there is a gap between housing that is available and housing that is suitable for low income families, how do you propose to narrow the gap? In other words, what programs do you have to provide additional housing?" Many programs result in dislocation and relocation of families. Many of our federal programs require certain relocation services before you are allowed to use federal funds to move a family. The community should look at all activities that result from relocation, not just at urban renewal programs or health programs, because a state or local highway program can be just as disruptive and completely overtax a community's relocation resources. The community should have a central relocation program that operates on a communitywide basis.

In the legislation of 1968 we were successful in getting the necessary changes in the law which permitted us to put renewal plans on a program basis instead of the restrictive project approach which we found so inflexible.

We still encountered problems in the administration of these programs through the Bureau of the Budget. The process required that our program be proposed and presented to the appropriate congressional legislative committee. If they authorized it, then we would have go to before the Appropriations Committee to obtain money to implement it. Having done all this, we would then be summoned before a representative of the Bureau of the Budget. This budget representative would tell us how we should apportion our funds. In other words, they recognized that we had an approval of a project or program, and that we had the authorization of Congress to implement it, but then the Bureau of the Budget would say, "You can only spend so much during this period of time." I greatly resented this procedure as it amounted to some career civil service employee overruling the Secretary of HUD, Congress and the administrative body responsible for the program. It is not responsible action. I considered it a most undemocratic procedure, but it prevailed. It stymied much of our flexibility.

The 1968 law authorized this program approach. We called it The Neighborhood Development Program. We tried to establish a program approach rather than a project basis to have it consistent with normal capital development programs in the locality. To do this, we allowed them to designate a much larger area; to allow projects that were not contiguous as previously required. This was particularly important as the housing programs often did not fit the planning program in the urban renewal area. We also permitted construction to proceed simultaneously with planning, rather than have a plan in detail before you could begin construction. This had been particularly onerous, in that an extensive program took several years to complete and by the time the plan was ready, conditions may have changed to the degree that it was no longer relevant. We advised the communities through the new housing programs that if they had an approved Neighborhood Development Program (and I want to emphasize that it was a program and not a project-by-project basis), we would allow them to start their planning program, at the same time start to purchase land that obviously was essential to the completion of the program.

In this way, we permitted simultaneous execution while the planning process was in effect. This saved years of time and made better use of our funds. This also fitted the local community methods of appropriation and procedure for redevelopment. It did have the disadvantage that there was no way we could promise that the federal government would continue appropriations to insure that the total program could be completed; however, the present plan did not either but purported to do so. We permitted the community to lay out a year's program, and if we approved their budget for the first year, we tentatively earmarked funds for the second year. This gave them some assurance that the federal government was planning on a continuation of the program. This required that the federal agency reevaluate at the end of each year what the community had done. If it had not completed its yearly program, but had spent the money set up for it, there could be no argument as to whose failure it was. In the past, the federal government had always been the scapegoat with the community saying they could have done the job if the federal government had given them more money. By the new approach, we achieved an automatic evaluation of their program every year, instead of trying to evaluate what actually happened after all the money had been spent. It also brought us closer to a cash basis instead of a reservation of monies being tied up for many years while other communities waited for funding. This change in urban renewal laws was enthusiastically accepted by the communities.

After President Nixon's election, the secretary, undersecretary and others had all submitted their resignations, including mine. I agreed to stay for a short transition for the incoming secretary. We continued to operate as we had in the past, but one day I received a frantic call from some of my employees in the Housing Department stating that $300 million worth of treasury notes were scheduled to be sold on the following Monday, but all delegated authority had been rescinded. Normal procedure was to sell treasury notes for a 90-day term and when they matured, sell other notes to redeem the expiring notes on a rollover basis.

I previously had authority to sign for the new notes, but suddenly we found all our delegated authority had been canceled by George Romney, the new secretary of HUD.

I immediately paid a visit to Secretary Romney and advised him that someone had to authorize the signing of these notes, or the government would be in the uncomfortable position of failing to meet its obligation on some $300 million worth of treasury notes, which would be very embarrassing for the administration. Secretary Romney then authorized me to continue signing. The Republicans were sure that we, as Democrats, were going to try to do something to embarrass them in the transition, and that was the reason for the secretive withdrawal of delegated authority. About two weeks later, when I was leaving, I dropped by to say goodbye to Secretary Romney. He was sitting at his desk in his sloppy blue sweater with urban renewal and housing files stacked up about a foot deep on his desk. His comment to me was, "If I hadn't taken away your authority, you'd be doing this." I said goodbye to the secretary and that was the end of my association with the Department of Housing and Urban Development.

Genee's Christmas Letter, 1968:

This year finds many changes in the Hummel family. The prospect of uncertainty of Don's appointment to HUD led us to decide to put Charlene and Clifford in a private school. They have been at Orme Ranch School, north of Phoenix, since September.

Cliff, a senior, played football, first as a lineman, then as a half-back. He likes school and is doing well scholastically. Just recently he was elected student body president. Char, a sophomore, was quite homesick at first, but is happier now and making a good adjustment. You might say the same for us. It's been twenty years since we have been without children. Quite a change. Uncertainty is still with us. Don will resign as of January 20th as do all Presidential appointees, although he has expressed a willingness to stay through a transitional period if that is desired. We will then head back to Tucson and national park activity.

It has been a particularly challenging, often frustrating, but always stimulating 2-1/2 years. Don feels that he has been able to make a worthwhile contribution while directing the low rent housing and the urban renewal programs for the U.S. Genee has enjoyed all the opportunities to learn about this part of the country, to partake of its many official, diplomatic, cultural and educational activities.

We've had many visitors, seen more good friends since we've been here than in many years. There were more visitors than ever in Glacier National Park this summer, too. The highlight of the summer came in August when the HUD secretaries with their families arrived for five days of meetings; the Don Fords and Dallas Dorts arriving simultaneously. Meetings were scheduled early and late to give maximum opportunity to see the park. The proverbial good time was had by all. The children worked in the park again this year. Donna stayed at East Glacier Lodge as front desk relief while the others stayed with Genee at the cabin on Lake McDonald, Dee and Cliff waiting tables in the dining room; Char clerking in the gift shop. Donna is just out of her teens, a junior at Oregon State. She was recently elected to the business women's and music service honoraries. Dee is a sophomore at Colorado College and working too hard to get her share of her favorite sport — skiing.

Don has traveled a good deal and Genee has been included in a number of trips. In October the whole family was together for a weekend in Denver and visited Dee's campus in Colorado Springs. Now we are looking forward to being together at Christmas at Rex Ranch for desert sun and Lassen National Park for skiing. Meanwhile, Don and Genee have trips scheduled for Puerto Rico, Mexico City and New Orleans, so we will wind up the year in a blaze of activity.

❄ ❄ ❄

Genee's Christmas Letter, 1969:

1969 draws to a close as we approach the holiday season.

For the Chinese it was the year of the Rooster, a year of good portent. For the U.S. it did not bode so well: a year of dissent and demonstration. A changing world saw change in us, but only the normal kind that comes with politics and maturing children, and so we join you again to visit and wish you well.

Don left the Department of HUD after a brief transition with the Nixon Administration amidst nostalgic and heartwarming dinners and receptions with the men who had dedicated their abilities to help solve the complex problems we call the urban crises.

We sold our house in Bethesda and are now refurbishing our home at 40 Calle Encanto in Tucson, but not before we took a delightful cruise with Dal and Betty Dort exploring the Bahamas, Eluthera and Exuma Islands on their yacht, the "Damosel." It was a new world of white sand beaches and crystal clear waters; a new experience to snorkel amongst the coral reefs, the unnumbered variety of tropical ferns and fishes; for us, a perfect vacation.

After a brief Maryland-New York visit from Donna and Charlene during their Easter vacations, we headed for Glacier National Park driving one car, towing a second. Donna finished her third year at Oregon State on the Dean's list and came to work for us at Glacier Park as information agent. Cliff graduated from Orme School and left for work at Lassen National Park, but spent the last month as a grill cook at Lake McDonald. Char was a motel maid and lived with us at Lake McDonald while Diane left from Colorado College to join a Lassen friend, Marty McClelland, on a student tour of southern Europe. A three month trip; it was a grand and broadening experience.

Don and Genee joined the Dorts and Don Fords on a two-week trip to Alaska in August going up Inland Passage to Skagway, the narrow gauge to Whitehorse, then to Anchorage, Fairbanks, Nome, Kotzebue, and McKinley National Park. We detoured to Valdez for salmon fishing and a wonderful visit with Bill and Helen Snedden of Fairbanks, returning with a freezer full of delicious salmon and dungeness crab. A fabulous trip, we recommend it to you for your next vacation.

This winter finds Cliff a freshman at Colorado College taking a pre-med course; Donna, a senior at Oregon State, graduating in June with a B.S. in Business Administration. Char is living with us attending Tucson High as a junior. Di, searching for a change from Colorado College, tried three months at Cambridge, Mass., but is now reentering C.C. as a junior. All but Donna were home for Thanksgiving. We will all assemble again for joint Christmas plans and continuing efforts to maintain a healthy family communion.

❄ ❄ ❄

23

U.S. Natural Resources -
Yosemite Park & Curry Company

UPON MY return to Glacier from Washington in 1969, I took over the operation when I was again contacted by George Fleharty who had joined U.S. Natural Resources. He urged me to open negotiations with them to merge the Glacier, Lassen and McKinley National Parks Concessions with U.S. Natural Resources.

U.S. Natural Resources was incorporated in 1926 and was largely involved in the exploration and development of oil and gas resources. It had interests in 434 producing wells and a lease on 1,700,000 acres for offshore drilling extending from Cape Town, South Africa, to a point 470 miles east following the shoreline for 5.5 miles. It had interests on the Alaskan North Slope as well as interests in leases in the continental United States.

On October 15, 1969, Irving Lundborg and Company, members of the U.S. Stock Exchange, touted the new management of this firm, citing the increased value of stock from $10.50 on May 1, 1969, to $31.08 six months later. The new management had completely changed the physical structure of the company and its goals. The company quoted Robert Lehman, "I bet on people more than balance sheets."

New management was listed as Robert L. Katz, former professor in the Graduate Business School of Harvard, Stanford and Dartmouth, and as consultant for such firms as General Electric, Castle and Cook, Standard Oil Company and Boise Cascade Corporation; Robert Halliday, former executive vice president of Boise Cascade; Stanley B. McDonald, president of Air-Mac Inc., William D. Eberle, president of American Standard and formerly executive vice president of Boise Cascade Company, and Charles F. McDevitt, president of Beck Industries.

341

The new management strategy called for development of selected segments of (1) forest products, (2) mining and minerals, (3) oil and gas, and (4) recreational lands. It was projected that sales would be $20 million and earnings of $1.00 per share pre-tax. As the previous company had operated at a loss, there was a tax loss carried forward of $4.3 million for the following four years. The new U.S. Natural Resources projected assets at the close of the year (December 1969) of $21,300,000, with a net worth of $13,950,000.

George Fleharty, together with Russell Olson, had joined forces to establish the Shasta Company, a TV station in Redding, California with an investment of $100,000. They subsequently sold the station for $1,300,000.

In their search for another investment, they purchased the Ice Follies, which they turned around and sold for $5 million. They next looked at Yosemite Park & Curry Company to invest their funds. They sought a merger of Yosemite with their Shasta Company. As this was unsuccessful, they tendered for Yosemite stock. There were 1,045,000 shares outstanding and they had acquired 395,000 shares when their funds were exhausted.

There were some negotiations by Shasta for the sale of Yosemite stock to Greyhound Corporation, which they were not able to consummate. Fleharty then approached and made a deal with U.S. Natural Resources for an exchange of Yosemite stock for U.S. Natural Resources stock.

George Fleharty contracted with U.S. Natural Resources to represent the latter's recreation division. He contacted Al Donau at Lassen about acquisition of the Lassen Company, and was referred to me. We entered negotiations for the purpose of merging Lassen, Mt. McKinley, and Glacier Park concessions with U.S. Natural Resources.

Agreement was reached on the Lassen and McKinley Companies, but stalled on the Glacier operation. I then signed an employment agreement with U.S. Natural Resources for a five-year term, whereby I was to be general manager of the Lassen/McKinley Companies and was to provide executive services for other U.S. Natural Resources subsidiary companies, as directed by the board of directors. It was understood that I was to reorganize the Yosemite

Park & Curry Company as soon as U.S. Natural Resources gained control. U.S. Natural Resources, as the largest yet minority stockholder of Yosemite, had only two seats on their board of directors.

This was a period of confusion and fluctuating policies engendered by controversies between the old board of directors and the compromise board reflecting ownership of 38 percent of the stock by U.S. Natural Resources.

The directors on the old board largely represented the Curry family and people from the San Francisco Bay area, which had been handpicked by the Currys. The staff of the organization reflected the close association of the employees and the Curry family. It was this loyal association which led to the defeat of George Fleharty and his associates' attempts to acquire control of the board of directors. Many employees declined to sell their Yosemite stock, even though the price of $11.00 a share far exceeded the price quoted by Dean Witter and Company, who made the market for this stock.

The discord on the board of directors started before U.S. Natural Resources involvement between George Fleharty and the Yosemite directors, in a special meeting held on August 5, 1969, for the purpose of discussing Shasta Telecasting Corporation's new purchase of Yosemite stock and the preparation of a press release and letters to shareholders by Yosemite Park & Curry Company.

Fleharty objected to the use of the words "thus far unsuccessful takeover activities" in the press release. Director Fleharty stated that Shasta did not intend to take over Yosemite, but acknowledged that if they received 51 percent of the stock this would give their directors control; however, Shasta did not intend to liquidate or sell Yosemite assets, or to merge or make major changes in its corporate structure.

Mr. Fleharty criticized the lack of decision on management succession; that there were no new programs nor new directions for the company which was declining in profitability.

After U.S. Natural Resources acquired the Shasta Company, Robert L. Katz, as president of U.S. Natural Resources, wrote the Yosemite board advising them of this acquisition on December 16, 1969. The Yosemite board established a committee under the chairmanship of Director Eric Stanford to propose ways and means of cooperation with U.S. Natural Resources. The committee recommended a merger with U.S. Natural Resources as the best way of protecting Yosemite's minority stockholders, pointing out that if U.S. Natural Resources acquired 51 percent of Yosemite's stock, the present board would lose all control.

At the annual meeting of the stockholders of Yosemite Park & Curry Company on January 16, 1970, U.S. Natural Resources elected six members out of 15 to the board of directors. This was by agreement of all the parties. I was one of the six from U.S. Natural Resources.

Directly after the stockholders meeting, the board met and elected the following officers: Honorary Chairman, Mrs. Mary Curry Tresidder; Honorary Chairman, Hilmer Oehlmann; President, Stuart Cross; V. P. Operations, Robert A. Maynard; V. P. Commercial, Charles N. Proctor; V. P. Administration/Secretary, Arthur P. Robinson; Treasurer, Roger J. Sandberg.

The new board of directors of Yosemite Park & Curry Company met again on June 26, 1970, and at this meeting it was agreed that Don Hummel would have active participation in the operations of the company. The executive committee was to have specific powers which explicitly acknowledged U.S. Natural Resources' control position.

A resolution was adopted to change the By-Laws thus creating an executive committee with power to act; Don Hummel as chairman and John Curry, Stuart Cross and Eric Stanford as members.

Genee's Christmas Letter, 1970

The 1970s have ushered in some changes for the Hummels. The children are growing up and away. Diane was married to David Ellis in May. As both are interested in education, they had their baptism in a small school for underprivileged boys near Houston, Texas, this summer. They are back to finish their formal education at Colorado College where they are juniors. Cliff, discouraged with his fling at Colorado College, dropped out and is working as a roofer in Tucson. He has moved into a small house with a friend and plans to go to the University of Arizona this winter semester unless his status of 1-A in the draft and number 49 in the call dictates service in the armed forces. After 3-1/2 years Charlene has completed all requirements for high school graduation.

Now she is planning to work at Yosemite this winter so that she and Genee can join Don there. Cliff will move back into the house.

Donna received her B.S. in Business Administration with Phi Kappa Phi honors from Oregon State. As a graduation present she and Char spent seven weeks in Europe using Eurorail tickets and youth hostels, seeing and enjoying friends and ten countries. A very successful trip and experience. Donna is now working in the credit department of a bottling machinery manufacturer and preparing for a Milwaukee winter, a first for her in the cold and in a full-time, experience-getting job.

Change has been the dominant theme for Genee and Don, too. After more than 30 years, the Lassen National Park Company and the Mt. McKinley National Park Company were merged with U.S. Natural Resources, a company on the American Stock Exchange with interests in oil and gas, mines and minerals, forest products, and recreational resources. Don's attempt to reduce responsibilities through the merger resulted in expanding obligations. U.S.N.R. is the principal stockholder in Yosemite Park & Curry Company and Don, as vice president of operations of Recreational Resources Division of U.S.N.R., became chairman of the Executive Committee of the Y.P.C. Board of Directors. This requires residence in Yosemite and separation from the family in Tucson. Not an ideal home situation, but Genee keeps busy with courses in creative stitchery and art history. Participating in current events, and electioneering in the Arizona political campaign. She reviewed "Man, the Manipulator" for her book club. An occasional trip to Yosemite and a visit to Washington, D.C., and New York fills out her scheduled activities beyond homemaking for Char.

Christmas was spent in Yosemite Valley.

❊ ❊ ❊

At a Yosemite Board Meeting, Secretary Robert Katz proposed, and the board approved, $125,000 to establish a shuttle bus system on an experimental basis for 10 weeks, beginning July 15, with the understanding that the Park Service may not be able to reimburse the company. This was the company's first step toward reducing automobile traffic in the valley by 1972. Conditions in the valley had deteriorated through the dramatic increase in automobile travel.

H.L. (Spud) Bill, deputy director of the National Park Service, informed the board that, to date, the service had been unsuccessful in getting a supplemental budget for the system. He was delighted when informed that the company had approved the funds to establish the service. Mr. Bill and Director Hartzog would inaugurate the system on July 9 and 10.

My first report as chairman of the executive committee was made to U.S. Natural Resources after visiting the park on three occasions and talking with the principal officials and supervisors of Yosemite Park & Curry Company. This included ten of the top management staff members. I also made a tour of all the facilities except Toulumne Meadows and the El Portal operations.

I reported that most of the units were over-staffed. I made a comparison of the number of employees used at Many Glacier Hotel in Glacier National Park and with the food operations, gift shops, etc. The number of employees per room was considerably higher at Yosemite. Several problems aggravated this over-staffing. For example, the employees at Yosemite only worked a five-day week, while they worked a six-day week at Glacier. Yosemite provided free meals in lieu of 50 cents per hour employee meal charge, and since employees were only working five days a week, and being provided food for seven days, the increase of costs was obvious. I suggested that we increase the wages to the employees and have them buy their meals at the cafeterias at a discount. I noticed the employees did not consider food as part of their remuneration, and often took more than they required, which, left uneaten, went into garbage cans.

My basic conclusion was that the operations were not only over-staffed, but there was little continuity existing in the organization, and there appeared to be a complete lack of supervision. Managers were always found in their offices and very seldom were out in the operations observing what was occurring. The only contact between top management and unit managers was accomplished through a weekly breakfast meeting. While attending one of these, I felt that it was more a social gathering than a management seminar.

In the personnel department I found a rather disturbing fact. They hired only by personal interviews and this limited the employment to those people who dropped by the company site. During this period of time, we had many stragglers and unemployed who dropped by and asked for jobs. The quality of these employees was far below that of those we hired at Glacier by application through college campuses.

Another area in which I thought the procedures were very costly was in the warehouse. Practically everything was delivered to a central warehouse which resulted in multiple handling and redelivery to the units. Many of these goods could have been delivered directly to the units where they would be utilized. Purchasing was not standardized throughout the warehouse; each unit ordered the type of product it preferred. As an example, each housekeeper specified the brand of cleaner she preferred. The result, of course, was that they were carrying multiple brands of supplies when one would have sufficed. This also prevented volume purchasing with consequent reduction in price.

I recommended that in order to control the staffing of units, we have each unit manager prepare a personal budget supported by schedules to show the personnel coverage, hours of operation and requirements. There should also be introduced, a pooling operation, giving each location a basic complement, with a reserve pool to draw from. Examples: The Ahwahnee and the Lodge should each have a basic staff and the pool to draw from to correspond to the peaks and valleys of room occupancies.

I felt a major reorganization was necessary, if we were get effective supervision. The lines of authority, as I encountered them, were indirect and ineffective and in some instances almost non existent. I felt this reorganization of the top structure with some changes in key personnel was essential. To implement these recommendations, it was obvious I would have to have some direct responsibility. This, of course, challenged some rights of the established management structure and would in time lead to conflict.

Report of the Executive Committee, July 20, 1970:

A thorough review of the financial position of the company was made, which recognized the inability of the company to raise further capital and the need for tight control of cash.

President Cross was instructed not to approve any further projects and to analyze present projects, particularly as to return on investment. The company's June statement revealed no working capital and that cash projections through September 30 (the end of the summer season) would be $300,000, less than the results of the 1969 operation. This was insufficient to meet the winter expenses as revenues drastically declined during the off-season.

Unfavorable profit plan variances for direct labor, deductions made from income and nonoperating expenses were discussed.

The committee expressed concern as to whether direct labor costs met normal resort standards.

It was noted that arrivals, house counts and meals served, had dropped substantially. An advertising plan was proposed and approved.

High inventory levels were criticized. Pension fund management was discussed, noting that the relationship between fund performance and company contributions was not good. This was the start of inquiry to be pursued by the executive committee designed to control costs and improve profitability. It would also bring the executive committee into conflict with the established management headed by Stuart Cross, the president of Yosemite Park & Curry Company.

The effectiveness of this closer supervision and tighter contracts was evidenced in an analysis by Director Eric M. Stanford in December 1971. The comparisons between the 1970 and 1971 results showed:

	1971 (%)	1970 (%)
Cost of sales decreased to	28.10	from 31.36
Company's margin increased to	71.70	from 68.64
Direct labor costs decreased to	23.00	from 25.89
Attendant costs decreased to	5.32	from 6.54
House profit increased to	33.70	from 25.23

Advertising had been increased by 14.42 percent; property taxes increased 10.73 percent; insurance costs increased 31.70 percent, with depreciation costs increasing by 17.54 percent.

Despite these increases, net profits before taxes increased by 11.39 percent, or $1,500,900 as contrasted with $492,900 in 1970.

This was not accomplished without personal cost. It was a difficult time for me; as chairman of the Conference of National Park Concessioners, I had worked closely with Stuart Cross and the people who had represented Yosemite for years before U.S. Natural Resources had become involved, but my job was to increase the profitability of the Yosemite Company. I attempted to divorce my personal feelings and emphasize the improvement of profits. Despite the conflicts, Stuart Cross always conducted himself in a gentlemanly manner.

This overlap of authority with the president, Stuart Cross, and other executives of the Yosemite Park & Curry Company, led to the appointment of an ad hoc committee, chaired by Director Bill Janss, and its recommendation for reorganization of the Yosemite Park & Curry Company. The changes recommended were as follows:

1) Revision of the By-Laws to reduce operations;

2) Assignment of Don Hummel to represent the company on a national level and to have consultant status on operations with residence outside the park;

3) Granting a leave of absence to Stuart Cross at full pay from September 1, 1971, to September 31, 1972, for service outside the park;

4) Election of Alan B. Coleman as chairman of the board, and of Robert A. Maynard as president; and

5) By-Laws which divided the responsibilities of the chairman and the president.

When this was presented to the full board of directors, it was voted down. In a compromise, Alan B. Coleman was elected president. I continued as chairman of the executive committee, but with residence in Palo Alto, California. This added further uncertainty and confusion to Yosemite employees. They knew of the discord on the board of directors following the tender for stock by Fleharty and the entry of U.S. Natural Resources into the company affairs. They had endured the riot which President Cross had fully reported as follows:

By now I am sure you have all read press accounts of the July 4th disorder in Yosemite Valley. In brief resume, this is what happened: Stoneman Meadow, which adjoins Camp 14 and is located near Curry Village, has been increasingly misused by young people who gather there to rap, sing, smoke pot and engage in activities both legal and illegal. These gatherings have become offensive to other users of the park, and have resulted in considerable destruction of the meadow area of the park.

Over Memorial Day weekend, the National Park Service one evening attempted to clear the meadow with a small force of rangers and were forcefully driven out by a jeering mob, egged on by what seemed to be hard-core anti-establishment dissidents.

In preparation for the Independence Day weekend, the Park Service made plans to strictly enforce the regulations that would close the meadow to public use every evening at 7:00 p.m. Signs were posted to this effect. On Thursday and Friday evenings the rangers succeeded in clearing the meadow with only a minimum of difficulty. On Saturday night a far larger number, perhaps as many as 400 or 500, gathered, obviously bent on confrontation. Shortly after 7:00 p.m. the Park Service moved in with 12 or 15 rangers mounted on horseback and were met with stones, empty bottles and other objects.

After some skirmishing, the rangers were driven from the meadow, back beyond the four-way intersection in front of Curry Village. Barricades were established and the Park Service found itself forcibly prevented from access to the upper end of Yosemite Valley. With advice and concurrence from FBI agents, who were present to augment the ranger force, an emergency call was sent to the police departments in nearby communities and more than 100 law enforcement officers responded. Sometime after midnight, they moved back into the meadow and took into custody over 100 persons charged with various offenses. By morning the Park Service was again in control of Yosemite Valley. No further trouble is anticipated at this time, although a force of United States marshalls and Border Patrol officers are presently in Yosemite augmenting the ranger force.

There was negligible damage and the only personal injury was the Sheriff of Mariposa County who made a wrong turn and ended up in the middle of the trouble-makers. The Sheriff was beaten and his car was burned.

The conduct of the Yosemite employees was exemplary and the cooperation with the National Park Service and the detachment of Fresno City Police was outstanding. It was agreed that the group was led by a hard-core group and not by innocent college students or other young people on a weekend spree.

The aftermath of this riot in the valley was to be felt for sometime thereafter. Undesirable elements, ignoring all park regulations and the rights of other visitors, continued to come into the valley. They would sit down in front of the entrance to the store and play their guitars or stretch out and sleep on the boardwalk to the store. They often ate their lunches in this manner, and made it very difficult for park visitors to get into the store. We had 500 arrests in a single week, as the pilferage from the store was tremendous.

This disorderly conduct carried over into the restaurants and cafeterias. Some of this group would come into the cafeteria and not go through the line, or, if they went through the line, they would buy a cup of coffee. They would then start scavenging food from what was left on visitors' plates and in some instances when a visitor would leave his meal to get a second cup of coffee, they would steal the food from his table. This required us to put on security forces. The Park Service objected to me assigning security forces with badges, stating that this gave the wrong impression. I advised them if they would assign their men and enforce the rules, we would withdraw ours, but we had to protect both our own property and the rights of the individuals who were our clients. They finally consented to us leaving our security officers in place in the cafeterias to control this unruly group.

Another area that suffered considerably from the influx of transients was the campgrounds. People could not leave anything unattached or not under lock and key in the car, as it was pilfered. This was partially solved by assigning a particular campground to this group, for which the rental fee per night was reduced to 50 cents; however, the 50 cents per night was seldom collected, as the Park Service feared to go into this group of young people. They were sometimes assaulted when they attempted to collect the fees. This became a no-man's-land and the smoking of pot and the use of narcotics was prevalent during the entire time that his camp was available for their use. Panhandling was rife throughout the park and the visitor found this very objectionable.

The conditions in the valley during the summer of 1970 were described by Mr. Cross in a memorandum stating:

> However much we may decry the distorted and adverse publicity which the Yosemite Valley was receiving, an objective look disclosed that the appearance of the valley during much of the summer, and particularly on the three-day holiday weekends, left a great deal to be desired.

He described it as one of confusion and noise, with Hells Angels cruising back and forth on their motorcycles and riding down the footpaths and bridle paths, waving to hippies in their old bread trucks, while other people were drinking wine on Centennial Bridge, invading the meadows, and panhandling in front of the Village Store. Automobiles dominated the valley with bumper-to-bumper traffic; during the days of maximum travel, as many as 10,000 vehicles were entering the park, carrying an estimated 35 to 40 thousand visitors. On these days the existing ranger force was extended to the absolute limit.

President Cross recommended that a program be instituted to man the entrance stations 24 hours a day throughout the year, or to return to the practice of closing the park entrance stations at 6:00 p.m. as an alternative. He proposed that a curfew be established on the floor of the valley, at least as far as road travel was concerned. He suggested that dogs and cats be banned entirely, as this was the old policy and worked very well for many years. He suggested that motorcycles be banned from Yosemite National Park and that law enforcement staff be expanded. He suggested that a control of automobiles in the valley be achieved and, if necessary, to ban the presence of cars from the valley.

Removal of Cars from Yosemite Valley:

The Master Plan team had proposed removal of all cars from Yosemite Valley. Their proposal called for very high government expenditures and the removal of most administrative functions and employee housing from the valley. As this was considered unlikely, an interim measure was proposed as a solution. This was to provide parking area or areas where the automobile could be left as the visitor entered the valley. The area of Big Meadow was one proposal and another was at Illilouette Ridge. This latter solution would have required a gondola to be constructed from Yosemite Valley to the Ridge. The Big Meadow solution required a mechanical transportation system. This was politically unacceptable and financially impractical. It was then proposed that they stop the automobiles at Bridalveil Falls. This, however, would have required a four-story parking building in the lower end of the valley and was not considered acceptable.

As all these solutions were expensive and appeared to be far in the future, Superintendent Hadley proposed a new system which, when combined with a greatly expanded shuttle bus system, would eliminate most of the movement of private cars and trucks in the eastern half of the valley. As a result, a one-way road system was established and a connecting road between Curry Village and the Ahwahnee was eliminated. This caused great confusion and a very difficult traffic pattern.

The minutes of the meeting of the Master Plan Study Team, of July 9, 1970, reveal that Ronald Mortimore, from Western Service Center, was the team captain. Several retired National Park Service people were on the committee, in addition to Dr. Morgan Harris, a professor of zoology at Berkeley, and Laurence C. Hadley, superintendent at Yosemite. The concessioner representatives were Stuart Cross, president of Yosemite Park & Curry Company; Robert Maynard, vice president; Hilmer Oehlman, honorary chairman; and Ansel Adams, of Best Studios. The National Park Service was further represented by the director, and deputy director of the Western Region, and the wilderness coordinator by the name of John Henneberger. He was also a member of the National Park Service from the Western Service Center.

George Hartzog, director, expressed the hope that the Master Plan team would consider all possible alternatives with respect to recommending public use programs, especially where significant patterns of public use were involved and important resource values were at stake. In this latter context he indicated the necessity for the team to consider the needs of society for outdoor recreations of the kind available in national parks, in view of increasing population and increasing leisure time, coupled with an expanding urban population, and the increase of a youthful society. He said the Yosemite of tomorrow must be responsive to these needs and pleasures.

The team was asked to consider and develop to the fullest extent possible, all possibilities of providing public access to this area that would meet the objectives of providing for year-round public use. These means would be integrated with a public transportation system providing access to and travel within Yosemite Valley.

In earlier remarks the director emphasized the necessity for the National Park Service to consider the provision of High Sierra camps or chalets in the backcountry or wilderness areas in the national parks. This concept was clearly expressed in Secretary Hickel's memorandum of June 18, 1969. In this context the team considered the possibility of development of additional such camps or chalets that would lie within a short walking distance of automobile trail-head points.

When the final report was completed, it was submitted to the public in three separate hearings, with an opportunity for the public to make such suggestions and changes as they believed necessary. It was this master plan that had been in process for five years and had received final approval. Assistant Secretary for Parks, Nathaniel Reed, threw out the plan as permitting too much use. He stated that it sounded as though it had been made by the concessioners.

As a result, a new plan was proposed, It started with a series of workshops at different locations throughout the country. The Sierra Club got on the bandwagon and in their release of March 3, 1975, reported that the Sierra Club's Yosemite Task Force was drawing up suggestions for the new master plan. The club invited those with expertise in the fields of planning, wildlife, biology, plant ecology, geology, sanitation and engineering, to prepare for the public workshops. The Sierra Club said that anyone could help, either with a contribution of time and energy, or expertise or via a donation to help finance the work. Thereafter there followed a "loading" of the workshops by Sierra Club members. They objected to the High Sierra camps being classified as enclaves in the wilderness, but rather wanted them designated as nonconforming wilderness areas, which could be removed. They also objected to Yosemite wilderness area being set back from roads or developed areas by buffer zones. They stated that Badger Pass Ski Area was a non-Park use and should not be expanded; that Glacier Point should be dedeveloped and the road to Glacier Point closed. They recommended the removal of housing facilities and support facilities to areas outside the park, and the gradual elimination of all private automobiles within the park. They especially recommended the feasibility of removing visitor accommodations from the valley, stating that the permanent solution to this problem would be the ultimate removal of facilities from the park. In the interim, it was suggested that profit-oriented businesses be replaced by nonprofit concessioners.

As the fortunes of U.S. Natural Resources declined, George Fleharty became more and more disgruntled. He finally proposed that U.S. Natural Resources sell him the Mount McKinley National Park Company. George had interested the owner of a television company in Sacramento, California, to back him in the purchase of Mt. McKinley. The price agreed upon was one million dollars, plus the assumption of the debt I had incurred of $300,000, to build the 50-unit wing to the McKinley Park Hotel. I do not know the details of the transaction, but assume that Fleharty exchanged some of his U.S. Natural Resources stock which he acquired when he traded his 38 percent of Yosemite stock for U.S. Natural Resources stock. George Fleharty left U.S. Natural Resources when he disposed of his interest in the company. He went to Alaska to run the McKinley Company.

This left only the Yosemite Company and Lassen in the U.S. Natural Resources Recreation Division.

U.S. Natural Resources' fortunes were not going well and Bob Katz was replaced as president of U.S. Natural Resources by John Del Favero. As U.S. Natural Resources did not have the required 80 percent ownership of

Yosemite, they were unable to file consolidated financial reports, so the board of U.S. Natural Resources instructed John Del Favero to either acquire the necessary stock to increase its interest to 80 percent or sell the company.

In 1972, U.S. Natural Resources tendered for additional Yosemite stock and was successful in acquiring 52 percent and, thus, control of the corporation. At a special meeting held at Wawona on June 25, 1972, I was elected chairman of the board and chief executive officer.

As chairman and chief executive officer at Yosemite, I made a number of changes in personnel assignments in an effort to improve our financial operations. Keith Whitfield, who had been bounced around the company, was put in overall charge of all lodging facilities. I felt that he was one of the more capable managers. Keith appeared to be making some progress until one morning I found his resignation on my desk. He was too embarrassed to give it to me personally. He had accepted a job as head of the Hotel Division at Park Central ski operation south of Salt Lake City.

Robert Maynard, the vice president for operations, was the only person I released. I learned that he had sent copies of Yosemite's financial reports to a friend, suggesting that they buy out U.S. Natural Resources' interest, saying "Keep my name out of this." Bob had sent the financial statement in a Yosemite envelope with no identification on the return address as to the department it had come from.

For reasons unknown, it was not delivered and was returned. Roger Sandberg, treasurer, opened the letter and immediately turned it over to me. I confronted Maynard and asked for his resignation. As he had a contract, he refused. I obtained his resignation through his attorney.

In the compromise between U.S. Natural Resources and the Yosemite board, Alan Coleman, a member of U.S. Natural Resources, had been elected president of Yosemite Park & Curry Company. Alan then moved to Yosemite. U.S. Natural Resources felt that Alan had abandoned any loyalty to U.S. Natural Resources and evidenced some hostility toward U.S. Natural Resources representatives.

In September 1972, when Stuart Cross moved out of the park, as he agreed to do when Coleman was elected president, Coleman started to move into the president's quarters. I was asked by John Del Favero to advise Coleman not to move as he was to be replaced at the annual meeting. Coleman did not take this very graciously. At the annual meeting on January 15, 1973, I was elected president and was told to return to the valley from Palo Alto where I had been banished as a result of the compromises proposed by the ad hoc committee.

Shortly thereafter, I was visited by Sidney Sheinberg, president of MCA, and Jay Stein, head of their recreation division. They advised that they were negotiating the purchase of the Yosemite Company. They stated that they had talked with the National Park Service, who advised them that the company was well-run and at the peak of its profits. We had increased profits from $232,000, to $1,500,000, after taxes.

They wanted to know what I thought about the company.

I replied that the company was at the bottom of its profit potential. I explained that 60 percent of the facilities were substandard and needed upgrading. I said we were encountering reluctance on the part of our employees and director in operating Wawona more than two and one-half months each year; that if improved and promoted it could be made a separate recreation area. I pointed out that by upgrading facilities at Curry Village by substituting modern cottages for the 406 dilapidated tents, you could quadruple the profits from this area alone. In fact, I had construction plans prepared and Park Service approval to replace 150 of these tents as the first complement.

I urged them to promote year-round occupancy; that we had started this, but with little funds and no real promotion, and had vastly reduced the deficits with which we began prior summers as a result of winter losses. As a start on this program, I had installed a chairlift at our winter operation at Badger Flats in substitution for a T-bar tow. This had materially improved our winter patronage and was the first step in upgrading the three tows that constituted our winter sports program.

M.C.A. consummated their purchase from U.S. Natural Resources and tendered for the balance of the stock.

I contracted to run the company for a year until they could hire an executive and build their organization. This started immediately, and a stream of specialists from M.C.A. began visiting the park.

Jay Stein assured me that these specialists had no operating authority, and if any of them intruded, I was to send them back to Los Angeles. As a result, I sent Roberta Ross home, as she was interfering with Louis Melicek, who was in charge of the Merchandise Division, including all gift shops. Shortly thereafter Jay called and asked if Roberta could return. I said yes, if she would stay out of the operations. I later learned that Roberta had been M.C.A. Chairman of the Board Lew Wasserman's private secretary and had direct access to him.

This had aroused some fear in M.C.A. personnel responsible for the Yosemite operation. Jay was true to his word and backed up my decisions.

The purchase of Yosemite Park & Curry Company by M.C.A. created a real furor among the environmental organizations. It came to a head, when in the process of filming a segment of "Sierra," the photographers painted a nine foot square space on a rock wall with washable clay paint. The location of the filming had been changed for reasons of safety and the light at the new location was inadequate. This film segment was to document a rescue operation by the park rangers.

The National Park Service not only encouraged this filming but assigned rangers for technical assistance. They envisioned a competitive series to rival the Forest Service's "Lassie."

The recent disapproval of the master plan was seized upon to claim that M.C.A. dominated the Park Service to further commercialize the park. As a matter of fact, the master plan that was disavowed was developed long before M.C.A.'s involvement.

An article in the *Los Angeles Times*, May 4, 1975, under the banner "The Battle Over Yosemite," outlined the conservation organizations' participation in influencing the Park Service's decision to discard its master plan and hold hearings for a new plan.

The conservation organizations' position was enunciated by Connie Parrish, the California representative of Friends of the Earth.

> The over-riding issue in the battle over Yosemite is the rights of an increasingly conservation-minded public vs. the projected profits of a privately owned conglomerate.
>
> Act one of the Agenda ended December 13th, when the Interior Department, pushed by major conservation groups, rejected the National Park Service's tentative master plan for Yosemite. The plan had gone back to the drawing board and the public's voice at last is being heard..."
>
> Thanks largely to the protests of Friends of the Earth, the Sierra Club and other conservation groups, the Interior Department rejected the draft master plan on the grounds that there had been no public participation.

As a matter of fact, there had been three widely advertised public hearings on the master plan, but the final results did not please the environmental organizations.

The article continues:

> A congressional investigation also grew out of our protests. Hearings were held in December by U.S. Representative John Dingell (D-Michigan), chairman of House Subcommittee on Energy and the Environment, in conjunction with the Subcommittee on Conservation and Energy. Dingell heard testimony that the Park Service let M.C.A. push it into recommendations which were overly commercial...
>
> What M.C.A. wanted to do, in our opinion, was to turn Yosemite into a year-round luxury resort. The company proposed to tear down 150 of the primitive tent cabins in Curry Village at park headquarters and replace them with modern lodge facilities with indoor plumbing — at higher rent.

The facts are that I made these proposals as president of the Yosemite Park & Curry Company and had Park Service approval before M.C.A. purchased the company. Upgrading of facilities was encouraged by the Park Service as consistent with visitor demands: the replacement of modern cottages for dilapidated tents which often went begging and were rented only as a last resort when all else was occupied.

There followed a whole series of articles concerning the use of Yosemite National Park. Rudy Aversa, a *Herald Examiner* staff writer, reported:

> The major conservation organizations seems to be putting up a united front against the Yosemite Park & Curry Company, a subsidiary of M.C.A., the prime concessioner and unnamed candidate to implement future development of Yosemite. There is a faction of conservationists and environmentalists such as the Sierra Club, Friends of the Earth, Wilderness Society and other "Save the Yosemite" groups who not only want no more development in the park, but want all development removed.

The *Christian Science Monitor* on August 13, 1975 summed up the controversy by asking:

> What is the public's will?
>
> The basic question lingers; just what is the public's will? What does the park visitor want — better and more modern facilities, easier access to hiking, camping and scenic wonders? Or is he or she more concerned with preserving the natural state of things, with restoring forests, protecting wildlife and maintaining a rugged outdoor ethic?
>
> The conflict between these divergent outlooks is what the Yosemite controversy is all about. It surfaces in terms of proposals to limit visitor use, ban concessioner facilities from the interior of the park and replace auto traffic with bus transit. The Park Service...says the issue gets down to preservation vs. use. They admittedly lean toward the former goal.

Jay S. Stein, president of Yosemite Park & Curry Company, and vice president of M.C.A., in a statement before the Subcommittee on National Parks of the Interior and Insular Affairs Committee, stated in unequivocal terms the philosophy of the concessioner with these quotes:

> We recognize that it is our duty not only to meet our contractual obligations to provide public service, but also to do so in a manner that preserves the priceless beauty that is Yosemite.

The National Park Service has long championed the necessity for master planning — the N.P.S. has historically followed the policy of involving the public and the concessioner in the planning process...

The public, the National Park Service and the concessioner all have a vital role to play as members of the planning team. By practical necessity the concessioner has traditionally played his role at an earlier stage in cooperation with the National Park Service. Subsequently the public reviews the draft. Our company was criticized for its involvement...centered on the contention that the concessioner should not be involved to any greater extent than the general public.... We submit this is an unjustified indictment of the process.

It seems reasonable to involve the concessioner in the early process of planning since he has a contractual relationship with the National Park Service, has developed expertise as a result of his experience in operating park concessions, and will be called upon to make some major capital investments.

We believe that the historical process above is an intelligent process. We submit concessioner involvement in the planning process with the National Park Service is neither an abrogation of National Park Service responsibility to Congress and the public, nor an anathema to the public interest.

In the search for a top executive, I was visited by a number of applicants sent to me by Jay Stein. I turned them down until they sent Edward Hardy, former manager of the Riviera Country Club. He was hired as chief operating officer and is now president of the company. After eight months, I said I was sure that Ed could run the company and asked to be released from my contract to enable me to return to the Glacier operation.Al Donau had run Glacier from the time I left in May 1966, to report as Assistant Secretary of H.U.D. It was May 1974, when I returned to Glacier.

24

A Christian Ministry in the National Parks

ALMOST EVERY National Park has a history of religious services. In the beginning local committees invited circuit riding ministers from surrounding towns to hold services. In 1949 a student ministry was developed by the Yellowstone superintendent's Church Committee under the leadership of David Condon, who sought the advice of Warren W. Ost, a United Presbyterian studying at Princeton Seminary and working summers as a bellhop at Old Faithful Inn.

At Warren's suggestion Mr. Condon requested student ministers from three seminaries. Princeton agreed. In 1950 Warren Ost and Donald Bower arrived in Yellowstone to initiate A Christian Ministry in the National Parks, administered jointly by the National Council of Churches and Princeton Seminary. Warren Ost was appointed Director.

Committees were formed in each park, composed of laymen, employees, staff and clergymen. In 1959 the National Committee was reorganized to include representatives from local committees and concessioners. Concessioners gave student ministers secular jobs as bellhops, waiters, maids, etc.

A Christian Ministry in the National Parks helped guide the rapid expansion of recreation-related ministries in the 1960s, participating in recreation and conservation movements. It was formally separated from research and consultation activities and worked under the Division of Chrisitan Life and Missions. The Ministry provided a framework for permanent ecumenical relationships in the parks. The local committees included many denominations including Catholics, Southern Baptists and others that were not members of the Council of Churches.

In 1969 Warren Ost invited me to chair the National Committee. I was hesitant. Although I was a member of the Presbyterian Church, I was not an orthodox practicing churchgoer. But in view of the strong ecumenical direction of the churches, I accepted. I served from 1969 through

1972. In 1971 during my term as Chairman the National Committee separated the Ministry from the National Council of Churches. The Council recognized the Ministry as a valid interdenominational movement and offered to serve as a conduit for funds. I wrote all the concessioners urging further financial support for the Ministry. This change put further financial burdens on the Ministry but fortunately it had attracted support from prominent citizens, among them the Rockefeller interests and Mrs. Walter B. Driscoll of Church Women United. Mrs. Driscoll subsequently became Chairman of the Ministry, followed by Holly Coors of the Coors brewing families, and then by James G. Watt, former Secretary of the Interior.

In 1972 the Board of Trustees of the non-profit corporation, the Trust for A Christian Ministry in the National Parks, was created to conduct the affairs of the Trust and serve and Budget and Finance Committee of the National Board. I was one of the original trustees. From the beginning the ministry was dependent on the generosity of those who worship in the parks -- one third each from local committees, cooperating denominations and foundations / corporations, including concessioners and individuals.

At the end of my three year term, Warren wanted me to stay on as trustee. I have made it a practice to never stay on a board after heading an organization. I believe it unfair to the incoming officer, but once again Warren prevailed.

At a national board meeting in Rocky Mountain National Park the Board voted to raise $5 million for the trust. A professional was hired to solicit funds to support student ministries. I opposed the program as a major digression from the Ministry's purpose and could even destroy it. The solicitation fell short and was scaled down.

I do not know if I made any contribution to the spiritual advancement of the program. I would like to believe that I contributed to its secular and financial stability. Warren Ost who still heads the Ministry has been the real driving power and spiritual head.. He has also provided the main financial solicitation and overall direction for the program. It could not have succeeded without his full dedication. His has been a real contribution to a better national park program. I'm pleased to have been asked to participate.

25

Centennial Commission for the National Parks

As THE national parks approached the centennial of their creation, President Nixon signed a law creating the National Park Centennial Commission. This was mandated by Public Law 91-332 on July 10, 1970. The Commission, or more accurately Director Hartzog, designated the National Parks and Conservation Foundation, an environmental organization, to organize, staff and direct a citizen's appraisal of the National Park System. The selection of this environmental organization automatically set the emphasis and the direction that the report on "National Parks for the Future" would take. It would be preservation as the dominant theme and limitation of visitor facilities as a means to reduce visitor use.

A 35-member advisory committee was appointed by the President and U.S. Senate. Thirty other individuals were selected by the Conservation Foundation to make up the five task forces which would set the tone for future park policies. All five task forces commented on the concession system adversely, and three of them recommended removal of concessions and/or government acquisition of concession facilities. It is interesting to note that environmentalists dominated the membership in the task forces, and no concessioner was named to any task force. As head of the Conference of National Park Concessioners, I was named on the advisory committee, but was never contacted nor notified of the opportunity to participate.

In fact, when I discovered I was a member, I asked that my name be deleted. Since I had been given no opportunity to voice my opinions, I did not want my name associated with the recommendations proposed in "National Parks for the Future." They never removed my name. I also requested that I be given an opportunity to speak at the plenary session of the symposium to be held in Yosemite

National Park Symposium as I felt it was necessary to have the concessioners' views expressed. I was promised 30 minutes. The symposium was the vehicle selected to receive the reports of the five task forces and other invited participants including, for the first time, a number of concessioners who in every instance constituted a minority on each panel. The stage was set by the book entitled "National Parks for the Future" by the Conservation Foundation.

The recommendations in "National Parks for the Future," which the Conservation Foundation admitted were their own, contained these admissions and proposals:

> The commentary and conclusions, while formed by the findings of all who contributed to the work, are the Foundation's own. They do not necessarily reflect the positions held by participants, or consultants—some of whose contributions are set forth separately in the remaining sections of the volume.

The recommendation bearing on the relationship of the concession system to the national parks stated:

> If the parks are to be meaningful to all Americans, everyone must feel welcome. For many visitors this requires a somewhat civilized base of operations; a dry room, a bed with sheets, a recognizable kitchen or public eating place. At the same time, resort accommodations and shopping centers do not belong in national parks. Nor do camping and picnic areas which are designed and congested to bring urban scenes with urban problems.

Relative to concessions, the report stated that:

> There was a time when concessions were clearly needed to provide basic services for accommodations, food and the like. Today, however, the concessioner has a disproportionate influence on planning and policy-making for the national parks. His objective is to generate as much demand for the services he provides as is possible. We recommend that a long-term program of concessioner replacement be started on a pilot basis and proceed according to an equitable timetable until the parks are free of major private entrepreneurs and the

public has regained full control of facilities planning and operations.

The task forces largely picked up the theme from the Foundation of removal of concessioner-provided facilities in the national parks. The task forces reported to the Symposium through panels. The panel on "The Role of National Park Concessioners" reported that on the issue of relocating or moving facilities outside the parks, one task force categorically recommended moving all facilities outside; another advocated the removal when practical; and the third, no facilities to be left in the parks other than those essential. The report contained this caveat:

> In determining the practicality of removal of visitor facilities from the parks, consideration should be given to: (1) geographic and aesthetic implications of alternate locations; (2) practicality of transporting huge numbers during primary entrance and exodus periods; (3) impact on visitor experience; (4) effect of scheduled transportation approach on individual's park experience; (5) insure against proliferation of undesirable development on the periphery; (6) inequalities of exclusion which might result; and (7) review of economic imperatives of concessioners and permitting of democratization of services and facilities.

These recommendations were the majority, but were not unanimous, as reported by Jack Strain, Director of the Nebraska Bureau of State Parks, and the chairman of a panel on "Facilities in the National Parks." He reported:

> With great respect and admiration for the purist and the highly skilled, whatever his special interest, but with a greater concern for the average American, we concluded that visitor accommodations are a legitimate part of the national park scene and make an essential contribution to the quality of the visit of most Americans.
> We oppose the banishment of visitor accommodations outside park boundaries on these grounds: (a) there is no effective means of quality control; and (b) without control, high quality environment outside the park equal to much of that within the area may suffer disproportionately.

He went on to say that the concessioner, to survive, must furnish desirable goods and services to make a profit. To resolve this and insure control, the panel endorsed public ownership with private operation with a subsidy, if necessary.

The task force panel on the "National Park System and Urban America" had these comments:

> Shall the National Park Service permit itself to become a "wilderness land bank" increasing concern with preservation and conservation and oriented only to the accommodation of people to the extent that they don't threaten the land? Or shall the Park Service look first to the needs of Americans and then place parks and recreation services to meet those needs, viewing the land as a resource?

> The wilderness in current National Park Service terms is neither available nor accessible to most of the urban population. Transportation is inadequate, education inappropriate and interpretation falls far short of providing the basis for identification among minorities of color and women. In addition, we are aware of a certain insular tendency on the part of the National Park Service to deal more closely and comfortably with those elements of society who are most sympathetic to the natural preservationist preference and supportive of its basic management approach. These individuals, as Roger Revelle has observed, are "more concerned with the enhancement of the resources than with the needs of the people." We think the full range of consumer preference needs representation on the National Advisory Board.

Other panels made recommendations:

Panel on "Park Service Responsibility to Meet Outdoor Needs":

Where Does It End?

> The group appeared to generally agree that the National Park Service should occupy a role of national leadership in assuring that all national park and recreation needs are met.

Part of the group...expressed the view that the National Park Service should be prepared to meet needs when other levels of government or private industry cannot or will not.

There was substantial support, perhaps nearly unanimous, for the notion of developing a system of large urban oriented parks at the edge of metropolitan areas.

Panel on "Planning Framework and Procedures for Units of the National Park System":

As to external affairs, we should like to see the Park Service take a much stronger position in the critique of development in the regions on the periphery of the park.

As to internal park planning procedures, we feel the master plans are highly conceptual and that it is difficult to perform environmental impact review...

Regarding public involvement:

...We will need more user surveys, but we would hasten to add that it is one thing to get a survey by a sociologist who tells you what he thinks people think should be done vs. the kind of thing when people are actually brought into the planning and design process and work it out for themselves.

After all the discussions concerning the problems of concession operations and the recommendations for removal from the parks, the Chairman called on me to make my presentation, except that the time had already elapsed and the meeting was scheduled to recess to take the participants on a sightseeing tour of Yosemite. Not exactly a propitious time to present the concessioners' views!

The time had expired and the crowd was restless, so I stood up in the audience and did not go to the speaker's podium. I asked everybody to remain seated, as I would take only two minutes of their time. I announced that I had filed a prepared statement for those who might be interested in a concessioner's point of view who had not had an opportunity for expression to this symposium. I said:

I have listened with interest to the recommendations to remove all visitor accommodations from the park so as to restore the pristine nature of the natural features without discussion of this effect on the park visitor.

I stated that I noted concessioners had not been included on any task force, although they were probably in the best position to report how the park visitor felt about having accommodations for his convenience and use removed from the parks.

I said:

I am curious and would like a show of hands of the participants who slept out in the open last night, rather than in the concessioner's facilities?

(The weather had been miserable, with one downpour after another.)

There was a gasp, loud laughter and clapping of hands. I was standing next to Director Hartzog, who turned around in his seat and said to a man in back of him: If you're going to clap that loud, warn me — I thought I had been shot!

Not one of those armchair environmentalists had raised his hand!

The concessioners' attitude toward the removal of visitor facilities from the parks was not included in any task force report. It was also denied when I was not called on for delivery until it was time for recess.

In order to get the concessioners' views in the record, I filed my statement. It was never included in the report. I believe it is important to emphasize that this report was not intended to protect the concessioner although it would have that result. The essence is the protection of the people's right to use and enjoy their national parks. This is the part of the charge to the National Park Service that has been completely ignored in "National Parks for the Future." Excerpts from my statement intended to correct this omission are:

It is my understanding that the charge to this symposium is to develop a statement of philosophy, long-range objectives and goals, and means of implementation for the national park system to enable it to better serve the needs of all American people. I stress the word all because the parks are for people — all of the people. They are not just for the ardent preservationists who would remove them from most of the people by expanded wilderness designations and by restricted access; not for just those who would use them as laboratories for scientific interpretations; not just for those who have the physical stamina to backpack, ride a horse, to hike; but also for those who, by reason of age, physical handicap, or temperament, can enjoy the grandeur from the seat of a sightseeing bus or from a chair on a lodge veranda. Nor have these areas been set aside for just the affluent but also for the poor and the minorities among us, for otherwise the system would not be truly national. Each segment of our population has a right to have its needs recognized, for we are dealing here in large measure with the natural, historical and cultural heritage of our nation.

We are under directive to preserve these resources for the use and enjoyment of all generations, and that means present as well as future. The dichotomy of preservation and use has been debated and fought over since the passage of the basic act. This debate will continue long after our recommendations and departure, for it is in the day-to-day balance between these potentially antagonistic concepts that solutions lie.

The solutions cannot be neatly packaged in a pristine formula for all time, as they must be flexible enough to respond to changing demands. The preservation and use of the days of Cornelius Hedges or John Muir are not the same as today, nor will today's solutions be the same in the next century.

Instead of deploring the conflict between preservation and use, we should welcome them as counterbalancing forces. As we look at today's problems we are faced with rising populations of urban-oriented, wilderness-inexperienced people with more leisure time and easier access to areas and remoteness of location. We are not acting responsibly if we project solutions that may or may not be required in the year 2000 if they adversely affect the enjoyment by today's generation and do not cause irreparable harm to the resource.

Many of the solutions proposed suggested that we serve fewer, not more, people.

I submit that those who propose quotas, limitation of access and wholesale removal of facilities to serve people present an easy solution that might prevail in an autocratic system, but is unacceptable in a democracy unless there is no other way to conserve the resource. The nation's heritage should be available to all on as diverse and as wide a basis as possible consistent with preservation.

I have read with interest the recommendations of some of the task forces who would dismantle the concession system. If there was any consideration of the reasons for the establishment and growth of the concession system, and how it serves the needs of most of the park visitors, it is not apparent in the reports.

The only reason for a concession system is to serve the needs of people. People have to have food and drink and some place to get shelter for the night. Removing these services from the park creates more problems than it solves and materially reduces the quality of the experience for a very large proportion of the visitors who now visit our parks. Last year services provided by concessioners were available to serve 117 million visitors.

The concession system has been peremptorily dismissed with a proposal that the services be moved to some peripheral area outside the park. There appears to have been no consideration of the time that would be traveled each day to and from the park's principal features; that moving facilities out of the park would require an enormously expensive and expanded public transportation system which would result in most of the park's visitors arriving and departing the park at about the same time. This would constitute a serious deterioration of the visitors' experience, as people are required to see the park on a group schedule rather than on their own time. Apparently no consideration has been given to how the people are to be fed while in the park. Are they all to carry brown bags?

Areas like Yellowstone, Yosemite, McKinley, Grand Canyon and others cover vast land masses, with park features located at great distances from each other and from park boundaries. Great expanses of land inside the park boundaries are no different in character than large areas outside. The location of the park boundary line in many instances was established by historical accident or some log-rolling legislative compromise. The boundaries include many acres of land which, of themselves, do not call for the same degree of preservation as the features for which the park was created. The development of concession facilities on these lands to help visitors enjoy their parks does not and should not impinge on the scenic values sought to be preserved.

The approach of some task forces appears to be concerned with the value of the land and the physical resources, and not with the needs and enjoyment of people. Even in the founding days of the park system, when men were more rugged and used to a minimum of physical comforts, Steve Mather had this comment:

> Scenery is a hollow enjoyment to a tourist who sets out in the morning after an indigestible breakfast and a fitful sleep on an impossible bed.

Or John Muir, in his letter to President Roosevelt, when he wrote:

> I am anxious that the Yosemite National Park may be saved from all sorts of commercialism and marks of man's use other than the roads and hotels, etc., required to make its wonders and blessings available.

Today, as we search for ways to allow more and more of our citizens who are more and more used to creature comforts to enjoy their parks, it is proposed to deny them the right to spend a night in their national parks unless they camp. This is rank discrimination against those urban-reared citizens who have had no opportunity or disposition to want to camp and constitute the preponderant majority of the park visitor.

Why is it meritorious to sleep under a tent but not under a lodge or cabin roof? Justification is attempted on the basis of damage to the resource. I believe a good case can be made for less damage in the controlled atmosphere of a stable concession-operated facility than the helter-skelter, repetitious erecting and dismantling of a tent at the camper's discretion.

Do not be misled, nature is not as fragile as some would have you believe. Yosemite has been singled out in horror as the epitome of an over-crowded, smog-ridden, desecrated area. While you are here, look at it. It has absorbed the living and the trampling of millions of men's feet for a century. It is still blessed with green meadows, beautiful forests, clear and sparkling streams, waterfalls and incomparable granite cliffs. One old-timer (the late Ansel Adams) says it is more beautiful today than it was a half century ago.

Less than a year ago the National Park Service was considering the limiting of the number of people, but they found that the mere expedient of removing some of the automobiles and substituting a shuttle system made a wonderful improvement. Who put up the money to start the experiment? The concessioner. That experiment has just begun but it opened opportunities to serve many more people in a more pleasant environment. There weren't too many people, just too many cars. Think what could be accomplished if we had an adequate public transportation system to the park, not just in the park, so that the problems associated with the automobile remained at home and did not have to be faced in the park.

Think what might be done just in the dispersal of people if, instead of only three entrances to Yosemite, we had six; that if those who really wanted the so-called raw wilderness experience didn't enter through the valley but came in through the forest wilderness surrounding the park. There are 708,000 acres surrounding the park dedicated to that kind of use. There are many solutions before we resort to limitations and exclusion. Think what might be done if we emphasized use throughout the year.

When developments to serve the guests are dispersed and properly located, you minimize the impact on the park, and by dispersal of the visitor concentration improve the quality of his experience. Isn't the selection of locations and dispersal the answer before we resort to exclusion?

The advantages of serving people where they want to be decreases the need for the expansion of transportation systems which in themselves impinge on park values. Can you imagine the congestion and Pandemonium of 30 to 40 thousand people all starting out at Mariposa in

buses to get into Yosemite Valley between seven and nine
in the morning, and all leaving the park at the close of the
day? Have you ever witnessed a Disneyland exodus? Is
that the atmosphere you want to create for the national
park visitor?

The concession system provides an opportunity to
plan the development and provide the services that are
consistent with park values. Buildings are located by the
National Park Service, who also control the architectural
design. The Park Service decides what services are rendered, where, and at what price. By scrapping the concession system you relegate the question of availability,
type and cost of services to the freewheeling, indiscriminate rules that now prevail adjacent to the parks. This
can result in substandard services and price gouging
when demands are high, and no service at the beginning
or end of a season when visitation is low. The present
satellite communities provide an entry to the parks that
remind me of the entry to cities through the railroad
yards of yesteryear.
How many West Yellowstones or Gatlinburgs do
you want? They do not promote a beautiful America,
and we should be thinking of all America, not just the
limited part we call parks and monuments.

Anyone familiar with the early history of the concession development is aware of the unsatisfactory nature of
the freewheeling competitive system that prevailed in the
park; the harassment of tourists; the gouging prices; the
lack of quality of the service; and the complete absence of
some desirable but uneconomic services. This chaotic
condition was replaced by a single controlled concessioner who was required to provide a balanced service at
reasonable rates. Are we willing to go back to the unsatisfactory system provided it occurs at the park entrance
rather than in the park?

Who shall provide these services rather than whether
they should be provided has been the subject of inquiry
by departmental, congressional, general accounting and
citizen committees. The questions have centered on
whether the government should own and operate the
facilities or whether the private sector should make the
investment and operate the facilities, or some combination thereof.

After two years of congressional hearings the Congress enacted Public Law 89-249, adopting private ownership and operation as being the most satisfactory and desirable way to provide those services that are necessary and appropriate for public use and enjoyment of the park consistent with preservation and conservation of the areas. In so doing, they supported the recommendations of the Outdoor Recreation Resources Review Commission.

The reasons are many. First, the private sector is more attuned to providing hotel, restaurant and other services required by the visitors. They are more responsive to people's needs. They can provide services more efficiently and cheaply. Government operations which rely on the appropriation system administered through civil service channels are not dependent on a satisfied customer, and they often reflect it. Have you ever been served in government commissaries or a PX system? Do you know of the government record of operating campgrounds? In one park last year they only collected forty percent of the fees. Do you know that the Golden Eagle Pass has not yet been extended by Congress, forcing park visitors to pay on a daily basis? What would happen, if you didn't get the appropriations in time to open the restaurants?

Suffice it to say that Congress thoroughly examined the alternatives and chose this course with Park Service and departmental approval. This does not foreclose other solutions. As a matter of fact, economic necessities require various combinations of ownership versus operations and other subsidy measures. Public ownership with private operations can be an acceptable alternative. The present concession system in 1970 produced only a 3.53 percent return on gross receipts—hardly what you would call a bonanza.

My real concern with the recommendations is the preeminence given the protection of physical values as opposed to people enjoyment. In this park it is proposed to set aside as wilderness 80 percent of the land for less than one percent of the visitors. This is bad enough, but now I hear proposals that the other 99 percent are to be excluded from the use of their park except on a day-use basis.

The recommendations made by some task forces go to who can enjoy their national parks and on what conditions. If one is elderly or incapacitated, or unwilling to rough it, they are to be excluded except on a day-use basis. I submit that this is not consistent with improving the quality of the experience. The denial of an opportunity to spend a night within the sound of tumbling waters from Yosemite Falls or the opportunity to view the moon coming over Half Dome cannot be substituted with a night at El Portal or Mariposa.

The role of the concessioner, whoever he may be or whoever owns the facilities, is to make the parks available to the ordinary American on terms that permit him the maximum of enjoyment and leave the park intact for future generations. To dismantle it is to deny the vast majority of Americans the right to use and enjoy their national parks.

Preserving A Heritage

The final report by the National Park Centennial Commission appointed by the President and Congress is entitled "Preserving A Heritage." It reaffirmed the duality of purpose in the following words:

> In keeping with the 1916 Organic Act and the tradition of the Service, the Commission strongly recommends that the dual purpose of preservation and use be maintained as the dynamic principles undergirding the National Park System.
>
> It is clear that Congress intended the national parks to be used by people to the fullest extent possible without impairing those features for which the parks were established to protect.

The Commission accepted but did not approve the report, "National Parks for the Future," but did reflect many of the recommendations in the Foundation report; namely, that the National Park Service commence a long-term program to buy up existing concessioner-owned facilities and ask Congress for a review of Public Law 89-249 and make appropriate amendments; they questioned the granting of possessory interest, and suggested the amortization of all equity in concessioner structures. They proposed that a task force be created by the Secretary of the Interior to make an analysis of existing private and quasi-public concession operations and the feasibility of direct operations by the National Park Service.

The Commission recommended that when a needed service is being well performed by a private concession, it be continued and upgraded; that when the facilities and services had outlived their usefulness, they be eliminated. They also recommended greater citizen participation and the creation of a Citizens Advisory Commission.

Under the title, "Protecting the Land," they recommended establishment of carrying capacity for fragile areas, stating that permanent loss cannot be permitted; however, they said there are many areas that can stand heavy use and will regenerate and thus be restored. The environmentalists have never acknowledged this fact but have included all areas within the boundaries of the national parks as sacrosanct for preservation.

The Commission recommended that the Park Service appraise all existing facilities and move outside the park boundaries all administration, maintenance, concession and housing facilities not related to direct protection of the resources and the visitors' enjoyment of the park.

The report called attention to the fact that the establishment of wilderness designation in the parks provides for a higher level of preservation than the 1916 Act establishing the National Park Service.

Under the title "Accessibility and Use" the Commission commented:

> Members of the Commission realize that many of their fellow conservationists feel that no development would be best. This is not realistic. The public will demand access to these areas and access requires certain improvements or development, if for no other reason than public safety. In addition, certain types of creature comfort are demanded and must be built. Excluding the public because they might cause damage is unacceptable.

Park Service Selective Implementation of the Commission's Recommendations:

It soon became evident that the Park Service was adopting, without public hearings and without approval of the

Interior and Insular Affairs Committee, selected recommendations which advanced their predisposition to emphasize preservation and ignore the obligation to make the parks available for use, leading to the elimination and reduction of visitor facilities in the national parks.

Protests by concessioners through their representatives in the Conference of National Park Concessioners were routinely denied. The Conference pointed out that these policies were in contravention to congressional policy established in Public Law 89-249. Here is the record:

1. Wilderness designations removed vast areas in the parks from the erection of any facilities.

2. Master plans called for restriction and removal of visitor facilities in areas declared to be for visitor use and further reduced the opportunity for visitors who required accommodations.

3. Contract terms were altered, which reduced the concessioner's ability to secure financing and, thus, the ability to perform.

4. Approval for visitor expansion was arbitrarily denied as contrary to master plan provisions.

5. National Park Service policy was adopted to discourage or prevent the erection of visitor facilities, contrary to the provisions of Public Law 89-249, which was passed to encourage and enable concessioners to provide visitor facilities in the parks.

The policy of reduction for visitor facilities was being promulgated through pressure on the National Park Service by environmental organizations such as the Sierra Club, Friends of the Earth and National Parks and Conservation Association. Scare tactics were used, claiming the destruction of the parks' natural resources. Concessioners were vilified in the press, claiming over-commercialization in the National Parks. The fact was that the visitor facilities had not kept up with the demand of the park visitors. Even attempts to upgrade existing facilities were halted, alleging over-commercialization.

Another device was the deliberate misinterpretation of visitation figures to the parks, which were quoted as 240 million during the season. This was to show overuse and threatened destruction of the parks. In fact, three-quarters of the visits cited were automobile traffic on national parkways, recreation use of reclamation areas, visits to historic battlefields, the White House, Washington Monument, etc. Less than 25 percent of visits were to the natural feature national parks that were said to be threatened by overuse.

Compare the Park Service's actual figure for 1985 which lists 38,345,450 visits through August 1985 and estimates 268,298,354 for the 1985 calendar year; however, only 9,255,704 of these are visits to the national parks. A far cry from the threatening 240 million visits claimed in the 1970s to show destruction of the national parks.

Joe Skubitz, a congressman from Kansas, and seven-term member of the House of Representatives, made a statement on the floor of the House on January 21, 1976. He said:

> During my seven terms in this house, I have been a member of the Interior Committee and I have spent considerable time on the problems of the national park system. Over the years, I have watched a growing national debate, arising like hot lava in the plumbing of a volcano. It is a debate between conservationists, who would restrict and limit the use of the national parks, and those like myself who believe that the parks are for people; that their use and enjoyment should be encouraged.
>
> Some extremists would only be happy when all man-made structures are completely eliminated from the national parks, right down to the roads and overlooks everyone uses to view the scenery. This course, if implemented, would eliminate all visitation except for a few young healthy backpackers.

He totally rejected this extremist approach. Scoop Jackson from Washington State also rejected this approach.

The Park Service Manual, released by Director Gary Everhardt in 1975, specified in writing the policy which had not been published but had been followed since 1970, namely:

> If adequate facilities exist or can be developed by private enterprise to serve the park visitors' needs for commercial services outside of park boundaries, such facilities shall not be provided within park areas.

It should be noted that this policy ignores the Centennial Commission admonition to protect "the visitors' enjoyment of the parks." The policy calls Senator Jackson's objections contrary to congressional intent. His plea for the right of the visitor to the superior experience of spending a night in the national parks is denied.

As most park visitors have expressed a desire to have accommodation facilities in the parks, and as the Park Service master plans were trending toward the removal of visitor facilities, the Conference of National Park Concessioners authorized the Stanford Research Institute, Menlo Park, California, in 1975, to conduct visitor use surveys in National Parks. The survey, conducted in 21 areas, was to ascertain present visitor attitudes as to desirability of maintaining overnight and service concession facilities in the parks. These questions were proposed to park visitors to determine the visitors' desires relative to overnight facilities.

	Oppose	Favor
1. Do you favor or oppose removal of <u>all</u> overnight hotel and lodge type facilities?	92.2%	5.6%
2. Do you favor or oppose removal of <u>some</u> hotel and lodge type facilities?	74.7%	20.6%
3. Do you favor or oppose removal of <u>all</u> established campgrounds?	83.5%	7.0%
4. Do you favor or oppose removal of <u>some</u> established campgrounds?	61.8%	26.1%

Despite the reaffirmation of the public's desire to have accommodation facilities in the parks and the passage of Public Law 89-249 to make it feasible for the private sector to provide these facilities, a methodical and persistent attack has been conducted by the National Park Service to discourage and reduce the concessioners' ability to perform. This can be demonstrated by examining the record and by the reduction or the elimination of the guarantees provided in Public Law 89-249 to encourage concession investments to make visitor facilities available.

26

Attempted Closure of Zion, Bryce Canyon and the North rim of the Grand Canyon

THE UTAH PARKS COMPANY, a subsidiary of the Union Pacific Railroad, had built the concession facilities in Zion, Bryce Canyon and the North Rim of Grand Canyon national parks. With the advent of better roads and shift to automobile travel, the financial health of these operations was declining. The Union Pacific Railroad expressed a desire to get out of the concession business.

My brother Gail contacted Union Pacific and made a proposal backed by the non-profit Up-With-People organization, which, if accepted, would thereby secure a tax advantage for the railroad while at the same time allowing them to get out of the concessions operations.

The President of Union Pacific accepted the proposal and told Gail to take possession. Gail prepared menus for submission to the Park Service with proposed rates. He worked with the Union Pacific Transportation Department on plans for renovation of the lodge and cabin facilities in preparation for opening the season. He made an appointment with Park Service Director Hartzog to discuss the changeover, which the Director failed to keep.

As the work progressed, Gail protested that he had nothing in writing but was assured by Union Pacific that he had no reason to worry, as the operations were his. He contacted the Chairman of the Board in New York to secure approval of the transfer.

President Evans telephoned Director Hartzog to secure approval of the transfer of their contract to Up-With-People. Hartzog, instead of accepting the proposal, prevailed upon President Evans to give the three operations to a quasi-governmental non-profit organization, the National Park Foundation, and leave Gail and Up-With-People out of the deal. The tax plan that Gail had devised was usurped by the Park Foundation through Director Hartzog for its benefit. The Park Service, through its foundation, took over the three operations.

After taking possession of Zion, Bryce and North Rim Grand Canyon operations, the National Park Service issued an operating prospectus. The prospectus was issued May 25, 1972. It stated that, among other things, lodging facilities would be phased out at Zion National Park at the end of three years, terminating in 1975; lodging facilities would be removed from Bryce Canyon National Park in five years, or in 1977; and that the need to continue service at the North Rim of the Grand Canyon would be reevaluated at the end of the 10-year contract in 1982. The prospectus stated that the:

> National Park Service is charged by law with the responsibility of conserving the scenery and the natural and historic objects and wildlife in national parks and monuments and in providing for the enjoyment of them in such a manner and by such means as will leave them unimpaired for the enjoyment of future generations. In carrying out these responsibilities, concession services are authorized by contract or permit granted private parties to provide the visiting public with such accommodations, facilities and services as are reasonably necessary for the full enjoyment of the area. However, under the present policy, where adequate accommodations exist, or can be built or developed by private enterprise outside such areas, similar accommodations shall not be provided within the area.

It then specified that the successful applicant will be assigned the following government-owned buildings, structures and improvements for use in providing facilities to the public. It described the rather extensive facilities which would be available in the three areas. It also provided for concessioners' rehabilitation and modernization programs at an estimated cost of $130,000, adding this provision:

> In order to avoid the concessioner acquiring a possessory interest in a government acquired or constructed facility to be assigned to the concessioner, the concession contract contemplated hereunder will require the conces-

sioner to relinquish and waive any right to possessory
interest in all government owned facilities which may be
assigned.

It specified that such improvements that are made by
the concessioner may be expensed or amortized, but provided the concessioner will acquire a possessory interest in
any new facilities constructed by him with approval by the
National Park Service.   It stated, however, that other than
as stated herein, no expansion of facilities will be permitted.

There were a number of companies who responded, but
some declined to make proposals due to the limits put on
the operations. I made a proposal on behalf of the Yosemite
Park & Curry Company, of which I was president, but
reserved the right to raise the question of removal of facilities. My proposal was summarily dismissed.

The National Park Service let a contract for the three
operations: Zion, Bryce and the North Rim of Grand Canyon, to TWA Services. These contracts specified the phasing out of the facilities as provided in the prospectus; but
before turning the facilities over, the Park Service removed
the cabins and camper service building in Zion and removed the camper services in Bryce Canyon. Gary Everhardt replaced George Hartzog as the Director of the National Park Service.

Use of Master Plan to Reduce Facilities in
Zion National Park

On September 26, 1974, I appeared in Salt Lake City on
behalf of the Conference of National Park Concessioners
relating to the master plan hearing for Zion National Park. I
quoted Public Law 89-249 with these words:

> The Secretary of the Interior shall take such action as
> may be appropriate to encourage and enable private
> persons and corporations (hereinafter referred to as
> "concessioners"), to provide and operate facilities and
> services which he deems desirable for the accommoda-
> tion of visitors in areas administered by the National
> Park Service.

I asked if there was anything in this wording which
would suggest or give the Park Service the authority to

remove visitor facilities — there isn't — yet the Act had been quoted by the Park Service as authority for the removal of visitor facilities from Zion National Park. I stated that master plans and environmental impact statements were being used to support the reduction of facilities in the national parks.

I then examined the master plan and environmental statements for Zion. I stated:

> Here is a prime example of how these instruments can be used to implement a policy of exclusion. You simply endorse development that fits your concept of park use and you damn development that is contrary to your objective. The Zion Plan is a classic of contradictions. The Plan calls for removal of 83 cabins that can provide overnight lodging for 372 people each night. This development occupies only 12 acres of the park's 187,000 acres. This, according to the Plan, is an intrusive development and therefore should be removed.
>
> On the other hand, development of 10 picnic sites and limited camping is approved with the statement that this development will disturb less than 25 acres of land. In other words, we approve development of 25 acres of land to serve 10 picnic sites and limited camping, but providing lodging for an overnight experience of some 372 people a night on 12 acres is objectionable.
>
> In order to justify as practical the other component of the policy, "that adequate facilities exist or can be developed by private enterprise to serve park visitors outside park bound aries," the planners had to strain to show that these facilities were available outside of Zion National Park. They faced some real problems; water is a major problem. In fact, there was a congressional act of May 28, 1928, which permitted the diversion of water from inside park boundaries to enable the community of Springdale to get water. As a result, Springdale is a very small community with limited accommodations. If a visitor facility was to be provided by the community of Springdale, it had to have Park Service cooperation. It should be noted that the water would still have to come from the park as it does now, just as it did when the Diversion Act of 1928 was passed. In other words, develop outside and use park water but do not use park water inside for visitor facilities!

In the environmental statement it was acknowledged that sewage was also a problem. It was solved by the simple expedient of removing the concession facilities and therefore the sewage problem in the park would be lessened. It was transferred to Springdale. It said that Springdale had no sewage system except for septic tanks, but this would be solved by a plan to be completed in July 1975. In other words, they transferred the problem from inside the park to another area immediately adjacent in Springdale, outside the park; by whom or how financed was not disclosed. If the problem was transferred out of the park it would not be a problem. There was grave doubt that the small community of Springdale could cope with the vastly expanded development caused by the transfer of park sewerage treatment from Zion to Springdale.

The report also stated:

The elimination in the park of concessionaire overnight facilities will allow Zion to implement a more meaningful concept of personalized visitor services.

What these services are and how they are to be accomplished was not divulged, nor does the report disclose why overnight facilities in the park interfere with this meaningful experience.

I submit that the opportunity to spend the night in the park and the opportunity to experience a sunrise or sunset on the multicolored Zion walls, or to observe the stars on a clear Utah night from the valley, is to enhance — not limit — the park experience.

I believe that it is clear that Congress intended to make these parks available for the use and the enjoyment of the people, and that people are entitled to those facilities they need to make the park available for their use and enjoyment.

A report from Stanford Research Institute definitely supports the provision that the people who use the national parks want the facilities maintained in the parks, whether they be lodging or campground facilities for their use and enjoyment.

Zion is being the guinea pig for those who advocate the reduction of park use by reducing the facilities. This is not because Zion is different from other parks, but because the government owns the facilities and feels that by removal, it can dictate the terms of park use. The decisions made here today in large measure determine whether our national parks may be used and enjoyed by all the people, or are to be reserved for an elitist few. It will also in measure determine whether Congress sets park policy or whether the use of our national parks will fluctuate with the attitude of the bureaucracy.

That closed my testimony at the Salt Lake City hearing on the proposed master plan of Zion.

TWA, the concessioner, had conducted the operations in these three parks until the approaching year, 1975, when the facilities in Zion National Park were to be removed. As this date approached, the Conference of National Park Concessioners, together with the TWA concessioner and other Conference members, contacted their congressional representatives, protesting this move to reduce concession facilities from Zion National Park. The chambers of commerce and other businesses surrounding Zion National Park protested at the public hearings, which were held in Cedar City, Kaibab and Salt Lake City. The public hearings stirred up a real controversy. The Governor of Utah and congressional delegation, led by Senator Moss, violently objected to the proposed reduction of, or moving of, facilities from Zion National Park. Senator Moss introduced Senate Resolution 232, calling on the Secretary of the Interior and the Director of the National Park Service to repudiate the policy of the removal of concession facilities from the National Parks.

Senate Resolution 232:
...WHEREAS the Congress of the United States enacted, and the President approved, Public Law 89-249, to provide for lodging, facilities and services to make these parks available for the use, enjoyment and benefit of all people;
WHEREAS the policies of Public Law 89-249 cry for reaffirmation,
NOW THEREFORE BE IT RESOLVED: that the National Park Service, as the federal agency entrusted with the responsibility for administering these areas, be advised that it is the sense of the Senate of the United States that the National Park Service should take all appropriate action to carry out the terms of Public Law 89-249 to

assure the availability of lodging and other services and facilities where appropriate in the national park system, thus enabling all of our citizens to use and enjoy their national parks, said use and enjoyment to be consistent with the obligation of said National Park Service to protect the parks from irreparable harm,

BE IT FURTHER RESOLVED: that this resolution be spread on the records of the United States Senate and a copy thereof be furnished to the Secretary of the Interior and the Director of the National Park Service.

Senator E. Jake Garn, from Utah, sent a letter to the other senators from the West calling for support of the Senator Moss resolution:

I am writing this letter to request your help in preventing the National Park Service from proceeding with their plans to close lodging accommodations inside Zion and Bryce Canyon National Parks.

The lodging facilities at Zion are slated to be closed at the end of this year, while those facilities at Bryce Canyon will be closed two years hence. This action is a direct result of the Park Service's interpretation of Public Law 89-249 to mean that when adequate commercial services exist adjacent to the national park, then such services will be unnecessary and inappropriate inside the national park. Furthermore, the Park Service has expanded their policies in their current Management Policies Manual, April 1975 edition, to include not only those areas where adequate commercial facilities exist, but also to where they can possibly be developed.

The ramifications of this alternative accommodations policy has a bearing on more than just Zion and Bryce Canyon. It applies to all national parks — Yellowstone, Grand Teton, Mesa Verde and Glacier National Park — are just a few examples of the parks with support communities in close proximity to present concession sites.

In order to calm the opposition to this policy, the Park Service utilizes an escape valve by saying that the policy is implemented only on a case-by-case basis, but if Congress tolerates and is pacified by this pretext, each time a new case arises, then the Park Service will remove concessions case-by-case from the entire national park system.

E. Jake Garn.

The *Salt Lake Tribune*, under date of June 14, 1975, and heading "Park Service May Close Zion Lodge," reported the following:

> According to a university researcher, no negotiation has transpired for a contract for overnight accommodations in Zion National Park for next year.
>
> Tom Wilson, a spokesman for the National Park Service in Washington, D.C., said Friday no final decision had been made.
>
> "However, a study of moving concessions out of the park and a tentative decision to eventually phase them out has been reached," he said.
>
> TWA Services' contract was predicated on this possibility, according to Mr. Wilson, who said it had been a long-standing policy to build up business on the outside of the park and try to cut down some park traffic. Unofficial reports this week say the National Park Service is moving ahead with plans to phase out concessions in most of the parks, including Yosemite and Yellowstone, with Utah's going first, because it would not cost anything to locate the services outside the parks.

Upon receipt of the reference to Yellowstone, Trevor S. Povah, President of Hamilton Stores, Inc., a concessioner in Yellowstone National Park, wrote Director Gary Everhardt on August 4, 1975, expressing his concern.

He referred to Associate Director Russ Dickenson's letter to Senator Moss, which appeared to endorse the *Salt Lake Tribune* article on June 14 as correctly stating the issues involved in this controversy. Since this article quotes unofficial reports saying the National Park Service is "moving ahead with its plans to phase out concessions in most of the parks, including Yosemite and Yellowstone, we are again concerned as to what is transpiring."

In response, Director Everhardt, in a letter to Trevor S. Povah, dated July 16, 1975, stated:

> Tom (Wilson) is the National Park Service Chief of Media Information in our Office of Public Affairs, and has dealt many times daily with the press for a number of years without controversy. I am satisfied that this flap resulted from a misunderstanding and I explained this the other day to Representative Allan Howe.

Allan T. Howe, a member of Congress from the 2nd District of Utah, responded to Mr. Povah's inquiry with the following language:

> I thank you for writing me your feelings concerning this most important issue. I have been trying for some time to extract from the National Park Service what their long-term policy is concerning the phase-out of facilities in the national parks, and as of this date I have as yet to receive a direct answer concerning this policy. However, in a conversation with the National Park Service Director (Everhardt), he did indicate that each park would be considered on its own individual merits as to whether a phase-out of facilities would become a reality.

Alarmed by the reference to removal of facilities in Yellowstone National Park, Trevor Povah, in a letter dated August 2, 1975, to Senator Clifford P. Hanson, United States Senator from Wyoming, quoted from the Yellowstone Master Plan and Environmental Impact Statement, which on Page 11 included this statement that the 9300 concessioner-provided pillow spaces in the park would be reduced to 8300.

Pertaining to Old Faithful, the report states that:

> High priority should be given to gradually converting the Old Faithful development into a scenic day-use area, an objective that necessarily will take many years to achieve.
> Master Plan, Page 18:
> Old Faithful should be restored to day-use area with the obliteration of all non-historic facilities. In the meantime, no overnight accommodations will be constructed.
> At Fishing Bridge, overnight facilities should be phased out of the Fishing Bridge area. The existing campground there, the Village Store and service station will, however, be retained for an interim period. At West Thumb, the gas station and other service facilities should be phased out.

Mr. Povah wrote in his letter to Senator Hanson:

> While the threat of removal in Yellowstone concerns the future, it is nevertheless a very real threat and when

combined with past and immediate situations such as those at Lassen and Zion and Bryce, serves to illustrate that congressional intent most recently enunciated in Public Law 89-249, is not being followed by the National Park Service.

The National Park Service position was stated by Director Gary Everhardt in a letter dated September 18, 1975, to Congressman Allan P. Howe, as follows:

> The National Park Service has no overall policy concerning the closure of all over-night facilities at all national parks which are in close proximity to the community that can accommodate the park visitor's needs.
>
> The determination to phase out facilities in a particular park is made for the protection of park resources and considers many factors, including the economic impact on the area, inconvenience to park visitors, and physical condition of the facilities. Each park is treated as an individual case study.
>
> With regard to the position that the National Park Service lacks the statutory authority for closing park facilities, we (NPS) offer the following comments:
>
> The Act of August 25, 1916, as amended and supplemented, directs the Secretary of the Interior to administer areas in the national park system in accordance with the fundamental purpose of conserving their scenery, wildlife, natural historic objects and providing for the enjoyment in a manner that will leave them unimpaired for the enjoyment of future generations. The Act of October 9, 1965, 79 Statutes 969, 16 USC Section 20 et seq.
>
> The policy of the Congress that such development shall be limited to those that are necessary and appropriate for public use and enjoyment of the national park area in which they are located and that are consistent, to the highest practical degree with the preservation and conservation of the area.
>
> In our judgment, this congressional mandate, as well as other authorities of the Secretary contained in 16 USC Section 1 et sec., as amended and supplemented, provides authorization pursuant to which the Secretary may exercise discretion as to the extent, if any, of permissible development within any park area. We consider that the exercise of this discretion is on-going and that if existing concession developments prove to be no longer consistent with the standards established by Congress, the Sec-

retary shall have the authority to eliminate such developments, so long as proper compensation is paid affected concessioners.

In response to Director Everhardt's explanation of the National Park Service authority, the congressional delegation from Utah responded in the following manner:

> You have previously stated that pursuant to Public Law 89-249, it is your policy to close down existing lodging facilities inside the parks when such facilities can be provided outside park boundaries. However, there is no provision in Public Law 89-249 which directs that lodging facilities within national park boundaries should be precluded when lodging facilities exist outside the park boundaries.
>
> The language which you cite in Section 1 of the Law — that concession development should be limited to that which is necessary and appropriate for public use and enjoyment of an area, is merely a word of caution against over-development and use, since Congress recognized that this law grants to the Secretary of the Interior increased discretion in promoting concessioner development. However, reading Public Law 89-249 in its entirety, reveals that the law is designed to provide for concession facilities — not to restrict them.

Senator Henry M. Jackson from the State of Washington, and Chairman of the Senate Interior and Insular Affairs Committee, placed in the Senate Congressional Record on September 23, 1975, the following, from which excerpts are taken:

> Mr. Jackson: Mr. President, I bring to the attention of my colleagues a matter which is of critical importance to the State of Utah at this time, but which could appear at any time to any other state in the country. I am referring to the policy of the National Park Service toward overnight accommodation in national parks. The National Park Service has recently announced in its Administrative
>
> Policy Manual, Chapter 8, page 2:
>
> If adequate facilities exist or can be developed by private enterprise to serve the park visitors' needs for commercial services outside park boundaries, such facilities shall not be provided within the park area.

The Park Service has initially singled out only lodging accommodations in implementing its policy of excluding commercial services inside the park, when they exist or can be developed outside the park; however, the language of the Park Service is much broader and more comprehensive. Commercial services such as campgrounds, restaurants and curio shops are not logically exempt from this recently announced policy and, therefore, could become victims also of such far-reaching decisions.

The ultimate effect of this policy may be that people will be allowed access to the parks only on a limited daytime basis. An aesthete standard is being imposed by this policy which specifically affects those people who believe that a park visit is enriched by being able to spend a night inside the park.

There is no adequate substitute for the overnight experience inside the park. There are only less desirable alternatives to this experience. Take the case of the park visitors who derive their greatest enjoyment of visiting the park by just being able to relax beside or near their cabin, taking in the park's natural beauty, and not having to rely on constant commuting to and from an external motel in the area. Such an alternative accommodation would not be surrounded by the beauty of the park in its natural setting, but would be surrounded by an environment similar to that of the city which he left.

While the policy that is currently being implemented may reduce the administrative problems of the National Park Service, it is in direct opposition to their charge to provide for the enjoyment of the national parks.

The lodging facilities being phased out in Zion and Bryce Canyon National parks are not for the purpose of protecting scenery, natural or historic objects or wildlife; in fact, the removal of log cabins at Bryce Canyon could be interpreted as a direct violation of the mandate to protect historical objects.

The Park Service, in its effort to conserve the park environment, has neglected the equally important duty to provide for the enjoyment of the environment. It must consider that there are different types of park visitors and that it should respond where reasonably possible.

Senator Jackson was the Chairman of the Interior and Insular Affairs Committee of the Senate at that time, and during the time Public Law 89-249 was passed. He should have a complete under standing of the provisions in Public Law 89-249 and what it was intended to accomplish.

The *Deseret News* reported, under the headline, "Closure of Facilities is Definite":

> The National Park Service considers its decision to close both Zion and Bryce National Parks a definite commitment, unless new evidence is turned up to refute the program.
>
> Deputy Park Service Director Russell Dickenson told the *Deseret News* Monday if the decision was sound in 1971, it would be arbitrary to change it now.
>
> Dickenson's remarks put into perspective the Park Service's attitude as it proceeded to advance plans to hold public hearings in the fall in Southern Utah on the closure. The Park Service also had contracted with the University of Utah to make an economic study of the plan, which had not been received as the University report was due August 15.
>
> Dickenson said:
>
> The chief reason to close lodging and other facilities in Zion is the high cost of up-grading sewage treatment there to meet the antipollution laws.
>
> I know it may not be valid to close the park facilities just because of the cost of sewage treatment. But we have to make some judgments where we put our resources.
>
> A Park Service public affairs officer said last night that the Park Service wants to close such accommodations and other unnecessary facilities as a move toward making the national parks pure and pristine.
>
> There would be strong opposition from conservation groups such as the Sierra Club, the National Parks and Conservation Association, etc., if the Park's closure decision is reversed.
>
> At the request of the Utah congressional delegation, the Federal Research Committee of the State of Utah was requested to examine this problem of the proposed closure of the facilities in Zion National Park.
>
> A report issued by this research committee stated that the law provides that the Secretary of the Interior was charged to limit concessioner development to those who are "consistent with the highest practical degree of preservation and conservation of the area," and that such facilities should be under carefully controlled safeguards so that the heavy visitation will not impair park values. It further specified that it is the policy of Congress that

further development shall be limited to those that are necessary and appropriate for public use and enjoyment of the national park in the area in which they are located. It is this section of the law that the Park Service cites for the discontinuation of accommodations in the parks. It must be recognized, however, that this section of Public Law 89-249 is merely a word of caution against over-development in a bill designed to encourage concessioner investment within the park boundary.

It is important to realize that Public Law 89-249 does not provide a basis for the Park Service to remove existing facilities within national parks simply because alternative accommodations are present or can be developed outside the boundaries of the national park. No other statute has been offered as a basis of this policy; yet this policy exists, and the decision- making authority for the future of the concessions is being exercised by the National Park Service in the present case. The Park Service has made a far-reaching policy decision that it is not entitled to make. Congressional mandate on the matter of removing concessions does not exist, even though decision-making at the congressional level is certainly needed.

It was further stated that:

It is apparent that the National Park Service first adopted this policy of eliminating lodging facilities within park boundaries several years ago, although the actual time of decision is quite uncertain. The policy was formulated and implemented unanimously and quietly as a routine result of bureaucratic planning process. Current concession policy originated with the National Park Service.

An assessment of the capability of peripheral communities to accommodate visitors was also anticipated with great interest. The entire question of what constitutes an adequate accommodation alternative is important; how close must the lodging be to the park, and what would be the character of the lodging with respect to character, aesthetics and price. Is a standard motel room within 50 miles of the park a reasonable alternative for the family traveler? Is it satisfactory to an elderly traveler who relies upon the convenience of an organized tour which utilized public transportation, or is a satisfactory alternative lodging located within five miles of the park boundary and visually and functionally compatible with the park environment required for a true alternative? Definition of these values in the single case of Zion and Bryce Canyon phase-out will undoubtedly have a bearing on other parks and other phase-outs, for it is difficult to identify many other national parks that are more removed from viable support communities than Bryce Canyon and Zion.

The *Iron County Record*, of Cedar City, Utah, on August 28, 1975, under the caption "Who's to Decide?", cites the following:

> The implication of the issue is that the Park Service is considering each park on an individual basis. The handwriting is on the wall, that the "phase-out" is a definite goal of the department in all national parks.
>
> Like Senator Jake Garn told a Cedar City Chamber of Commerce meeting, "The departments are very courteous to congressmen. They answer their questions and respond to their letters; then they do just as they please."

The political pressure brought to bear by the Utah Congressional Delegation and the state's governor forced the Park Service to retract their proposed closure of Zion National Park's visitor facilities. However, the Park Service still retains its policy, "if adequate facilities exist or can be developed outside the park, they will not be permitted in the park." This despite the fact that congressional representatives including Scoop Jackson, Chairman of the Senate Interior and Insular Affairs Committee, said the Park Service had no such authority; an arrogant disregard of the law of the land.

27

Lassen Closure

MANZANITA LAKE, in Lassen Volcanic National Park, suffered the greatest setback. The people lost their national park in April 1974. In a presentation to the Park Service Advisory Committee, the planning department of the Western Regional office proposed the removal of visitor facilities to two miles outside of the park, based on a six-year-old geologic report stating that the concession facilities were in the path of a possible rock slide from Chaos Crags. This was based upon the fact that some three hundred or more years ago, a rock slide had taken place. The cause was unknown, but it was speculated that the volcanic extrusion which built Chaos Crags had reached too great a height and had tumbled, or a buildup of steam had caused an explosion causing a rock slide. If this were to reoccur in the summer, when occupied, and if it were to happen fast enough, it would create its own cushion of air and the rocks would travel 2 1/2 miles, devastating the concession facilities. Remarkably, the government campground adjacent to the concession facilities was closed and then reopened, as not being affected! No effort was made to reexamine the so-called danger to concessions.

The report used by the National Park Service to close the facilities in Lassen Volcanic National Park came from a U.S. Geological Survey Report made in 1968 by Dwight Crandall, Donald Mullineaux, Robert S. Sigafoos and Meyer Rubin, of Denver, Colorado. This was the report used for justification, but an investigation and subsequent report by *The Redding Record Searchlight* reporter, Glenn Hassenpflug, confirms that this was used in justification to support a previously made decision by the National Park Service to reduce facilities in the park and to eventually eradicate them entirely.

The U.S. Geological Survey Report, under the heading "Potential Volcanic Hazards," stated:

> A potentially more hazardous event than an eruption would be the formation of another rockfall-avalanche at Chaos Crags, or from a newly erupted dome. Such avalanche could be caused by volcanic explosion during the eruption of the dome or by an earthquake unrelated to volcanism. A rockfall-avalanche might not be preceded by any warning and an extremely high velocity would surely preclude evacuation in time to prevent loss of life. Because of this, we regard as hazardous, the area within a distance of about five kilometers down-slope from Chaos Crags to the east and to the west.
>
> There seems to be no way to warn or protect persons in the path of such an avalanche and we think that future use of the area which might be affected should be restricted.

While the main park road passed immediately under the Chaos Crags, which was the alleged scene of a rockslide, the road has never been closed.

The Park Service ordered the closure of visitor facilities at Manzanita Lake in April 1974. Unfortunately, there was not a concessioner interested in fighting for the people's right to accommodations at Manzanita Lake. The concessioner, U.S. Natural Resources, a conglomerate, had sold its concession at Yosemite, leaving only Lassen, which was considered to be too small for their concern. They welcomed the chance to sell the Lassen concessions.

There was considerable suspicion in the surrounding communities that the full story supporting the closure of concession facilities at Manzanita Lake had not been revealed. This was engendered by the haste in ordering the closure without prior notice, the vague and conflicting statements made by National Park Service representatives and the fact that a master plan had been in the planning stage for a considerable time (revised draft was dated November 12, 1973), and curious references to uses not related to geologic hazards.

Master Plan - Lassen Volcanic National Park:
Lassen Volcanic National Park, a park already hosting near capacity crowds at times of peak travel, cannot

face the future passively or in isolation. The National Park Service must consider new systems of receiving the public so that visitors may enjoy a quality experience in a manner not leading to degradation of an outstanding national resource.

At the north entrance on the trans-park road, the Manzanita area will continue to serve as the major developed center of the park. However, in view of the rockfall-avalanche hazard, and increasing human pressures on a primary and limited scenic site, all functions other than those necessary for reduced day-use activities will be relocated to sites outside the present park boundary (the only exception is the campground which will be retained in its present location south of Manzanita Lake) (p 29).

As a result of these suspicions, the *Redding Record Searchlight* assigned its reporter, Glenn Hassenpflug, to make an investigation to "dig out the real story" of the closing of visitor facilities in Lassen Volcanic National park.

The results were reported in a five-part series. The first series was entitled "Volcanic Hazard Study Leads to Shasta."

The first article posed the question: "Why did the Park Service really close Manzanita Lake?"

That question has nagged at county officials and users of Lassen Volcanic National Park since the National Park Service, in April 1974, shut down the visitor center and resort at Lassen.

The Park Service had other motives that in time could have limited access to Manzanita Lake. This was the best reason, and the distinction is important: First, Ben Avery, a member of the park's advisory council, pointed out at a meeting in Redding last August:

It is a hazard because the U.S.F.&G. says so. Howard Chapman, on April 26, 1974, said:

The evidence at hand is so compelling that no other decision than closing out the operations at this location is consistent with our responsibility.

Dwight Crandall, Chief of the U.S. Hazards Projects, said:

I don't think the Lassen situation is unique. We have right now the towns of Weed and Mt. Shasta and McCleod around the base of Mt. Shasta. The idea is that once a community or town becomes established in a hazard area, it becomes a little hard to pack them up and move them out. Indeed, the citizens of Weed, McCleod and Mt. Shasta might frown upon such an enterprise.

The U.S. geologist from Denver, Dan Miller, who is doing the Shasta field work, commented that:

The citizen didn't learn of the Shasta hazard study over after-dinner drinks with his neighbor, the bureaucrat — he might have gotten it from the Bureau of Mines office in Sacramento. The information was not actually kept secret — it was on file there. This is part of the planning and not one that is generally communicated by the government.

Part II - Lassen: Fear of Law Suit Ended Foot-Dragging

The Service (referring to the National Park Service) did not actually lie, but it did not tell the whole truth. In the current planning for the future use of Lassen Park, it is quoted that:

If the Manzanita Lake development is replaced, the Park Service wants it done outside of Lassen National Park, probably on Forest Service Land.

Between 1968 and 1975, the Park Service reacted to expressions of puzzlement and outrage by the public with all the patient paternalism of a colonial government which had been summoned for a native uprising in some back-water province. Regional Director Howard Chapman said:

"We did it for your own good."

What forced the announcement of the closure was a letter written on April 5, 1974, by John Del Favero, president of the company that ran the Lassen National Park Company Resort. Del Favero gave the Park Service an ultimatum to announce its steps to protect employees and visitors by April 15, or he would shut the resort himself. He said:

"We will, of course, hold you responsible and liable for all damages."

There was another stimulus, and it was not concern for human life, but a prod from the Service's planning arm, the Denver Service Center, followed by this threat from Del Favero.

The Denver office was then working on the Lassen Master Plan. Planning representative Frank Collins told a group:

The planners have strongly indicated that they must reduce the hazard to the visitor by removing the visitor from the hazardous area

Within weeks of the reading of the U.S. Geological Survey Report, Superintendent Boyer, on April 29, 1969, appealed to Chapman for "a hard and fast administrative decision." Boyer said, "Actually, there are only two alternatives: do we go, or do we stay?" Boyer favored staying. By 1971 Boyer was complaining that the Service's lack of a decision was hampering his ability to administer the park. Mr. Chapman, on May 12, repeated his opinion that the service should take "a calculated risk to keep the development open." Superintendent Boyer was transferred from Lassen to Washington, D.C., in late 1971.

Robert J. Murphy took Boyer's place as the superintendent of Lassen Volcanic National Park. In a memorandum to Regional Director Chapman, he advised that he thought the matter should be communicated to the public. He told Chapman that:

The lack of an action plan appears to be long overdue and any attempt to further defer positive solutions, in view of longstanding recommendations, could prove embarrassing to the service.

The public knew nothing until the closure announcement on April 26, 1974, six years after the U.S. Geological Survey finished its study. Ralph G. Mihan, San Francisco field solicitor for the U.S. Department of the Interior, rendered a legal decision calling attention to the government's liability under the Tort Claims Act if there was injury to person or property. In a later interview Mr. Mihan stated he did not know why the service, if it cared deeply either about human life or liability, took six years to act.

Part III - Many National Parks Closing Concessions

Don Hummel, Lassen National Park's first concessioner, stated that he thought he knew why the National Park Service waited six years to close the visitor center and private visitor facilities at Manzanita Lake. Hummel said:

I think that the National Park Service intended to use

this hazardous report as a leverage to remove the concession facilities.

The response from the advisory group, after it was presented to them by the planning department, was much greater than the Park Service anticipated and the Park Service found themselves out on a limb, saying:

"If this is that bad, we'll have to do something."

They never intended to go that far, in my opinion.

All the overt steps to deal with the avalanche threat occurred between January and April 1974, although the Park Service was alerted in 1968.

Currently, Hummel is Chairman of the Conference of National Park Concessioners. He sees the Lassen closure as one more example of the Park Service's intent to end concession operations.

I have examined 12 Master Plans for 12 national parks, and every one of them called for either a reduction or removal of concession facilities out of the park.

Hummel is not alone in his suspicions.

In practical terms, the Service has summed up a variety of local reasons to justify the same result.

Lassen: The elimination of all lodging and most other commercial services.

Zion, Bryce & Cedar Breaks: The elimination of overnight lodging.

Yosemite: The removal of all non-essential services.

Grand Canyon North Rim: A review of overnight facilities for 1982.

Part IV - Lassen "Hazard": Only an Excuse to Close the Park?

Without a hazard survey, the National Park Service probably would have needed years to close the private resort at Manzanita Lake in Lassen Volcanic National Park. The survey, entirely funded and conducted by a separate federal agency, gave the Park Service a solidly practical reason to begin carrying out at Lassen in 1974, one of its own long-range philosophic changes in the ecology to restore the parks as "vignettes of primitive America."

Superintendent Richard Boyer was flabbergasted when he sensed in 1969 that the Manzanita Lake development might be closed. He argued against the possibility and complained of being excluded from the decision making. He stated:

What I was concerned about is that we may have many, many areas in the National Park Service that are located in probably just as critical locations — water courses and flood plains — that it just seems very strange to me that such a big push would be made on our little area here, with an end to effect closure of it.

Shortly after his transfer and his replacement by Superintendent Robert J. Murphy in 1971, a new set of management objectives was outlined. They were:

1) Restore park lakes to their natural condition where recent use, visitor use or fish stocking has adversely affected the normal ecosystem.

2) Actively promote the development of campgrounds, trailer courts, overnight accommodations and associated recreational facilities outside the park.

3) Limit campground development and the total number of campsites to those presently existing.

4) Eliminate concessioner overnight accommodations from the park and limit Manzanita Lake and Drakesbad facilities to their current overnight capacity as long as they continue to operate.

It should be noted that the concession facility at Drakesbad is located some 10 air miles across the hill from the alleged danger of Chaos Crags. The management objective calls for:

1) Relocation of the concession and service operation from Manzanita Lake to a less geographically hazardous area, and;

2) Phase out the concession operation at Drakesbad and restore the site.

These facts clearly show that the Service intended to shut down the concessioner's overnight accommodations, hazard or no hazard.

The Park Service objective of closing the facilities was denied to Rush M. Blodgett, M.D., of Redding, California, a patron of Drakesbad, in a letter dated June 10, 1974, from Imogene B. LaCovey, Acting Assistant Director of Concessions Management in Washington, D.C. She said, and I quote in part:

In regard to the Drakesbad and ski areas,the National Park Service has not proposed or encouraged the closure of these facilities. U.S. Natural Resources, the present operator, has taken action to close these facilities.

With congressional intervention, the Park Service, through Regional Director Chapman, stated:

In the event the concessioner expresses a wish to continue the Drakesbad and expand the ski operations, as there was strong public political pressure to continue, they could be continued in operation on their concession contract or through a successor concessioner.

Chapman knew full well that there had been a strong push to expand a ski area with some major additions and that the public would not stand for a closure of the ski area. The much harassed Chapman assured Doctor Blodgett that the resort's (Drakesbad) continued existence depended upon its ability to pay its own way. Blodgett had his accountant prepare a financial statement to prove that Drakesbad was not a loser. The Park Service denied that there was a desire to move concession facilities out of the park and that that was not a factor, nor was such a desire considered in arriving at their final decision.

Part V: Park Service Vows to Change its Ways

Interview with Park Superintendent Robert J. Murphy, who outlined the goals for Lassen, brought to light the Service's covert motives for closing the Manzanita Lake development. These objectives or goals were approved by the Service in May of 1973. In the 1970 publication of the administrative report on the avalanche danger in Lassen, and the 1974 publication of the official version in the *Journal of Research* of the U.S. Geological Survey, the following is stated:

One of the objectives was to eliminate overnight accommodations for visitors to the park. Another was to phase out the concession operation at Drakesbad, a small guest ranch operation across the park from the hazard area.

The emphasis throughout the report was on erasing man-made changes and restoring Lassen to its natural state. The avalanche hazard was mentioned only once briefly in the six-page report. The tone of the report was established in the introductory paragraph which states:

Current and projected visitor use statistics indicate that, if continued, they jeopardize the integrity of park value and quality of the visitor experience.

Visitation to Lassen had increased from 399,000 to 500,000 during 1962 to 1972. In 1970, the Lassen concession had merged with U.S. Natural Resources, who also had Yosemite Park & Curry Company, operating the Yosemite National Park, and was involved in an ecology dispute with the Park Service.

The concessioner, in a letter dated August 13, 1972, stated to the Park Service:

Lassen does not appear to be in any overuse danger at the present during the summer season.

It said that projections over the next five years showed an essentially continuing non-pressure visitation. By contrast, the Park Service was already thinking of closing the Manzanita Lake development for a reason that had nothing to do with a possible avalanche.

Superintendent Murphy explained his proposal to close the Drakesbad operation in this manner:

That particular action comes from the development of a policy where certain concessioners were marginal.

I think we were taking the total visitation as opposed to Drakesbad, where they were accommodating guests in the primary purpose of a dude ranch.

There was some feeling that private interests had a desire, in some areas, to develop their facilities quality-wise above those existing in the park. In such instances, it was viewed in the best interest to encourage private development outside and reduce private development inside, where it proved marginal or of limited interest.

The public knew nothing of Murphy's objection until it was published in the appendix of a master plan draft in late 1973. When it came into view of the public and the Park Service was asked to explain, Regional Director Chapman and other administrators responded only with some variation of the standard line:

We have no policy as such; when such possibilities exist they must be considered on a case-to-case basis.

Upon completion of the five series of reports, the editor of The *Redding Record Searchlight* published the following:

Last In a Series: A reporter's job is to report facts as he finds them and the opinions of others as they are expressed to him. When it comes to his own opinions, the disciplines of his profession require that he put them on the shelf, neither expressing them directly nor allowing them to color what he writes.

The *Record Searchlight* reporter, Glenn Hassenpflug, spent several months recently probing both the steps and the motivations involved in the National Park Service closure of visitor facilities at Manzanita Lake in early 1974. His five-part report appeared in the newspaper early this month. We asked Hassenpflug to share with our readers the personal impressions and opinions that he formed as a result of his investigation.

Here is his report:

As a reporter, I have spent hours trying to get a specific question answered, been shuttered from desk to desk, disconnected, lectured to about who's doing what and who isn't, and finally been given the answer "off the record." Had I not been a reporter, but a mere citizen, I would not have gotten the answer at all.

It is the news media's dubious distinction to have become an institutionalized information collector for the citizen and, conversely, information dispenser for the government.

The closure of the Manzanita Lake development in Lassen National Park is an excellent example of how the system functions. When the National Park Service, without notice, shut down this visitor center and private resort, they told the public, "We did it for your own good, to save you from a possible hundred miles per hour rock slide off Chaos Crags."

Partly because the closure was made so suddenly, while the Crags had stood unmoved for centuries, many citizens and Shasta County officials suspected that they were being avalanched by the Park Service. They were!

The Park Service spokesmen stuck to their justification. It was another good one, sealed and delivered by another government entity, the U.S. Geological Survey, but not understood or seriously challenged. On request from county officials, the Service even released its file of memoranda, telephone calls and lectures on the closure, or at least enough of the files to start a damning, circumstantial case for the prosecution. But Shasta County lacked the time to flush out the file with endless telephone interviews and inquiries to Utah, Denver and San Francisco, and, had it assembled the case, it lacked a forum for pressing it effectively.

By contrast, a newspaper is a forum and it has the time if it chooses. An investigation of several weeks revealed the true reason why the Park Service closed Manzanita Lake. Everything else was sheer pettifoggery. It wanted to, because human population pressures had begun to imperil the natural ecology, and because commercial pressures at other parks, such as Yosemite, had embarrassed it politically.

Quietly, and for the public's own good, it had decided to limit public access to the parks and to begin buying out the private interest. Yet how painfully hard it was to make the Park Service explain its intention. Service spokesmen took refuge in bureaucratic loyalties and in elaborate quibbling over terms, in manufactured statements and appeals to altruism, and in buck-passing, both petty and grand.

The combined effect was obscurity — a tangle of words and circumstances that could hardly have been more difficult to separate had they been designed deliberately to obscure. I don't think Park Service officials sat in their offices and decided "Let's deceive the public." I think instead the Service — like the bureaucracy in general — had learned its functions with the greatest freedom in a climate of obscurity. For example, Regional Director Howard Chapman, who acted as the Service's field marshal, is uniformly described by his fellow bureaucrats as honest, conscientious and a hard worker; but county officials and private citizens who dealt with him describe him as a very different man — aloof, hard to reach, non-committal.

The point about the whole Lassen controversy is not just whether people's access to the park should be limited, or whether the Service made the right decision in closing Manzanita Lake's complex.

The point is that the people cannot afford to let administrators whom they can't locate or understand make their decisions for them.

The government doesn't need more good men — it needs more responsive men. It doesn't need better reasons — it needs more clarity. Thus, the investigation disclosed that the National Park Service implemented its over-all objectives of reducing or eliminating visitor facilities in the national parks. In the case of Lassen, they seized upon a report of possible hazard and utilized it to close the facilities at Manzanita Lake. Their real objective is poignantly disclosed in the proposal to also close Drakesbad, which is 10 air miles across the mountain from the park and not involved in any claim of danger.

Despite petitions submitted to the congressmen and congressmen's intercession, Lassen remains closed, the result of bureaucratic action, implementing the desires of the environmental purists who have been putting pressure on the National Park Service to remove all visitor facilities from the parks and return them to their pristine nature.

The result was that the government closed and paid for the concession facilities, tore down the buildings and the Park Service objective of eradicating the concession facilities was accomplished. Park visitors can no longer stay in Lassen Volcanic National park except at a dude ranch complex at Drakesbad, unless they camp. As a result, few people visit the park and businesses adjacent to the park have failed. The public has been denied the use of their national park by this spurious act of the National Park Service. The public lost its national park.

Lassen is a clear-cut case documenting what the Conference of National Park Concessioners had been complaining of for years; namely, that the Park Service was pursuing a policy of reduction and removal of visitor facilities from the national parks. The Park Service's response was always the same:

> We have no policy as such on closing out concession facilities. When such possibilities exist, they must be considered on a case-by-case basis.

This policy flies in the face of and demonstrates contempt for Public Law 89-249, wherein Congress established concession policies for areas administered by the National Park Service and which directs that:

> The Secretary of the Interior shall take such action as may be appropriate to encourage and enable private persons and corporations (hereinafter referred to as "concessioners") to provide and operate facilities and services which he deems desirable for the accommodation of visitors in areas administered by the National Park Service.

It should be quite apparent to any objective person that there is an unauthorized, unpublished, underlying policy of removal of concession facilities and that Park Service personnel are less than honest with the public as to their objectives.

Lassen experienced a drastic reduction of visitation since there were no facilities at Manzanita Lake to accommodate overnight lodging unless one camped.

This also adversely affected the Park Service's ability to conduct ranger and naturalists' services and to provide a visitor contact point. Some park personnel and others interested in Lassen sponsored a solicitation program to build a visitors center at Manzanita Lake in 1985.

This solicitation acknowledged that the situation was aggravated (more aptly described as caused) by the removal of concessioner facilities in 1974.

The sequel to this closing is the formation of Lassen Park Foundation to solicit funds to erect a visitor center in the Manzanita Lake area and to support the reestablishment of ranger and naturalist services there.

The solicitation address to me contained the following excerpts:

Dear Mr. And Mrs. Hummel

LASSEN VOLCANIC NATIONAL PARK is a very special place, but threatened. Like so many things, we expect Lassen to remain as we remember it. But appropriations for operation of the park are not keeping pace with increased operating costs and inflation. This shortfall creates delays in repairs, reductions of naturalist activities and the elimination of ranger services—conditions that are felt by all of us who love the park!

The whole picture has been aggravated by the closure of Lassen's major visitor center complex at Manzanita Lake in 1974.This area was the hub of summertime activities at Lassen; now little remains of what was once a memorable national park experience there. The park is still without an appropriate visitor facility, and federal funds for a planned replacement are not likely to be available in the near future.

Only direct action by those of us who care deeply can protect the quality of our experiences at Lassen and help bring the park back to its former quality and beauty. The

Superintendent's Fund, Lassen Volcanic National Park, is a non-profit undertaking that has been organized by a group of Lassen Supporters headed by former park Superintendent Bill Stephenson. This organization is soliciting tax deductible contributions to help supplement the park's annual appropriations. In the very near future, this organization will officially become The Lassen Volcanic National Park Foundation. This action will allow for greater fund-raising capacities and program management.

Among the initial goals will be the construction of a visitor center that will replace the Loomis Museum and return ranger services and naturalist activities to the level that we have come to appreciate and expect.

This is an exciting time for Lassen. There is a spirited rebirth of the private initiative that created our national parks and aid in protecting their precious natural resources. Continuing a portion of the protection in the face of limited governmental funding is again in the hands of the American people. Each of us, through your active support, can join in the same effort that Peter Lassen, John Raker, Arthur Conrad and Stephen Mather worked so tirelessly to achieve.

Sincerely yours,
W. Stephenson
Former Superintendent

My response follows:

Gentlemen:

I am in receipt of your solicitation for funds to construct a visitor center to replace the Loomis Museum at Manzanita Lake, and reestablish the Ranger and Naturalist services there. You say the situation has been aggravated by the closure of Lassen's major facility at Manzanita Lake in 1974.

How painfully aware I am, since I built all the visitor facilities which you closed and are having removed. How outraged I am at the perfidy of the National Park Service in the use of the U.S.G.S. report as an excuse to close the facilities to reduce an alleged threat of visitor overuse. Through your closure, the people lost their national park and the Park Service lost the support necessary "to put it back to its former quality and beauty";

and, I might add, the people's right to visit and enjoy.

You say:

"There is a spirited rebirth of the private initiative that created our National Parks and aid in protecting their precious natural resources."

The Service should have considered this when it neglected to provide for the people's right to use and enjoy, as set forth in the National Park Service enabling act. I suggest you contact Regional Director Howard Chapman. He said Manzanita Lake was closed for the public's own good. Is this request for funds an acknowledgment that the closure was not good for the people?

I am curious: Has the danger of the Chaos Crags rock/avalanche declined since the concession facilities have been removed, as you now propose erecting a visitor center in this alleged danger area? If so, why not use the Manzanita Lake Lodge as a visitor center? It is built of native stone and was cited by the National Park Service when it was built for its design integrity.

Or better still, why not return the park to the people and reestablish concession facilities? You reopened the adjacent campground; you could reopen the concession facilities. This would solve your problem and make the park available for the people's use and enjoyment. I should not have to remind the Park Service that this is part of their charge.

Sincerely,
Don Hummel, Former Park Ranger and Lassen's First Concessioner
cc: Editor, *Redding Record Searchlight*

The lodge had not been torn down at the time this letter was written. It was destroyed later in the same year.

28

Return to Glacier Park

I RETURNED to Glacier from Yosemite in May 1974. Our patronage was increasing but our profits were not. I set about to trim our expenses and reorganize some of our departments. I reduced the number of employees and merged the purchasing department by combining all purchases under Louis Melicek, who had been released from Yosemite after the MCA purchase of the company.

This required the release of Frankie Donau who was our gift shop purchaser coming to Glacier after we merged the Lassen operation with U.S.N.R. Jay Joplin, who did the institutional purchasing was also released. Al Donau resigned to take a position with Hamilton Stores Inc., a concession operation in Yellowstone National Park. I hired Robert Eaton as our Controller. He had been with me in Yosemite. Bob and Henry Varner clashed, so Bob left after one season. I brought O. A. (Pappy) Gamble in to reorganize the transport division as it had greatly deteriorated. Hugo (Bud) O'Neill was hired to take over the garage and motor maintenance which was in a shambles.

Reorganization was not our only problem. Shortly before opening in June 1975, we had another flood. This was not as bad as 1964 as it caused physical damage only on the east of the Divide. It cut off all through traffic over the Going-to-the-Sun Road. This closed Rising Sun as the road from St. Mary's was washed out. Many Glaciers could not open until its access road was reestablished nine days later.

East Glacier was the worst hit as we again lost our water system with the collapse of the dam and the wash-out of the water flume leaving the hotel and the community of East Glacier without water.

Cy Stevenson established a temporary system on a side stream with a pump to put water into the remaining system. The pump broke down, and Herb Sammons, a friend and local resident, acquired another pump from a rancher by the name of Keil. We had a small convention in the

Lodge when Keil and his lawyer brother came to my office on a Sunday at about 6:00 p.m. They demanded that I sign a lease of the pump for 30 days at an exorbitant rent. They threatened immediate removal of the pump. In addition to loss of nominal services, I would have had no fire protection for our guests. Since I had about 250 guests in the Lodge, I signed under protest.

Two days later I canceled our agreement as it had been signed under duress. We were sued and lost the case. It cost us over $15,000. Keil's tactics were comparable to those attempted by the linen supply companies after the flood of 1964 except that he was successful in holding us up.

We reestablished our water system and the County and Park Service repaved the washed out roads. We opened for business after losing about two weeks of our season.

Genee's Christmas Letter, 1975

It's early to start a Christmas letter, but since we have another new address, it seems like a good idea. Apartment living didn't seem the right answer for us in Tucson. We started to look for townhouses in the fall. After several trials, in February we decided on a most attractive unit. It is an end unit with natural desert surroundings and a fine view of the Catalina and Rincon Mountains. We modified the plans to our taste. The townhouse was to be completed in early July, but in mid- August was not even complete enough to store our furniture when Genee flew down from Glacier to vacate the apartment. We moved in September 28th and are now settled.

In January we enjoyed a two week cruise down the Eastern South American coast. Then there was a HUD reunion in New York City in February, trips to Washington, D.C. and several to Glacier before we departed for the Park on May 12th for the summer. Our Glacier season started with beautiful weather, only to be followed by rain and more rain. On June 19th it flooded. It was not quite as damaging as the 1964 disaster since the West side of the Park was not deluged; however, roads were washed out, the Many Glacier Hotel and Swiftcurrent Motor Lodge were isolated for nine days, and Rising Sun Motor Lodge for five. The water system at East Glacier was severely damaged, and we had to rely on a temporary system to get through the season. The laundry was hampered all summer with heavy glacial silt in the water. We really could have used a lot of Duz to conquer the tattletale gray. The rainy days persisted all summer except for two weeks in mid-July. It was the wettest, coldest summer in

Montana's recorded history. Morale remained high during the emergency, but cold and wet made operations difficult with low employee morale and guest restiveness. Despite the problems, travel was good and we closed on September 15th with a good financial season.

Diane and Dave Ellis managed the Lake McDonald Lodge and got their baptismal under difficult conditions. Cliff managed the Prince of Wales Hotel and had to contend not only with employee shortages, but rising Canadian nationalism. It is encouraging to have some of the family learning about and interested in the Park operations. Cliff will stay at East Glacier this winter to assist in the maintenance program. He cooked and guided in the same wilderness hunting camp that he was in last fall. Dave and Diane plan to job hunt in California. Donna is still with the Bank of America as an auditor in Los Angeles. She visited in the Park in late August. Char never did get to Glacier as she had the opportunity to go to New Zealand for two summer months with her dance professor and several New Zealand artists on an education and interpretive tour. Quite an experience for her. She will be graduating from the University of Pacific this December. She is part of a small independent dance company in Stockton and will continue on with dancing — performing and teaching. In November the company presented it's first full production. Don and Genee were delighted and pleased at her progress. All the children were home for a happy reunion over Thanksgiving.

❄ ❄ ❄

Genee's Christmas Letter, 1976:

This year has kept Don shuttling between Tucson, Montana and Washington, D.C., on park affairs. Public clamor about too much government is given full credence in park operations. Genee tended the store by working on the garden and our new townhouse. In mid-March Donna joined us for a trip to Bogota, Lima, Cuzco and Machu Picchu. The whole trip was fun, but the highlight was the fabulous Inca citadel. Rarely do reports measure up to expectations, but Machu Picchu inspired us all. We were fortunate to get lodging quarters which permitted us to explore at leisure the myriad buildings and terraced grounds. What an incredible achievement and still steeped in mystery.

Middle May found us back in Glacier faced with repairs to storm-damaged buildings. The huge powerhouse stack at the Prince of Wales had to be replaced. Cliff became construction supervisor, repairman and carpenter, erecting the new smokestack, building additional fire escapes and alarm systems before settling down to manage the hotel. As snow was light, the Going-to-the-Sun Road opened early, giving us a good start for the season. We experienced our best occupancy despite a wet and cold August. Visitation from the East was the highest ever which we attributed to Easterners' desire to escape the Centennial crowds.

Genee's selection of new drapes, spreads, carpets and upholstery paid off with a fresh look for the lodges. This year will put the emphasis on motel and cottage units. Operating problems still plague us with early employee departures and too much alcohol in the kitchens, but we are encouraged as we detect an increasing sense of responsibility on the part of employees.

After the close of the season, Cliff served again as cook and guide in the hunting camp in the Bob Marshall Wilderness. He will join us in Tucson after the first of the year to assist in the hiring and purchasing for next year's operations, while attending UofA to take some accounting courses. Donna plans to resign from her job as auditor with the Bank of America and finish her MBA at USC. She has been attending night school so the course is half completed. Charlene is teaching modern dance on a part-time basis at the University of Pacific and hopes to secure full time employment there while pursuing a Masters in dance. She purchased an old house in Stockton and is in the process of remodeling it with Diane and Dave's help. Dave is applying for admission to several law schools with the hope of pursuing a legal career.

❄ ❄ ❄

In 1977 I entered into negotiations to sell our Glacier operations to TWA Services. The vast expansion of government regulations, the appointment of concessions specialists and the general bureaucratic intervention in the operations took out all the fun. The advantages to be gained by private enterprises were being eroded. It was no longer a partnership to provide service to the public with the Park providing government services and the concessioner the seasonal hospitality services.

TWA and I came to tentative agreement on a sale, but as they did not want to buy the whole company but only the national park portion, excluding East Glacier and the Prince of Wales, I conditioned my approval on an acceptable tax solution. This could not be accomplished so the deal fell through.

As I had to inform the Park Service of our negotiations the press became involved.

The *Hungry Horse News* contacted me and I confirmed that the sale was in progress but not finalized. Dick Munro, Glacier Parks Acting Superintendent, released the following story:

> Don Hummel and his associates rebuilt the business into a successful venture in spite of a 70 to 80 day visitor season, old facilities and an inflationary economy. Over the years Glacier Park visitors have been well served by the company. This is evident by the lack of visitor complaints. Written complaints averaged less than 10 per year.
>
> When we consider that in 1977 Glacier Park Inc. housed over 98,000 persons and served approximately 448,000 meals to visitors, the complaint faction is infinitesimal. Glacier Park Inc. has provided valuable services to Glacier National Park visitors and will be missed.

Upon release of this story, the Montana Tourist Promotion Bureau asked me to attend their annual conference. They prevailed upon me to continue our operations in Glacier National Park.

Genee's Christmas Letter, 1977:

January found us back in Washington, D.C., for President Carter's Inaugural. Such an array of activities; many of them free and well attended; a real "peoples'" gathering. Everywhere huge crowds jostling good-naturedly. In March we returned to D.C. for the Conference of National Park Concessioners. Don was reelected Chairman, though he says this is positively the last time. Other meetings and short trips during the spring filled out our year until it was time to return to Glacier Park in May.

The season started well despite sporadic rain that lasted all summer. Increasing governmental regulations and personnel problems plagued us. There seemed to be more employee unrest for some unknown reason. Perhaps it was the four deaths from accidents at the start of the season. The frustrations were eased by good business which is slowly extending the season into September. A mid-year concessioner's meeting at Yosemite in October disclosed similar widespread difficulties and exasperation with increasing government regulations that impede rather than serve the park visitors. The paper record has become all-important.

Cliff again managed the Prince of Wales Hotel and this winter is serving as caretaker-maintenance man in Waterton. Char was married to John Casserley in April. It was a family home wedding with Donna as a bridesmaid and our good friend, Judge Tony Greco, officiating. All the family was present, so it was a very happy occasion. They are now living in Palo Alto. Char is getting her masters in dance at Stanford and John is teaching dance at Lone Mountain College in San Francisco. Donna resigned her auditor's job at the bank and received her masters in business from USC in May. She has been job hunting, but took time out to help Cliff at the Prince with his financial records in August. She also took a Thanksgiving week's trip to the Virgin Islands and Puerto Rico with us. Diane and Dave spent four months in France visiting with friends. They had a marvelous time and loved it, but returned to the U.S. more appreciative of the opportunities and freedoms here. They are now with Dave's family in Houston in an effort to determine where they want to settle. We all plan to be together in Tucson over Christmas. We planned to be in Yosemite, but as the snows appear uncertain, we have canceled. We had that experience at Aspen when lack of snow limited our skiing to two days out of fourteen. We did ice skate and enjoyed our time together.

This year closes with encouraging signs of peace in the Middle East. The President and Congress are finally grappling with the big problems of energy, welfare and tax reform. There is hesitant, but hopeful, turn up in the economy. We are optimistic that 1978 bodes well for our nation for peace and for you.

❄ ❄ ❄

Genee's Christmas Letter, 1978:

While we liked our townhouse, we have been looking for a hilltop to build a home. During the process Genee found a home with a commanding view of the Catalina Mountains and the city. The owners were looking for a townhouse. We exchanged. Our new address is 5870 North Campbell Avenue, zip 85718.

The season at Glacier went surprisingly well despite the coldest, wettest season in our 18 years. Cliff disagreed with company policy at the Prince of Wales and resigned. This precipitated a number of changes and some disruption. His plans are quite indefinite.

Dave is studying diligently and making perfect grades at the University of Houston Pre-Vet School. Diane is keeping books for an interior decorator and taking dancing lessons. They bought an old home and are in the process of remodeling and refurnishing.

Char received her masters in Education with specialization in dance at Stanford this spring. John taught dance at Lone Mountain College in San Francisco while Char was finishing her schooling. They jointly managed Switfcurrent Motor Lodge in Glacier last summer and are now at the winter offices in Tucson to decide if the hospitality industry will be their future.

Donna was promoted at Hughes Aircraft in Los Angeles to the position of financial forecaster analyzing project costs. She acquired a townhouse in Bellflower, a Los Angeles suburb, last August. She did not limit her forecasting exclusively to financial matters as she announced her engagement to John Bodie, a project coordinator for Hughes. They plan a family wedding in Tucson on February 17.

Our trip up the Nile was fascinating as we went by riverboat from Cairo to Aswan. The pace of life on the Nile is measured by donkeys, camels and hand carts. The dwellings house both the animals and the family with less than acceptable health standards. In the cities where the automobile and the animal-drawn vehicles compete with the pedestrians, the result is chaotic and exciting. Missing by inches is the standard. It strains the nerves.

There were numerous stops to visit the pyramids, temples and tombs. The number and extensive art work is overwhelming. If half the energy used to prepare for the Pharaohs' resurrection had been directed to benefit the people, it would have been one of the world's paradises. Likewise, the Coptic Christians would have been well advised to expend their effort constructively instead of meticulously destroying the figures of the pagan gods. Today there's still more emphasis on maintaining the necropolises for the dead than on the living.

❄ ❄ ❄

At the Annual Spring NPS/Concessioners Meeting on April 23, 1979, views were exchanged and plans announced for the coming season. Superintendent Iverson announced that Pat O'Mary, Concessioners Specialist, was being transferred to Denver and Dick Munro, the Management Assistant, was retiring for medical reasons arising out of a car accident when he was hit by a truck on an icy road. No criticism was expressed of any of our concession operations for the previous year. In fact, Superintendent Iverson had publicly lauded GPI's performance and cheered our continuance as the concessioner.

As a result of the National Park Services purchase of the assets of the Yellowstone Park Company, the General Accounting Office made a survey of these newly acquired assets. They were very critical of the lack of adequate fire and safety conditions and censured the National Park Service for their lack of enforcement.

As a result, Director William Whalen issued a memorandum requiring the Park Service to make a thorough inspection of all park and concessions facilities, particularly where there were older buildings. This was to be a special survey over and above the annual fire and safety inspection programs which had been made once or twice each season.

On September 1, 1979, a team of 16 people arrived at Glacier Park headquarters to conduct a survey of the Park's and our facilities. We all met in the Park Service conference room. I had arranged to have Cy Stevenson, our retired Chief Engineer, join us as he was the most knowledgeable person concerning our facilities.

At this meeting, it was agreed that we would all meet again in five days at which time this survey team would give us an oral report alerting us as to what to expect from their written report. Their first stop was to be at our largest hotel at Many Glacier.

That night, I received a call from Cy Stevenson saying, "I don't know what I can contribute. This gang of 16 arrived at the hotel and scattered like a covey of quail. Each one has a notebook and is making his own inspection."

Five days later we all assembled in the Park Service conference room, as agreed, to hear the preliminary reports but none were forthcoming. Despite our protests no recommendations were made. The reason became obvious later. There had been no coordination and no one knew what was in the 16 notebooks. Both the Superintendent and I protested without avail.

Three months later we received a 300 page report from the Park Service Regional Office. It was one of the most biased reports initiated to discredit our operation. For example, they indicated that the facilities and general condition at the Rising Sun Motel were in good condition but the matching photograph was of a series of plastic bags used by the cabin crew to pick up trash in the cabins. These bags were then left behind the laundry to be picked up by the garbage trucks. This photograph was cited as evidence of our bad housekeeping at the cabins.

The facilities at Swiftcurrent were stated to be generally in good shape but the photograph was of a table which required repainting of its splashboard. The report called for extensive replacement of pots, pans and dishes which had nothing to do with fire and safety of the facilities. I strongly objected to the report. Its objective was to discredit our operation and not just to ascertain fire and safety hazards.

Upon delivery of this 300 page report, Buddy Surles, from Washington, D.C., James B. Johnson, Assistant Regional Director, and John Spurgeon, Chief of Concessions, both from the Denver Regional Office, met with me in Glacier. I advised them that

I thought the demands were excessive and as the projected costs for the fire and safety requirements were estimated to be $1,750,000, I could not make the investment without a new contract.

I called attention to the fact that I only had five years remaining on my contract and the law provided that I could not be required to make an investment without a reasonable opportunity to make a return on the investment. I pointed out that this $1,750,000 would not produce an additional dollar of revenue.

They said, that it would not be possible to approve a new contract in the time allotted. They suggested that they extend my present contract. I agreed to proceed upon their assurances that my contract would be extended.

The report was so extreme that Superintendent Iverson set up his own task force consisting of a retired fire chief, Bill Pentila, a retired state fire marshall and a safety engineer out of Denver who had made prior inspections of our facilities for the Park Service.

I was called to fly up from Tucson, Arizona, for this urgent meeting. The meeting started at 9:00 a.m. Superintendent Iverson announced that he had a Rotary Club meeting and departed at 10:30 a.m. This task force was out only two days and returned. It was too cold to spend any more time.

On January 16, 1980, I received their preliminary report. The demands were onerous but more reasonable than the 300 page report. However, that was not the end; Superintendent Iverson advised me that those were the interim demands but I still had to comply with all the recommendations of the 300 page report or I would not be permitted to open.

I protested that this was impossible as there were 20-

foot snow drifts at Many Glacier and as temperatures dropped to 30-35 degrees below zero, I could not get a qualified crew in there to complete the work before opening date on June 7th.

Glen Bean, the Regional Director, and John Spurgeon from the Denver office, flew to Tucson with a five-year extension. They stated that the maximum term of a contract was 30 years and since my contract was for 25 years, they could not give me more than a five-year extension. I protested but agreed to proceed until they showed me the so-called extension. It was not an extension as it contained many new provisions. I refused to accept it and demanded a long-term contract if I was to proceed. They agreed but when the proposal was released, they had added another three million dollars of improvements.

When they insisted that the work had to be performed, contract or no contract, I contacted my congressman, Morris K. Udall, Chairman of the House Interior and Insular Affairs Committee. Mo called Secretary Andrus and a meeting was set up with an assistant secretary, Robert L. Herbst, two of his staff members, Director Bill Whalen, Assistant Director Jim Tobin and Buddy Surles. Mo sent the Committee counsel, Lee MacIlvain, with me. This was a signal that he expected fair treatment. The meeting adjourned and Surles, MacIlvain and I worked out what would be required to be completed by the time we opened and what could be delayed. It was still onerous but possible.

The Park Service was to proceed with notice for a new contract and I was to start on the Life/Safety Programs.

As if I did not have enough problems I had to fire the newly hired Chief Engineer because he was padding purchase orders for equipment. Ray Wyatt, the Location Engineer at Many Glacier, resigned as work started. We soon found out why. He had not drained about half of the hotel. We had 176 broken pipes in the walls and ceilings. Fire extinguishers had not been drained and had burst and the auxiliary steam pump for the fire sprinkler system suffered the same fate. It was a trying time and Many Glacier was only one of six locations that required changes to permit us to open on June 7th.

It was soon obvious that I would not get cooperation

from the Park Service but active opposition. When Dick Munro retired on medical disability, Superintendent Iverson appointed Robert Reyes as his replacement. Bob was third out of 10 on the eligibility list. He was also an Hispanic and entitled to preference. While the appointment was Iverson's, he acceded to Buddy Surles' demand to appoint Joe Shellenberger. Shellenberger was retired and not in the Park Service. He was appointed as a ranger and assigned as management assistant in charge of concessions. He had never been to Glacier before. Bob Reyes planned to file a complaint of discrimination but finally decided against it. He said to me, "I'm told that if I do, my career with the Park Service will be ended." The Service placated him by appointing him as the Superintendent of a small monument.

C. W. Brinck had been the sanitarian assigned by the Public Health Department for the past two seasons. He was told to return and a house was assigned to him. Schellenberger remanded this and had James Lodge, whom he had worked with in the State of Washington, assigned as the Sanitarian.

Although we were fighting against time to comply with the Park Service demands, we were subjected to constant inspections. Some lasting up to six hours extended throughout the season. The new sanitarian was obsessed with the temperature of food. Anything between 45 and 140 degrees was considered dangerous. He would go into a refrigerator and insert a thermometer and regardless of when the food had been stored, we would be written up for improper storage. On one occasion, he went into the dining room and stuck a thermometer into a guest's plate of food. While previously we had always been scored in the middle- to upper-90s, we were then scored at 50 to 60 and usually accompanied by a dissertation from the Sanitation Code.

One chef with over 40 years' experience in top restaurants resigned rather than be subjected to this harassment. Another with 45 years' experience threatened to resign if he had to deal with the sanitarian. We solved the impasse by having the storekeeper deal with the sanitarian.

James Miller, concessions specialist, was sent from Yellowstone to assist in inspections. He was known in Yellowstone as a "nitpicker." We found him even more disagreeable. His inspections often lasted six hours and included taking pictures during mealtimes, disrupting service and antagonizing employees and guests. He often went into kitchens when no one was present and without notice. I protested this to his superiors without result.

Miller based his actions on the government's right to make unannounced inspections. I told him unannounced did not permit surreptitious entry. He also persisted in issuing instructions to managers. One young inexperienced manager painted the front of a coffee shop without my permission and in a color objected to by the Park Service.

The operation in the summer of 1980 was of harassment. This was a new experience for me as we had always cooperated with the Park Service. I had protested the consistent inspections and criticisms which our employees were subjected to as we attempted to serve our guests and respond to the demands of the Park Service. Superintendent Iverson and Shellenberger called me into the office and threatened to give me an unsatisfactory rating. I replied that I thought we were entitled to cooperation and assistance but had only had criticism and obstacles from Park Service personnel. That in times past the Park Service had cooperated but the attitude now appeared to be one of opposition.

In response, Superintendent Iverson wrote me a letter dated July 11, 1980:

> You have often lamented the decline and deterioration of relationships between the National Park Service and concessioners throughout the system. There could be numerous explanations for this change, but the change is not necessarily bad. We have evolved from a sort of buddy system to a more professional relationship. The Service now employs more specialists and professionals, i.e., sanitarians, law enforcement specialists, concessions specialists, building fire experts. You are encountering these professional people more often and obviously resent, not least regards this as an intrusion into your domain.

The professionalism the Superintendent referred to is exemplified in Glacier concessions specialist Pat O'Mary.

Pat was an auditor in the Yosemite Company accounting office when I directed those operations. I complained to the Controller, Roger Sandberg, about his performance. He was later released by the Yosemite Company when MCA purchased the company. He then was assigned to Glacier as a "concessions specialist."

Buddy Surles, the Chief of Concessions in the Washington Office, had a brief experience in the guest ranch business and went broke. He then became a concessions specialist in Yellowstone and then was assigned as Chief of Concessions in the Washington Office.

Superintendent Iverson's letter continued:

> In bygone days park concessions operated more independently. Let's face it, some of the big companies, Union Pacific, Great Northern and Santa Fe Railroads barely acknowledged the presence of the National Park Service. They played a dominant role in establishing some of the parks, provided a great service to the public but at the same time displayed a possessory interest in the real estate.
>
> During George Hartzog's era, this term "partnership" between concessioners and the National Park Service became a pet phrase. I think it was not so much an acknowledgment of the concessioner's role as a new assertion of NPS responsibility. Today, the Service has reached, in my opinion, a proper position of responsibility.

The Park Service issued a prospectus calling for a new contract. It called for not only the $1,750,000 life/safety program, but for improvements estimated to cost another $3,000,000.

There were two responses to the prospectus: ours as a satisfactory concessioner entitled to a preferential right of renewal under the law; and one from a newly formed corporation made up of some of our past and present employees. They were disqualified as ineligible since their assets consisted of $3,500 and pledges from other employees of another $8,000 and with no history of having supervised a major business operation.

It was obvious to me that continued operation with the present National Park Service was impossible so I began negotiations to sell the stock of Glacier Park Inc. to the Del

E. Webb Corp. The stockholders signed a contract for the sale of their stock. Del Webb signed with two conditions. They had to sell their half-interest in the Rosenzweig Center in Phoenix or get permission from a consortium of banks to whom they were indebted for loans for two hotel casinos in Atlantic city.

I immediately notified the Director of the intention to sell as required by our contract.

On September 1, 1980, I telephoned Lorraine Mintzmyer, Regional Director in Denver, and asked if I could come to Denver to negotiate a contract. I told her I had reservations to take my wife to China starting September 10th. She said she needed 30 days to evaluate the responses to the prospectus. I called to her attention that ours was the only acceptable response and that we had a preferential right to a renewal under the law.

Mrs. Mintzmyer said she would not be able to negotiate until the end of September and urged me to continue with our travel plans. I left for China.

On September 24, 1980, the Denver Regional Office wrote me as follows:

Dear Mr. Hummel:

We have reviewed the proposal submitted on August 26, 1980, by Glacier Park Inc. for the negotiation of a contract for the operation of accommodations, facilities and services within Glacier National Park.

While Glacier Park Inc.'s proposal offers some additional commitment to maintain and improve facilities, it does not provide sufficient consideration to justify abandonment of the present contract and entering into a new long-term contact. Our position is, therefore, that the present contract with Glacier Park Inc. should remain in effect for the time being.

Sincerely yours,
James B. Thompson
Acting Regional Director
Rocky Mountain Region.
Enclosure: letter from R. E. Dickenson
dated September 24, 1980.

Director Dickenson's letter, also dated September 24, 1980, addressed to David L. Johnson, Executive Vice President, Del Webb Recreational Properties Inc.

Dear Mr. Johnson:

The National Park Service has determined through extensive analysis that a long-term contract is needed for a private operation to economically return the investment required to accomplish improvements in concessions facilities and services in Glacier National Park.

In accordance with the stated intention of Del E. Webb Corp. to purchase the stock of Glacier Park Inc. for a term of 25 years, providing that the agreed-to contract contains adequate consideration from the government's interest to justify the length of term, and further provided the stock transfers of Glacier Park Inc. to Del Webb is consummated.

Sincerely,
Russell E. Dickenson, Director.

It should be noted that the Park Service letter to me states that "it does not provide sufficient consideration to ... enter into a long-term contract." And the same day Director Dickenson says if Del Webb buys Glacier Park Inc.'s stock, there is justification for a 25 year contract. Note that both letters refer to the same contract. Del E. Webb Corp. never responded to the prospectus and had no standing except Glacier Park Inc.'s and then only if they bought its stock!

John Spurgeon, Regional Concessions Specialist, advised the press that they had rejected both responses to the prospectus. On October 1st, Lorraine Mintzmyer advised the press that Glacier National Park and her staff had recommended that the proposal not be accepted.

It had already been agreed that the expenditure of $1,750,000 for the life/safety program alone was justification for a long-term contract by Associate Director Daniel Tobin in a letter to me dated August 10, 1980. Glacier Park Inc., in its response, also had agreed to the improvements which the Park Service had estimated to cost an additional $3,000,000.

Lorraine Mintzmyer refused to negotiate with me stating she "would rather negotiate with Del Webb." I advised her that Del Webb had not responded to the prospectus and until they bought Glacier Park Inc.'s stock, they had no standing. She still refused to negotiate with me. As Rex Maughan, Chairman of the Conference of National Park

Concessioners, had represented me while I was in China, I called him and told him to have Director Dickenson straighten out Mintzmyer or I would sue the Park Service.

As a result, Lorraine Mintzmyer wrote me on October 10th, 1980, establishing October 17-18th to negotiate a contract stating:

> Since the proposed sales agreement for the transfer of stock to Del E. Webb states that the terms of the negotiated contract must be agreeable to Webb we assume a representative of Del Webb will be present.

On the same day, Mintzmyer wrote Del Webb,

> "We hope to begin negotiations for a new concessions contract for Glacier with Del E. Webb Corp. as soon as possible. We propose to meet with you and other Del E. Webb representatives in Denver."

We met in Denver Colorado, and negotiated a contract for 25 years based on Glacier Park Inc.'s proposal, the same proposal which their office had advised did not contain sufficient consideration to justify a new long-term contract and that we would have to continue on the contract with the five years still remaining.

On October 22, 1980, I signed, on behalf of Glacier Park Inc., a 25-year contract with the National Park Service. It was then submitted, as required by law, to the congressional committees for 60 days to allow them to comment.

The Glacier Park Foundation, whose proposal had been rejected, sued the National Park Service to enjoin them from signing the contract with Glacier Park Inc., challenging the right of the National Park Service to negotiate a contract with Glacier Park Inc., after having rejected Glacier Park Inc.'s proposal.

A hearing was conducted before the United States District Court in Missoula, Montana, and John Spurgeon, chief of concessions of the Denver Regional Office, was called as an adverse witness by the Foundation. John Spurgeon admitted under oath before the court that he had used the term "rejected" as related to Glacier Park Inc.'s proposal in talking to the press, but denied that it was a real rejection.

It is obvious that these maneuverings by the Regional

Director's office were for the purpose of denying Glacier Park Inc.'s right to a new contract, which by law Glacier Park Inc. had a preferential right as it had been declared by the Park Service to be a satisfactory concession. Rex Maughan warned the National Park Service that they were proceeding illegally and that their position could not be sustained. At the close of Glacier Park Foundation's case and before any testimony was submitted on behalf of Glacier Park Inc., on a motion for a directed verdict, the district judge denied the Foundation's request for an injunction.

Del E. Webb Corporation notified the National Park Service that it was dropping its attempt to purchase the stock of Glacier Park Inc. This occurred when the Del E. Webb Corporation was unable to sell their interest in the Rosenzweig Center in Phoenix, Arizona, and the refusal of their bankers to permit Del E. Webb to incur any more debt. These were the conditions which would permit the Del E. Webb Corporation to back out of the contract to purchase Glacier Park Inc.'s stock. Buddy Surles, chief of concessions in Washington, D.C., had made the statement to Rex Maughan that they had no intention of signing a contract with Glacier Park Inc. unless we sold our stock to the Del E. Web Corporation. When this occurred, Rex Maughan, on behalf of Glacier Park Inc., entered negotiations with Greyhound Food Management company to purchase Glacier Park Inc.'s stock. This deal was successfully negotiated and agreements signed to take over all the stock of Glacier Park Inc.

After Glacier Park Foundation lost its bid for an injunction in the United States District Court, they appealed to the Ninth Circuit Court of Appeals in San Francisco questioning the National Park Service's right to negotiate a contract with Glacier Park Inc., after having announced that they had rejected our proposal. The Ninth Circuit Court of Appeals supported the Foundation's objection and advised the National Park Service that they were remanding it to the District Court to determine whether or not the decision had been made on the merits of the case. And if they had, the Park Service would be required to solicit new proposals, as they had violated their own regulations.

The United States District Court reset the case for trial in Great Falls, Montana, before Judge Hatfield. The court called the session to order with all parties present for trial. This included the United States Attorney's office, attorneys for the National Park Service, attorneys representing Glacier Park Inc. and attorneys for the Glacier Foundation. In addition, there were some 12 witnesses. After the court permitted opening statements and called for the Foundation to put on its first witness, the court shocked the entire group by asking what interest Greyhound had in this case. They were advised that Greyhound owned the stock of Glacier Park Inc., whereupon Judge Hatfield said that he owned $100 worth of Greyhound stock which he had inherited from his mother and he recessed the court for five minutes; went back to his chambers, returned immediately with a law book in his hand, read a decision and disqualified himself. This, after all the parties had been notified, comprehensive briefs filed and the case set for trial.

The case was reset several months later before U.S. District Judge Cordova, who had been called in to hear the case. Upon submission of all of the evidence, including a great deal of irrelevant material, the judge found for the National Park Service which permitted them to proceed with the contract which Glacier Park Inc. had negotiated. Shortly thereafter, in March 1981, Glacier Park Inc. stockholders sold all their stock to Greyhound Food Management company. Thus ended my 47-year career that had been praised as exemplary and which opened expanded opportunities through Park Service intervention to take over other concessions in Mt. McKinley and Glacier National Park. There was no bar to action — both legal and illegal — to discredit me when government bureaucrats were antagonized.

Genee's Christmas Letter, 1979:

The holiday season is fast approaching despite our balmy 70 degree days. We were pleased to see it snow in Colorado as we are planning to ski at Aspen the week before Christmas (there was no snow for our last visit). David will have completed his pre-vet course in time for him and Diane to join us.

There was lots to do at our new home to be ready for Donna's marriage to John Bodie on February 17. It turned out to be a perfect day for an outdoor wedding and reception. After a Mexico City honey moon, they returned to Los Angeles where they both worked for Hughes Aircraft. They gave notice and in June joined Glacier Park Co., Inc., Donna as financial planner and assistant manager of Glacier Park Lodge, John as assistant to the vice president of marketing. Now they are settling into a new home in Tucson.

We left for Glacier in early May as we opened Glacier Park Lodge pre-season for the film crew of Cimino's "HEAVEN'S GATE." Weather was exceptionally good ameliorating the difficulties of an inexperienced crew, physical hotel problems after a severe winter, and changing demands of the movie company. It was an "experience." The excessive TV coverage of the supposed gas shortage slowed our June auto visitation, but bus and train tours increased enough to make up the loss and we felt lucky to have matched last season. More and more government regulation makes operation in the Park less and less attractive and takes much of the joy out of running the Park.

Char and John worked in the Tucson office last spring, bought and fixed up rental property. They jointly managed Lake McDonald Lodge in Glacier last summer and are spending this winter there. Cliff helped a friend repair his house last winter, spent time in the wilderness south of Glacier this summer. His plans are still indefinite.

Donna, John, Genee and Don went on a Mediterranean Cruise in November. There were stops at Turkey, Malta, Crete and Rhodes, where ancient civilizations flourished in elegant splendor. We also had glimpses of Athens, Rome and Florence. It was all too brief, but fascinating.

Now as we write, hostages are still being held in Teheran. Religion, that could bring peace, brings only terror and threat. Thousands are starving in Cambodia. We seem far away from political solutions. As the world becomes more explosive, the closeness and caring among friends seems ever more precious.

❄ ❄ ❄

Genee's Christmas Letter, 1980-81:

This early November finds us in a holiday mood ready to send you our warmest greetings and catch you up with 1980 and 1981. If you think we missed you last Christmas, we did. There was such turmoil in the Hummel family that we could not quite get into the Christmas Spirit. It all culminated this year when we disposed of our operations in Glacier National Park, closing 46years as a concessioner. Fun had given way to frustration as government regulations overwhelmed us and service to people have become subservient to protecting animals and ecosystems. Greyhound acquired our Glacier operation in March of this year. This followed the tragic death of our only son, Cliff, in a powered hang-glider accident in Kalispell on February 11th. It's hard to accept why one who had so much to offer was allowed so little time.

It was not all heartbreak and frustration last year. The two of us had a most interesting trip to China in September. It was too controlled, but we saw the famed palaces in Peking, the unbelievable Great Wall, the bustling Shanghai waterway. Don even found the old hotel in which he stayed during World War II. Kweilin, with its up and down mountains, was even more picturesque than he remembered. We trained, bussed, and boated mixing with the happy and responsive Chinese people.

Last Christmas we had a good holiday with Diane and Dave in Houston. In March the Conference of National Park Concessioners made Don President Emeritus. We have just returned from the mid-year conference meeting in Banff, Canada. This summer Don was consultant to Greyhound, a far easier experience giving advice than being responsible for all the results. We are ambivalent about the sale, but on balance, believe it was the right thing to do. Our future is uncertain as we do not want to completely retire.

Donna was controller for Glacier until this summer when she was made assistant to the president for finance. Her husband, John Bodie, is assistant to the purchasing director. They are ambivalent about their future. Char and John have bought a home in Coram, just outside Glacier Park, and have been busy raising animals and renovating their property. Diane has decided she wants to study more dance and theater. Dave finished his pre-veterinary program, but decided not to continue when there was so little hope of getting into a vet school for several years. Now he, too, is uncertain. They had just returned from a six week trip to France and will not be joining the rest of the family on our December trip to South Africa.

❄ ❄ ❄

Genee's Christmas Letter, 1982:

This holiday will find us separated; Bodies and Ellises opting to have a quiet Christmas in their own homes. We two fly to Montana to join Char and John and our first grandchild, Julian Hummel-Casserley, born on October 12th.

Don is still involved in national park affairs in a consulting capacity. We attended the Washington Conference and he is now on the Board of Directors of Hamilton Stores, Yellowstone. Genee continues with water color classes, house projects, and book review.

Diane has become interested in drama, studying diligently (she and Genee flew to New York for a theater binge). Dave is working on commercial real estate in Houston. Donna and John have opened a Property Management office in Tucson.

Our first summer without direct responsibility went surprisingly fast. There was work on the Lake McDonald cabin, and our first summer vacation ever, with a trip to the Balkans. We visited Yugoslavia, Bulgaria, Romania, Hungary, returning through Vienna, Austria. They were beautiful countries, but reflect the stultifying effects of Communist suppression.

We arrived in Tucson later than usual, staying for a surprise birthday party for Don's 75th, and to welcome the new baby. Now, Tucson has for the first time honored its pioneers, Don among them, in a permanent plaza with appropriate plaques. He was also selected for the first Tucson High School Hall of Fame. He was one of five, including three teachers and astronaut Frank Borman. Honors a long time coming that really pleased us.

We hope the new Year strengthens our economy with less politics and greater attention to solving our national problems; with restoration of sanity by the elimination of terrorism, poisoning and unreasoning assault on innocent people and the return of Peace on Earth, Good Will to Men.

❉ ❉ ❉

29

Incorporation of Conference of National Park Concessioners

Attempts to Circumvent the Conference Representation

IN EARLY 1975, the Conference of National Park Concessioners voted to incorporate as a non-profit organization. The informal structure that had been followed over the years was not considered adequate in view of the problems we were having with various congressional committees and the fact that a new law required that any organization which in any manner attempted to influence legislation, was considered to be a lobbying organization and had to register as a lobbyist.

As a result of this we instructed Edward M. Lightfoot, who had been hired as our Washington representative, to prepare Articles of Incorporation for approval by the membership. These were submitted on February 3, 1975. In addition to the Articles, Ed Lightfoot presented a proposed set of By-Laws. I objected to the By-Laws as departing from the normal organizational structure in that they vested the day-to-day administration and management of the Conference in an executive director, a radical departure from the historic conduct of the Conference's business.

The By-Laws specified that the Chairman was not charged with executive or administrative responsibilities in the management and continuing conduct of the daily affairs of the Conference. They stated that he was only the chief policy spokesman. This placed the executive director, a hired staff member, in control of the conference on all administrative matters. This obviously was not consistent, in that the responsibility should have been vested in the position elected by the Board of Directors; namely the Chairman.

I changed the By-Laws to read:

> The Chairman is charged with the executive and administrative responsibilities in the management and continuing conduct of the affairs of the Conference. He shall be the chief policy spokesman for the Conference.

I pointed out that there is a great difference in having responsibility for and actually performing the administrative duties. The Chairman, as the top elected office, can delegate the performance of any of these responsibilities, but he is still responsible. This was just one of the changes that I proposed in the By-Laws before the adoption by the Conference. The attempt to put control in the executive director alerted me to the fact that there was to be a struggle ahead as to who would make the Conference decisions. This matter was to surface again at a later date.

When Gary Everhardt was named the Director of the National Park Service, I contacted him as Chairman of the Conference and asked for an opportunity to discuss the problems we were facing in the relationship between the Conference and the Service. I tried on some six different occasions to arrange a meeting with Director Everhardt, but he declined to set a meeting date. I offered him the Conference's full support and advised that in the past we had always conducted Conference affairs through the Chairman and that the Conference position had always been the collective voice of the concessioners. After many attempts, Ed Lightfoot and I met with Director Everhardt in an attempt to improve the relationships.

At this meeting the Director requested that the Conference support legislation which would permit the use of franchise fees to maintain government buildings. This was identified as the Stevens Bill, but instead of providing funds for the maintenance of government buildings, it provided for the use of franchise fees to buy concessioners' possessory interests. This was an entirely different bill than the one we had discussed with the Director. It would permit the Park Service to buy out the concessioner without Congressional appropriations.

Phillip Stewart, who had been in charge of land acquisition, was named as our contact to discuss all contract changes. Stewart was not only arbitrary, but was also unfamiliar with the background of the relationships between the Conference and the Park Service. Most of our members objected violently to negotiating with Mr. Stewart, as he was inflexible and arbitrary. All prior Directors had agreed to submit proposed contract language changes to the Conference for comment before adoption. This was not followed under the Everhardt regime. Proposed contract changes were submitted as a *fait accompli* without any opportunity to discuss their relevance or effect on the concessioners' operations or their compliance with Public Law 89-249.

On March 10, 1976, I met with Lightfoot and Secretary Reed and Ms. Montinko (whose first name I don't recall), Assistant Solicitor for the Park Service. We discussed our problems of communicating with Director Everhardt. This was deplored by Assistant Secretary Reed. He suggested that we meet in Denver to discuss the rising problem. We welcomed this, but the meeting was never scheduled and did not take place even though promised by Assistant Secretary Reed.

Edward Lightfoot met with Director Everhardt and newly appointed Associate Director William Briggle. Lightfoot advised them that he had heard from over half of the concessioners that they could not deal with Phillip O. Stewart, and that relations would be bad as long as Stewart remained in that position. Director Everhardt responded that he (the Director) could not talk with me. Lightfoot responded that the quid pro quo for excluding Stewart was Hummel's expulsion as Chairman of the Conference. This was without authority from the Conference and consistent with Lightfoot's attempts to make the Washington representative the Conference spokesman. There was agreement to meet and a meeting was scheduled.

The principal reason for the deteriorating relationship between the Conference was the concessioners' inability to work with Phillip Stewart, who was now designated as the Concessions Management Representative. The Park Service released its policy to the effect that:

> If adequate facilities exist or can be developed to meet people's commercial needs outside park boundaries, such facilities will not be provided in the park.

Director Everhardt denied that the policy was to be applied nationwide but that it was to be administered selectively, park-by-park. We questioned this interpretation by pointing out that present plans called for the reduction of facilities in Zion, Bryce, North Rim of the Grand Canyon and the Lassen Closure, the reduction of facilities in Mammoth Cave and the proposal to remove some so-called nonessential facilities from Yosemite. The Master Plan for Yellowstone called for phasing out of several locations.

Director Everhardt's attention was directed to Master Plans that were being proposed without concessioner participation although they vitally affected the concessioners' operations. All prior Directors had provided for some, if sporadic, concessioner participation at the beginning before the plans were approved. Director Everhardt said the concessioners' role should be the same as the general public's. It was also pointed out to the Director that the approach to franchise fees had been drastically changed, from providing good services at reasonable rates to requiring a six percent return to the government on the appreciated value of all government buildings and that this was contrary to the law.

Other principal objections with Director Everhardt's administration were the proposed reduction of contract terms to five to 10 years and the fact that he had asserted that the granting of possessory interest was not required, as the government had the option to waive its inclusion. When asked at the meeting whether he supported the concept of possessory interest, he refused to reply. These were just a few of the problems that we had with the Everhardt regime.

On September 2, 1976, at Hamilton Stores in West Yellowstone, Montana, I reported to a specially called meeting of the Board of Directors. I reported that a request had been received from Director Everhardt and Deputy Director Briggle, that representatives of the Conference meet with Deputy Director Briggle to discuss ways and means of improving communications between the Conference and the Park Service. This oral request had been made to Executive Director Lightfoot and was passed on orally by him to me. It specifically included a stated desire that neither Director Everhardt nor Chairman Hummel be present at this proposed meeting.

It was agreed by the Board of Directors that Director Hardy and Director Vern Johnson, together with Executive Director Lightfoot, be instructed to arrange a meeting with the following instructions:

> 1) That no matter of substance would be discussed at the meeting.
> 2) That Director Everhardt and Acting Assistant Director Stewart and Chairman Hummel be excluded from this meeting.

The meeting with Deputy Director Briggle was held on September 27, 1976, in Dulles Airport in Washington, D.C. Vern Johnson, Trevor Povah and Ed Lightfoot represented the concessioners. The minutes of this meeting were reported as follows:

> Deputy Briggle was asked why he had asked for the meeting and what he thought it would accomplish and what, in his opinion, had caused the impasse in which the Conference and the Service found itself. The answer was:
> Obvious answer — there are personality clashes in this — we recognize Hummel has been an outstanding member and Chairman of the Conference almost since its conception. He has more than satisfactorily operated several of our finest concession operations. He literally has more background and knowledge regarding the concessions operations and problems than anyone else today. His devotion to the concession cause is legendary and we wish we could work with him and utilize his wealth of information he holds. He is highly respected for his knowledge and his views should be considered, but there appears to be an uncompromising attitude by Hummel that we can no longer accept. There must be some compromise on some issues. Hummel represents two sets of elements; himself and the Conference. There needs to be an independent leader of the group who has no personal axe to grind. We are concerned about the Conference really representing all concessioners as long as Hummel is in the Chair. Hummel is brilliant, but dogmatic. The Conference needs to give Ed Lightfoot more authority so he can act for them. He is here; he gets along very well with Gary. The Hummel problem is of

course aggravated by Everhardt, who is a compromiser. He plays on human relations. A specific system of positive communication should be developed using your Washington office (Executive Director). If you need to change your rules, do so and change them.

Here again was a bid, with the help of the National Park Service, for the Executive Director to take over control as spokesman of the Conference and resolve the problems for the Conference, rather than through the Conference's elected Chairman. It should be noted that all these suggestions arose out of and were communicated by the Executive Director of the Conference. It appeared to me to be more than coincidence that this was consistent with the By-Laws proposed by the executive director for the Conference which I had objected to and the Conference had disapproved.

> The question was asked, "Why is Gary Everhardt so uptight?" Answer:
> He can't be pushed; he must be led. Hummel has tried to push him. Hummel doesn't seem to recognize nor want to recognize the N.P.S problems; also the N.P.S. personnel must be made aware that the concessioners are not bad people just because they are concessioners. The concessioners really need to police their own operations by establishing standards and insisting on adherence to those standards.

It should be noted that the Conference specifically repudiated a policy of policing its own members and that the chairman offered full support to Director Everhardt. I could not have pushed the Director as he had refused on several occasions to even talk with me.

> Deputy Briggle continued: The very essence of better communications is communication. You just can't refuse to talk, even under the very worst of circumstances and still hope to establish satisfactory communications.
> It was the Director not the Chairman that refused to talk.
> Question: Under what conditions will Everhardt relax his repeated statement, that he just won't talk more with Hummel?

Answer: The Conference must impress on Hummel that there is a problem; that he is a contributor to the problem and that to reopen a satisfactory discussion, there must be a capability and a desire to recognize the Park Service's side of the problem, and discuss it from both points of view.

Question: Why can't Everhardt more easily and quickly say "yes" or "no," and then stand by it?

Answer: It is the very nature of the guy — he ponders and ponders and ponders. He is a brilliant man, but he allows fear and concern of bad reactions somewhere to influence his actions.

Question: Why, after so many years of mutually satisfactory operations, do we suddenly have so many more costly, effort-consuming controls placed on us?

Briggle's answer: The pressure from outside groups, environmentalists and all, highlighted by Dingell/ Brooks Committee actions, and focused on the M.C.A. and Yellowstone situations have pressured Gary into the action being taken. The Conference has not endeavored to be of assistance, but has steadfastly, unpleasantly, objected to any proposed or adopted position. The Conference could help us a great deal in the Yellowstone Park Company situation.

Lightfoot: Why didn't you ask us to help you draft proposed contract language?

Answer: We should have, but unfortunately, this was done at the lowest ebb in our communications cycle. I acknowledge it was a mistake.

Question: Why has N.P.S. so suddenly, in the last 18 months, apparently acceded to the great pressure from the environmentalists?

Answer: We had to because it came to us from all sides, as well as from above.

Conclusions: He believed it showed progress. Everhardt believed, and Briggle concurred, that Hummel must be replaced by a less uncompromising Chairman. There was no positive action formulated regarding Phil Stewart's removal. The N.P.S. would like this or a similar group from the Conference to be perpetuated and to meet with them two or three times a year. A self-policing program that was enforced should be developed. Finally, a positive system of communications was needed. All communications both oral and written should flow through the Conference's Washington Office into the Executive Director's. This would expedite action.

This was an obvious bid to circumvent the Conference and its elected representatives and deal with a more amenable group.

The report was signed by Vern Johnson, Edward Lightfoot and Trevor S. Povah. Povah insisted that a letter of his to Lightfoot be appended to the meeting report which is quoted in part:

> I would like to go on record that although the minutes do not reflect this, we did not just listen to Bill's answers. We did discuss the issues and spoke out in favor of our Chairman's position. Nobody can deny that our Chairman knows more of the concession system policy, history and why the original policies were enacted than Don Hummel. He has also been the one person who has devoted more time and effort to the concessioners' problems than any one of us in the concessions business today. I am sure everyone agrees we all appreciate Don's hard work and the continued help he will give us all in the future.
>
> /s/ Trevor Povah

It had become obvious to me that the Conference was making no progress with Director Everhardt. I had made up my mind that at the next meeting I would decline to be a candidate for Chairman of the Conference, but when it became obvious to me that the National Park Service, with some collaboration from our Executive Director, was attempting to push me out of representing the Conference, I decided that this was the Conference's decision, and not the National Park Service's nor our Washington representative. I therefore ran for office again and was re-elected Chairman of the Conference. I resented the attempt by the National Park Service to dictate who would represent the Conference of National Park Concessioners. This was extremely important as the policies being enacted and the contract changes that were being proposed, all were at the concessioners' expense. They jeopardized the concessioner's security of his investment, which Public Law 89-249 attempted to guarantee. The policy of limitation, exclusion and removal of concessioner facilities, was in full swing.

30

Committee on Government Operations
and
Committee on Small Business

WHILE THE Interior and Insular Affairs Committee was the proper committee to handle all matters concerning the National Parks, confusion resulted when a number of other committees got in on the act. One of these was the Conservation, Energy and Natural Resources Subcommittee; and the Small Business Subcommittee on Government Operations. This was often referred to as "The Dingell Committee." John Dingell is greatly opposed to the concession policies adopted by Congress in Public law 89-249. This subcommittee was part of the Government Operations Committee, chaired by Jack Brooks. You will recall it was Jack Brooks who attempted, but was unsuccessful, in having President L. B. Johnson veto Public Law 89-249, which established the concessions policies.

The Committee on Government Operations was held on July 25, 1975, and John D. Dingell presided at the hearing. The subject of the hearing was National Park Service management of concession operations. It should be of interest to note the opening statement by Congressman Dingell, as I believe it adequately expresses the climate that existed when this committee held its hearing. His statement is as follows:

> I think the nature of the matter before us demonstrates gross indifference of the National Park Service of its responsibilities under the law, and one of the functions of this gathering today is hopefully to procure — I must confess I say this with some doubt — statements from the Park Service indicating a change in the handling of their responsibilities to protect the public interest from predaceous actions of the concessioners.
>
> The Chair is delighted to acknowledge at this time

the Chairman of the distinguished Government Operations Committee, who is a very good friend of us all here. We are certainly glad you are here, Mr. Chairman, and if you would like, we would be glad to have you join us.

Jack Brooks, Chairman of the Committee on Government Operations, said:

> I am going to have to go to another meeting, but I would just like to commend you, Mr. Dingell, and Mr. Moorehead, for this look at the concessions operations of the National Park Service, which for 20 years has been a disgrace. I tell you, I know from personal experience and personal investigation, that the Park Service gives, not by trade or by sale, but by inheritance, concession rights to the major park facilities in the United States. Families just inherit them from generation to generation, and there is no refuting the evidence. It has been clearly laid out before us. I am very delighted that both committees are now looking at it. It may be that now, on a bipartisan basis, we can reestablish some kind of equitable competition in the granting of these concessions and help protect the rights of people who drive with their kids to see the beauties of this nation.

Mr. Dingell:
> Mr. Chairman, we are in entire agreement with you. We would be delighted if you would sit with us. I believe your thoughts and views are certainly identical with my own on these thoughts and viewpoints.

Mr. Brooks:
> Well, I have confidence in you — get after them, John. My theory is, "if they won't follow the law, maybe you can cut their appropriations." We can get the Appropriations Committee in here with us as well. Surely the Park Service will pay some attention to Congress, now that we have Republican and Democratic awareness of the problem of third generation and fourth generation concession operators.

Mr. Dingell:
> Mr. Chairman, you echo our thoughts. As a matter of fact, you say them first. We are proud of you, Mr. Chairman. Thank you very much for being with us.

Mr. Brooks:
> I want it to be a fair and objective hearing.

This exchange did not impress us that we would have a fair and objective hearing!

> Honorable William S. Moorhead, Chairman, Conservation, Energy and Natural Resources Subcommittee of the Committee on Government Operation:
> Mr. Chairman, I would first like to commend you and my predecessor, Mr. Reuss, for the hearings you held last year. I think they have already had some results. I would also like to join you in commending the G.A.O. and I want to welcome them before this joint hearing. We appreciate the amount of time and effort the G.A.O. has put forth in carrying out a request to have them evaluate the National Park Service concession operations.

(Note: The G.A.O. has always objected to the terms and negotiation of concession contracts. They expressed this at hearings on Public Law 89-249, but were overruled by Congress.)

Mr. Henry Eschwege, Director, Resource and Economic Development Division, G.A.O., testified next on concession operations:

> The Concessions Policy Act of 1965 established policies and procedures for administering concession operations in the National Parks. In essence, this act said concession operations should be limited to those necessary and appropriate for public use and enjoyment, while maintaining the preservation and the conservation of the park areas.

He stated that the Park Service had no guidelines to judge the adequacy of franchise fees, and acceptable rate of return for concessioners. Because of these shortcomings, the Park Service could not determine whether the visitors, the concessioners and the government were being treated equitably. Mr. Eschwege testified that, based on his review of the concession operation at Yosemite National Park, he concluded that the Park Service does not have sufficient information to determine whether existing concessioners are performing satisfactorily and, therefore, are entitled to consideration when the contract is expanded or renewed. He criticized having one large business control all the concessions in the parks, stating that from a practical point of view, the Service cannot close down the concessioner to force compliance, because the concessioner's sizable investment makes it difficult for the Service to obtain funds to buy them out. He recommended that the Park Service request the concessioner to waive his possessory interest, stating that this was proper under the act. He said:

> We believe that the Act allows the Park Service to institute a policy of asking the concessioner to waive his possessory interest. This would obviate some of the problems of acquiring concessioner facilities.

He further testified that the Concessions Policy Act encourages continuity in concession operations; that if Congress wished to provide for more competition in the award and renewal of such contracts, it could do so by encouraging construction of facilities by the government whenever possible, lessening potential funding problems in buying out large concession interests and by amending the Act to limit preferential renewal rights.

As Chairman of the Conference of National Park Concessioners, I testified before the Committee. I pointed out that I had testified before a number of congressional committees and that the concessions movement had probably been investigated more than any contractor for government services in the history of the country. Its policies had been challenged on at least three separate occasions, two of them before congressional committees and, despite any weaknesses the system may have, that the system has, on each occasion, been reaffirmed.

The question was raised as to the concessioner's rights in government improvements. The National Park Service had announced a change of policy, under which the concessioners would no longer be permitted to acquire possessory interest in government improvements. I testified that this attempt to deny recognition of concessioner's interests flies in the face of the congressional act granting it in Public Law 89-249, and that it had the joint support of the Department of the Interior, the National Park Service and the concessioners. It was designed to enable the concessioner to provide accommodations desired by the public and approved by the National Park Service. I testified that attempts to reverse what the Interior and Insular Committee had provided and which had become part of the law, had resulted in great confusion. I read from a letter written by the Honorable Morris K. Udall addressed to his brother, Secretary of the Interior Stuart Udall, and I quote:

> Implementation of Public Law 89-249 has been one of my more frustrating experiences since coming to Washington. To pass a bill with overwhelming support, send it to the President and then get an approval which sounds like a veto, and finally for the administering agency to extract the opposite meaning from what was intended by its author, has left me a little shaken. I thought in view of this whole history, which seems to me to go unchecked, I would call your attention to the latest development and provide you with the copies of the letter by Mr. Cross and the memorandum prepared by Mr. Hoss.

In a letter, dated June 21, 1968 Congressman Udall wrote the Secretary as follows:

> At the heart of this exchange, of course, is the question of whether the Park Service is following both the letter and intent of Public Law 89-249. In my judgment, as author of the act, it is not. It seems to me that the Park Service position on length of contract, which was criticized here this morning, as well as on the handling of possessory interest, which has been criticized here this morning, and the government improvements, is at variance with the letter and intent of that act. The situation at Lake McDonald Lodge in Glacier National Park, about which I wrote you on March 27th, is a case in point.

I added an "amen" to Congressman Udall's letter, stating that even when Congress, after prolonged hearings, adopted a concessions policy, we had experienced difficulties in having it administered consistent with the intent of the act. I called attention to the fact that the Public Land Law Review Commission in 1970, had endorsed the soundness of these policies and recommended that the concept of possessory interest be expanded to private investments in other federal agencies. Yet we hear today that the Park Service intends not to recognize possessory interest for investments made on government facilities in the parks.

In the letter to Director George Hartzog, Stuart G. Cross, Chairman of the Conference of National Park Concessioners, wrote as follows:

Dear Mr. Hartzog:
Your recent letter to the Regional Directors on the subject of concessioner maintenance to government improvements reiterates your policy concerning the possessory interest of the concessioners in such improvements. As you are aware, the Conference, as a group, and individual members in the course of their contract negotiations (as well as specific controversies involving such properties at Lake McDonald Lodge), have consistently protested this policy. At the time of our annual meeting in Washington last March, you and I engaged in a lengthy discussion on the topic. At the conclusion of that discussion we agreed to present to you a memorandum setting forth our position.
Briefly, it is our contention that Public Law 89-249 intends the concessioner may acquire a possessory interest in structures which he has built or will build upon government land. No distinction is made in the law between new structures, constructed entirely by the concessioner and structures attached to or made part of existing government improvements assigned for use by the concessioner. While the desirability for the possessory interest concept was set forth in detail — it was recognized by all parties at the hearing: the Park Service, the concessioners and the Majority Committee, that the possessory interest concept was to be encouraged and be enabled to carry out the will of the Secretary.

In a meeting with the Director, Chairman Cross commented on the fact that fact sheets were being released with the prohibition of possessory interest in government buildings.
Director Hartzog stated:

As everyone knew, he did not believe in dual ownership in the same facility; that this policy position was taken in 1964, before the Policy Bill.

This had been raised with the Secretary. If he (the Secretary) reverses the policy, Hartzog will carry it out, but he personally will not change the policy.

Enclosed with Stuart Cross' letter to Director Hartzog was a memorandum prepared by Herman H. Hoss, Attorney for the Conference of National Park Concessioners, entitled "Possessory Interest in Government Improvements." The memorandum is as follows:

> The National Park Service has announced a change in policy on which concessioners will no longer be permitted to acquire a possessory interest in government improvements. This change of policy appears to be based on a misunderstanding of the concept of possessory interest, and particularly of the distinction between government improvement and concessioner improvement. The Park Service statement on the subject consistently referred to "government owned buildings" and to "mixed ownership of property." The concept of possessory interest, developed some 20 years ago for the purpose of giving the concessioner reasonable assurance of the security of its investment in buildings, fixtures and other improvements, had become part of the realty and property of the United States, because they were affixed to or rested upon, land owned by the United States. By definition, there is no possessory interest in improvements which are not owned by the government.
>
> The distinction between government improvements and concessioner improvements is not a matter of ownership, but a matter of who acquired, or constructed, the improvements. The term "government owned buildings" frequently being used informally to mean buildings acquired or constructed by the government, but the shortcut in language should not be permitted to obscure the basis of the distinction between government improvements and concessioner improvements. Both are owned by the government, both are possessed and used by the concessioner under the provisions of the concessioner's contract. They differ in the source of the funds under which they were acquired or constructed.

The foregoing principles were thoroughly explained to the Subcommittee of National Parks and Committee of Interior and Insular Affairs of the House of Representatives, when I testified as follows:

> These provisions for security of investment are necessary because of the unique conditions under which the

concessioners' investments are made. Legal title to all improvements in government land is in the United States by operation of law. The location, character, design and use of all concessioner improvements may be used only for the purpose of serving visitors, and for that one purpose only, to the extent and for so long as authorized by contract and approval under it. Any recovery of these investments, whether by use or by sale, requires not only the approval, but also the active assistance of the Secretary. Only he, or a person he selects, is a potential buyer. These unusual conditions justify unusual provisions for security of investment.

Possessory interest is the name given to the whole group of rights of concessioner in its improvements recognized in present contracts and confirmed in Public Law 89-249. Briefly, it means alternative right either to use the improvements as contemplated by the contract, or to be compensated for their value, if the right to use them is terminated for any reason.

The standard language of concession contracts, as adopted in about 1950, is an indispensable part of the definition of possessory interest. That standard language, and the foregoing description of possessory interest makes no distinction between the concessioner's improvements to government improvements, and the concessioner's improvements, wholly constructed or acquired by the concessioner.

From the foregoing, it is apparent that there can be no mixed ownership as a result of recognizing possessory interest to concessioners to improvements to government improvements. It is possible that there may be a few instances of mixed right to possess or use. The government may reserve, or be given a right to use, a portion of an improvement for a government activity, but such arrangements should not affect the concessioner's right to reimbursement under the possessory interest concept.

As a practical matter, there appears to be no advantage to the government or the public in denying a possessory interest in concessioner improvements to government improvements, so long as the concessioner continues to use such improvements for the purposes contemplated by the contract. The only problems which may arise are those related to the desirability of proposed betterment or additions. Such problems are not significantly different from those arising from proposed betterments or additions to concessioner's improvements, which are also subject to the approval of the government.

In our discussion of the subject, there have been references to difficulties in arriving at fair compensation upon termination, but no cases of such difficulties have been presented. Some questions are expected in evaluating any possessory interest upon termination, and no reason appears for expecting greater difficulty when a government improvement is involved. The concessioner using the government improvement must determine the value of such possessory interest for the purpose of the balance sheet or depreciation, for local property taxes, and for insurance. No significant problem will develop.

The position of the Conference of National Park Concessioners may be summarized as follows:

1. So far as ownership is concerned, there is no distinction between concessioner improvements and government improvements, and there can be no mixed ownership in either.

2. The recognition of possessory interest in concessioner's improvements to government improvements has been established policy ever since the adoption of the concept of possessory interest, and is now confirmed in Public Law 89-249.

3. So far as the general policy of encouraging and enabling private capital is concerned, there is no distinction between concessioner improvements to government improvements and other concessioner improvements.

4. There are no practical problems in the recognition of a possessory interest in concession improvements to government improvements that are not also present in the relation to possessory interest in other concessioner improvements.

5. The reason for relying on private capital rather than government funds to provide facilities desirable for the accommodation of visitors in the national parks applies with equal force to government improvement and to other concessioner improvements.

Signed by H. H. Hoss, Attorney

The matter came to a head in the case of the demand by the Superintendent of Glacier National Park that certain improvements to the balcony be made at the Lake McDonald Lodge, and demanding that in the event that the concessioner did not provide that renovation, that the Park Service would do so. If provided by the concessioner, the Park, Service demanded that the concessioner waive his possessory interest for the capital improvements made to this government-owned facility. On refusal by the concessioner, the Superintendent, through Regional Director Reynolds, in Denver, Colorado, requested that Glacier's contract be amended to provide for waiving by the concessioner of his possessory interest for these proposed capital improvements. The Assistant Director in Washington responded to the Regional Director, stating:

> We shall, of course, be pleased to amend the contract as proposed by Mr. Neilsen, if the concessioner requests it, or advises that he is willing to accept such an amendment, however, we cannot unilaterally amend the contract as requested.
>
> In this connection, we would like to correct the references made by Mr. Neilsen, that Public Law 89-249 does not permit concessioners to acquire possessory interest in government-owned buildings. On the contrary, the Act provides for such possessory interest, making it necessary for the concessioner to waive it if it is not to acquire the interest.

When I, as the concessioner, refused to agree to a waiver of this interest or to perform the work without recognition of my possessory interest, the matter was referred to the Secretary In a letter to Secretary Stewart L. Udall, dated March 26, 1968, Congressman Morris K. Udall, advised as follows:

> Dear Stu:
> Reference is made to the complaint made by the Glacier Park Company concerning the replacing of the balconies on the Lake McDonald Lodge in Glacier National Park.
>
> The Glacier people have advised me that the National Park Service has demanded that they repair or replace the balconies by the opening of the summer season, or close the facilities to public use in toto, or at least 22 of the 31 rooms. The Glacier people responded in accordance with the terms of their contract with the government; this work, which constitutes a major capital investment is to be done by the Park Service, or if per-

formed by the park company, they are entitled to a possessory interest in the building, to the extent of this new capital investment. The concessioner already has a substantial possessory interest in this building.

The Park Service refuses to do the work, or to acknowledge the company's investment requiring that the company waive its rights under the law and the terms of the contract, under threat of closing of the facilities.

Public Law 89-249, which I authored, specifically provides that the concessioner shall be given a possessory interest representing its interest in the Park, which is not to be terminated without just compensation. The law is clear and Glacier's contract is clear, that the company is acting within its rights; and a demand to the company to waive this right under threat of closing is a flagrant violation of the law and its contract with the government.

This is not the first time that the concessioners have complained to me that the Director of the National Park Service is violating both the spirit and the terms of the law. This is not consistent with the reasons for the adoption of this law, which was intended to encourage private investment in concession facilities in the parks to serve the public by giving the concessioners security for their investments.

The continued disregard of the terms and intent of law is largely negating the purpose of encouraging private investment to serve park visitors.

Sincerely, Morris K. Udall

Secretary Udall telephoned me stating that Director Hartzog felt very strongly that the Glacier Park Company should not get a possessory interest for the renovation of balconies on the Lake McDonald Lodge. I said: Stu, I feel strongly, too, and if the Park Service insists on its waiver or closing of the facility, I would have no alternative but to sue you as Secretary of the Interior and the National Park Service. Secretary Udall said, "I'll call you back." He did, and asked me if I had any objection to the Park Service doing the work. I said: Only as a taxpayer, as I believe it is our responsibility, but the Glacier Company could not object to the government making the improvement on their own building.

The issue was resolved by the Park Service renovating the balconies on Lake McDonald Lodge. I also testified concerning some questions that had been raised in the morning session of the "Dingell" Committee, particularly preferential renewal rights (referred to by Congressman Brooks as transfers by inheritance).

Preferential renewal rights were granted for the purpose of providing continuity of operations. If the concessioner hires a good employee, he cannot keep him if he has only a five-year contract as is being proposed. A man who is raising a family who you want to employ, is not going to stay with you if at the end of five years he is out of a job. Good employees want some tenure and a chance of continuity of their employment. It has also been demonstrated in every inquiry into the concessioners policy that continuity results in better service to the visitor.

I commented that there are people who recommend for other reasons removal of all facilities from the national parks. They have zeroed in on and criticized the concession operations, because they have to discredit the concessioner before they can get the facilities removed.

I identified them as extreme preservationist organizations, who recommend in public statements and in their periodicals, the removal of all facilities. I said the effect would be to deny 90 percent of the people an opportunity to spend the night in a national park. Congressman John Burton, a member of the committee, interceded, stating that he was from California, and that he had yet to hear anyone suggest that we remove facilities from the national parks. He stated that he was from Marin County, which is the home of the Sierra Club and John Muir, and said that if anyone would have heard the conservation organizations make this suggestion, he would have heard it. I responded by asking for an opportunity to present, in writing, the names and the comments of these organizations to be included in the record. They follow:

Connie Parrish, California Representative of Friends of the Earth TV Interview, KABC-TV, June 14, 1975, 12:30 p.m.:
What Friends of the Earth, Sierra Club and other conservation groups have proposed is to phase out accommodations.

Sierra Club Bulletin, March 3, 1975:

We urge that the following actions be taken regarding Yosemite Valley Facilities: Removal of concessioner housing facilities and support facilities to a location outside of the park — possibly El Portal. Removal of NPS staff administrative housing and support facilities from the Valley is also recommended... Study of the feasibility of removing visitor accommodations from the Valley.

Above all, the Park Service must not be hindered in the fulfillment of its public trust by permitting the concessioner, with its own financial interests at heart, to unduly influence NPS management decisions. The permanent solution to this problem will be the ultimate removal of facilities from the park. In the interim, thought should be given to the replacement of profit-oriented businesses by non-profit concessioners.

**The Wilderness Society,
"Wilderness Report" (April 1975):**

The Wilderness Society...recommends that the National Park Service adopt and implement a firm policy of phasing out unnecessary concession facilities in the parks, and of relying in most cases on private enterprises to provide tourist services outside the park boundaries.

Statement of Brock Evans, Director, Washington Office, Sierra Club, to Interior Committee, March 14, 1975:

We share the view of the Conservation Foundation that visitor facilities within the parks are ideally to be operated by a nonprofit, quasi-public corporation, whose primary allegiance is to appropriate public use of the parks. Where private enterprise is required, it should operate facilities outside the parks.

National Parks & Conservation Association Magazine, June 1975:

...Likewise, many Yosemite concessioner services would be more appropriately located at such a peripheral location instead of in the heart of scenic Yosemite Valley.

Sierra Club Letter dated May 3, 1975, distributed to all Bay Area Master Plan Meetings:
We urge the following actions be taken regarding Yosemite Valley facilities to a location outside of the park — possibly El Portal...Study of the feasibility of removing visitor accommodations from the Valley.

Anthony Wayne Smith, President of National Parks & Conservation Association:
The place for the big hotels, motels and urban-accommodations is in the communities beyond the great public land holdings. Recreation resorts can be built by private enterprise on private land in these communities...

Mailing of Sierra Club Yosemite Task Force, dated April 1975:
We urge that ... feasibility of reducing or relocating visitor accommodations be studied.

Connie Parrish, California Representative of Friends of the Earth, in Los Angeles Times, May 4, 1975:
... We realize that it may take years, but all present-day planning should aim at restoring the park to its natural state. To do this, we urge these steps: Remove from the park all facilities that are not essential to the enjoyment of the scenic resource. Congressional mandates and National Park Service administrative policies make it clear that visitor facilities are supposed to be located away from scenic attractions, and, when possible, outside the boundaries ... Accommodations should be nearby, outside the park boundaries.

The Conservation Foundation, National Parks for the Future, Page 22:
We recommend that a long-term program of concessioner replacement be started on a pilot basis

and proceed according to an equitable timetable until the parks are free of major private entrepreneurs and the public has regained full control of facilities planning and operations.

In response to questions from the Chairman about the concessioner's role in planning, criticizing that the concessioner was given a preference over the general public by participating in planning before the general public had an opportunity to comment, I pointed out that the concessioner is not just a member of the public, but a part of the park team attempting to respond to the needs and desires of the park visitor.

I stated that if anyone wanted to know what the park visitor wanted, that the concessioner was in the best position to provide that answer. In fact, he has the closest personal contact with the visitor or anyone including the National Park Service. The recent disapproval of the Yosemite Master Plan was seized upon by environmental organizations to claim that M.C.A. dominated the Park Service to further commercialize the park. As a matter of fact, the master plan that was disavowed was developed long before M.C.A.'s involvement. An article in the *Los Angeles Times*, May 4, 1975, under the banner "The Battle Over Yosemite," outlined the conservation organizations' participation in influencing the Park Service's decision to discard its master plan and hold hearings for a new plan. The conservation organizations' position was enunciated by Connie Parrish, the California representative of Friends of the Earth.

> The overriding issue in the battle over Yosemite is the rights of an increasingly conservation-minded public vs. the projected profits of a privately owned conglomerate.
>
> Act One of the Agenda ended December 13th, when the Interior Department, pushed by major conservation groups, rejected the National Park Service's tentative master plan for Yosemite. The plan had gone back to the drawing board and the public's voice at last is being heard...
>
> Thanks largely to the protests of Friends of the Earth, the Sierra Club and other conservation groups, the

Interior Department rejected the draft master plan on the grounds that there had been no public participation. As a matter of fact, there had been three widely advertised public hearings on the master plan, but the final results did not please the environmental organizations.

The article continues:

> A congressional investigation also grew out of our protests. Hearings were held in December by U.S. Representative John Dingell (D-Michigan), Chairman of the House Sub-Committee on Energy and the Environment, in conjunction with the Subcommittee on Conservation and Energy. Dingell heard testimony that the Park Service let M.C.A. push it into recommendations which were overly commercial...
>
> What M.C.A. wanted to do, in our opinion, was to turn Yosemite into a year-round luxury resort. The company proposed to tear down 150 of the primitive tent cabins in Curry Village at park headquarters and replace them with modern lodge facilities with indoor plumbing — at higher rent.

The facts are that I made these proposals to upgrade these substandard facilities as President of the Yosemite Park & Curry Company in 1972 and had Park Service approval in 1973 before M.C.A. had expressed interest in purchasing the company. Upgrading of facilities was encouraged by the Park Service as consistent with visitor demands: the replacement of modern cottages for 150 of the 409 dilapidated tents which often went begging and were rented only as a last resort when all else was occupied.

31

Reducing Concessioner Ability to Perform by National Park Contract Provisions

IN THE last analysis the test of the National Park Service's adherence to congressional policy on concessions is revealed in the provisions in the concessions contracts. The test is whether these provisions encourage and enable, as required by law, or discourage and inhibit the providing of visitor facilities. The concessions contract is the legal basis for the relationship between the National Park Service and the concessioner. The terms of this relationship were clearly stated in Public Law 89-249. The underlying basis for this law was to encourage and enable the private sector represented by concessioners to provide facilities for the accommodation of park visitors as approved by the Secretary of the Interior.

This was brought about through Congress' decision not to provide public funds for visitor facilities and the inability of the concessioner to get equity or loan capital for investment in these visitor facilities. This was difficult as buildings attached to park lands vest legal title in the United States, and as the government retains almost complete control of the concessioner's operations. The Enabling Act establishing the Park Service authorized the Secretary to provide facilities for the people's use and enjoyment of the parks. In fact, it was dictated subject to the requirement to preserve the natural resources.

The designation of wilderness and the adoption of restrictive master plans were effectively used to halt expansion of visitor facilities. To get effective reduction of existing facilities required the acquisition of concessioners' facilities which were protected by contract provisions supported by Public Law 89-249.

To accomplish this, a methodical assault was made through changes in contract provisions. Following are some of the basic changes forced on concessioners. The agreement with Congress that changes would be agreed upon between the Conference of National Park Concessioners and N.P.S. had gradually been abandoned. A contract presupposes agreement between the parties, freely arrived at, and not imposed by one of the parties.

Terms of Contract

The term of contract had been considered crucial if funds were to be available, and 20-year terms were the accepted norm, if a substantial investment was required. The footnote to the old standard language contract provided:

> While the term of the contract is left blank, it is the policy of the Department to grant a contract for a 20-year term when the concessioner is to provide a substantial investment.

The Park Service removed this footnote and Director Gary Everhardt stated to the Subcommittee on Energy and Environment of Small Business on December 3, 1976:

> We intend to limit their rights by contract revision. We have not yet formalized a policy respecting the term of contracts to achieve shorter durations than in the past.

This was subsequently proposed to be set at 10 years. The irony is that this was a committee charged with protecting small business. The small business concessioner must rely on his contract for financing and the shorter the term, the greater his inability to secure a loan or amortize his debt. The large concessioners do not rely solely on their contracts to secure financing. They have independent credit-standing and other sources of capital for their concession operations.

The purpose for providing a long-term contract is several-fold:

First, a 20-year contract for a 100-day seasonal operation compares with the revenue potential of a five-year, year-round operation. It also gives assurance to the banker that the concessioner has time to repay his loan. Twenty-year terms also permit continuity of operation, and have demonstrated a capacity to provide better service. Most employees are seasonal and inexperienced, consisting largely of college students. It gives the concessioner the ability to attract and retain competent permanent supervisory employees as a necessary stabilizing component. A long-term contract permits lower rates to park visitors as the capital invested can be amortized over a longer period. An objective of the National Park Service is good service at reasonable rates.

The attitude of the Department of the Interior is aptly summed up in the response in House Report 94868, dated June 4, 1976, on Energy and Environment Committee of Small Business, by Assistant Secretary of Fish, Wildlife and Parks Nathaniel P. Reed, on term of contracts as follows:

> The appropriate term for renewal (of contracts) is one of the several considerations now under review.
>
> We have under consideration generally, two courses of action: First is to change our contract to provide for advance notice to be given the Secretary in the event a concessioner is trying to arrange a sale.
>
> The second is the possibility of attempting to influence existing contracts in this fashion by proposed rule-making and the issuance of an appropriate regulation. We have just started to study this latter matter with our Solicitor while the first has actually been drafted in the proposed changes to the standard contract which we are making to tie down loose ends and eliminate ambiguities.

Possessory Interest

This is the term which acknowledges the concessioner's property interest in facilities constructed by him in the park and is considered the basic security for the concessioner's investment.

Section 6 of Public Law 89-249 provides:

> A concessioner who has heretofore acquired or constructed, or who hereafter acquires or constructs pursuant to a contract and with the approval of the Secretary, any structure, fixture or improvement on land owned by the United States within an area administered by the National Park Service shall have a possessory interest therein which shall consist of all incidents of ownership except legal title...
>
> The said possessory interest shall not be extin-

guished by the expiration or other termination of the contract and may not be taken for public use without compensation.

The Park Service's proposal to reduce that security was enunciated by Director Everhardt to the House Subcommittee on Energy and Environment on Small Business on December 9, 1976:

> For new ones (contracts) we have the option of waiving this (possessory interest) administratively, as it is not mandatory.
> Therefore, we envision that future long-term contracts will be held to those that are totally new or where expenditures are major and no possessory interests are granted.

Another reduction of this security was achieved by seizing on an exception that if the facilities were not to be replaced, the contract specifies that the concessioner was to be paid tax depreciated book value. This exception had been included in the law to take care of old dilapidated buildings that had lost their usefulness. It is now applied to any facility that the park, in their planning process, wants to get rid of, and when coupled with the present policy applies to every concessioner facility as opportunities arise "on a case-by-case basis."

"Agreement" of the parties was achieved by government fiat on a take-it or leave-it basis. You "agreed" or you did not get a contract!

Capital Additions to Government Buildings
The Park Service administratively decided that improvements, regardless of how extensive, made to government buildings did not entitle you to a possessory interest; your investments were to be amortized. This was based on a misconception by Director Hartzog of the concept of possessory interest and the adoption of a policy refusing to acknowledge possessory interests in capital improvements made on government buildings unless it was amortized. The interests were to be paid at book value.

The Land Law Review Commission established to identify and coordinate laws covering the use of federal public lands for public accommodations criticized this as contrary to the Policy Act of 1965, but the Park Service continues to insist on this interpretation.

Public Land Law Review Commission, June 1970: "One-Third the Nations' Land"

The security of investment offered under the Concessioners' Act of 1965 should be extended. The 1965 Act recognizes a possessory interest in facilities constructed by concessioners and provides for compensation for their values upon termination of the concession agreement. We believe that this policy is sound and should be uniformly applicable. However, we understand that the National Park Service does not recognize such an interest where the concessioner improves or adds to government-built facilities. Since all such concessioner improvements become the legal property of the United States, we see no reason for any distinction and believe that the concessioners in such cases should be recognized as having a compensable interest.

Amortization of Possessory Interest

Another administrative approach to reduce the concessioners' security in his investment is to force the amortization of possessory interest over the term of the contract vesting title in the government without paying for the facilities. This flies in the face of providing security for the investments, forces higher rates to consumers, undermines continuity and the willingness to invest in improvements as the contract approaches termination. It "discourages" investment when the law dictates that the Secretary shall "encourage" and enable the concessioner to provide and operate facilities which he deems desirable for the accommodation of visitors.

The purchaser of an existing facility from a concessioner is prohibited by contract terms from reevaluating the interest consistent with the purchase price. This also discourages sales, an important property right particularly for the individual entrepreneur.

A recent provision added to contracts came as a result of an Appropriations Committee rider without hearings and without consultation with the Interior Committee that is charged with the Department's prime legislative authority.

This provision forces the concessioner to agree to take tax book value in the event of default or failure to perform to the satisfaction of the Secretary, contrary to Public Law 89-249 which provides for sound value. As the Secretary has complete discretion in determining whether the services have been satisfactory, there is little left of the security that Congress provided in Public Law 89-249.

The law provides that the concessioner is entitled to sound value at the time of taking in case of termination, unless otherwise agreed to by the parties. The "agreement" with concessioners has been attained unilaterally by government fiat, on a "take it or leave it" basis, set forth in the standard language contract.

When you consider that possessory interest was to be the concessioner's guarantee of security for his investment, contract provisions forced on the concessioners on a take-it or leave-it basis leaves little substance to Congress' attempt to protect the concessioners' investments to enable him to provide the facilities.

Compensation

While the law unequivocally grants the concessioner the right to be compensated at sound value (reconstruction cost less actual depreciation) at the time of taking contracts now force the concessioner to take book value in the following situations:

1) Improvements made on government buildings. (This was criticized by the Land Law Review Commission as contrary to the law.)

2) When the Secretary chooses at the time of expiration of contract to discontinue any operation, concessioner is forced to take book value.

3) Termination of any contract for default. If the concessioner is declared unsatisfactory, he receives book value. (The Secretary has complete discretion to determine whether the service are satisfactory.)

4) If concessioner's interest (possessory interest) is sold to a successor, the purchaser is held to book value.

5) If the successor is a government agency, the Secretary has complete discretion as to the value of the concessioner's interest.

6) The Secretary has the right to withdraw any assignment of land or buildings at any time during the

contract, if in his judgment, such assigned land and improvements are no longer necessary to conduct the concessions authorized hereon, and the concessioner receives book value.

Preferential Right of Renewal

is also dictated by the law in Section 5, Public Law 89-249, to provide continuity in the following words:

> The Secretary shall encourage continuity of operation and facilities and services by giving preference in the renewal of contracts or permits and in the negotiation of new contracts or permits to the concessioners who have performed their obligations under prior contracts or permits to the satisfaction of the Secretary.

The Park Service watered this down to a right of first refusal, introducing a bidding process which was explicitly repudiated when the law was enacted. Director Everhardt, to Chairman, Subcommittee on Energy and Environment, Small Business, December 3, 1976, advised that the Service planned to further reduce these rights by stating: "We intend to limit their rights by contract revisions."

Franchise Fee

The concessioner shall pay to the Secretary on or before the last day of each month of the operating season during the term of this contract, a franchise fee for the preceding month as follows:

A fee (to be paid monthly in equal installments during the operating season) for the use of any government improvements assigned to the concessioner for the purposes of this contract. Such fee will not exceed the annual fair value rental of the government improvements as determined by the Secretary. This fee is not subject to renegotiation as hereinafter provided and such fair value is subject to such adjustment by the Secretary as provided in the contract to reflect increases or decreases as the case may be, on an annual or other basis as specified.

It should be noted that the government wants to collect fees for the use of its buildings based on the fluctuating present day value of its buildings including inflation, but insists on the concessioner agreeing to take the depreciated book value for its assets. The government also reserves the right to change the rent on these buildings without concessioner approval and these fees are not subject to renegotiation at each five-year interval!

Insurance

Notwithstanding any other provision hereof, the concessioner shall not acquire a possessory interest in, or otherwise be entitled to compensation for any government improvements constructed with casualty insurance proceeds. In the event that government improvements are underinsured, the concessioner shall be liable for such underinsured value and, notwithstanding any other provision hereof, shall not acquire a possessory interest in or otherwise be entitled to compensation for government improvements constructed in whole or part with concessioner's funds pursuant hereto.

General Provisions

Notwithstanding any other provision hereof the Secretary reserves the right to provide directly or through cooperative or other non-concession agreements any accommodations, facilities or services to park visitors which are considered by the Secretary as part of or contributing to a park interpretive or other program.

This conflicts with the interpretive programs conducted on all sightseeing buses and tour boats. It allows the government to give competitive contracts just by calling them interpretive, or which he says contributes to a park program.

Disputes

Except as otherwise provided in this contract, any dispute, or claim concerning this contract which is not disposed of by agreement shall be decided by the Director, National Park Service, who shall reduce his decision to writing and mail or otherwise furnish a copy thereof to the concessioner. The decision of the Director shall be final and conclusive unless, within 30 days of the date of receipt of such copy, the concessioner mails or otherwise furnishes to the Director a written appeal addressed to the Secretary. The decision of the Secretary or his duly authorized representative for the determination of such appeals shall be final and conclusive unless overturned by a court of competent jurisdiction to have been fraudulent, or capricious, or arbitrary, or so grossly erroneous as necessarily to imply bad faith, or not supported by substantial evidence.

The requirement to establish that the decision was "fraudulent, capricious, arbitrary or so grossly erroneous as to imply bad faith" is a burden of proof almost impossible to meet since courts are reluctant to reverse any decision which has a measure of discretion. The effect is to deny access to the courts.

For the Convenience of the Government

Another approach which would limit the concessioners' security and reduce the term of contract was proposed contract provision which would permit the government to terminate the contract at any time "for the convenience of the government." This was bitterly opposed by the Conference of National Park Concessioners as destroying the whole concept of Public Law 89-249. It would result in a contract by sufferance with no continuity, no ability to obtain financing, and would destabilize the entire concession system. It should be noted that Public Law 89-249 was to make a "bankable contract" to enable the concessioner to borrow money for his operation to provide those services that the National Park Service required.

As a result of this protest, Assistant Secretary of the Interior Nathaniel Reed submitted the draft contract for evaluation to the Bank of America and the Chase Manhattan Bank. Their responses are as follows:

Bank of America, to National Park Service, in a letter dated December 2, 1976, and signed by Winfield Jones, Vice President and Assistant General Counsel:

> It is my understanding that your specific question is: "Does our proposed modification of contract language in any way change the loanability as contrasted with the existing contract, disregarding the capital position of any particular concessioner?"
>
> As you may know, loans to such concessioners have never been as attractive to lenders as loans to most other businesses. In making loans to a business, two of the fac-

tors in which the lender is interested are:

a) assurances that the business will continue in existence to produce income to pay the loan; and,

b) the existence of business assets in which the lender can take a security interest and which are readily salable at foreclosure and fully usable by a purchaser at the foreclosure sale. The extent to which these factors exist, in the case of a loan to the concessioner, is very limited because the continued right of the concessioner to operate the concession and the right of a purchaser or encumbrancer to use assets of the concessioner acquired through foreclosure must necessarily be limited by the department in order to accomplish its purposes (sic).

With the foregoing in mind, my comments with reference to your question are as follows:

1) Section 2(c)(2). The more or less arbitrary authority granted to the Secretary for additional facilities and to authorize others to provide such facilities without resorting to the procedure previously set forth in Section 16, and thus create competition for the concessioner, might give lender some concern.

2) Section 4(a). The clear right of the Secretary expressed in this Section to withdraw the right of the concessioner to use assigned land and government improvements, and thus deprive the concessioner of the use of some of the facilities used in the operation of the concession, would probably give the lender some concern.

3) Section 9(d). The right given to the Secretary by this section to increase franchise fee and thus increase the concessioner's cost might give a lender some concern.

4) Section 11(a). The right given to the Secretary to terminate the contract "for the convenience of the government" would probably make a lender very reluctant to lend.

5) Section 13. This section, in both the current and the proposed contract is one of the primary reasons for reluctance for lenders to lend to concessioners, as the security taken in assets of the business, and particularly concessioners' improvements, cannot readily be foreclosed upon when statutory procedures, such as those existing in California relating to security interests in real property, require public sale to the highest bidder, since the bidder at a public sale acquires no rights to use the assets purchased unless the Secretary has accepted the bidder as a concessioner. The detailed procedures and require-

ments set forth in the revised Section 13, tend to complicate this problem.

6) Section 15(b). A lender might object to this provision, since the indemnity could impose substantial obligations on the concessioner which he might not otherwise have and thus impair his ability to service his loan.

Chase Manhattan Bank of North America, in a letter to Assistant Secretary Reed, dated December 2, 1976, addressed as "Dear Nathaniel" (brother) and signed by J. V. Reed, Vice President and Assistant to the Chairman, stated:

I have had several people read the proposed contract and I have read it a couple of times myself. Overall, the consensus is that the contract leaves decisions in it, most all of the key financial areas, totally to the discretion of the Secretary of the Interior. This is most clear in Section 11, "Termination." Quite frankly, this entire section gives the Secretary extremely broad powers and leaves the concessioner in a rather tenuous position. Section 11, in conjunction with Section 12, "Compensation," leaves very little that can be relied upon as an asset value against which a banker would prudently lend money.

As an example, the Secretary can abrogate the contract unilaterally on the basis of "unsatisfactory performance" in which instance the concessioner must sell his "possessory interest in Concessioner's Improvements" at "fair value," a figure which may well become a matter for arbitration under the mechanism provided in the contract. Going into a lending situation where such valuation procedures look to be a possibility is generally (or should be) unacceptable to most commercial bankers. Several other instances, particularly in the termination, inspection and compensation areas just cited, could be developed. Everything from the concession costs to the prices allowed to be charged, to the manner of valuation on the balance sheet, etc., are restrictively defined and generally left to the discretion of the Secretary in the event of a dispute. Indeed, it appears that the lender to such a concessioner would be providing funds for the support of assets which would pass out of the control of the concessioner as they are placed in a national park. Thus, any loan for such assets would probably have to be supported by other assets (i.e., non-national park assets) outside of the control of the contract.

In my opinion, then, it does seem that should the

Department of the Interior insist that the Secretary retain as much control over the concessioner's operations as is presently embodied in the proposed contract, then possibly the Department of the Interior should provide the funds to support the concessioner's assets, or else construct and own those assets directly.

The cumulative total of these contract provisions forced on the concessioner under the euphemism of "agreement" in large measure nullifies the protection afforded in Public Law 89-249. Congress, as the policy agency of our government, directed that:

> The Secretary of the Interior shall take such action as may be appropriate to encourage and enable private persons and corporations (hereinafter referred to as concessioners) to provide and operate facilities which he deems desirable for the accommodation of visitors in areas administered by the National Park Service.

These contract terms discourage private investment in the parks and in many cases, prevent access to capital to provide the facilities even when the concessioner is willing to proceed.

The forced amortization of concessioner assets and the payment of book value not only ignore inflation, but tend to vest full beneficial title in the government at bargain prices at the expense of the concessioner. In this manner the National Park Service can acquire ownership without appropriations which Congress has always refused to provide.

It is a classic case of the National Park Service bureaucracy dominated by environmental purists usurping the power of Congress.

The National Park Service is effectively pursuing a long established policy of removing visitor facilities from the National Parks and thereby ignoring a basic precept when the parks were established to provide for people's use and enjoyment.

As the security which we had achieved with the passage of Public Law 89-249 was seriously being eroded by contract provisions which were not reached by agreement but were imposed by the National Park Service, the Conference members refused to accept their contracts. As Chairman of the Conference, I was the spokesman, not just for the Conference, but also for individual concessioners who sought my help.

This crystallized Park Service opposition and I became the target. Director Everhardt continued to refuse to talk with me and devised an approach to isolate me from the Conference. This approach fitted in with the Conference's Executive Director who thought he should be the Conference representative on all matters between the Service and the Conference.

The policies being enunciated together with these changes in contract language set the stage to limit the expansion of concession facilities in the parks and to acquire title without the necessity of congressional appropriations. The master plan over time would assist in the removal of unwanted visitor facilities. The reduction in the length of contract would discourage investments. The problem facing the environmental/Park Service consortium was how to get rid of existing facilities. The Park Service insists that there is no overall policy to remove visitor facilities but that as occasions arise each park will be considered on a case-by-case basis.

32

Master Plans:
Instruments to Reduce Visitor Facilities

THE ATTEMPT to remove all visitor facilities in Zion, Bryce and North Rim Grand Canyon national parks started with their Master Plans. This attempt was thwarted when the governor of Utah and its congressional delegation forced a retraction of the plan.

Lassen's plan, calling for the removal of visitor facilities at Manzanita Lake, did not have this kind of support, as U.S. Natural Resources, the concessioner, welcomed the opportunity to sell the park concessions to the government. They did not attempt to mobilize the opposition to removal. The Park Service was aided by a six-year-old U.S. Geological Survey report that said the area was hazardous.

The Park Service retreated from their attempt to remove visitor facilities from the Drakesbad area when it was challenged by a patron of Drakesbad as not being a loser, as claimed by the Service.

Following are a few examples of other master plans which I believe demonstrate that the Park Service, contrary to their assertions, has an overall policy of removal of visitor facilities. It is administered on a case-by-case basis. In other words, when circumstances permit, the Park Service will reduce or remove visitor facilities. They are consistently ignoring a fundamental charge to make the parks available for the use and enjoyment of people, except for those uses approved by environmental organizations as appropriate.

This policy, if allowed to continue, will deprive the vast majority of our citizens an opportunity to spend a night or enjoy a restful period in a manner consistent with their capabilities and desires. These policies will exclude the elderly, the handicapped and those urban dwellers who by inexperience or choice require facilities for their comfort.

Yellowstone National Park
Old Faithful

The reference to removal of visitor facilities in Yellowstone National Park that Trevor Povah complained of to Director Everhardt and Congressman Hanson during the attempt to remove visitor facilities from Zion National park are now being implemented.

Most of the overnight facilities at Old Faithful are being removed and the area is being restricted to day use.

West Thumb

All the overnight facilities at West Thumb are being removed. The campground and the service station are gone. The store was scheduled for and was eradicated in 1986. The removal of visitor facilities at West thumb is predicated on the basis that this will protect the mating ground for grizzly bears. These facilities have been in existence for over 50 years and the bears apparently continue to mate, as the grizzly bear population is reported to be increasing.

Fishing Bridge - Bridge Bay

Consider this memo from Yellowstone's superintendent:

> Removal of facilities at Fishing Bridge must be in concert with overall operations of public facilities in Yellowstone National Park. It must be recognized that our intent to remove all facilities from Fishing Bridge must be politically and soundly accepted.
>
> John A. Townsley, Superintendent
> January 26, 1981

The overnight facilities at Fishing Bridge are the next target for eradication. Director Gary Everhardt justified their authority to remove visitor facilities in his letter to Congressman Allan P. Howe:

> The National Park Service has no overall policy concerning the closure of all overnight facilities in all na-

tional parks...The determination to phase out facilities is made for the protection of park resources...Each park is considered as an individual case study.

Director Everhardt further justified this removal by stating that the discretion to determine the facilities that are required is an "ongoing" authority that includes elimination of existing facilities. This appears to be an open-ended claim to remove any and all visitor facilities.

This was challenged by members of Congress as beyond the Park Service's authority and contrary to Public Law 89-249, but the Park Service continues unabated. Senator "Scoop" Jackson, chairman of the Senate Interior and Insular Affairs Committee, warned in a statement to the Senate that this is an open-ended policy with the ultimate effect that:

> The people will be allowed access to the parks only on a limited daytime basis.

He further stated:

> The Park Service, in its effort to conserve the park environment, has neglected the equally important duty to provide for the enjoyment of the environment.

The Yellowstone Master Plan includes this statement:

> The anticipated shift of terminal overnight accommodations to surrounding gateway towns might ultimately dictate a similar shift in the location of evening interpretive programs. Each case is to be considered on an individual basis.

Couple this with the policy:

> ...that when facilities can be developed outside the park, they will not be permitted inside.

It should be obvious to any objective person that Director Everhardt was less than honest in responding to Trevor Povah, Congressman Allen Howe and Senator Clifford Hanson when they inquired as to the plans for removing facilities from Yellowstone National park:

The Yellowstone Master Plan provides:

> With the conversion of Old Faithful to day use, the opportunity will exist for restoring Old Faithful Inn to its historic and architectural integrity.
> West Thumb will become a day use area for visitor observation of lakeside thermal features.
> Because of proximity to choice grizzly bear habitats in the Pelican Valley and in the lake outlet areas, as well as the outstanding environmental education opportunities, overnight facilities should be phased out of the Fishing Bridge area.
> Consideration should be given to relocating the Mammoth Campground. Concessioner support facilities that now duplicate services in Gardiner should be removed.

According to Federal Parks and Recreation Bulletin Volume 3, Number 18, September 1985, the newly appointed National Park Director William Penn Mott Jr. has a new plan which will accelerate the closing of Fishing Bridge campgrounds in Yellowstone National Park.

It is interesting to note that the facilities constructed in Grant Village to substitute for facilities being removed from Thumb is also a grizzly habitat. Here, again, the Park Service has a facile approach, i.e., if it fits with your plan, cite it in support, if it does not, ignore it.

Grant Village was selected during the Mission 66 program for development. The Park Service spent millions installing utilities. Concessioners resisted building there, as it was a mosquito-infested area with a very short season. It receives the earliest snowfall and is one of the last places to clear.

It was the refusal of the Yellowstone Park Company to build in Grant Village that led to that company being declared in breach of its contract and the purchase of its facilities by National Park Service. The government then assumed the responsibility to build visitor facilities in Grant Village, contrary to long established policy of relying on the private sector to furnish visitor accommodations.

Yosemite National Park

In 1972, the environmental assessment plan called for 666,915 acres to be classed as wilderness, and 4,211 acres as potential wilderness or 671,126 acres out of 760,000 acres or 88 percent to serve the one percent of the visitors to the park whose use is acceptable to the environmentalists.

The National Park Service contracted with V.T.N. Consolidated, Inc. of Irvine, California, to conduct transportation and relocation of facilities surveys. Contrary to the scare tactics being released by the national Park Service that the parks were being desecrated by overuse and projecting high increases in travel, the report disclosed that travel to Yosemite over the Memorial Day weekend the days of greatest visitation had decreased 25 percent from 1972 and 12 percent from 1971. They also disclosed that the Park Service was using a formula of 3.5 persons per car to ascertain visitation, while V.T.N.'s figures showed 2.76 persons per vehicle on Memorial Day and 2.93 during August. The Park Service refused to revise their formula.

The report also stated that "traffic volumes were about 10,000 vehicles on a two-way section of the northside drive between Sentinel Bridge and the entrance in a 24 hour period. The northside and southside volumes ranged between 6,000 and 7,000 vehicles per day." V.T.N. reported that "traffic volumes are well within roadway capacities in Yosemite Valley."

During a typical summer week an average of 30 percent were day users which increased to 44 percent on Memorial Day weekend.

The Attitudinal Survey indicated that most Yosemite visitors do not consider transportation-related problems as being critical or of severe magnitude. Of selected activities, 73 percent said that sightseeing by automobile was their chosen activity. The second most popular was picture-taking, followed by riding the shuttle to sightsee, shopping in village stores and having food service in restaurants.

On the cost of removing so-called nonessential facilities from the Valley to El Portal, the cost of site development at El Portal was estimated to be $110,019,000. The removal costs were estimated to be an additional $2,693,700, which did not include the cost of purchase of the Yosemite Park & Curry Company facilities as required by contract.

The Master Plan for Yosemite approved in September 1980 contains these conclusions:

Appropriate activities—activities such as picknicking, hiking and camping which will take advantage of the parks' natural features rather than manmade facilities or mechanized equipment, are the most appropriate uses of the park.

The V.T.N. report showed that hiking was listed as preferred by only 43 percent, while sightseeing by car was listed as 73 percent; picknicking was listed by 28 percent, while eating in restaurants was preferred activity by 52 percent, but the Park Service has never felt that they were bound by visitor preferences.

The Master Plan provides:

Visitor Use Levels - Appropriate overnight and day use levels for the various developed areas of the park will be achieved by limiting the number of overnight accommodations, campsites, and day use parking spaces available to visitors. Access will be restricted when these capacities are reached.

The day use level for Yosemite Valley will be lower than the level of use that is currently provided for because the significant amount of parking that will be removed from the Valley will be more than offset by the new parking with bus service at El Portal, Crane Flat and Wawona.

Transportation and private vehicles will ultimately be excluded from Yosemite Valley. The immediate steps to be taken include the removal of more than 1,000 parking spaces from the Valley and enforcement of an automobile carrying capacity.

Pursuant to the Master Plan, the following visitor facilities are scheduled for removal: Degnan's restaurant, delicatessen, fast food and gift sales; service station, car rental and garage; heavy maintenance and warehouse facility, concessioners head quarters building, lower Tecoya residential houses; the Ahwahnee row house and Camp 6; remove facilities and restore the Church Bowl area to natural condition; remove 52 cabins with bath and 33 cabins without bath; remove Pine Cottage containing 16 units with bath and 16 without bath; remove clothing sale use space for interpretation/information; remove 48 company employee tent cabins; remove 83 visitor tent cabins; remove Foster

Curry cabin; remove permanent ice rink (provide portable rink in winter); remove 25 parking spaces at ice rink; remove 68 housekeeping units; remove tennis court and golf course.

Mammoth Cave National Park

As in other cases, the drive to reduce automobiles and visitor facilities in the park started during mid-1960. The approach was the same. The Master Plan was the vehicle; the projected increase in visitation would swamp the roads, parking lots and visitor facilities. The solution was to remove visitor facilities to the periphery of the park. In this case, from the Historic Entrance in the park to the periphery at Union City where visitors would leave their cars, board buses to take them to the cave entrances or to hiking areas.

It also called for closing of some intrapark roads to private vehicles, permitting public buses exclusive use. Government and existing concessioner facilities at Historic Entrance were to be continued without expansion until their functions terminate and then the area would be restored to its natural condition.

The Park Service emphasized in response to congressional inquiry that the removal of any concession facilities were not imminent, but the facilities would be retained during their economic life.

In the case of Mammoth Cave Lodge at the Historic Entrance which provided food, lodging and the concessioner's general offices, Superintendent Albert A. Hawkins, angered by the concessioner's opposition to the Master Plan, "expedited" the economic demise of the lodge.

He ordered a safety inspection and then served notice to make certain improvements or vacate the premises. The concessioner made the requested improvements. He next ordered the concessioner to vacate the second floor, which was complied with. The concessioner was then told to vacate the building, which was to be demolished. It was — under protest.

The number of entries into the caves were to be expanded which they asserted would give the visitor a higher quality experience. On the contrary, the use of the surface of the park was to be restricted. Visitors to Historic Entrance were crowded when visited by 4,000 visitors during a given day. The projection was that this would increase to an average of 13,265 visitors per day by the year 2000. It was said that Mammoth Cave alone could accept 26,000 cave entrances each day. The congestion was on the surface, with automobiles and park visitors.

Other visitor needs, such as lodging and food, would be provided by the private sector outside the park. In a reply to inquiry by the Senate Judiciary Committee, the Park Service stated:

> In the meantime, private enterprise is providing, very near the park, many of these services now available near the cave entrance. Expanded developments planned by private enterprise present excellent prospects for the economic growth of nearby communities where much of the visitors' nonrelated park recreation needs would be served. At the same time the park would be relieved of the pressures of overcrowding. And development by private enterprises would not involve taxpayers' money.

This is less than an honest reply, as concessions in the park are built and maintained by the private sector and do not involve taxpayers' money. The result to be achieved is to remove visitor facilities from the park to outside communities. The method is to reduce or eradicate concessions facilities.

Here again, as in the Zion and Bryce Canyon National Parks, the intercession by the congressional delegation prevented the full implementation of the Park Service Master Plan for eradication of visitor facilities. The means employed was a rider to the Interior Appropriations Bill by Congressman William H. Nather of Kentucky, prohibiting the use of government funds to implement the Master Plan.

The Master Plan approved in 1983 acknowledged the inappropriateness of the proposals urged in 1976 with these words:

> Since this proposal was made, circumstances have occurred that question the need or advisability of relocating visitor use facilities to a peripheral site:
>
> 1) Since the 1976 plan, the park has experienced a significant drop in annual and peak day visitation, with no appreciable increase projected in the foreseeable future;

2) Recent discoveries have found that contrary to earlier assumptions, the proposed Union City staging area is underlaid by caves and major underground streams that are components of the overall Mammoth Cave system. Consequently, based on resource considerations, the Union City site appears less suitable for development and intensive use than the existing headquarters site (Historic Entrance).

This plan provides for the continuation of existing commercial visitor services at the park. Lodging, food and beverage, shuttle transportation to and from caves and basic shopping and automotive service facilities will be operated under concession contract.

Rocky Mountain National Park

The Rocky Mountain Master Plan emphasizes the desire to reduce the impact of visitors to the park by reducing facilities erected for people's use and pleasure in visiting the park. The thrust is to protect the environment with little, if any, concern for the enjoyment of people.

Trends on a parkwide scale are amplified by the steadily increasing number of people:

1,774,000 visitors in 1962, rising to 2,520,000 in 1972. It now shows the greatest increases in the spring and fall, along with the usual summer vacation peak period. There is an increasing impact on the environment as measured by the effects on vegetation and wildlife. And there is a growing impact on the experience as demonstrated by crowding and conflicts in lifestyle.

Ever increasing numbers of visitors with contemporary comfort standards are a growing threat to the land. The total amount of the park that has been visibly altered is small, but it is the most used and obvious part. The alpine tundra is highly fragile and particularly susceptible to man's impact as is evident near parking areas along Trail Ridge Road.

Development Concepts

Physical facilities and means of access will be minimized so the visitor will focus on the park experience itself.

More day-use picnic facilities are needed. Most campgrounds will be retained with tent camping gradually replacing some, but not all, vehicle camping. Group camping will not be expanded.

Some 91 percent of the park's land is classified as primitive. As defined by the National Wilderness Act of 1964, a wilderness is "an area where earth and its community of life are untrammeled by man, where man himself is a visitor who does not remain." That is where the forces of nature dominate the landscape "in contrast with those areas where man and his own works dominate."

No addition or expansion of campgrounds will be attempted. Vehicle camping will be encouraged by private enterprise outside the park. Overnight tent camping will be favored within the limits of existing campgrounds. More picnic facilities will be provided at day use areas by converting parking lots, campgrounds and acquired holdings.

This will allow the removal of facilities and structures in Moraine Parks, Hallowell Park and Green Mountain areas.

Although current agreements provide for operation of existing concession facilities, plans must be initiated to eliminate those facilities that are degrading to park resources. The Hidden Valley Ski area provides family recreation during the winter and generates public use of the park in the off-season. But the use of these sizable facilities has produced severe visual and physical impact with little relative benefit in terms of park objectives.

Therefore, action will be taken to eventually eliminate or limit this facility to existing levels. Downhill skiing in the park will not be expanded. Ski touring and snowshoeing will be allowed to increase.

The Fall River Pass store, situated adjacent to a key interpretive facility, provides food services to visitors. During peak use periods, this development is a source of severe traffic congestion. Large volumes of pedestrian activity generated by the facilities are eroding the surrounding alpine tundra. Sanitation facilities, parking, water supply and trash removal have all reached their limits. The curio and novelty sales section of the store is unnecessarily large and contributes to the length of time the visitors stay. This results in an impact on all of the facilities. It is proposed that the concession operation be limited to supplying food services and minor visitor needs such as film sales and restrooms.

People are anathema to the Park Service! They even changed the boundary of Rocky Mountain National Park to exclude Grand Lake Lodge from the park. As a result, there are no overnight facilities for the accommodation of park visitors unless they camp.

Glacier National Park

The Park Service recommended that 927,550 acres be designated as wilderness with an additional 3,360 as potential wilderness, which will become wilderness when their nonconforming uses are eliminated.

This leaves only 82,600 acres of the 1,013,500 acres for all other uses, including roadways, campgrounds, Park Service and concession facilities. I protested this without avail at the time of the hearing as an unfair allocation of resources; i.e., 930,900 acres for use by one percent of the visitors and 82,600 for the 99 percent.

To add insult to an already misallocation of land, the Master Plan provides:

> As visitation increases, new facilities both overnight and day use, will be needed. Adequate space exists for the future developments in locations convenient to all resources outside the park boundaries.

The National Park Service is now limiting the number of lodging rooms that will be permitted to those now in existence. This, despite the fact that there are fewer overnight facilities today than there were before World War II. There has been no claim of overcrowding in Glacier National Park even with 91 percent set aside as wilderness.

Sun Point Lodge was removed after World War II by the concessioner. This took out 50 rooms for overnight lodging. The overnight facilities at Two Medicine Lake, containing 40 rooms, were destroyed. Later, 10 cabins containing 18 rooms were removed from Swiftcurrent to Lake McDonald and converted from visitor overnight lodging to dormitory space for employees.

In 1979, I requested permission to add 50 lodging rooms at Lake McDonald, as traffic during the period of emphasis on fuel conservation was switching from individual to group travel. This switch was welcomed by the Park Service not only for fuel conservation, but for relief on the Going-To-The-Sun Road through the park.

Superintendent Iverson denied my request, citing

Glacier's Master Plan that "concessioner-provided over-night accommodations are considered adequate." I pointed out to the Superintendent that this section was not intended as a cap on visitor facilities, but a statement on the adequacy of facilities at the time of approval of the Master Plan. I referred him to the discussion on visitor use:

> With the general concept of park use a basis, the resources' capacity to accommodate visitors must be carefully analyzed. The eventual result will determine the total capacity for the entire park.
>
> ...This analysis and the resulting capacity figure must be part of a continuing program. As additional data on the resources are obtained, the entire park complex will be monitored to determine the effect of use and whether or not a change (either up or down) is necessary.

I pointed out that I was consulted on the Master Plan when it was adopted and this language was chosen to indicate that the facilities might be increased or reduced in the future. My request was again denied, even though we were attempting to bring a better balance between the facilities on each side of the continental divide, to improve visitor services. We had 380 rooms in the park on the east side and only 136 on the west side. This resulted in backtracking to accommodate guests which further congested park roads and diminished the visitor experience.

In 1985 the Park Service changed its position; i.e., the concessioner can build more lodging facilities at Lake McDonald, on the west side, if they remove an equal number from Rising Sun or Swiftcurrent on the east side. There is no claim that either location is overbuilt or desecrating natural resources.

This decision puts the lie to the justification for the previous rejection and supports a policy of limitation of visitor facilities in the park.

The Master Plan contains this conclusion:

> Appropriate lodging facilities are now and will continue to be provided outside the park in locations convenient to destination points within the boundary. As visitation increases, these exterior developments will probably be expanded.

Despite the fact that there is over a million acres of land in Glacier National Park, the number of visitors to be accorded an opportunity to spend a night in the park is being restricted to the number of facilities now extant. A bold repudiation of the Park Service's responsibility to make the park available for people's use and enjoyment.

33

Glacier Personnel

WHILE RECITING events, it is difficult to acknowledge the contributions of each of our permanent employees. They were a competent and loyal crew. We could not have succeeded without these, despite the financial strictures under which we operated and which dictated close control of expenditures with salaries and performance always under strict scrutiny. I am indebted to them for their dedicated and loyal devotion to Glacier Park Inc.

Emily Moke, my private secretary, also served as my administrative assistant. Her loyalty and sound judgment substituted for me whenever I was absent. If employees needed advice or guidance, the standard guide was "Call Emily." Her contribution to overall success was immeasurable. She never let me down. Emily was undoubtedly the most popular of our employees, not only with our employees, but the Park Service and people in the East Glacier community. This was an added asset for the company.

Al Donau, my general manager during the sojourn in Washington, D.C., made it possible for me to accept the appointment as Assistant Secretary in the Department of Housing and Urban Development. With Al at the head of Glacier Park, Inc., I could concentrate on my government job, as I knew the company was in good hands and my personal interests secured. His common sense and sound judgment gave me confidence in my absence.

In addition to his duties at Glacier, he had oversight responsibilities for Lassen, including the negotiations of a new contract. He performed to my complete satisfaction.

Cyril W. (Cy) Stevenson was my chief engineer, coming to us from Great Northern, where he had served since a youth. Cy was undoubtedly the best maintenance man in Montana, and probably in the west. He not only knew mechanics, steam, electricity and plumbing, he knew the theories behind them and could repair them when they failed to function. He was a strict taskmaster, and if anyone

489

did not work fast enough, look out! Cy would show him how. Hours meant nothing to Cy—the job had to be done and done right. We sorely missed him when he retired after being with us for 17 years.

Ian Tippet was manager of the Lake McDonald Lodge, the smallest hotel, when we acquired Glacier. I immediately assigned him as manager of Many Glacier Hotel, our largest facility. Ian is superb in working with young people and service to guests is his hallmark. He was trained in the British hotel schools and reflected their traditions. During the winter, Ian took over personnel director. It was generally conceded in National Park circles that Glacier hired the best. **Marjorie Lillibridge** was his good right arm. Ian appeared to be a frustrated theatrical manager, as he spent many hours on his own time to produce such plays as "Brigadoon," "South Pacific," "Fiddler on the Roof," "The Girlfriend," etc. They were often compared with Broadway productions.

Marvin Twamley, the location engineer at Lake McDonald, is unsurpassed in his dedication and devotion to making "his place" the best in the system. While he often had to "make do" with less than adequate facilities, his performance was always out standing. His willingness to "lend a hand" has endeared him to both company and Park Service personnel. This, despite his intolerance toward shoddy workmanship or lack of common sense or diligence. He calls a spade a spade. We never worried about McDonald while Marv was on the job.

Hugh (Bud) O'Neill had the challenging job of keeping the motors running and the crushed and dented fenders repaired. This is no small achievement when looking after 30-35 gear jammers and truck drivers whose main interests were getting home, regardless of speed limits, and whose driving attention was often obscured by anticipation of that night's date. Bud's body repair and painting ability has kept a fleet of 50 buses, five over-the-road trucks, plus a compliment of pickups and sedans running and looking like new. These included the famous "Red Buses" of Glacier. Bud was Glacier's "company man." Always loyal to his employer.

Kenneth Hammes and I became friends when I was Assistant U.S. Attorney and he handled accounting for the

U.S. Bankruptcy Court. Ken came to Glacier in 1965, when I was desperate for someone I could trust to handle our accounting records. Ken filled the bill. A meticulous accountant. I could always rely on Ken to provide accurate figures. He was immensely loyal and dedicated. We sorely missed him when he resigned to join Frampton Cafeteria. We often called him socially after he left our employ. **Emily Hammes**, his wife, was a strong support to Ken and to us. She continued to assist Glacier operations after Ken's demise, a loyal Glacier employee.

Kemper Meriam served as our auditor and independent accountant. His knowledge of the tax laws protected us from many a pitfall. He served us well even after he migrated to Florida, where he taught at the University of Florida. We relied upon his expertise and loyal support.

Henry Varner followed Ken Hammes as our controller. Henry was a real workhorse, putting in untold hours to assure the completion and adequacy of our reports. Henry had the capacity to instill loyalty in his staff, which inured to Glacier Park, Inc.'s performance.

Louis Melicek came to us from Yosemite Park & Curry Company. Louis had a long and illustrious career as manager of such department stores as Rhodes, Meyer & Frank, and George Wyman and Company. Louis was our purchasing agent and in charge of our warehouse. This was a demanding job that covered the full range of institutional foods, gift stores, camper services, film and hotel supplies. His knowledge of merchandising was invaluable; his ability to represent the company's interest was a source of confidence to me in this field, which has traditionally been a source of abuse.

Randi Peterson was in charge of our reservation department — a meticulous and demanding job where mistakes can escalate into disaster as occupancy reaches capacity and guests alter plans and shift between the seven locations we served. Randi was known and respected by the numerous tour agencies who looked to her for protection of their guests' accommodations. She never let them or us down over her years of service.

The late **Robert Hayes,** manager of the Prince of Wales Hotel, was our Canadian representative. Bob had a knack of adapting to conditions prevalent in Canada. Bob had been employed by Great Northern to run the Village Inn when we took over. I hired him to manage Rising Sun Motor Lodge. One day Bob said to me, "My experience has primarily been in hotels. They say that the Prince of Wales is a stuffy place and I have a reputation of being a stuffy person. I'd like to manage the Prince of Wales Hotel." I assigned him to the Prince where he served us in an exemplary fashion until his death.

John Fabian was the location engineer at Lake McDonald when we acquired the company. He worked for us for eight years. We never had any concern as long as John was with us. We felt that we could never fill his shoes when he resigned. It was a great relief when **Marv Twamley** took his place. He filled John's shoes admirably.

Jay Joplin came to us from Carlsbad Cavern. Jay was our purchasing agent handling the institutional purchases until we combined all purchasing under Louis Melicek. Jay gave us good loyal service for the many years he was with us.

Ralph Erickson was a tradition at Glacier, serving at Glacier Park Lodge and ending his service as manager of Lake McDonald Lodge. He was with us through the flood of 1964. He left to take a permanent position as hotel manager in Florida. He was a popular and loyal employee.

I do not want to ignore the loyal services of my family. My reticence in singling out individual service is predicated on my fear of being accused of prejudice. On the other hand, to completely ignore their services would be unjust. They all started young as dishwashers, help in affixing price tags and help as maids. As they were too young to be on the payroll, I paid them personally. Learning work habits at an early age is important but neglected in our modern society. They learned that no job is beneath them as they worked their way up the ladder.

Let me then just acknowledge their employment and willingness to serve in any position they were needed. **Donna** filled in as manager at the Village Inn, the Prince of Wales Hotel and finally became the controller; **Diane** managed the Lake McDonald Lodge; **Cliff** managed both the Swiftcurrent Motor Lodge and the Prince of Wales Hotel; **John and Charlene Casserley** managed the Lake McDonald Lodge and **John Bodie** headed the warehouse.

With dedication and without pay, my wife, **Genee,** was the company decorator and floral arranger. She provided the training of dining room personnel. It was always amazing to me how girls and boys from middle-class families, who sat down to a table three times a day could not properly set a table! The teas that she gave for women in the communities are still remembered and served to cement our local relationships. Genee was also the eyes and ears in the company where employees felt free to confide information to her that they would not provide me.

While not permanent employees, **Ade and Joy Abbott** were traditional managers of the Village Inn. A demanding job, that provided no time off and was subject to midnight calls for rooms and services. I never worried, as I knew they provided good and loyal representation for Glacier Park, Inc. Their personal loyalty gave me confidence.

Genee's Christmas Letter, 1983

In March Jeanne and Tony Greco joined us on the Love Boat for a fabulous trip through the Panama Canal with Caribbean stops. We were intrigued to learn that the canal locks are operated by gravity water and no pumps are required. We also learned that John Stevens, the engineer who built the Great Northern Railway and discovered Marias Pass south of Glacier National Park, was the engineer who solved the problem that made the Panama Canal possible. Ships are raised 85 feet above sea level in transit.

Dal and Betty Dort joined us on a trip we had longed to take to the Galapagos in May. These volcanic islands have never been connected to the Equadoran mainland. The bird, reptile and animal life are surprisingly varied not only from the mainland but between the islands. These mutations were an inspiration for Darwin's "Origin of the Species." Turtles weighing several hundred pounds, red and black iguanas — remnants of a prehistoric age, flightless cormorants, courting frigate birds with their huge red pouches, blue and red footed boobies and even foot high penguins — all ignoring us as we watched as they do not fear man.

We were back in Tucson for four days where Dee joined us for our long-dreamed of float trip down the Colorado river. Seven days and 280 miles through the Grand Canyon from Lee's Ferry to Lake Mead. The river was twenty feet above normal and three times as rapid which reduced the number of rapids, but increased the danger for the two principal ones. Gay and Joy Stavely piloted us on this marvelous trip.

Only after the U.S. District Court's last minute fumbling display, when a Federal judge disqualified himself because he owned $100 worth of Greyhound stock, did the Glacier Park Foundation's challenge to Greyhound's contract for the concessions in Glacier Park finally come to trial with vindication for Glacier Park, Inc.

On November 19 we welcomed Michael Rowley into our family at a quiet family wedding in Tahoe when he and Diane were married. Michael is vice president of a fruit processing plant that has machines in 19 countries throughout the world. Michael is in charge of sales and services which translates into world travel

A new addition arrived to John and Donna Bodie's family on October 29th. Christine Elena is a bright-eyed baby girl. This means a granddaughter balances the grandson born to John and Charlene a year ago in October, also.

We are delighted that the whole family with all additions will gather at the Bodie's new home in Tucson to celebrate this holiday season.

While tragedy stalked much of the world in 1983, the United States is again asserting its leadership role for peace — the peace promised by the brotherhood of man.

❀ ❀ ❀

Genee's Christmas Letter, 1984

During the year Don has been working on his autobiography and the history of the National Park Concession System. Our new Apple McIntosh promises help with Word Processing when we learn how it operates. Genee has had watercolor workshops, training classes for a docent at the Museum of Art, sewing projects with Charlene.

The winter passed quickly with trips to Florida, Fresno, Hawaii and to Southern India and Sri Lanka. The Indian trip was by ship with long bus rides into towns with Buddhist, Hindu, and Jinn temples. There were special traditional dance programs and a wild melee of water buffalo races. Don became so sick on his return that his doctor hospitalized him. The doctor was shocked to learn after tests that Don had Typhoid Fever, but he responded well to medicines and was soon back to normal.

We drove to Lake McDonald the end of May. Pete Donau visited to discuss the upcoming contract for Glacier Bay as did Gaylord Staveley on his Trail Guide Permit in Grand Canyon. Don serves on Glacier home owners committee and there were numerous meetings with and without the Park Service. We had a good visit with Sol and Bia Barsy before we attended Hamilton Store's board Meeting in Yellowstone. All good timing before Dee and

Michael's baby girl was born August 7. Little Charlene had her first dinner party at three days and her first sail on San Francisco Bay at five days — off to a flying start. There was another celebration: Don and Siri Ann's 50th wedding anniversary in Costa Mesa. Don H. was in this wedding party. Before we left the Park, Marvin Twamley, Lake McDonald's longtime maintenance engineer, suffered a heart attack after the excitement of a lodge kitchen fire. He has now had a single bypass operation and is doing well.

Genee's mother broke her hip in early October, so there have been several trips to Kingsburg. She was some better after an operation so we could join Dee, Michael and Charlene on the Queen Elizabeth II. We had a wonderful time despite the three-day delay in the mid-Atlantic caused by power and then engine failures. Dee and Michael continued on to Italy without us. With only a few days left we stayed in London. It was interesting to watch our election coverage from the British point of view and then witness that same Tuesday all the pomp and ceremony as the Queen opened their Parliament. We returned on the Concorde in three hours and twenty minutes from London to New York at Mach 2.2. No jet lag on that trip.

Early December we fly to Montana to help with Julian after Char has her second child. There will be another Hamilton Stores Board Meeting in Santa Barbara. The Bodies will have Christmas with us. Char and John will remain in Coram. Dee and Michael will be with his family in Tahoe.

❋ ❋ ❋

Genee's Christmas Letter, 1985

Spring found Don still working on his concessions book, giving several talks, traveling for interviews. Genee reviewed Lin Yutang's book, "Importance of Living" and studied for her Docents' class at the Museum of Art. Our trip to Washington, D.C., Conference of National Park Concessioners was enhanced by a trip to Florida to visit the Barsys and the Dorts.

Late May and early June at Glacier were cold and rainy. Don moved his "office" near the fireplace and made real progress on his book. Genee sewed for Christmas. She and Char met often to launch a new business getting final design, working on supplies and readying the ad for December 5th "Family Circle" for fitted, velcro-closed flannel diapers. Genee completed the brochure for Do-Little Diapers. To date, slow start. Glacier Park was celebrating its 75th year and there were many extra events. Don gave an historic talk, one of a series. Diane and baby Charlene visited for several events, as did Don's niece, Trudy, and her new husband, Mark. The last two weeks in July we flew off to the Scandinavian countries, a trip we had long wanted to take. Our favorite country was Norway, with its stunning fjords, granite mountains, friendly atmosphere. Imagine so much water that there is no use-charge, only flat rate, and all cross country trains are hydro-electric.

We flew back to Tucson in late August to attend the 14th Air Force Convention (14th served in China).

John Bodie had a serious pancreas infection and was in his fourth week in the hospital. We stayed longer to bolster Donna's morale. He is much improved now, studying for a broker's license, but still not back to work. We also spent a wonderful Labor Day with the Grecos in Denver. Tony was recovering from brain tumor and shunt surgery, and Jean from aspirin poisoning. Both are doing remarkably well.

Char and John found equestrian riding as challenging as dance, and good for John's hip. Tane arrived at the end of June and is now spending the winter with them, so they are a family of five. Diane and Michael are still doing a lot of traveling. They have just bought their first house in Belvedere, California, and are getting settled. They are thrilled.

Genee and her brother have been dissatisfied with the nursing home care for their Mother. This fall, Genee found a four patient private home with a compassionate practical nurse and made arrangements to bring her Mother to Tucson late November. Don completed the first draft of his concession history, "Wake Up! - You're Losing Your National parks" and is looking for a publisher. Also in late November the first water from the Central Arizona Project was delivered to Phoenix. Don got the first recognition for his role in bringing CAP water to Tucson in a public ceremony in Phoenix.

All the Hummel families, except Casserleys, and all the Rowley families are joining in Yosemite for a reunion over the Christmas holidays. We are hoping for a white Christmas to close another full year.

❄ ❄ ❄

Genee's Christmas Letter, 1986

We will be in Hawaii for the holidays visiting Char and John Casserley. They sold their Coram home and moved to Maui August 1st. John's arthritis and the cold gray winters finally forced a move. Now they are settled in. Char is finishing a course in real estate. Donna and John will be with John's family in California. Dee and Michael will be in Tahoe.

Last fall Genee moved her mother from the Kingsburg nursing home to a well-run private home with a compassionate practical nurse. On December 31 she died peacefully. A memorial service was held in Kingsburg. Friends, a busy schedule and several trips helped ease the loss.

In one of those perfect timings we visited the Yucatan peninsula with its fascinating ancient cities. On our return we visited the Dorts and Barsys in Florida, then attended the Conference of National Park Concessioners in Washington, D.C. In the spring Char, Dee and Mike, Trudy and Mark Allen visited us. Our trip to Glacier was delayed as Don had appointments with his urologist and specialists at the University of Arizona's Cancer Clinic. Experimental medication recommended by the UofA's doctors has checked or at least slowed the spread of the disease. While we waited for the reaction to the new drugs, we flew to Maui to attend our condo's board meeting. We finally left for Glacier June 10th.

Don has found a publisher for his book "Wake Up America, the Environmentalists are Stealing the National Parks." The publisher wanted to combine Don's story with his personal history. This resulted in days of writing and rewriting with many hours on the telephone. Genee collaborated on the rewrite plus sewing and gardening. Dee and Michael will be moving to Pueblo, Colorado, where their new manufacturing plant will be located. For the first time Dee left Charlene in a strange place with her grandparents. She adapted beautifully and we had our first real chance to get acquainted with her.

We stopped off briefly on our way back to Tucson in Yellowstone where Al Donau gave Don a splendid birthday dinner. We also attended several social functions celebrating the 40th anniversary of the Christian Ministry in the National Parks. There was more rewriting and phoning on the book 'til mid-October. It's publication release date is scheduled for January. Genee continues her volunteer work at the Museum of Art and will review Don's book December 10. Every spare minute she has had has been editing 20 years of 8mm movies dating from 1950 when Donna was three months old. For years we thought all those films had been stolen from the office. Lo and behold, when Don cleaned out a back storage area, they turned up. Now we hope to have them video-taped.

❄ ❄ ❄

34

National Parks for a New Generation

IF THERE still remains a doubt in the minds of my readers that the environmental organizations are the motivating force back of the National Park Service to reduce or remove visitor facilities from the national parks, read "National Parks for a New Generation."

It is a report just released by the Conservation Foundation strongly endorsed by the National Parks and Conservation Association, the Wilderness Society, the Sierra Club and significantly by William Penn Mott, Jr., the newly appointed Director of the National Park Service.

The comments on concessions endorse the familiar pattern of removing visitor facilities to outside the park boundaries.

> Many of the major concessions facilities would almost certainly not be permitted today if they did not already exist. Park Service policy has for years favored the provision of new commercial services outside the parks whenever possible, not within them.
>
> The major facilities that already exist raise continuing management issues. Not only do the facilities take up park land, but some of their functions (for example selling souvenirs) have been criticized as inappropriate to park areas. What most concerns critics is their perception that the concessioners' continued influence on the planning process within their parks will result in a drive for more facilities and urbanlike services.
>
> Although removal of many major installations remains an appropriate long-term goal, there is little likelihood that large-scale removal will occur soon. A few facilities have become historic structures in their own right. Others are protected by long-term contractual guarantees that make buyouts expensive. All serve large numbers of visitors, some of whom are likely to join with concessioners in appealing to politics and custom in resisting removal.

The Foundation's suggested solutions:

> 1) Release information on concession profitability.
> 2) Avoid excessive protection in concessionnaires contracts.
> 3) Contracts should require the Service to pay only unamortized book value and not fair market value.
> 4) Preferential right to provide additional services in the parks should be granted only in the most unusual circumstances, if at all.
> 5) Law changed to make renewal of contracts discretionary rather than mandated when a concessioner has performed satisfactorily.

In other words, the Park Service should further reduce the security provisions which Congress provided in Public Law 89-249 to assure visitor facilities in the National Parks. The environmental organizations now feel that they have sufficient support to publicly avow a policy that was covertly imposed over the last decade and a half and is contrary to congressional enactment.

When questioned by the Stanford Research Institute, the park visitor overwhelmingly expressed his desire to be able to spend a night in his national parks. He must be alerted to the fact that this right is about to be taken from him.

Parks are for people — not just the conservationist who would set them aside for their use in wilderness designations; not just for those who would use them as laboratories for scientific interpretations; not just for those who have the physical stamina to backpack, ride a horse, or hike; but also for those who by reason of age, physical handicap, or just temperament, can enjoy the grandeur from the seat of an automobile or a sightseeing bus or from a chair on a lodge veranda. Each segment of our population has a right to have its needs recognized for we deal in part with our nation's heritage in a democratic society.

I am told that these parks should be preserved for posterity. My question is: When does posterity begin? Does posterity begin tomorrow? Next year? One hundred years from now? Or shouldn't it begin with this year's senior citizen? The parks are already 100 years old.

The people must be informed about the restrictions being imposed on their use of the national parks which if continued will prevent them from spending a night in the national parks unless they camp. This will be particularly harsh on the older and handicapped citizens.

The Park Service must be called to account for their flagrant disregard of congressional policy and for the violations of the provisions and the spirit of Public Law 89-249. Policy must be changed.

This book is our legacy to America. It has turned into more than we expected. We truly hope our readers have enjoyed these ramblings and sketches of the American journey from wagon wheels to the space age that has been our lives. We have tried to put everything in it from our experience that has permanent meaning. We hope you reflect upon our message, chew on it and mull it over long after you put our book down. Your own conclusions, your own thoughts, your own actions, are the real final chapter of our story. As Goethe said, "Experience is only half of experience."

If there is any lesson to be drawn from these pages, it is that the people who make our nation work, and who make our national parks work, are not perfect — but that they must ever strive for that unreachable perfection. We want *our* legacy to America to be National Parks for a New Generation — but in a wider, more inclusive, less ideological framework than envisioned by the Conservation Foundation and its allies. We must insure a return of the parks to the people. They were set aside for the use and enjoyment of all of the people. And when we say *all*, we mean *all*.

Index

Adams, Ansel, 353

Advisory Commission on Intergovernmental Relations, 182, 192, 224, 234, 237, 239, 307.

Ahwahnee, The, 111, 267, 347, 353, 480.

Alaska Railroad, 195, 197, 199, 203.

Albright, Horace M., 110, 140, 142, 183, 286.

Albright, John, 164.

American Municipal Association, 155, 163, 182, 189ff., 208-209, 224, 233, 236, 239, 250, 303.

Appropriations Committee, House, 255, 285ff., 333, 336, 446, 465.

Arizona Daily Star, 146, 153, 157ff.

Arizona, University of, 21, 31ff., 43ff., 68, 132, 148, 165, 344, 497.

Army Corps of Engineers, 245, 298.

Aspinall, Wayne N., 288, 292-293.

Aszmann, Adolph A., 144.

Baxter, Lawson, 31ff., 43ff.

Bean, Glen, 424.

Beetson, Frank, 18, 21.

Bemiss, Gerry, 260.

Bill, Harthon L. "Spud", 276, 345.

Birch, John 90ff.

Blackfeet Indian Reservation, 229, 241.

Blossom, Wilson A., 36.

Borman, Frank, 28.

Boyer, Richard, 403-04.

Briggle, William, 439ff.

Brooks, James P., 293ff., 443, 445ff.

Bryce Canyon National Park, 284, 383ff, 475.

Bureau of the Budget, 291ff., 298ff., 336.

Bureau of Land Management, 297.

Carver, John A., Jr., 125, 253, 257, 259-60, 283ff., 294.

Cedar Breaks National Monument, 404.

Central Arizona Project, 216ff.

Chiang Kai-shek, Gen., 91ff.

Chandler, Tom, 217.

Chapman, Howard H., 401ff.

Chapman, Oscar, 120, 253

Chennault, Gen. Clair, 88ff.

Christison, Marion, 67ff.

Church, Wade, 181ff.

Civilian Conservation Corps, 54.

Collins, Clem, 109.

Collins, Frank, 402.

Collins, George, 38, 41, 195.

Collins, Walker, 44ff.

Concessions Advisory Group, 109ff.

Concession Policy Act of 1965, 280, 283ff., 297ff., 376ff., 385ff., 410, 439, 444, 445ff., 461ff. 500.

Concessions,
Origins: 139ff.; Attacked by environmentalists: 341ff., 365ff., 445ff., 499ff.
Conference of National Park Concessioners, including all precursor names: 139ff., 273ff., 283ff. 437ff.
Conservation Foundation, 365ff., 457-58, 499ff.
Cramton, Louis C., 139-40.
Crawford, Fred L., 113ff.
Cross, Stuart G., 261, 264, 344, 348ff., 449ff.
Curry, Mary, 344.

Davidson, C. Girard "Jebby", 111ff.
Davis, Luther, 164.
Del Favero, John, 205, 355ff., 402.
Demaray, Arthur E., 57, 105ff.
Denali National Park, See Mount McKinley National Park.
Department of Housing and Urban Affairs, U.S., 303ff.
D'Ewart, Wesley A., 114.
Dickenson, Russell E., 390, 395ff., 428ff.
Dingell, John, 359, 443, 445ff., 456.
Donau, Al, 56, 123ff., 196ff., 222, 240, 250, 261, 305, 342, 361, 415, 489.
Donau, Mary Frank, 123ff., 305, 415.
Dort, Dallas W., 49ff., 60, 62, 105, 340, 493.
Doty, Dale E., 116, 259-60.
Drakesbad, 132ff., 148, 152, 163, 193, 207, 223, 296, 405, 475.
Drury, Newton, 117.

Echo Lake Trail, 47.

Edelstein, Harry, 115ff.
Edwards, John H., 140.
Eisenhower, Dwight D., 76-77, 145, 178, 180-81, 192.
Emery, Fred, 146, 149.
Energy and Environment Subcommittee, 462ff.
Engle, Clair, 114.
Environmental Impact Statements, 391.
Eschwege, Henry, 447.
Evans, Brock, 457.
Evans, James H., 383
Evans, Steve, 97.
Everhardt, Gary, 380, 385, 390ff., 438ff., 462ff., 476ff.

Fleharty, George, 204, 341ff., 355.
Flynn, Frank, 129.
Flynn, Thomas F., Jr., 117, 258, 264, 272, 276.
Ford, Don, 45, 107-08, 227-28, 233.
Forest Service, U.S.D.A., 65, 250, 298, 300, 358, 402.
Fred Harvey Company, 34, 36, 39, 261.
Friends of the Earth, 359-60, 379, 456, 458-59.
Gable, Charles, L., 36, 37, 49.
Galloway, Claude, 57.
Galusha, Hugh, 258, 260.
Gannon, George, 62ff.
Garn, Jacob Edward, "Jake," 389-90, 397.

Genee's Christmas Letters, 130, 131, 136, 146, 147, 151, 155, 162, 192, 207, 222, 233, 236, 239, 248, 295, 305, 315, 338, 339, 344, 416, 417, 419, 420, 432, 433, 434, 493, 494, 495, 496.
General Accounting Office, 285, 421, 447.

Geological Survey, U.S., 399, 400, 403, 406, 408, 475.

Glacier National Park, 186-87, 193, 225ff. 339-40, 346, 363, 389, 415ff., 449, 453ff., 485ff., 481ff.

Glacier Park Foundation, 430ff.

Glacier Park, Inc., 419ff.

Glacier Park Lodge, 226ff., 433, 492.

Glacier Park Transport Company, 226.

Government Operations Committee, House, 445ff.

Government Services, Inc., 56, 105.

Grand Canyon National Park, 23, 34ff., 43ff., 195, 250, 260ff., 268ff. 284, 305, 372, 383ff., 440, 475ff., 493.

Grand Teton National Park, 163, 261, 278, 389.

Great Northern R.R., 144, 225ff., 284, 437, 489.

Great Smoky Mountain National Park, 296.

Greco, Anthony F., 72, 420, 493.

Greyhound Company, 342.

Greyhound Food Management Company, 431-32.

Griffith, E.J., 64ff.

Hall, Ansel, 119.

Hamilton Stores, Inc., 119, 258, 390, 415, 434, 440, 494-95.

Hanson, Garner, foreword.

Hanson, Clifford P., 391, 476-77.

Hardy, Edward C., 361.

Hartzog, George B., Jr., 117, 125, 250, 256ff. 264, 271ff. 283ff., 294ff., 305, 346ff., 365ff., 383ff., 415ff.

Harvey, Daggett, 196, 261.

Hassenpflug, Glenn, 399ff.

Hays, Howard, 120.

Hawkins, Albert A., 481.

Hearst, William Randolph, 8.

Herbst, Robert L., 424.

Homer, Porter, 150ff., 180, 210

Hoover, Herbert, 52.

Horace M. Albright Training Center, 250, 305.

Hoss, Herman, 115ff., 258, 291, 453.

Howe, Allan T., 390ff.

Hummel, Don:
Ancestors, 1-7; Assistant U.S. Attorney, 121ff.; Assistant Secretary of H.U.D., 303ff.; Children, *see under* Genee's Christmas Letters; Glacier concession, 225ff., 415ff.; Lassen concession, 43ff., 121ff., 391ff., 399ff.; Mayor of Tucson, 145ff., 177ff., 189ff., 207ff.; McKinley concession, 195ff., 341ff.; Siblings, 7-24; Testimony before Congress, 109ff., 283ff.; Yosemite Park & Curry Company, 341ff.

Hummel, Gail, 4, 9ff., 128, 185, 225ff., 296, 383ff.

Hummel, Genee, 127ff., 190, 196, 303ff. See also under *Genee's Christmas Letters*.

Ickes, Harold L., 112, 143.

Interior and Insular Affairs Committee, House, 113, 260, 283ff., 360, 379, 424, 445ff., 451.

Interior and Insular Affairs Committee, Senate, 393ff., 477.

Interior Department, 110ff., 121ff., 139ff., 195ff., 225ff., 253ff., 263ff., 267ff., 283ff., 391ff., 365ff., 399ff. 415ff., 437ff. 445ff., 461ff., 475ff.

Iverson, Phillip, 421, 423ff.

Jackson, Henry M. "Scoop," 380, 393-94, 397, 477.
Jenkins, Elmer, 109.
Jensen, Ben F., 112-13.
Johnson, Lyndon B., 179, 182ff., 293, 300, 305, 326ff., 445.

Katz, Robert L., 204-05, 341ff.
Kautenburger, Lambert, 145-46.
Keathley, Charles, 47ff., 124.
Kenady, James, 225ff.
Kennedy, John F., 178, 180ff., 193, 233, 237, 250, 304-05.
Kings Canyon National Park, 128, 267, 284.
Kirwan, Michael K., 255ff.
Knutson Construction Co., 231ff.

LaCovey, Imogene, 405.
Lake McDonald Lodge, 228-29, 242, 251, 417, 433, 449ff., 490.
Lassen National Park Camps, Ltd., 50.
Lassen National Park Company, 121ff., 221-22, 283ff., 399ff.
Lassen Volcanic National Park, 44ff., 105-06, 117, 143ff., 146ff., 121ff., 399ff.
Lightfoot, Edward M., 437ff.
Lloyd, Jimmy, 122-23.
Lodge, James, 425.
Los Angeles Times, 167, 358, 458, 459.

MacIlvain, Lee, 424.
Mammoth Cave Lodge, 481
Mammoth Cave National Park, 481-83.
Manzanita Lake Lodge, 50ff.

121ff., 148, 156, 193, 221-22, 306, 399ff., 475.
Master Plans, 265, 352ff., 385ff., 400ff., 475ff.
Mather, Stephen Tyng, 142, 284, 286.
Mather-Albright Concession Principles, 120, 122, 253, 257, 288, 290
Matthews, William, 146ff., 211.
Mauger of Sequoia, 260, 267
Maughan, Rex, 429, 431.
Meier, Jack, 65.
Merriam, John C., 35-36.
Merriam, Lawrence C., 197.
Mesa Verde National Park, 119, 240, 389.
Metcalf, Lee, 283.
Michigan, University of, Law School, 43ff.
Miller, Dan, 402.
Miller, James, 425-26.
Mintzmyer, Lorraine, 428ff.
Mitchell, Eugenia, See Hummel, Genee,
Molloy, John, 145
Morris, Gen. Winslow, 85ff.
Moss, (Senator) Frank E., 388ff.
Mott, William Penn, Jr., 499.
Mount Hood, 64.
Mount McKinley National Park, 195ff.
Mount Rainier National Park, 64, 143-44, 261, 284, 294.
Muir, John, 373.
Munro, Dick, 419ff.
Murphy, Robert J., 403ff.
Music Corporation of America (MCA), 357ff.

National League of Cities, 189ff.
National Park Centennial Commission, 365ff.

National Park Concessions,
Inc., 109, 143, 196.
National Park Operators
Conference, 139ff.
National Park Service, 35, 41,
49, 109, 139ff., 195ff., 225ff.,
253ff., 263ff., 267ff., 283ff.,
297ff., 341ff., 365ff., 383ff.,
399ff., 415ff., 437ff., 445ff.,
461ff., 475ff., 499-500; De-
molishing visitor facilities,
383ff., 399ff., 475ff.
Neilsen, Keith, 454.
Nicholson, Rex, 183ff.
Nixon, Richard M., 145, 179,
327, 338, 340, 365.
North Rim Grand Canyon, 60,
404
Northern Pacific Railroad,
225ff., 284, 415ff, 445ff, 487-
88.

Oehlmann, Hilmer, 105, 126,
228, 255, 258, 260, 267, 269ff.,
344ff.
Office of Price Administration,
73ff.
Outdoor Recreation Resources
Review Commission, 289ff.

Parrish, Connie, 359, 456, 458-
59.
Patton, Harold "Porque", 26ff.
Paulus, Sylvester, 26ff.
Peterson, J. Hardin, 113ff., 258.
Phantom Ranch, 36ff.
Possessory Interest, 297ff.,
451ff., 463ff.
Potter, Earl, 124ff.
Povah, Trevor S., 114, 260,
268, 271, 390-91, 441ff., 476-
77.
Price, Jackson E., 115, 258, 271.
Prince of Wales Hotel, 225-26,
230, 235, 247, 252, 417-20,
491.

Public Land Law Review
Commission, 449, 465ff.
Public Lands Committee,
House, 113, 116, 121, 288.

Raker, John E., 134, 412.
Redding Record Searchlight,
401ff.
Reed, Joseph V., Jr., 471.
Reed, Nathaniel, 354, 439,
463ff.
Rising Sun Motel, 229, 243,
249, 252, 415ff, 486, 491.
Rocky Mountain National
Park, 363, 483.
Rogers, Nathaniel, 61ff.
Romney, George, 338.
Ronstadt, Carlos, 171ff.
Roosevelt, Eleanor, 64.
Roosevelt, Franklin D., 64, 67,
79, 91.

Santa Fe Railway, 284, 427.
Sceva, Paul, 64, 143-44, 261.
Scott, Les, 260.
Sheinberg, Sidney, 357.
Shellenberger, Joe, 425-26
Sierra (television series), 358.
Sierra Club, 354ff., 379, 395,
Sifford, Roy, 132ff.
Smith, George D., 109.
Solicitor's Opinion (1946),
111ff.
Southern Pacific Railroad, 7,
13, 48, 157, 214.
Spurgeon, John, 423ff.
Standard Oil Company, 123,
198, 341.
Stanford, Eric, 344, 348.
Stanford, Leland, 8.
Stanford Research Institute,
381, 387.
Stanford University, 8, 59, 105,
296, 306, 341, 420
Stein, Jay S., 357ff.
Stevenson, Adlai, 177ff.

Stevenson, Cy, 228ff., 415ff., 489-90.
Stewart, Phillip O., 438ff.
Surles, Lloyd "Buddy," 423ff.
Swiftcurrent Motor Lodge, 229, 241, 250, 416, 422, 485-92.
Symposium in Yosemite, 365ff.
Taber, Fred L., 105, 126.
Taft, Charles P., 109.
Taft, William Howard, 2, 11.
Tillotson, Minor R. "Tilly", 34ff.
Timberline Lodge, 64-65.
Tippet, Ian, 228, 500.
Tobin, Jim, 424.
Tomlinson, Owen A., 122.
Tower, Dudley, 227.
Tresidder, Donald, 105, 112, 142.
Tucson Daily Citizen, 149ff.
TWA Services (includes TW Services), 385, 388, 390, 418.

Udall, Morris K., 183-84, 283ff., 424ff., 449, 454.
Udall, Stewart, 124-25, 182ff., 241ff., 253ff. 279, 294,
Union Oil Company, 227-28, 232-33,
Union Pacific Railroad, 255, 284, 383ff., 427.
U.S. Natural Resources, 204ff., 341ff.
Utah Parks Company, 228, 383ff.
Verkamp, Jack, 268.
Vint, Tom, 195.

Waterton-Glacier International Peace Park, 225, 230, 247, 419.
Watt, James G., 364.
Webb, Del E., 428ff.
Whalen, William, 422, 424.

White, Mastin G., 111.
Wilbur, Ray Lyman, 139ff.
Wilderness Act of 1964, 263ff., 379, 484.
Wilderness Society, 360, 457, 499.
Wilson, Tom, 390.
Wirth, Conrad L., 118, 125, 258ff., 268.
Works Progress Administration (WPA), 59ff.
World War II, 77ff.
Wyatt, Cliff, 21.

Yellowstone National Park, 3, 114, 147ff., 163, 195, 238, 258, 261, 278, 284, 372, 390ff., 415, 421, 425, 427, 434, 440ff., 476-78, 494, 497.
Yosemite National Park, 204ff., 341ff.
Yosemite Park and Curry Company, 204ff., 341ff.

Zion National Park, 284, 383ff., 475.